D0679566

Cleburne And His Command

—Courtesy Gerard O'Brien, West Hyattsville, Md., from the Meserve Collection.

PATRICK R. CLEBURNE
Major General, C.S.A.
from photograph taken in Mobile, Ala., in January 1864.

Cleburne And His Command

By *Capt. Irving A. Buck*

ASSISTANT ADJUTANT GENERAL, CLEBURNE'S DIVISION, C.S.A.

AND

Pat Cleburne

Stonewall Jackson of the West

BY THOMAS ROBSON HAY, Editor

FOREWORD BY BELL IRVIN WILEY

Broadfoot Publishing Company

MONOGRAPHS, SOURCES, AND REPRINTS IN SOUTHERN HISTORY

Wilmington, North Carolina 1987

This edition, Broadfoot Publishing Company, 1987

Library of Congress
Catalog Card No. 58-14212

Broadfoot Publishing Company
Route 4, Box 508C, Wilmington, North Carolina 28405

FOREWORD

THE EMERALD ISLE was well represented on both sides in the American Civil War. That regiment was a rarity which did not have on its rolls a Finegan, an O'Brien, an O'Connor, an O'Malley, a Sweeny or some other native of Ireland. Both the Northern and Southern armies had their "Irish Brigades," several "Irish Regiments" and numerous organizations of lesser size made up in large part of sons of Erin. All-told, nearly 150,000 Irishmen were scattered through the Union ranks. The total number who wore the grey cannot be ascertained but it is known that in 1860 Irishmen living in the South aggregated some 85,000 and that Ireland contributed more soldiers to the Confederacy than did any other non-American country.

Irish soldiers were reputed to be quarrelsome, insubordinate and overly fond of pillage. But they were rated high for generosity and good humor, and as fighters they were said to be unexcelled.

On the Federal side natives of Ireland including Thomas F. Meagher, Thomas W. Sweeny and Jeremiah T. Boyle, rose to brigadier. The Confederacy also had several Irish brigadiers, including Patrick T. Moore, Walter P. Lane, and Joseph Finegan. At the battle of Ocean Pond, Finegan was greatly upset when his son, a member of his staff, rushed forward with the troops into the thick of the fight. "Go to the rear Finegan me B'ye, go to the rear," he was said to have exclaimed, "ye know ye are ye mither's darlin'."

The Irishman who achieved highest rank on either side was Patrick R. Cleburne of the Confederate Army of Tennessee. On the basis of his demonstrated superiority as a division commander, Cleburne should have been made a lieutenant general and he possibly would have attained that rank had he not made himself suspect by his early advocacy of making soldiers out of the slaves and freeing those who rendered faithful service in the ranks.

In Cleburne, and a younger brother in grey, were found the very best qualities of the nationality into which he was born. He was modest, considerate, well-mannered, generous, honest, industrious, and temperate. He was devoted to his men. He was not a slaveholder, but his attachment to his adopted Southland was so great that he once declared in an impassioned and eloquent speech to his command: "If this cause which is so dear to my heart is doomed to fail, I pray heaven may let me fall with it, while my face is turned to the enemy and my arm battling for that which I know to be right."

Cleburne knew not the meaning of fear and so compelling was his personality and so dynamic his leadership that he was able to impress his gallantry and dauntlessness on those whom he commanded. When he fell at Franklin, he was with his men in the forefront of battle, setting a pattern of heroism.

Truly he deserved the soubriquet given him by his admirers, "Stonewall of the West." And it is wholly fitting that the only full-scale study of him ever to be written should now be rescued from the rare book rooms and collectors shelves and made available to all who may be attracted by the sterling character, magnificent leadership and shining heroism recorded on its pages.

BELL IRVIN WILEY

CONTENTS

CONTENTS (Continued)

ILLUSTRATIONS

PATRICK R. CLEBURNE, age 25, from an ambrotype done in Helena, Ark., from Confederate Memorial Museum, Richmond, Va.

CAPTAIN IRVING ASHBY BUCK
(November 24, 1840-September 8, 1912)

When Buck was wounded, Cleburne wrote the doctor: *"You must save Buck. He is the best adjutant general in the army."*

—Courtesy Welford Ashby Buck, Baltimore, Md.

PAT CLEBURNE
STONEWALL JACKSON OF THE WEST

PATRICK RONAYNE CLEBURNE[1] was one of those rare civilians with little military training who during the Civil War developed unusual attributes of leadership both on and off the battlefield. He generated confidence in his judgment and ability and attracted men to him. His reputation as a leader, disciplinarian and fighter spread throughout the Southern Confederacy and was not unknown to the opposing armies of the Union.

He was the idol of his command, "a division unsurpassed for courage, energy and endurance by any other in the Confederacy." His personal courage, though "cool and calculating, was electric in its influence upon his men," who literally worshipped him. The morale of his command, whether in camp or on the battlefield, was always high when their leader was with them. In acknowledging a complimentary letter written to him by a refugee lady from Tennessee, he replied: "To my noble division and not to myself belong the

---

1. The pronunciation of General Cleburne's name appears to have varied from C*lee*burne in the eastern part of the Confederacy to C*lay*burne west of the Mississippi, particularly in Arkansas and Texas. In some of the official reports the name is spelled "Claiborne," which would seem to support C*lay*burne as the usual pronunciation. On the other hand, Cleburne E. Gregory, Director, Georgia Historical Commission, whose father, Captain Edward Gregory, 9th Kentucky Infantry, Orphan Brigade, writes that his father "was temporarily on the staff of General Pat Cleburne." He states that "my father always called General Cleburne C*lee*burne with emphasis on the C*lee*." (Cleburne E. Gregory to T. R. Hay, May 26, 1958.) At this late date it is not possible to say with any certainty what pronunciation General Cleburne used.

praise for the deeds of gallantry you mention."[2] It was this man and soldier whom General Robert E. Lee called "A meteor shining from a clouded sky" and whom President Jefferson Davis and others characterized as the "Stonewall Jackson of the West." *The Arkansas Gazette* of November 22, 1937, included Cleburne among the ten most famous men in Arkansas history. It is of this man, an Irishman by birth and an American by adoption, Patrick Ronayne Cleburne, and the command he fashioned and led that this book, *Cleburne and His Command* by Captain Irving A. Buck, is concerned.[3]

In April 1861, three young men from the village of Front Royal, in the Shenandoah Valley of Virginia, enlisted in Company B of the 17th Virginia Regiment of Infantry, then being recruited for service in the Virginia forces and soon to be transferred to the Confederate Army. Three months later, under command of their colonel, Montgomery D. Corse, they participated in the battle of the First Bull Run. All three, T. B. Roy (1838-1910), George A. Williams (1842-1929) and Irving A. Buck (1840-1912), were soon afterward detailed as clerks at General P. G. T. Beauregard's headquarters and in February 1862 went with Beauregard to the Confederate Army of Mississippi, later the Army of Tennessee, then in Kentucky and Tennessee. Each of them remained throughout the war on staff work with the Army of Tennessee. Roy, on General W. J. Hardee's staff, attained the rank of lieutenant colonel, A. A. G., and soon after the close of the war, married one of General Hardee's daughters and later wrote an excellent account of the "Operations of General Hardee in the Atlanta Campaign."[4] Williams, as captain, A. A. G., served on the staff of General St. John R. Liddell and later of General D. C. Govan, and after the war settled in New Orleans.

---

2. William J. Hardee, "A Sketch of General Patrick R. Cleburne," *Southern Historical Society Papers,* XXXI (Richmond 1903), 157. Henceforth cited as *SHSP.*

3. It is of interest to note that General Cleburne was one of the very few Confederate leaders whom Colonel G. F. R. Henderson, the English biographer of Stonewall Jackson and distinguished military critic, singled out for favorable mention in his critical studies on the *Science of War.* See Jay Luvaas, ed., *The Civil War: A Soldier's View* (Chicago, 1958), 184, 186.

4. *SHSP,* VIII (1880), 337-87.

Irving A. Buck, the author of this book, *Cleburne and His Command,* served from December 1862 until he was wounded at the battle of Jonesboro, September 2, 1864, on Cleburne's staff as a captain, A. A. G., and after the war engaged in business in Baltimore.

Cleburne and His Command, first published by The Neale Publishing Company, in a limited edition, in 1908, has long been out of print. For the period from late 1862 until shortly before Cleburne's death at Franklin, November 30, 1864, the book is based on the author's personal contact with and observation of General Cleburne and his brigade and division. For information about Cleburne's early life and the three months before the battle of Franklin, the author relies on published accounts.

The first published account of Cleburne, other than contemporary newspaper notices, was a brief sketch, probably by General D. H. Hill, one of Cleburne's former commanders, in the April 1867 issue of *The Land We Love.* Several months later the New Orleans *Times Picayune* in the issues of July 12 and 19, 1867, published a longer and more authoritative account of Cleburne and his command written by Cleburne's friend and long time commander, General W. J. Hardee.[5] This sketch was several times reprinted, wholly or in part. Another early account, largely extracts from General Hardee's sketch, was printed in 1867 in John Francis Maguire, *The Irish in America.* Nothing of consequence seems to have been published until twenty years later. The *Kennesaw Gazette,* of May 15, 1887, contained a nine page summary of Cleburne's career by Colonel I. W. Avery, commander of the 4th Georgia Cavalry. Avery saw much of Cleburne throughout the war and, therefore, could write from personal knowledge and observation. A month later, June 15, 1887, the *Kennesaw Gazette,* published an excellent account of Cleburne—"His Early Career and Last Battle" —by his former law partner in Helena, Arkansas, and a member of his staff, Judge L. H Mangum.

---

5. See for example, *SHSP,* XXXI, 157-63 and *The Confederate Veteran,* XII (Nashville, 1904), 17.

In the *Kennesaw Gazette* of November 15, 1888, Mr. J. M. Brown, a son of Governor J. E. Brown of Georgia, who at the time was president of the Western and Atlantic Railroad and who used the *Kennesaw Gazette* as a promotion medium for the railroad, announced: "Mr. J. M. Brown of Atlanta has secured through Judge L. H. Mangum [then] of Washington, D. C. . . . a number of papers which give the history of General Cleburne and his magnificent division during the War Between the States. We will begin publication of the Cleburne papers in our issue of January 1, 1889. There are some things in these papers that have never been published before."

Among the "papers" was a biographical sketch of General Cleburne by Major Calhoun Benham, A. A. G. and chief of staff of Cleburne's division The sketch covered the period from mid-December 1862 until the end of the fighting at Ezra Church, near Atlanta, July 27, 1864. It ended at this point, presumably because of the wounding of Benham on that day by a shell fragment. Major Benham wrote that this biographical sketch was written during the war, much of it "composed under [Cleburne's] eye" and with his approval. Probably Benham later planned to continue his narrative to Cleburne's death at Franklin, but he evidently was unable to secure the necessary information.[6] Soon after the close of the war Benham went to San Francisco, where he was living when the war began, to resume his law practice and where he remained until his death on June 12, 1884. Benham's narrative was published in twenty installments of varying length in nearly consecutive issues of the *Kennesaw Gazette* from January 1 to November 15, 1889.

Apparently Judge Mangum had kept in touch with Major Benham, and when Benham died his war papers were sent to Mangum. These papers included Benham's sketch of Cleburne, an autobiography of General M. P. Lowrey, one of Cleburne's brigade commanders, and perhaps the sketch of Cleburne by Colonel I. W.

---

6. See Calhoun Benham, New York, to Robert Tarleton, Mobile, Ala., June 5, 1867, in Tarleton Papers, Yale University Library; San Francisco *Call,* June 13, 1884.

General B. F. Cheatham
(October 20, 1820-September 4, 1886)

"A fighter, not a general."

—Courtesy Library of Congress

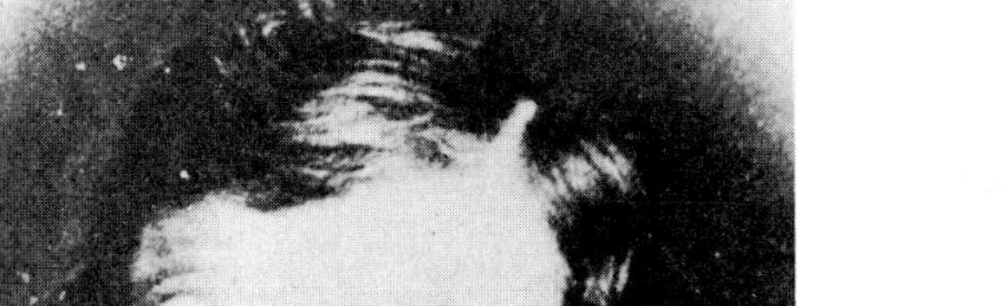

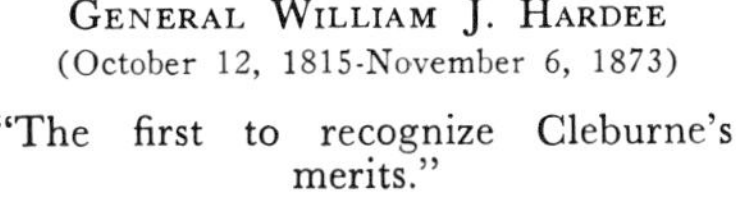

General William J. Hardee
(October 12, 1815-November 6, 1873)

"The first to recognize Cleburne's merits."

—Courtesy Library of Congress

—Courtesy Library of Congress

GENERAL HIRAM BRONSON GRANBURY
(March 1, 1831-November 30, 1864)

"A Mississippian commanding a Texas brigade."

—Courtesy Library of Congress

GENERAL STATES RIGHTS GIST
(September 1, 1831-November 30, 1864)

"Leading his brigade on foot he fell pierced through the heart."

—Courtesy Library of Congress

GENERAL OTHO FRENCH STRAHL
(June 3, 1831-November 30, 1864)

A native of Ohio, commanding a Tennessee brigade. *"Keep firing,"* was his last command. "Shot in the head, he was being carried to the rear when he received another shot and directly a third which killed him."

—Courtesy Ezra J. Warner, LaJolla, Calif.

GENERAL JOHN ADAMS
(July 1, 1825-November 30, 1864)

"Shot through the thighs, he tried to crawl away, but soon died in Federal hands."

Avery. Also included was Cleburne's memorial of January 2, 1864, advocating arming of the slaves of which more later, and perhaps other papers that are not known or that were never printed.

Major Benham's sketch was not complete in that there is no mention of Cleburne's service at the battle of Shiloh and in the Kentucky campaign. His account begins with the battle of Murfreesboro and ends with the close of the Atlanta campaign. The reason for this, undoubtedly, is that Benham only wrote of that part of Cleburne's military career of which he had personal knowledge. The portion treating of Cleburne's life before and shortly after he joined the Confederate Army was included, presumably, because it was obtained in personal discussions with Cleburne himself. Benham apparently completed his series of articles about Cleburne before he returned to California in the late 1860s.

In this connection it is of interest to note that all accounts of Cleburne's career, with the possible exception of that by Judge L. H. Mangum and that by Captain Buck, were written shortly after the close of the war when the events narrated were fresh in the minds of the writers and when participants and friends of Cleburne were available for consultation. However, except for the sketch in *The Land We Love* and General Hardee's longer sketch first printed in the New Orleans *Times Picayune,* none of the sketches mentioned was printed until some twenty years after their preparation. Captain Buck in this book relies on all of the printed accounts of Cleburne either to supplement or to verify and strengthen his own observation and knowledge.

Cleburne's career is well portrayed in Buck's account. He was born in the county of Cork in southern Ireland, March 17, 1828, of Protestant parents. His mother died when he was four years old and his father married again. Cleburne got on well with his stepmother, studied at Trinity College in Dublin, and at the age of 17, enlisted in the 41st Regiment of the British Army, stationed in Dublin. He served for something over three years and attained the rank of corporal. He purchased his discharge sometime in 1849, and on November 11, 1849, he with his elder brother, William, and his sister, Anne, sailed from Queenstown for New Orleans, where they arrived, December 25, 1849. Cleburne went on alone to Cincinnati, Ohio, followed by his brother and sister, remained there for about six months and then moved down the Mississippi River to Helena, Arkansas. He worked first as a prescription clerk and then as part owner of a drug store in Helena. He found the place congenial and made friends, studied oratory, became a Mason and read law. He was admitted to the bar in 1856 and began practice of the law in Helena. An ardent Whig when he first came to Helena, he joined the Democratic party several years later. He was badly wounded in a street fight in Helena in 1858 when he came to the aid of his friend, T. C. Hindman, who was attacked and shot by political opponents. He was a vestryman in St. John's Protestant Episcopal Church in Helena.

Cleburne owned no slaves, but as the threats of civil conflict became more menacing he did not hesitate to array himself at the side of his friends and neighbors. Probably early in April 1861 he wrote his half-brother Robert, who had followed him to America: "I hardly know what to say about politics. This state [Arkansas] has ordered an election for delegates to a convention. I cannot say what course they will adopt, but the fever of revolution is very contagious and if blood is spilled and passion excited the reckless riflemen who inhabit our woods, will inevitably take a hand. Even if the State should not secede it will be impossible to prevent armed volunteers from rushing to the scene of action. My own opinion is that the first blood shed on Southern soil in a collision between the Federal troops and the State authorities of any Southern State will be the signal for a civil war which must ultimately array the fifteen Southern states against the Northern states."

"As to my own position," he continued, "I hope to see the Union preserved by granting to the South the full measure of her constitutional rights. If this cannot be done I hope to see all the Southern states united in a new confederation and that we can effect a peaceable separation. If both these are denied us, I am with Arkansas in weal or in woe." Several weeks later, in a letter dated

May 7, 1861, Cleburne again wrote his brother Robert: "I am with the South in life or in death, in victory or in defeat. I never owned a negro and care nothing for them, but these people have been my friends and have stood by me on all occasions."[7]

A man of firm convictions, absolutely indifferent to danger and cool and self-controlled when exposed to it, he had joined a military company called the Yell Rifles formed in Helena in the summer of 1860 and was present at the surrender of the United States arsenal in Little Rock in January 1861. Upon the call of the Arkansas Military Board for troops in the spring of 1861, Cleburne, then serving as a private, entered the Arkansas State service. He was later elected captain. When the Yell Rifles and other companies were taken into State service at Mound City in May 1861, Cleburne was chosen colonel of his regiment which was designated as the 15th Arkansas Infantry. In July 1861 the regiment was ordered to a rendezvous at Pitman's Ferry in northern Arkansas, just south of the Arkansas-Missouri state line. At this point General W. J. Hardee was in command and here began a friendship and an association that continued, almost without interruption, for over three years until just prior to Cleburne's death at Franklin.

Almost from the beginning Cleburne commanded Hardee's confidence by his attention to duty and care for his men and because of his intelligence, ability, fearlessness and discretion. He not only cared for his men but was scrupulous in recognizing the rights and protecting the property of civilians in areas where his command was stationed or through which it marched. On November 16, 1861, reporting on foraging done by men of his command, he wrote: "I have paid out of my own pocket for the articles stolen by our men. . . . Confidence is restored, all the houses open, and families returned."

The winter of 1861 and the spring of 1862 were spent at Bowling Green, Kentucky, where a Confederate army was being assembled by General Albert Sidney Johnston. Hardee, now a

7. MSS in possession of General Cleburne's grand-niece, Mrs. Isabella Connelley, Huntington, W. Va.

major general, was in command of a division, Cleburne, as the ranking colonel, was in command of the second brigade of the division. In this capacity Cleburne engaged in drilling and disciplining his command and preparing it for combat. On March 4, 1862, while at Shelbyville, Tennessee, he was promoted to the rank of brigadier general. This honor came to him through his own performance and on the recommendation of General Hardee. Within a month Cleburne and his command received their baptism of fire in the bloody battle of Shiloh. Thereafter, as long as Cleburne lived, he and his command were distinguished in every battle and campaign in which the gallant Army of Tennessee participated.

On December 13, 1862, Cleburne was promoted to major general and assigned to command a division in Hardee's corps. One of his first acts in the new position was to form a competent staff. His first chief of staff, Colonel W. W. Kirkland of North Carolina,[8] was succeeded by Major Calhoun Benham, A. A. G., who joined Cleburne's staff just before the battle of Murfreesboro. Irving A. Buck was appointed a captain, A. A. G., at about the same time. One of his aides, Lieutenant J. K. Dixon, who was wounded at Murfreesboro, after his return to duty was promoted to major and assigned as divisional inspector general in the place of Major Calhoun Benham, appointed chief of staff. The chief of artillery was Captain, later Major, T. R. Hotchkiss. Lieutenants L. H. Mangum and S. P. Hanly, both of Helena, Arkansas, were aides to the general. Captain, later Major, C. S. Hill of Mississippi was the divisional chief of ordnance. Another aide, a young Englishman, C. H. Byrne, who may have come to the United States with Lieutenant Colonel J. A. L. Fremantle, volunteered his services and was with Cleburne at least through the Atlanta campaign. Cleburne identified him as a captain and sought to have him commissioned

8. It is probable that Colonel Kirkland, still disabled by a wound received at the battle of Winchester, Va., May 25, 1862, was visiting at General Hardee's headquarters. Kirkland's wife was Hardee's niece. His short term of duty on Cleburne's staff was probably at the recommendation of General Hardee. Lieutenant L. H. Mangum, one of Cleburne's aides, was a fellow townsman, both Kirkland and Mangum being from Hillsboro, N. C.

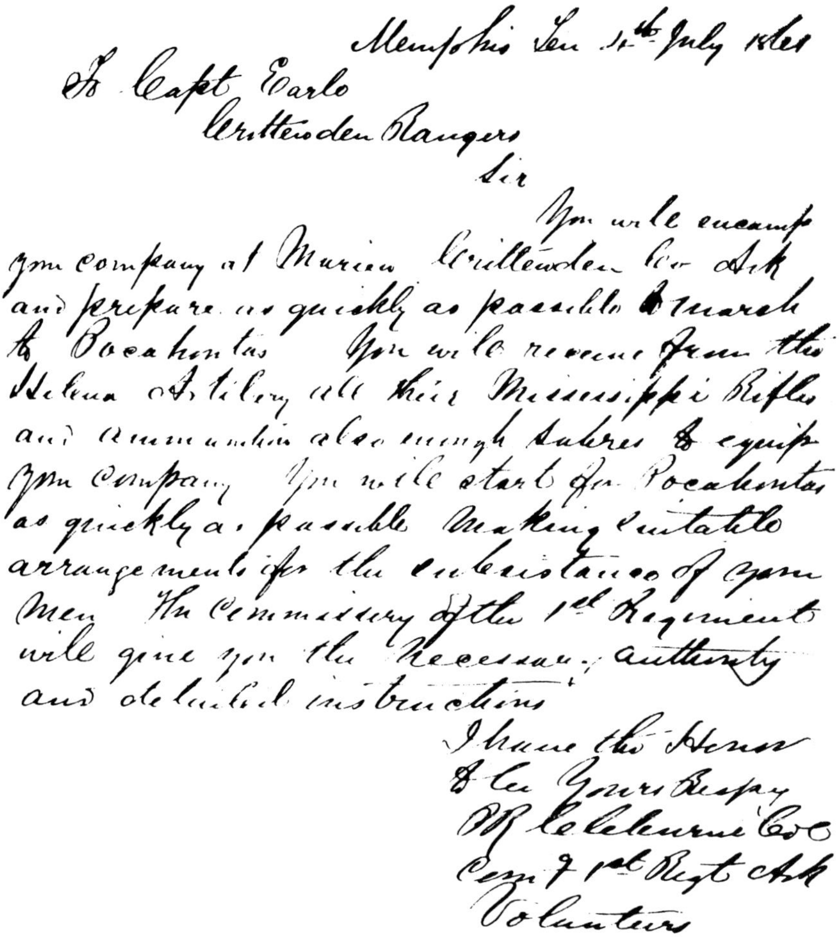

Memphis Ten 10th July 1861

To Capt Earle
Crittenden Rangers
Sir

You will encamp your company at Marion Crittenden Co Ark and prepare as quickly as possible to march to Pocahontas. You will receive from the Helena Artillery all their Mississippi Rifles and ammunition also enough sabres to equip your company. You will start for Pocahontas as quickly as possible making suitable arrangements for the subsistance of your men. The Commissary of the 1st Regiment will give you the necessary authority and detailed instructions

I have the Honor
to be Yours Respy
P R Cleburne Col
Com of 1st Regt Ark
Volunteers

—Courtesy Arkansas Historical Commission

Earliest known Civil War letter written
and signed by Cleburne

General John C. Carter
(December 19, 1837-December 9, 1864)

Mortally wounded at the battle of Franklin, November 30, 1864, he was removed to the Harrison house, near Franklin, where he died.

—Courtesy John R. Peacock, High Point, N. C.

—Battles and Leaders of the Civil War

The Carter House (headquarters, Gen. J. D. Cox, commanding 23rd Corps), was the center of bitter hand-to-hand fighting.

Cleburne Division battle flag—A blue field with a white center and border. The flag became known to friend and foe alike. It clearly marked the presence and place of Cleburne's Division in the line of battle.

❖❖❖

The Carter gin house and screw near which Cleburne fell. From a drawing reportedly made by a wounded Confederate soldier the morning after the battle of Franklin.

—Courtesy John R. Peacock, High Point, N. C.

Cleburne's Repulse of Sherman at the tunnel, November 25, 1863. Cleburne's stand here covered the retreat of Bragg's army from Missionary Ridge.

—The Mountain Campaigns in Georgia (Atlanta, 1890)

in the Confederate Army, but without success. He wrote that Byrne "left England to volunteer his service in our cause" sacrificing "an opportunity of being commissioned in the British Army." Cleburne found "him a brave and gallant officer, highly intelligent and devoted to our cause."[9]

With the exception of Colonel Kirkland, who served only briefly with Cleburne, and Major Benham all the others mentioned, were members of his staff until his death at Franklin. Major Calhoun Benham (1823-1884) was the oldest and most experienced member of the staff. Born in Cincinnati, Ohio, a brother-in-law of George D. Prentice, long time editor of the *Louisville Journal,* a lawyer by education and training and a veteran of the Mexican War, Benham had gone to California in 1849, practiced law in San Francisco and served as principal second to Judge David S. Terry in his duel with Senator David Broderick. He was a member of the Committee for Law and Order in San Francisco, an unsuccessful candidate for Congress, and United States Attorney General in California, 1860-1861. In the fall of 1861, he sailed for New York in company with J. L. Brent and former Senator William Gwynn. General E. V. Sumner, who had relieved Colonel Albert Sidney Johnston in command of the Department of California, was on the same vessel with United States Army troops returning to New York. Just before reaching Panama, Sumner arrested Benham, Brent and Gwynn and on arriving on the eastern seaboard, they were confined at Fort Lafayette, Delaware, until released early in December 1861, largely through the efforts of Benham's brother-in-law, George D. Prentice.

A week later Benham and Prentice, after an interview with President Lincoln, went to Prentice's home in Louisville. Soon afterwards Benham attached himself to the staff of General Albert Sidney Johnston, whom he had known in California, as a volunteer aide. When Johnston was killed at the battle of Shiloh, Benham was one

---

9. P. R. Cleburne, Missionary Ridge, Tenn., to David Urquhart, Lt. Col., A. A. G. on General Braxton Bragg's staff, Nov. 8, 1863 copy of MS provided through the courtesy of John R. Peacock. See also J. A. L. Fremantle, *Three Months in the Southern States, April-June 1863* (Mobile, 1864), 78-80.

of those who accompanied his body to New Orleans for burial. Returning to Kentucky he attached himself to General P. G. T. Beauregard's staff, again as a volunteer aide, but early in October 1862 he was assigned to General J. C. Breckinridge's staff with the rank of major. When Cleburne formed his staff Benham joined it, although he knew Cleburne only by reputation. He was slightly wounded at the battle of Chickamauga in September 1863 and again at Ezra Church, near Atlanta, on July 27, 1864. Soon afterwards Benham went to Louisville for rest and recuperation and did not again return to active duty. Late in 1864 or early in 1865 he joined his friend, Senator William Gwynn, in his colonization project in northern Mexico, but, after the surrender at Appomattox, he again returned to Louisville, where on November 28, 1866, he took the amnesty oath. In the next few months he employed his leisure time completing his sketch of Cleburne and his command. He went to California in 1867, resumed practice of the law and died in San Francisco, June 12, 1884.

Another interesting member of Cleburne's staff was Joseph Koger Dixon, a native of Noxubee County, Mississippi. He entered West Point in July 1857, was found deficient twice, but managed to secure restoration. When he learned of South Carolina's secession, he telegraphed the Governor of Mississippi on Christmas Eve, 1860: "The war is begun. I leave to-morrow." As soon as he arrived at Jackson, Mississippi, he tendered his services and was commissioned a 3d lieutenant of the "Noxubee Rifles" and was soon en route to Pensacola as a member of an expedition that took over that city early in January 1861. He was mustered out in February 1861 and returned to his home in Mississippi.[10] Soon afterward he was appointed a 2d Lieutenant, Confederate States Army and participated in the unsuccessful defense of New Orleans in April 1862 and was taken prisoner. He was paroled, and after his exchange in the summer of 1862, at the request of General Braxton Bragg, he joined the

10. Morris Schaff, *The Spirit of Old West Point* (Boston and New York, 1907), 178; Mississippi Historical Society *Publications,* IX (Jackson, 1906), 18.

Army of Tennessee and was assigned to duty as an aide to General Cleburne. As previously noted, he was appointed major and inspector general of the division in place of Major Calhoun Benham when that officer was made chief of staff to General Cleburne and served in that capacity until Cleburne's death. He was wounded at Murfreesboro, December 31, 1862. He served Cleburne loyally and effectively.

Cleburne's chief of artillery, T. R. Hotchkiss of Mississippi, had entered the Confederate Army as a private of artillery. He had come to the attention of General Albert Sidney Johnston, who recommended his promotion to command a battery, and soon afterward he was assigned to command the artillery battalion attached to Cleburne's division in which capacity he served throughout the remainder of the war, attaining the rank of major. He was a firm disciplinarian and expected strict obedience of his orders. One of his battery commanders, Captain T. J. Key, recorded in his Diary that "a captain under this battalion management is a perfect automaton." Hotchkiss was "fearless" under fire and "too reckless at times when it is unnecessary." He was wounded in action at Murfreesboro and at Chickamauga. On July 21, 1864, at Atlanta, he received "a severe wound through the hip bone." He was a brave and efficient officer whose artillery battalion's fighting effectiveness matched the well known fighting ability of Cleburne's famous division.[11]

Another member of Cleburne's staff, Lieutenant L. H. Mangum, was born in Hillsboro, North Carolina, May 26, 1837. After graduating from Princeton University in 1857, he settled in Helena, Arkansas, and became Cleburne's law partner in the firm of Cleburne, Scaife and Mangum. He enlisted in the Yell Rifles, at the company's formation in 1860, along with Cleburne. When Cleburne was elected captain, Mangum was appointed sergeant. After the company was mustered into the Confederate service as a part of Cleburne's 15th

---

11. Wirt Cate, *Two Soldiers* (Chapel Hill, 1938), 32, 64-66, 95; *War of the Rebellion: Official Records of the Union and Confederate Armies* (Washington, 1880-1901), series 1, XX, part 1, 850 and XXX, part 2, 158. Henceforth cited as *O.R.* The series unless otherwise indicated is series 1.

Arkansas Infantry, Mangum remained as a sergeant and as such participated in the battle of Shiloh, where he was severely wounded. On his recovery he was offered a captaincy, but preferred to join Cleburne's staff as an aide with the rank of lieutenant, in which capacity he served for the remainder of the war. He received seven wounds during the battle of Perryville, October 8, 1862, but none of them "touched a vital spot." After the war Mangum resumed his law practice in Helena, was a probate judge in that town and then served in the United States Treasury. He died in Washington April 28, 1903.

In addition to Captain Buck other members of Cleburne's staff included Lieutenant S. P. Hanly, a son of Judge T. B. Hanly, in whose office Cleburne studied law, and Major C. S. Hill of Mississippi, divisional chief of ordnance, who after the war held political offices in Mississippi and in the nation's capital.

It will be seen that Cleburne's staff, with minor changes of personnel and the occasional absence of members on account of wounds or sickness, served him throughout his career as a division commander. This continuity in staff personnel undoubtedly added to the efficiency and effectiveness of the division as a combat unit. As time passed the staff not only became more skilled in their duties, but also became better acquainted with their chief and with each other. Orders were promptly and properly prepared and delivered to brigade and regimental commanders in such detail and manner as to enable prompt execution. Mutual confidence between the division commander and his men, discipline and effective staff work combined to create a fighting unit that was hardly surpassed on either side for its effectiveness in attack and defense and ability to meet changing circumstances and conditions with confidence. In a large degree this proficiency was a reflection of the personality, character and ability of Cleburne, the division commander, who instilled in his command the benefits of discipline, resourcefulness and the ability to meet any situation with unflinching courage, confidence and determination.

—Tennessee Historical Society, Nashville, Tenn.

General Cleburne's cap which he is believed to have been wearing when he was killed at the battle of Franklin, Tenn., Nov. 30, 1864. There is a hole in the cap, presumably made by a bullet that passed through it, as he charged forward with the cap on the point of his sword.

—Tennessee Historical Society, Nashville, Tenn.

Combination spoon and fork believed to have been used by General Cleburne.

Battle of Ringgold, Ga., Nov. 27, 1863. Cleburne stationed his troops on the ridge; their fire was destructive; huge rocks were rolled down the mountain slope; confusion and heavy losses were inflicted on the attacking Federals who withdrew to await reenforcements. Cleburne's command retired unmolested.

—The Mountain Campaigns in Georgia (Atlanta, 1890)

The division's superior qualities were repeatedly demonstrated in a positive manner at Richmond, Kentucky, Murfreesboro, Chickamauga, Chattanooga, Ringgold, Pickett's Mill, Atlanta and finally at Franklin. In these engagements, it may be noted that most of the actual fighting took place at close range either from intrenchments as at Pickett's Mill, at the tunnel at Chattanooga and at Ringgold, or in open manœuvre as at Richmond, Kentucky, Murfreesboro and at Atlanta. Frequently the opposing lines were scarcely 100 paces apart. Cleburne's knowledge and use of fire power combined with the effective use of his artillery as at Missionary Ridge were decisive in their effect. Largely because of Cleburne's superior leadership, his division turned in an outstanding combat performance in every battle in which he commanded it.

Soon after the battle of Shiloh and the withdrawal of the Confederates to Corinth, General Braxton Bragg superceded General P. G. T. Beauregard and the Army of Mississippi was divided, part of it under General Earl Van Dorn being left in Mississippi, while the larger portion, commanded by Bragg, was moved by rail to Chattanooga and from there into central Tennessee. From this point it was decided to invade Kentucky. In the campaign that followed, Cleburne and his brigade served under the general direction of General E. Kirby Smith. Cleburne, commanding his own and General T. J. Churchill's brigade, successfully engaged Federal troops at Richmond, Kentucky, August 30, 1862. Cleburne was wounded and incapacitated for over a month, but rejoined his command in time to lead it in the battle of Perryville, October 8, 1862, where he was again wounded, but remained with his troops. Several days later, while the army was in process of withdrawing into Tennessee, Cleburne directed the successful retreat over Big Hill of Bragg's train of some 4,000 wagons.[12] Soon afterwards the army was removed to the vicinity of Tullahoma and Murfreesboro, Tennessee. Here the troops remained encamped facing the Federal Army, now commanded by General W. S. Rosecrans, who had replaced General

12. *O.R.*, XVI, part 2, 943, 949, 951f; *SHSP*, XXXI (1903), 154.

Don Carlos Buell. Bragg reorganized his army and divided it into two corps under Generals Leonidas Polk and W. J. Hardee. General S. B. Buckner's division, formerly commanded by Hardee, and including Cleburne's brigade, was assigned to Hardee's corps.

On November 20, 1862, the name of the army was changed from Army of Mississippi to Army of Tennessee. On the same date, Bragg included Cleburne's name among a number recommended for promotion characterizing him as "young, ardent, exceedingly gallant, but sufficiently prudent; a fine drill officer and the admiration of his command as a soldier and a gentleman." Soon afterward President Davis visited the army in an effort to alleviate some of the criticism against Bragg on the part of his principal subordinates as well as to see for himself the condition of affairs. While at Bragg's headquarters Davis personally directed the promotion and assignment of Cleburne to command the division in place of Buckner, who was transferred.[13]

Davis proposed to meet some of the criticism against Bragg by putting his army and that of General J. C. Pemberton at Vicksburg under the general supervision of General J. E. Johnston. As matters turned out Johnston commanded neither Bragg in Tennessee nor Pemberton at Vicksburg. Several weeks later the inconclusive battle of Murfreesboro was fought. Cleburne again was distinguished for his personal conduct and leadership. Bragg, in his report, "especially commended [him] to the government for valor, skill and ability."[14]

After the battle of Murfreesboro the criticism of Bragg was renewed with increased vehemence. Seeking moral support, Bragg wrote his principal subordinates, including Cleburne, asking for a frank opinion concerning his conduct of the campaign. Cleburne, in his reply, stated "with regret" that, in his observation, Bragg did "not possess the confidence of the army." Others expressed similar

13. *O.R.* XX, pt. 2, 449, 508; W. J. Hardee, "Sketch of Patrick R. Cleburne," *SHSP,* XXXI, 154.

14. *O.R.* XX, pt. 1, 670; *Ibid.,* XXIII, pt. 2, 613; Thomas Robson Hay, "Confederate Leadership at Vicksburg," *Mississippi Valley Historical Review,* XI (Cedar Rapids, 1925), 543ff.

sentiments, but General Johnston thought it best that Bragg remain in command of the Army of Tennessee and so arranged matters that no change was made.[15]

At this period in his career Cleburne was described by one who knew him as "a blunt, impassive, rather heavy man . . . who only needed the flames of battle to kindle his dull features, to stir the depths of his strong nature and to show forth a soldier for stoutness of heart, for stubbornness of fight, for shining valor and forgetfulness of self rarely to be matched."[16]

Late in June 1863, Rosecrans moved to force Bragg out of Tennessee. By early September, as a consequence of skillful manœuvreing, Bragg had been compelled to yield Chattanooga to the Federals. On September 4, Bragg, writing to General D. H. Hill, who had been placed in command of Hardee's corps when that officer was sent to aid in the defense of Vicksburg, suggested to him that in making a proposed movement against "a Federal corps opposite," he consult Cleburne, stating, "He is cool, full of resources and ever alive to a success."[17] These operations of Bragg culminated in the barren victory at Chickamauga, September 19-20, 1863.

The outcome of the campaign and the failure of Bragg's leadership to accomplish anything of positive benefit to the Confederacy caused increased friction between Bragg and his subordinate commanders. Another petition to President Davis asking for Bragg's removal from command of the army was sent to Richmond. Many of the general officers, including Cleburne, signed the petition. Cleburne had no ill feelings toward Bragg, but having reluctantly reached the conclusion that Bragg was not suited to command an army in the field, he felt it his duty to express his opinion and to make clear his position. On October 9, 1863, after receiving the petition, President Davis again visited the army and at army head-

15. *O.R.* XX, pt. 1, 699, 284; *Ibid.,* XXIII, pt. 2, 613; J. E. Johnston, *Narrative of Military Operations* (New York, 1874), 165.

16. Archer Anderson, "The Campaign and Battle of Chickamauga," *SHSP,* IX (1881), 390.

17. *O.R.* XXIII, pt. 2, 918 and XXX, pt. 4, 594.

quarters, with Bragg himself present, met the leading officers of the army to ask each of those present their opinion as to Bragg's qualifications to command. Cleburne, in his turn, was said to have expressed the opinion that Bragg had lost the confidence of the army and that a change of commanders should be made. No written record of the meeting was kept. Davis, in the end, decided to leave Bragg in command and to recall Hardee from Mississippi to replace General D. H. Hill, whom Davis felt was largely responsible for the petition asking for Bragg's removal. When Hill was relieved on October 9, 1863, Cleburne and other division and brigade commanders in his corps wrote him letters of appreciation. Cleburne wrote: "Allow me to express to you the sincere regard and high confidence with which you succeeded in inspiring both myself and, I believe, every officer and man in my command."[18]

In the six weeks that followed Davis's visit to the army, Bragg unsuccessfully attempted to starve Rosecrans' army shut up in Chattanooga. On October 17, 1863, General U. S. Grant was placed in command of the Federal forces at Chattanooga. Rosecrans was relieved, re-enforcements from Mississippi under the command of General W. T. Sherman and from the Army of the Potomac under General Joseph Hooker arrived and a supply line to Chattanooga was opened. Bragg, instead of concentrating his available forces and taking a vigorous offensive before the Federal re-enforcements could arrive, had elected to detach a force under General James Longstreet to take Knoxville, while his remaining troops maintained an ineffective siege of Chattanooga. Grant, under great pressure

---

18. For the petition, see *O.R.*, XXX, pt. 2, 65 and LII, pt. 2, 664, 666; *SHSP*, XXI (1893), 143; James Longstreet, *From Manassas to Appomattox* (Philadelphia, 1908), 465; William M. Polk, *Leonidas Polk: Bishop and General*, II (New York, 1893), 291; A. C. Avery, "Life and Character of Lt. Gen. D. H. Hill," *SHSP*, XXI, 110-50; on Oct. 9, 1863, on Hill's relief from duty with the Army of Tennessee, Cleburne and other division and brigade commanders in Hill's corps wrote him letters of appreciation. Cleburne wrote: "Allow me to express to you the sincere regard and high confidence with which you succeeded in inspiring both myself and, I believe, every officer and man in my command." quoted in A. C. Avery, "Life and Character of Lieut. Gen. D. H. Hill," in *SHSP*, XXI, 145.

Battle of Pickett's Mill—"The Hell Hole," May 25, 1864. One of Cleburne's bitterest fights.

—The Mountain Campaigns in Georgia (Atlanta, 1890)

from the Washington authorities to take the offensive, worked energetically to complete his preparations to attack Bragg, whose troops were stationed along Missionary Ridge and at its base. When Grant learned that Bragg had ordered Cleburne with his own and Edward Johnson's division to entrain for East Tennessee to report to Longstreet, he directed an immediate attack on Missionary Ridge. Cleburne's troops were promptly recalled and he was ordered to report to General Bragg. His division was assigned as a reserve, but when Bragg learned that Federal troops under Sherman were threatening the Confederate right, he directed Cleburne to post his division in a position defending the railroad tunnel through Missionary Ridge.

Cleburne placed his infantry and artillery skillfully and was able to beat off Sherman's repeated attempts to dislodge him. Bragg's men, however, were driven from their positions at the foot of and along Missionary Ridge. Cleburne's command was the only organized unit to hold firmly against all attacks. As the victorious Federals pursued the fleeing Confederate troops along Missionary Ridge, Cleburne was charged with covering the retreat of the army southward to Dalton, Georgia. He was directed to take position in a pass in the hills at Ringgold and "to hold [it] at all hazards and keep back the enemy until the artillery and transportation of the army is secure, the salvation of which depends upon him." During the morning of the next day, November 27, 1863, attacks from all sides were made and repulsed. About noon, Cleburne on orders, his mission accomplished, was directed to retire as soon as he could break off the fight. By mid-afternoon he began to withdraw southward to previously chosen positions. No further pursuit followed. For his skillful leadership and determined stand against odds, Cleburne received the thanks of Bragg's army and of a grateful government. Within a few days, Cleburne and his division rejoined the army and went into winter quarters at Tunnel Hill, ten miles north of Dalton.[19] Bragg was soon afterward replaced by General Johnston.

19. I. A. Buck, "Cleburne and His Division at Missionary Ridge and Ringgold Gap," *SHSP,* VIII, 464-75.

Despite the fact that Cleburne personally led his men where the fighting was hottest in battle after battle and sometimes at heavy cost, he himself was wounded only twice, once at the battle of Richmond, Kentucky, August 30, 1862, when several of his teeth were knocked out by a rifle ball that entered through his cheek, and again at Perryville, October 8, 1862, when he was wounded in the leg by a cannon shot that killed his horse. He passed unscathed through fierce conflict at Murfreesboro, Chickamauga, Missionary Ridge, Ringgold Gap and the battles of the Atlanta campaign. Finally at Franklin, in the thick of combat, while charging with his men on foot, he met his death.

Cleburne's reputation extended beyond that of a successful combat leader. Confidence in his administrative capacity was evidenced when General E. Kirby Smith, with whom he had served during the Kentucky campaign, named Cleburne as one of those who might be sent to him to command the District of Arkansas in the Trans-Mississippi in place of Lieutenant General T. H. Holmes, who had asked to be relieved. No reply to Kirby Smith's request has been found. General S. B. Buckner was finally sent to the area.[20]

Cleburne's leadership, skill and conduct on the field of battle were twice noticed by the thanks of the Confederate Congress, first as a consequence of his conduct and leadership at the battle of Richmond, Kentucky, August 30, 1862 and again for his successful conduct of the rear guard at Ringgold Gap, Novembr 27, 1863.[21] Cleburne many times earned the proud title of the "Stonewall Jackson of the West" bestowed on him by President Jefferson Davis and others. John Fiske characterized him as "the ablest division commander in all the Confederate army west of the Alleghenies."[22]

20. See "Indorsement" by Gen. E. Kirby Smith, March 1, 1864, on Holmes' request of Feb. 1, 1864, to be relieved of his command, *O.R.* XXXIV, pt. 2, 935; see also E. Kirby Smith, Shreveport, La., to R. W. Johnson, Confederate Senator from Arkansas, Jan. 15, 1864, *Ibid.*, XXXIV, pt. 2, 869-70.

21. *O.R.* XVI, pt. 1, 1161; *Journal of the Congress of the Confederate States of America, 1861-1865,* II (Washington, 1904), 620, 665, 689, 698.

22. Jefferson Davis, *The Rise and Fall of the Confederate Government,* II (New York, 1881), 577; *The Land We Love,* II (Charlotte, 1867), 460;

General Hardee "was the first to recognize [Cleburne's] merits and was mainly instrumental in securing his promotion successively to the brigade and the division which Hardee had himself commanded. With brief exceptions Cleburne served under Hardee continuously. . . . Their personal relations were close and intimate, and Cleburne's attachment to Hardee and his admiration for him as a soldier were well known to every one acquainted with him." Cleburne was characterized as "one of the most loyal of men . . . he was a man of rare intelligence, but excessively guarded in speech."[23]

Cleburne made his division what it was, a well drilled and well disciplined force, able and willing at all times and under all conditions and circumstances, to carry out the directives of its commander. As General Hardee said: "When [Cleburne's] division defended, no odds broke its lines; where it attacked, no numbers resisted its onslaught, save only once, and there is the grave of Cleburne." He was the idol of his command, constantly on the alert to see to it that his men were as well fed, well clothed, well housed and well armed as circumstances permitted.

He instituted or originated the order of the "Comrades of the Southern Cross" about which little is known. The organization was reported to be partially philanthropic in its object and "was intended to bind together as one man the soldiers of the Southern army, obligating themselves to stand by each other and never to desert their comrades in distress or the cause of their country in any adversity." General Cleburne "attributed the valor of his troops mainly to the effect of this organization." He is said to have remarked. "Had this order been disseminated throughout the Southern army, they could march to the Ohio River without a check."[24]

Another interesting fact in connection with Cleburne's division is that when at Wartrace, Tennessee, near Murfreesboro, when new

---

John Fiske, *The Mississippi Valley in the Civil War* (Boston and New York, 1900), 167.

23. T. B. Roy, "General Hardee and Military Operations About Atlanta," *SHSP,* VIII, 381, 386.

24. *The Land We Love,* II, 462.

flags were ordered to be issued to the troops of the Army of Tennessee, Cleburne's men objected to giving up their distinctive colors —a blue and white flag with a white moon in the center on which were "crossed cannon inverted" with the number of the regiment carrying the flag. It had been designed and adopted by General W. J. Hardee, previous to the battle of Shiloh. The protests to giving up the distinctive colors for the newly adopted St. Andrew's Cross flag were finally heeded and the division was allowed to retain its own distinctive flag, the only division in the army permitted to do so. This was a high compliment alike to the division and its commander. The flag became well known to friend and foe alike and always clearly marked the presence and place of Cleburne's division in the line of battle.[25]

While in camp at Tunnel Hill during December 1863 Cleburne gave serious thought to the worsening position of the Southern Confederacy and to possible means to improve its situation *vis a vis* its Northern opponent. To crystallize his thoughts, Cleburne composed a lengthy memorial setting forth his ideas which he planned to read to an assembly of leading officers of the Army of Tennessee.

Cleburne had been a signer, with others, to two previous memorials, one addressed to the Adjutant General of the Confederate Army at Richmond and the other to the Confederate Congress, urging that steps be taken to add strength to the Confederate armies. The first, dated July 25, 1863, from army headquarters in Middle Tennessee, urged particularly that the substitution regulations be overhauled

---

25. *Ibid.*, II, 462; Carlton McCarthy, "Origin of the Confederate Battleflag," designed by General P. G. T. Beauregard in 1862, *SHSP*, VIII, 497-99; A. L. Rogers, "The Confederate Flag," *Ibid.*, IX, 155-62; "Facts about 'The Cleburne Flag,'" *Confederate Veteran,* XVII (1909), 328; General S. B. Buckner says General Albert Sidney Johnston "wanted a battle flag so distinctive in character that it could not be mistaken . . . a blue field and a white centre. . . . My wife made such a flag for each regiment at Bowling Green. . . . The first time the battle flag was used was at [Fort] Donelson. The troops that I commanded mostly fell to Hardee's command afterwards, they continued to use the flag, and it came to be known as Hardee's Battle Flag." Quoted from Nashville *Banner* of Dec. 11, 1909 in Arndt M. Stickles, *Simon Bolivar Buckner: Borderland Knight* (Chapel Hill, 1940), 172.

—Courtesy John R. Peacock, High Point, N. C.

"Carnton"—The McGavock House, Franklin, Tenn. When found, Cleburne's body was taken to the McGavock house, but soon afterward was removed to Ashwood Hall.

The Absalom Thompson House, Spring Hill, Tenn.—Hood's headquarters during the late afternoon, evening, and night of November 29, 1864.

—Courtesy John R. Peacock, High Point, N. C.

—Courtesy John R. Peacock, High Point, N. C.

Ashwood Hall, Maury Co., Tenn. The home of General Leonidas Polk. Cleburne's body was brought here for burial.
"Fare thee well, departed chieftain. Passed so soon through death's dark vale."

—Courtesy John R. Peacock, High Point, N. C.

St. John's Church yard, Ashwood—"Almost worth dying for, to be buried in such a beautiful spot." Cleburne, Granbury and Strahl were buried here. Later all were removed to their respective homes.

Monument to General P. R. Cleburne, erected by the Phillips County Memorial Association on Confederate Hill in Evergreen Cemetery, Helena, Ark., and dedicated on Confederate Memorial day, May 10, 1891. From a recent photograph. The Confederate monument is in the background.

CONFEDERATE CLEBURNE

to curb the loss of army personnel by desertion and malingering of substitutes and by reducing the number of details for non-combatant duty.[26] The second memorial dated soon after the disastrous loss of Chattanooga and the retreat to Tunnel Hill and Dalton was also signed by many of the high ranking officers of the army, Cleburne signing with reservations. The memorial, addressed to the Confederate Congress, was referred to the Committee on Military Affairs of both the House and the Senate for consideration and debate, but no action was taken at the time.[27]

Undoubtedly, the discussions among the officers coupled with the disasters and demoralization that had overtaken the army, prompted Cleburne to present for consideration a memorial of his own. To a man of his intelligence and perception, it seemed only rational to use the slaves as soldiers. Out of this conception grew his proposal to arm the slaves, making emancipation a reward for their service. Accordingly, consulting with the brigade and division commanders in Hardee's corps as well as with Hardee himself, he prepared a proposal to this effect. It was signed by many of the leading general officers of the army and was read to an assembly which was called to meet in General J. E. Johnston's headquarters. As noted in Captain Buck's account, there was some approval and some dissent. One of those present, General W. H. T. Walker, violently objected to the proposal and with Cleburne's permission forwarded the memorial to President Davis. Walker also planned to write "to each of the gentlemen present at the meeting" asking "their sentiments in so grave a proposal," but the only such letter that has been found is Walker's letter to General T. C. Hindman and Hindman's reply in which that officer declined to comply with Walker's request because he did not recognize Walker's right to make such a request. He did say, however, that "whenever my proper superiors see fit to propound any interrogations to me touching matters as to which

26. See *O.R.*, series 4, II, 670-71.

27. See memorial and remarks concerning it by Senator H. S. Foote, in Richmond *Examiner,* Dec. 30, 1863; see also *Journals of the Confederate Congress,* Dec. 29, 1863, III, 494.

they are entitled to inquire, it will be my duty to answer directly, and I shall do so."[28]

President Davis did not feel that the military situation was so bad as to justify consideration of such an extreme measure as that proposed by Cleburne. Through Secretary of War James A. Seddon, President Davis asked that the proposal be suppressed. When Cleburne heard of Davis's reaction he banned all discussion of the proposal and did not again mention it. Few in Richmond or elsewhere, at the time, knew much, if anything concerning Cleburne's memorial. Locally, however, General Bragg wrote ". . . Great sensation is being produced . . . by the Emancipation project of Hardee, Cheatham, Cleburne & Co. It will kill them." Less than a year later, Davis was moved by circumstances and events to propose to the Confederate Congress, as a military measure, the arming of the slaves almost along the lines proposed by Cleburne. By the time Congress got around to adopting Davis's proposal it was too late.[29]

An interesting comment on the memorial and the secrecy with which it was surrounded is to be found in a letter written from Newnan, Georgia, January 30, 1864, by Colonel A. S. Colyar, a member of the Confederate Congress from Tennessee, to his cousin, Albert S.

---

28. Walker to Hindman, Jan. 9, 1864, *O.R.* LII, part 2, 593, and Hindman's reply of the same date, in *Ibid.,* XXXII, part 2, 594. Hindman wrote that "So far as the looked for thunder bolts are concerned, I am ready to meet them by a distinct avowal at the proper time and in the proper way, but 'not on compulsion' of this sort."

29. For Cleburne's memorial, see *O.R.* LII, part 2, 586-93. See also Irving A. Buck, "Negroes in Our Army," in Richmond *Dispatch,* Aug. 5, 1901 and *SHSP,* XXXI, 215-28; J. W. Du Bose, *General Joseph Wheeler and the Army of Tennessee* (New York, 1912), 256-59; W. M. Polk, *Leonidas Polk: Bishop and General,* II, 339-43; Thomas Robson Hay, "The South and the Arming of the Slaves," *Mississippi Valley Historical Review,* VI (Cedar Rapids, 1920), 39-50; Bell Irvin Wiley, *Southern Negroes, 1861-1865* (New Haven, 1938), 150; N. W. Stephenson, "The Question of Arming the Slaves," *American Historical Review,* XVIII (Lancaster, 1913), 295; Bragg to M. J. White, Feb. 5, 1864 in University of North Carolina Library—Marcus J. Wright Collection. For general ignorance of the contents of Cleburne's memorial in Richmond see J. B. Jones, *A Rebel War Clerk's Diary* (Philadelphia, 1866), II, 146 and Edward Younger, ed., *Inside the Confederate Government: The Diary of Robert Garlick Hill Kean* (New York, 1957), 177-78. See also Cate, ed., *Two Soldiers,* 16-18, 33.

Marks, Colonel of the 17th Tennessee in Cleburne's division. Colonel Colyar wrote: "While at Atlanta I saw General Cleburne for the first time, and spent some time with him at his room. He spoke in high terms of you. I found him to be apparently, and I suppose really, a very modest man. I was very much surprised to hear him say that he considered slavery as at an end. That we ought to put many of the negroes in the service, but that we could not risk them and the consequences without changing our relations with them. That no half-way measures would do—that an entire change of our relations to the slaves, not by military law, but by action of the states, was necessary. That as soon as this was done, the effect would be upon the North such that they could not keep their armies in the field; and certainly it would insure our recognition at once by the principal powers of Europe. That if we take this step now, we can mold the relations, for all time to come, between the white and colored races and we can control the negroes, and that they will still be our laborers as much as they now are, and, to all intents and purposes, will be our servants at less cost than now. His great argument is that if the Yankees succeed in abolishing slavery, *equality and amalgamation will finally take place*. General Cleburne says he submitted his views in writing to a number of the officers of the army, at a meeting some weeks ago. That the paper was signed and approved by most of the officers of his division; that many officers at the meeting seemed favorably inclined to his views, and but one man, Major General [W. H. T.] Walker, took decided ground against him, and a few days afterward wrote him a note (which he showed me) asking for a copy of the paper to be forwarded to the Secretary of War. General Cleburne answered him, saying he would take pleasure in furnishing a copy; had no objection to the Secretary of War knowing his views; that he did furnish the copy, signing his own name, saying to General Walker that he had not consulted the other gentlemen, and did not feel authorized to give their names as they signed the paper for the purposes of that meeting. General Cleburne promised to send me a copy of this paper (25 pages).

Battle of Atlanta, July 22, 1864—The capture of De Gress's battery—"A single line of Confederate troops from Hardee's corps, with no support, stormed the works and overwhelmed the gun crews."

—Mountain Campaigns in Georgia (Atlanta, 1890)

The Battlefield of Franklin, Tenn., looking north from General Cheatham's headquarters.

—Battles and Leaders of the Civil War

"I admire General Cleburne's boldness and the fearless manner in which he comes up to a question which he must know may overwhelm him in ruin; but I cannot agree with him in the necessity for such a move. I have no doubt about the effect on European Powers; but I do not believe the negro could be used to much advantage after he was freed. (But, General Cleburne says, writing a man 'free' does not make him so, as the history of the Irish laborer shows). We are fast approaching a crisis in this revolution when we may look for bold moves on the chess-board. No man need be surprised at anything. I am always hopeful." A week later, on February 5, 1864, Colyar wrote again: "I have just received a letter from General Cleburne in which he excuses himself from sending me a copy of the paper referred to in my letter to you, by saying that he had a communication from the Secretary of War saying: 'The President was of the opinion that the promulgation of such opinions under present circumstances of the Confederacy can be productive only of discouragement, distraction and dissension;' and urging the suppression, not only of the Memorial itself, but, likewise, of all discussion growing out of it. General Cleburne further says: 'After such an opinion from the Commander-in-Chief of the Army and the highest officer of our Government, I feel it my duty to suppress the Memorial and to cease to advocate the measures mentioned.' "[30]

General Walker, who had violently opposed Cleburne's proposal, wrote General Bragg, then in Richmond as personal military adviser to the President, that the "proceedings . . . would ruin our cause and disgrace our country." He commended Davis's prompt action in suppressing Cleburne's "extraordinary document." After the meeting Walker had written each of those present asking their attitude toward "the proposition and sentiments of General Cleburne." Some of the replies favored Cleburne's proposal; some did not. Others, including General Hardee, did not reply.[31]

---

30. Quoted in E. L. Drake, ed., *Annals of the Army of Tennessee* (Nashville, 1878), 339-45.

31. MS in Bragg Papers, Western Reserve Historical Society; see also W. M. Polk, *Leonidas Polk: Bishop and General,* II, 339-43; O.R. LII, part 2, 598.

In the midst of the excitement caused by his memorial, Cleburne became an important participant in a fully non-military event. General W. J. Hardee, his corps commander, was making preparations to be married. Without hesitation he invited Cleburne to be his best man and Cleburne promptly accepted. General Walker, in his letter to Bragg above mentioned, was scornful of Hardee's action in choosing Cleburne. He wrote: "[Hardee] *introduced t*he Gentle*man* [Cleburne] to the meeting and took him after *knowing* his sentiments and hearing his paper read to perform a very confidential and intimate office no less than playing Brides Man at his wedding, an office which is only intrusted to a *particular Friend*."

Hardee was 48. The bride-to-be was Mary Foreman Lewis, then nearly 26 years of age. She was the daughter of a wealthy cotton planter who lived at "Bleak House" in Marengo County, Alabama, on Prairie Creek, a tributary of the Black Warrior River. Her brother was Ivey Foreman Lewis, who served throughout the war in the Jeff Davis (cavalry) Legion. The bride-to-be, "born an heiress and educated abroad"' was reported to have had "a wonderful personality and magnificent eyes. She would have been a beauty but for her extreme thinness."

Bleak House, said to be up-to-date for the time, was located in the black belt of Alabama. There were few roads, in places wooden causeways crossed the streams and the mud was "so deep that in places a man might sink until only his hat was showing." The marriage was most unusual and romantic and the wedding was a grand event for the wealthy planters in the county. "The ladies coming to the wedding had to be carried from their carriages to the house through the mud by darkies" on the plantation. Many guests came from Mobile, Selma and other points in the area. The refreshments too came from Mobile. General Hardee and his staff as well as other invited officers were in full uniform. Champagne added to the festivities, so much so, it was reported one general could not find his trousers the next morning.[32]

---

32. This account of Hardee's wedding is from a letter of a niece of Mrs. Hardee—Mrs. Allen C. Jones, Birmingham, Ala.—to the writer, May

Among those attending the wedding, which took place, January 13, 1864, was a girl of 24, Miss Sue Tarleton from Mobile, who was the maid of honor. She thus stood up with General Cleburne, the best man. She has been described "as a young maiden of rare accomplishments and intelligence, the daughter of a cotton factor of Mobile." For Cleburne it was a case of love at first sight. After the ceremony the bride and groom, Cleburne, Miss Tarleton and other members of the wedding party went to Mobile, presumably by boat on the Black Warrior River. The Mobile *Daily Advertiser and Register* of January 22, 1864, noticing Cleburne's presence in the city, commented that he was "as modest and unassuming as a girl, he has shunned the crowd of parasites and puffers, unfortunately found around headquarters. Hence, while columns are devoted to the exploits of tenth rate men, but little has been said about this extraordinary man."

Cleburne remained only briefly in Mobile to pay court to Miss Tarleton. By the end of January he was back in camp at Dalton. He at once began a correspondence with Miss Tarleton, at the same time enlisting the help of Miss Sallie Lightfoot, also of Mobile, who was soon to marry Miss Tarleton's brother Robert. On March 6 Cleburne returned to Mobile. Five days later he wrote Miss Sallie Lightfoot that Miss Tarleton, after keeping him "in cruel suspense at length consented to be mine and we are engaged." Whether Cleburne ever saw his affianced again is not known, though perhaps he returned to Mobile or Miss Tarleton may have visited the army in camp at Dalton. After his death at Franklin some of Cleburne's personal belongings were sent to her by his aides and by his friend of Helena days, C. E. Nash, who was then living in Selma, Alabama.[33]

4, 1942; for a description of Bleak House, see J. W. Du Bose, "Chronicle of the Canebrake, 1817-1860," *Alabama Historical Quarterly*, IX (1947), 534, 543-44.

33. J. W. Du Bose, *General Joseph Wheeler and the Army of Tennessee*, 402; Irving A. Buck to his sister, Lucy, Feb. 9, 1864, MS in private hands; Cleburne to Miss Sallie Lightfoot, March 11, 1864, MS in Tarleton Papers, Yale University; also printed in *Arkansas Historical Quarterly*, I (Little Rock, 1952), 157-58; L. H. Mangum, "*General P. R. Cleburne*," in

Just what effect Cleburne's action in suggesting the arming of the slaves and their enrollment in the ranks of the Confederate Army had on consideration of his promotion to the rank of lieutenant general is not known. Within eight months after he presented his memorial three vacancies in this rank occurred in the Army of Tennessee to any one of which Cleburne could logically have been promoted. The first came when Leonidas Polk was killed on Pine Mountain, Georgia, June 14, 1864; the second when J. B. Hood superseded J. E. Johnston as commander of the Army of Tennessee, July 18, 1864; the third when W. J. Hardee, at his own request, was relieved from command of the corps of which Cleburne's division was a part, September 23, 1864.

In the first case, the promotion went to Major General A. P. Stewart, then commanding a division in Hood's corps. In the second instance, the promotion and assignment went to Major General S. D. Lee, who had not previously served with the Army of Tennessee, but who was then on duty in Mississippi. Cleburne ranked both Stewart and Lee as a major general and had a more consistently successful record than either of them.

No promotion was made to fill the position vacated by Hardee but Major General B. F. Cheatham, the ranking division commander in Hardee's corps, was assigned to the command. Hood apparently recommended that Cheatham be promoted to the rank of lieutenant general, but later withdrew the recommendation.[34] Cheatham had a good record, but his performance had not been as brilliant and successful as that of Cleburne. Both men, for short periods, had commanded the corps in Hardee's absence, Cleburne as late as September 1864 in the operations about Jonesboro. Cheatham, though a hard

---

Kennesaw Gazette, June 15, 1887; C. E. Nash, *Biographical Sketches of General Pat Cleburne and T. C. Hindman* (Little Rock, 1898), 111.

34. Hood wrote Seddon, Dec. 7, 1864: "I withdraw my recommendation in favor of the promotion of Major General Cheatham for reasons which I will write more fully." Hood blamed Cheatham for the failure at Spring Hill on Nov. 29, 1864, but no letter explaining "more fully" his reasons for withdrawing the recommendation has been located. See J. B. Hood, *Advance and Retreat* (New Orleans, 1880), 289.

fighter, was known to be addicted to strong drink. One newspaper commented: "Cheatham is only a fighter, not a general, and a better horse jockey than either. Cleburne, who has been raised to the rank of major general against a great deal of opposition, is perhaps the best man in Hood's army at this time, at least possessed of more of the sterling qualities of a man and experience as a soldier."[35]

While the soldiers in the army generally opposed Cleburne's proposal to arm the slaves, they did not believe that this action should stand in the way of his promotion. Many attributed his being passed over to President Davis's disapproval of his memorial and to Hood's resentment of Cleburne's opposition to his appointment as successor to General Johnston. General Braxton Bragg, though he had repeatedly commended Cleburne's ability and conduct under fire, would hardly have advocated his promotion to lieutenant general. He knew that Cleburne had expressed lack of confidence in his competency to command the Army of Tennessee and that he was a close friend of Hardee, who had voiced similar sentiments. There was also opposition to the promotion of General S. D. Lee, who it was reported "assumes command with the prejudices of the army against him." On the other hand, Judge J. P. Young, an authority on the history of the Army of Tennessee, who, as a youth of 15 or 16 served in Forrest's cavalry, wrote: "as a soldier in that Army [of Tennessee], I personally knew that the troops in general coincided in the views of their superior officers and President about making soldiers of negroes, though there were a few of the opposite opinion . . . I am sure that the [Cleburne] memorial incident had nothing to do with any failure by the military authorities to promote General Cleburne to the rank of lieutenant general."[36]

Cleburne was repeatedly distinguished in the Atlanta campaign, which began, May 5, 1864, with a flanking movement by Sherman's

35. New York *Herald,* quoted in Charleston *Daily Courier,* Aug. 15, 1864, commenting on A. P. Stewart's promotion to lieutenant general.

36. E. T. Sykes, "History of Walthall's Brigade," Mississippi Historical Society *Publications,* centenary series, I (Jackson, 1916), 551; Cate, ed., *Two Soldiers,* 103—entry July 27, 1864; J. P. Young to T. R. Hay, May 29, 1918.

forces. In successive operations, particularly at Pickett's Mill, May 27, at Kennesaw Mountain, June 27, and in the operations about Atlanta in the last two weeks of July 1864, Cleburne was in the thick of the fight and was constantly distinguished by his conduct and leadership. Though he had not favored Johnston's replacement by Hood, neither this nor his ebbing confidence in the new commander diminished in any degree his loyal support of Hood and his attempt, to the best of his ability, to carry out orders as directed.

All of Cleburne's important battle reports survived and are printed in the *Official Records* with the exception of a complete report of the Atlanta campaign. There is only a report of the battle of Pickett's Mill, May 27, 1864. General Cleburne's reports are complete as to the action of his own command. He always cited outstanding individual conduct of members of his division and never failed to mention by name and thank the members of his staff.[37]

Cleburne's report of the "Atlanta Campaign, May 5 to August 30, 1864," was his last one. This report, dated at "Baugh's House, near Atlanta, Georgia, August 16, 1864" was addressed to Cleburne's corps commander, General W. J. Hardee, and was captioned as covering the period from the opening of the Atlanta campaign "to the date of General J. E. Johnston's being relieved from the command of the army," July 18, 1864. Actually, the report is in two parts, the first part is the usual *Official Records* type covering the period from May 6 to May 27, 1864. The second part, which is in smaller type, is dated May 30, 1864, "Paulding County, Georgia," and is addressed to General J. B. Hood under whom Cleburne and his division served during the battle of Pickett's Mill. It is an account of Cleburne's participation in that engagement. At the end of the report to General Hood is a statement by the editors of the *Official*

37. For Cleburne's battle reports see: Shiloh, *O.R.*, X, part 1, 580-84; Richmond, Ky., *Ibid.*, XVI, part 1, 944-45; Perryville, *Ibid.*, LII, part 1, 51-53; Murfreesboro, *Ibid.*, XX, part 1, 843-52; Chickamauga, *Ibid.*, XXX, part 2, 155-58; Missionary Ridge, *Ibid.*, XXXI, part 2, 745-53; Ringgold Gap, *Ibid.*, XXXI, part 2, 755-58; Atlanta Campaign through the battle of Pickett's Mill, May 27, 1864, *Ibid.*, XXXVIII, part 3, 720-25. All Cleburne's battle reports except for Shiloh, Richmond, Ky., and Perryville are given in full in the Appendix.

Records: "The continuation of this report has not been found," nor have any other of Cleburne's reports after this date been found.[38]

In his book, Captain Buck states concerning Cleburne's report of May 30, 1864, that it was "in my handwriting" and that "It was the last battle report made by him [General Cleburne]." Buck makes no mention of the previous portion of the report covering the period from May 6-27, 1864.

Was this previous portion and the "report . . . also prepared and examined and approved [by Cleburne] . . . which gives the history of his division in the Dalton to Atlanta campaign" prepared by Major Calhoun Benham, his chief of staff? If so, did Benham prepare any report of the operations of Cleburne's division subsequent to the report of May 30, 1864 on the battle of Pickett's Mill and is this latter portion that which Benham refers to in his letter to Robert Tarleton in which he states: "It being known that I have in my possession the life of Major General Cleburne brought down to a period shortly prior to his death and composed under his eye, I am requested by many of his best friends to finish it as something towards his biography. Of course I do not feel at liberty to do so. But the account of the General's career will be imperfect if left at the point where the narrative mentioned ends, and can only be completed by the addition of a report which I also prepared and he examined and approved and which gives the history of his division in the Dalton-Atlanta campaign.

"That report Mr. [L. H.] Mangum, one of the General's aides-de-camp, tells me, is in the possession of Miss [Sue] Tarleton, your sister. I feel that it is a very delicate step for me to approach Miss Tarleton to obtain the report—particularly as I have not the honor of her acquaintance, and could not consequently be sure of dealing considerately with the possible susceptibilities of her character.

"I therefore apply to you. Will you do me the favor to procure me the report and I will see that it is published. This is the more proper as it is the only authoritative account which can now be

38. *O.R.*, XXXVIII, part 3, 720-726.

given of the exploits of the Division which rendered so much service to the South, and reflected so much honor upon itself and its distinguished and lamented commander. I know that it was the earnest wish of the General the report should be made public as a testimonial which he conceived his duty required him to give of the conduct of his officers and men. History too requires it. The Division is entitled to its publication. It will be a grateful consolation to them to have their praises from the lips of their dear General and brother in arms, dead on the field of honor.

"Without my certification the report is imperfect. I alone of his officers can certify it, and it is important I should annex to it a statement explanatory of its incompleteness. If Miss Tarleton is willing to entrust the paper to me I will see the manuscript returned if she desires it." In conclusion, Benham wrote: "You will not of course need my assurances that in preparing the General's life, a discreet reticence will be observed as to his relations with Miss Tarleton of which you will have expected I am informed."[39]

Apparently Captain Buck did not have, did not know of, or had forgotten, that portion of Cleburne's report, dated August 16, 1864, prepared, probably by Major Benham, covering the period from May 6 to May 27, 1864. At the end of this portion of the report as printed in Major Benham's sketch of Cleburne in the *Kennesaw Gazette* of June 15, 1889, is a "Note by Major Benham" in which he states: "The foregoing account of the operations of Cleburne's Division was prepared and published by General Cleburne, though not in fact signed, because it remained to add the history of his operations from May 27th to the date of General Johnston's being relieved from command. I make this statement to certify the document as official. The fact is well known to the whole of General Cleburne's staff."

In view of the date, it is reasonable to presume that Major Benham did prepare a report of the operations of Cleburne's division to the time of General Johnston's replacement by Hood, and

39. Calhoun Benham, New York Hotel, New York, to Robert Tarleton, Mobile, Ala., June 5, 1867, MS in Tarleton Papers, Yale University. For Cleburne's report, see Appendix, p. 352-356.

perhaps through the battles about Atlanta to the end of July 1864. If Benham did prepare such a report and if the latter part, which is now missing, was that "in the possession of Miss [Sue] Tarleton" of Mobile to whom Cleburne was engaged at the time of his death and for which Benham wrote Miss Tarleton's brother, Robert, what became of the report? Did Miss Tarleton agree to have it sent to Benham and, if so, did he return it or did he retain it? If the latter, was the report in Benham's papers at the time of his death in San Francisco, or, if returned to Miss Tarleton, what became of it? These are questions not likely to be answered at this late date.

In the days following the loss of Atlanta Hood's Army of Tennessee, including Cleburne and his command, was camped about Lovejoy's Station, Georgia. Both Hood and Sherman were confronted with the problem of what to do next. In the midst of the lull in military operations, President Davis paid his third visit to the Army of Tennessee to investigate the advisability of removing the commander of the army. After careful inquiry his decision was to leave Hood at the helm, but he acceded to Hardee's oft-repeated request for relief as corps commander, and B. F. Cheatham was named as Hardee's successor.[40]

Following the visit of President Davis, Hood moved his army northward through Georgia to the Tennessee River, where he delayed for three weeks until November 19 when the advance into Tennessee was begun. The events of the next ten days ending in the failure to cut off the Federal army at Spring Hill on November 29 and the bloody defeat at Franklin on the following day were the most tragic in the long history of the Confederate Army of Tennessee.

For nearly a week after Hood's army began its northward march into Tennessee, General J. M. Schofield, commanding the opposing Federal troops, was uncertain as to his opponent's intentions. Had Hood carried out his plan of operations with energy and expedition, he probably could have cut off Schofield from his base at Nashville and forced him to fight at a great disadvantage or disperse his army. But, because of a lack of energy in direction and in a period of

40. See *O.R.*, XXXIX, part 3, 842, 859, 979-80.

indecision and failure to exercise personal command, Hood failed and Schofield's troops in the dark of the night of November 29, marched past the waiting Confederate troops at Spring Hill and went safely into Franklin. In a fit of disappointment and frustration at his failure to intercept and cut off Schofield, Hood the next day, November 30, threw his troops, practically without artillery support, against the entrenched Federals in front of Franklin. The attacks, beginning about 4 o'clock in the afternoon, failed to drive Schofield's men from their positions. After dark the Federal troops withdrew across the Harpeth River and retreated hastily to Nashville, some thirty miles distant. Hood's losses in both officers and men were among the heaviest of the war in proportion to the number of men engaged. His losses in killed and wounded and missing were four and one half times the Federal losses. Five general officers—Cleburne, John Adams, O. F. Strahl, H. B. Granbury and States R. Gist—were killed; General John C. Carter died of his wounds several days later. Five general officers—J. C. Brown, A. M. Manigault, F. M. Cockrell, W. A. Quarles and T. M. Scott—were wounded. General G. W. Gordon was captured.

The attack had been made without artillery preparation because, Hood later wrote, "of the women and children remaining in Franklin." Only two batteries of artillery participated in the action—Guibor's Missouri battery and Slocomb's Louisiana battery, commanded by Lieutenant J. Adolphe Chalaron. A careful study of Hood's report and of his book, *Advance and Retreat,* leave the impression that Hood either did not know how to use his artillery and cavalry or did not think of these arms of the service as necessary to his success. He seemed to depend almost entirely on the shock effect of his veteran infantry.[41]

---

41. On November 28, 1864, at Columbia, Tenn., General Hood issued the following circular to his corps commanders: "If you have any batteries of artillery whose animals you consider too weak to continue on this expedition, General Hood directs that you leave them here [at Columbia] to form a garrison of the place."—Circular, *O.R.*, XLV, part 1, 1255; Hood, *Advance and Retreat,* 328, 330; D. W. Sanders, "The Tennessee Campaign," *Southern Bivouac,* new series, I [1885], 8, 9 and 13; Bate's report, *O.R.*, XLV, part 1, 744-45.

Thus Cleburne ended a brilliant military career in an unnecessary assault carried out in the late afternoon in an effort to atone for Hood's hesitating leadership of the day before and to satisfy his wounded pride. Men's lives were sacrificed in the vain hope of retrieving errors of the high command that were committed, primarily, because of the lack of personal supervision on the part of the one responsible for the prompt execution of orders.

Hood later wrote, seemingly in self-justification, that Cleburne "knew in what manner my orders at Spring Hill had been totally disregarded," and said that "he would never again allow one of my orders for battle to be disobeyed, if he could prevent it." Hood also wrote that while Cleburne was preparing his division for the charge at Franklin, he expressed himself "with an enthusiasm which he had never before betrayed in our intercourse" saying: " 'General, I am ready, and have more hope in the final success of our cause than I have had at any time since the first gun was fired.' " These alleged remarks are at variance with Cleburne's usual manner. He was a realist and he could not help but see that the task set for him and his division and the others who were to participate in the projected assault against a brave, veteran infantry behind entrenchments, with their backs to a river and well supported by artillery, was anything but an easy one. In addition, as General J. C. Brown later wrote, Cleburne believed that Hood held him responsible, in large measure at least, for the failure to attack Schofield's passing troops at Spring Hill and "was quite angry and evidently deeply hurt." Cleburne certainly was in no way responsible for the failure to attack at Spring Hill, nor was Cheatham. Hood, at first, blamed Cheatham, but later withdrew his accusation because, he said, an order directing him to make a night attack on November 29 was never delivered. He did charge that "the best move of his career was made for nothing because of *the failure of a subordinate* [whom he did not name] to properly execute his orders."[42]

---

42. Hood, *Advance and Retreat,* 289-90, 297; B. F. Cheatham, "The Failure at Spring Hill," *SHSP,* IX, 538-39; Thomas Robson Hay, *Hood's Tennessee Campaign* (New York, 1929), 88 note no. 35, p. 95, 130; The

Hood's statements as to Cleburne's feelings are contradictory. Hood was on the defensive. His leadership had ended in the complete defeat of his army with terrific losses and he was anxious to relieve himself of as much of the blame as he could. Cleburne had been killed in the action and could not defend himself. There is evidence that "the befuddlement of intoxication might account as much as anything else for the otherwise inexplicable confusion and paralysis at Spring Hill."[43]

A variety of reports give different versions of the cause of Cleburne's death. That he had two horses killed under him as he led the charge of his division against the Federal works at Franklin is generally stated. However, some accounts state that his body was pierced by a score of bullets from Federal rifles, others that he was shot through the head and still others that he fell from a single bullet through the heart. The most credible reports state that he was killed by a single bullet through the heart. General D. C. Govan, one of his brigade commanders wrote, some fifteen years after the battle, that when Cleburne's second horse was killed under him he charged

---

estimate in which Cleburne was held by his men is illustrated by an anecdote told by Gen. Randal L. Gibson, who said that the morning after the fight at Franklin he heard an Arkansas veteran discussing the battle. "You see," he said, "we kept getting over, but they would reenforce and drive us out. Finally we said, 'let's . . . keep quiet till General Cleburne gives the word to charge so we'll all get over together.' . . . we waited and waited and waited. And the boys kept crying for the word and wondered why it didn't come. But when it didn't come, I knew Pat Cleburne was *dead;* for if he had been living he would have given us that order.'" W. P. Johnston, *The Life of Albert Sidney Johnston* (New York, 1878), 354.

43. Stanley F. Horn, *The Army of Tennessee* (Indianapolis and New York, 1941), 392. The posthumous publication of Hood's book, *Advance and Retreat,* in 1880, brought forth a number of articles by participants in the campaign, notably articles by General Cheatham in the *Southern Historical Society Papers* and by Major D. W. Sanders of General A. P. Stewart's staff in the *Southern Bivouac.* Probably the best account of the failure at Spring Hill is that of Judge J. P. Young in the *Confederate Veteran.* The Spring Hill controversy is also discussed in Hay, *Hood's Tennessee Campaign.* General J. C. Brown is reported to have written out a statement of his part in the affair, but though it was announced for delivery before the Southern Historical Society at its May 1883 meeting in Nashville, Tenn., it was neither delivered nor published.

forward on foot with a pistol in one hand and with his sword, his cap on its point, in the other. The cap, now in the museum of the Tennessee Historical Society at Nashville, has a bullet hole in it. How and when it was made is not known. In his book, Captain Buck states that Cleburne was killed by a single bullet through the heart. Cleburne's uniform coat is in the Confederate Memorial Museum in Richmond, Virginia, but it is not certain that it is the coat he was wearing at the time of his death or because of its tattered condition that it has any bullet holes in it. One contemporary statement reported that Cleburne was buried "in plain clothes," which would account for the statement that his uniform coat had been saved and later deposited in the Confederate Memorial Museum.[44]

There have been occasional statements that Cleburne gave his boots to a soldier who had none and that he charged forward against the Federal trenches in his stocking feet, but the best evidence indicates that his boots were stolen from him after he was killed. No trace has been found of the sword presented to him by his former regiment, the 15th Arkansas, in the summer of 1863, although there are varying reports as to what became of it. Likewise, the diary that Cleburne kept has never been found. He is said to have had it with him when he was killed.[45]

As nearly as can be determined Cleburne fell in front of the 16th Kentucky (Federal) infantry regiment of J. W. Reilly's brigade, J. D. Cox's division of the 23d corps, near the old Carter gin house at a point 90 paces south and nearly in front of the gin house and 290 feet east of the Columbia pike.[46] Cleburne's body is reported to have been found by a newspaper man who was going over the battlefield. The body was taken first to the house of John McGavock,

---

44. Statement of Mrs. John McGavock in a newspaper clipping pasted in McGavock Confederate Cemetery book according to information furnished the writer by John R. Peacock.

45. Cleburne's diary is quoted, probably from memory, by Buck, by Benham in *Kennesaw Gazette,* Jan. 1, 1889, and by Mangum in *Ibid.,* June 15, 1887.

46. J. P. Young to the writer, May 5, 1921; Mangum in *Kennesaw Gazette,* June 15, 1887; G. W. Gordon in *SHSP,* XVIII (1891), 267; W. J. Hardee in *Ibid.,* XXXI, 158.

south of Franklin and just to the southeast of the battlefield. Later, a coffin having been procured, Cleburne's remains were removed to the residence of William Julius Polk. Together with the bodies of General H. B. Granbury and Colonel R. B. Young, they were laid in the parlor of the Polk home near Columbia, Tennessee. It was recorded that when his body was brought to the Polk home "a bloody handkerchief was over General Cleburne's face, but one of his staff took from his pocket an embroidered handkerchief and said, 'Cover his face with this; it was sent him from Mobile and I think he was engaged to the lady.' "[47] During the night preceding burial, Miss Naomi Hays, a niece of President James K. Polk and afterwards wife of Major W. R. Moore, Chief Commissary, Army of Tennessee, wrote and placed upon General Cleburne's coffin, a poem as follows:

"Fare thee well, departed chieftain
Erin's land sends forth a wail;
And oh! my country sad laments thee
Passed so soon through death's dark vale.

Blow, ye breezes, softly o'er him,
Fan his brow with gentle breath;
Disturb ye not his gentle slumbers;
Cleburne sleeps the sleep of death!

Rest thee, Cleburne; tears of sadness
Flow from hearts thou'st nobly won;
Memory ne'er will cease to cherish
Deeds of glory thou hast done."[48]

The next morning burial took place in Rose Hill Cemetery, Columbia, Tennessee, Generals Cleburne and Granbury and Colonel Young being buried alongside the bodies of General O. F. Strahl and his aide, Lieutenant John March. "It was soon discovered that

47. Mary Polk Branch, *Memoirs of a Southern Woman* (Chicago, 1893), 47; Mangum, *Kennesaw Gazette,* June 15, 1887; C. T. Quintard Diary, entry Dec. 3, 1864, in The Library of the University of the South, Sewanee, Tenn.

48. Quoted in Mangum, *Kennesaw Gazette,* June 15, 1887.

the resting place that had been chosen by the sexton was in that part of the cemetery known as the potter's field, where criminals and the lower classes rested." Mangum later wrote that General Lucius E. Polk, a nephew of General Bishop Leonidas Polk, "offered a lot" in St. John's churchyard, the family cemetery of the Polk family at Ashwood Hall, about six miles south and west of Columbia. The bodies of Generals Cleburne, Granbury and Strahl and those of Colonel Young and Lieutenant Marsh were disinterred and re-buried in St. John's churchyard.[49]

The day before the battle of Franklin the line of Cleburne's march to Spring Hill went by Ashwood Hall and St. John's churchyard. Cleburne is reported to have reined in his horse and paused for a moment to admire the beauty of the setting, saying to one of his staff that it was "almost worth dying for, to be buried in such a beautiful spot."[50]

Cleburne's remains were removed from St. John's churchyard to Helena, Arkansas, in 1869. A simple slab marked his grave on Confederate Hill in Evergreen Cemetery overlooking the Mississippi River. On it was inscribed: "Major General P. R. Cleburne of the Confederate Army. Born in the County Cork, Ireland. Killed at the battle of Franklin, November 30, 1864." On May 10, 1891, a monument provided by the Phillips County Memorial Association of Helena was dedicated, the feature of the occasion being an address by General George W. Gordon, who commanded a brigade in General J. C. Brown's Division of Cheatham's Corps and who was captured at the battle of Franklin.[51]

Cleburne's friend, Colonel I. W. Avery, 4th Georgia Cavalry, has well stated his character, leadership and ability: "Cleburne rose

---

49. *Ibid.;* Quintard Diary, entry Dec. 3, 1864.

50. Ashwood Hall had been owned by Bishop General Leonidas Polk, but about 1850, if not before, he had sold it to his brother, Andrew Jackson, who remodeled the house and made it into one of the finest houses in Tennessee. St. John's church was jointly built and owned by the four brothers—Lucius Julius, Leonidas, George Washington and Andrew Jackson Polk. It was consecrated Sunday, September 4, 1842, by Bishop James H. Otey, Bishop Leonidas Polk and others participating in the ceremony.

51. *SHSP,* XVIII, 272-81.

to be a military authority in our army. He knew the very rudiments of fighting and had the genius to use his knowledge. Always ready and watchful, never depressed, beloved by his good men, feared by his bad ones, trusted by all, indomitable in courage, skillfully headlong in attack, coolly strategic in retreat, thorough master of detail, yet with large Generalship, obedient to the letter, capable in any crisis, modest as a woman, a resolute disciplinarian, Cleburne was a gem of a warrior. He could do anything with his division. General Hardee once said: 'When his division defended, no odds broke its lines; where it attacked, no numbers resisted its onslaught, save only once, and there is the grave of Cleburne.' "[52] His name is permanently recorded by two counties, one in Texas and one in Arkansas, and by two towns, one in Texas and the other in Kansas.

Captain Irving Ashby Buck, son of William Mason and Elizabeth Anne Ashby Buck, was born November 24, 1840, at Front Royal, Virginia. As previously mentioned, he enlisted in the 17th Virginia Infantry in April 1861, participated in the battle of the First Bull Run as a messenger at General P. G. T. Beauregard's headquarters and went with Beauregard to Tennessee. Buck served at the battle of Shiloh as a headquarters messenger and subsequently was successful in obtaining a commission as a captain and was assigned to General Cleburne's staff in time to participate in the battle of Murfreesboro. His brother, Alvin, then also seeking a staff appointment, wrote their sister that the sights and scenes of battle "cured him of any love he ever entertained for fighting." Irving Buck wrote his sister that he found General Cleburne and his staff as constituted on his joining it "a very pleasant set of gentlemen."

For nearly two years, Buck served as an active member of Cleburne's staff. His relations with Cleburne, he later wrote, were "close and confidential. I habitually messed with him and shared his tent and often shared his blankets." Captain Buck was severely wounded in the fighting near Jonesboro, September 2, 1864, and was

52. *Kennesaw Gazette,* May 15, 1887.

taken to a hospital at Americus, La. General Cleburne is reported to have written the surgeon in charge of the hospital: "You must save Buck. He is the best adjutant general in the army." This was high praise indeed from a soldier of Cleburne's ability, high standards and reputation. Buck's wounds did not heal in time for him to rejoin Cleburne before that officer's death. So far as known, Captain Benjamin F. Phillips, A. A. G. of Arkansas, then serving with Cleburne as an aide, and who was wounded at the battle of Franklin, assumed Captain Buck's duties and was with Cleburne and his command during the Tennessee campaign.

After the close of the war, Buck returned to his home at Front Royal, but subsequently engaged in business in Baltimore, Maryland. On January 31, 1871, he married Frances Ricards from North East, Maryland, a small village near Havre de Grace, Maryland. Captain Buck remained in Baltimore until the early 1900's when he sold his business and returned to live in Front Royal, where he died, September 8, 1912.

From available evidence, it is apparent that Buck's book, *Cleburne and His Command,* was composed over a period of years, beginning probably in the 1880s. It is reported that all his papers, including those which he used in the preparation of his book, were destroyed, with the exception of several small packages, about 1937, because they were in the way. Their value was not appreciated. As a result, surviving papers relating to Buck and his career are scarce.

In the preparation of this introduction, I am particularly indebted to John R. Peacock of High Point, North Carolina, who has made many helpful suggestions and answered many questions, particularly with reference to the circumstances, place and manner of General Cleburne's death. Mr. Peacock has also been generous in furnishing photographs of Confederate general officers killed and wounded at the battle of Franklin and of places in the area with which Cleburne was associated both in life and in death. His unfailing interest is much appreciated. My thanks are also extended to Bell Irvin Wiley, who has read the Introduction several times, for his helpful comments and suggestions. Likewise, the enthusiastic attitude and help of the publisher, Seale Johnson, both in the selection of illustrations and the re-printing of this book are acknowledged. My thanks are also due to Mr. Charles L. Dufour of New Orleans for supplying war-time letters written to Captain Buck's sister and to Mr. Ezra J. Warner of La Jolla, California, for photographs, particularly that of General John Adams. Thanks also are extended to Miss India Thomas of the Confederate Memorial Museum, Richmond, Virginia for the ante-bellum portrait of Cleburne and to Ted R. Worley, Executive Secretary, Arkansas History Commission, Little Rock, for supplying the first known letter written by Cleburne as a Confederate soldier. I am indebted to Mrs. Alene Lowe White, Librarian, Western Reserve Historical Society, Cleveland, Ohio, for a photostat of General W. H. T. Walker's letter to General Bragg, to Mrs. Grace P. Butterworth, Office of the Secretary, Princeton University, for biographical data concerning Judge L. H. Mangum and Mr. Robert Tarleton, and to Mr. Allan R. Ottley, California State Library, Sacramento, California, for biographical data concerning Major Calhoun Benham. Miss Laura Virginia Hale of Front Royal, Virginia and Mr. Welford Ashby Buck of Baltimore, Maryland, have furnished useful biographical data concerning Captain Buck.

THOMAS ROBSON HAY.

Locust Valley, N. Y.
October 2, 1958.

Cleburne And His Command

AUTHOR'S PREFACE

IN WRITING this book all has been subordinated to plain and simple narrative of the life and services of that most remarkable man, General Patrick Cleburne, and his command. Where incidents stated are not matters of personal knowledge, no pains have been spared to verify them by official records, correspondence and verbal information from those who are familiar with them. To the Century "Battles and Leaders of the Civil War," the Southern Historical Papers, Hoods "Advance and Retreat," Taylor's "Destruction and Reconstruction," *The Kennesaw Gazette,* and *The Confederate Veteran,* I am deeply indebted for data.

As far as practicable the pronoun *I* has been avoided, but where used, it is for the purpose of making plain incidents which otherwise would be somewhat obscure, and my personal relations with General Cleburne for over two years were so close as to make entire self elimination difficult, if not impossible.

Defective as the book may be, it is the history of "Cleburne and his Command." It may possibly too much vaunt our dear old division, but if so, that is a trait easily pardonable in all old soldiers, who love, or *should* love, their own.

The Author.

CHAPTER ONE

Early Life

FROM THE FOUNDATION of the American Republic the Irish people have largely contributed to its upbuilding. Want of space forbids a recital of their services in the pulpit and in the forum, in commerce, agriculture, finance, and government. The military is the only one which can be treated in any degree of detail, for in this the natives of the Emerald isle have ever been conspicuously distinguished. Of this is written by an accomplished Confederate soldier: "Strange people, these Irish. Fighting every one's battles and cheerfully taking the hot end of the poker, they are only found wanting when engaged in what they believe to be their national cause. Except the defense of Limerick, under the brilliant Sarsfield, I recall no domestic struggle in which they have shown their worth."[1] And Gen. D. H. Hill says: "Poor Pat, he has fought courageously in every land, in quarrels not his own." And the same author, to illustrate the *esprit-de-corps* of the Irish soldier, his pride in his command, and affection for it, relates that he found on the field of Chickamauga a desperately and shockingly wounded Irishman, to whom he said: "My poor fellow, you are badly hurt. What regiment do you belong to?" "The Fifth Confidrit, and a dommed good rigimint it is," said the wounded man promptly.[2]

1. Richard Taylor, *Destruction and Reconstruction* (New York, 1879), 76.

Note—Those footnotes that are numbered are by the Editor; the starred footnotes are the Author's.

2. D. H. Hill, "Chickamauga—The Great Battle of the West," *Battles and Leaders of the Civil War,* (New York, 1905) III, 659. Henceforth cited *Battles and Leaders.*

To go no further back than the war between the States, it is found that those of Irish birth or descent, on the Federal side, were Sheridan, Meagher, and Sweeny; on the Confederate side, Cleburne, Finegan, and Dick Dowling. And in both armies thousands of less rank, or none at all, while not so conspicuous, were none the less gallant. But among all these the career of Patrick Cleburne was most brilliant and phenomenal. From the local reputation of a young lawyer of high standing, Patrick Ronayne Cleburne, in less than four years, rose from a private soldier, and at the early age of thirty-seven years died holding the rank of major-general, and with a military record to be envied by the most illustrious, and after having gained from the public the well-earned *sobriquet* "Stonewall of the West." But by his idolizing command, he was only spoken of as "old Pat."

It may appear strange that one so prominent should not have had more mention among the leaders of the South, and that he is so little known beyond the Western Army. This seeming omission or neglect can in a measure be attributed to the fact that he was killed in the last months of the war, and the surviving participants, after the war closed, were too busy repairing their broken fortunes to pay much attention to literary affairs. It has required the lapse of decades to give suitable opportunity for historical or biographical justice to those who staked their all for the South.

The following sketch was written for the *Arkansas Gazette,* by Judge L. H. Mangum, Cleburne's law partner before and his aide-de-camp during the war:

> Gen. Patrick Ronayne Cleburne was the third child of Joseph and Mary Ann Cleburne. He was born at Bridgepark Cottage in the county of Cork, ten miles west from the city of Cork, March 17, 1828. His father was a physician of considerable eminence in his profession; a graduate of medicine of the University of London, and in surgery of the Royal College of Surgery, Dublin. He was of an old Tipperary family. * * * Dr. Cleburne was noted for his generosity and unselfishness; was beliked alike by rich and poor; and left behind him a name which lives in the memory of the old inhabitants of West Cork.

His wife was the daughter of Patrick Ronayne, Esq., of Annebrook, on the Great Island, Cork, after whom General Cleburne was named, a name that has survived through six generations of that family. On his mother's side General Cleburne was therefore of an old Irish stock, and being born on St. Patrick's Day his claim to the ancestral name rests upon a double association. By a singular coincidence the name which was destined in after years to shed splendor on the annals of heroism and arms was crowned in its very birth by the three ideas dearest to the Irishman who bore it—patriotism, pride of honorable lineage, and filial love.

Patrick was but little over two years of age when his mother died. His father's second marriage found him still a child, but he was kindly and tenderly treated by his step-mother, with whom he was a favorite. Dr. Cleburne's first family consisted of three sons and one daughter—William, the eldest, now (1886) engineer in charge of the Oregon Short Line Railway; Anne, now Mrs. Sherlock, formerly of Cincinnati, Ohio; Patrick Ronayne, the subject of this sketch; and Joseph, the youngest. All of these are now (1886) living except Patrick.

The second marriage was contracted about a year after the first Mrs. Cleburne's death, with a Miss Isabella Stuart, daughter of a Scotch clergyman. The children by this marriage were four—Isabella, Edward Warren, who went to sea and died of yellow fever on the west coast of Africa; Robert Stuart, and Christopher. This last named half-brother followed General Cleburne to America, who at the beginning of the war bought his younger brother a fine horse and sent him to General Morgan.* He declined, after his own rule, to furnish any letters of introduction, but Morgan soon found the worth of the young man, and he became captain in the Confederate Second Kentucky Cavalry. He was killed at the battle of Cloyd's Farm, near Dublin, Virginia, May 10, 1864, in the twenty-first year of his age. In the words of his commanding officer, "He rests in the State whose valor has given luster to the age, and his memory is cherished by his comrades as that of the brave, chivalrous and true man."

---

*Judge Mangum makes an error as to the time Christopher joined General Morgan's command. It will be seen later that he was serving as a private in Polk's brigade, of his brother's division, at Ringgold, Georgia, on November 27, 1863.

Young Patrick received instruction at home from a tutor until he was about twelve years of age, when he was sent to a school in the neighborhood kept by a clergyman of the Established Church named Spedding, whose memory is preserved in the recollections of his pupils by the terrors of his rule rather than by the force of his scholarship, or by the taste for learning which his system of instruction inspired.

Patrick was fond of boyish adventures, but he avoided companionship and preferred his dog, his horse, his rod or his gun to other company. Even in those early days he was noted for his high sense of honor and his keen sense of disgrace. In literary taste he was fond of history, travels, and poetry, but whether it was due to some peculiar mental inaptitude or to the disgust created within him by the pedagogue who had dealt out the classics by the rule of iron, he was very deficient in Latin and Greek.

His father was in the receipt of a good income from the practice of his profession, but had one expensive taste in a fondness for amateur farming. He cultivated a farm of 500 acres on this principle and practiced his profession at the same time. As he was a better doctor than farmer the result was that what the profession brought in the farming absorbed. When he died he left but a small estate to be divided between his widow and his eight children. Two years later, when Patrick was eighteen years old, he turned his thoughts to the selection of an occupation for life. He had a taste for chemistry and he chose the business of a druggist, intending to make that a stepping-stone to the study of medicine. With this in view he apprenticed himself to a Dr. Justin, who kept a drug store in the little town of Mallow.

Had chemical tastes or pharmaceutical studies been the only requisites for advancement in that line, the future general might have lived a respectable Mallow druggist or been a dispensary doctor in some quiet Irish village. To secure a diploma, however, it was necessary for him to pass a severe examination in Apothecaries' Hall, Trinity College, Dublin, which included Latin, Greek, and French. Here the Societies of Apothecaries attacked him in his weakest point, and here the embryo hero met the first and only defeat of his life. The sense of disgrace overwhelmed the boy of eighteen, and resolving that his family should never know more of one who, as he conceived in his infinite humiliation, had brought a blot upon the family escutcheon, he immediately enlisted without communication with his friends and became a soldier in the Forty-first Regiment of infantry, then stationed in Dublin. It was rumored at the time that these troops would be ordered on foreign service, and this thought influenced him in selecting that particular regiment.

A year elapsed before his friends knew where the boy was, and the information came then from the family of Captain (now General) Robert Pratt. This officer was the son of the rector of the parish adjoining that in which the Cleburne family lived, and the rector was a warm personal friend of Dr. Cleburne. Captain Pratt was not in command of the company to which young Cleburne was attached, and it was only by accident that Patrick's identity was discovered. He has been heard to say with emphasis in alluding to this incident of his life that he would have enlisted under an assumed name had he known of Captain Pratt's presence in the regiment.

The Forty-first was not sent out of the country and the young soldier's life was uneventful. After above three years' service he had been promoted through the grades of lance-corporal and corporal, but further promotion had been checked by the escape of a military prisoner whom he had in charge. Captain Pratt had secured his transfer to his own company and showed him many acts of kindness and courtesy uncommon in those days between a commissioned and a non-commissioned officer. When Cleburne made up his mind to quit the Army, Captain Pratt remonstrated with him strongly and assured him if he remained he would ere long win a commission. The brilliancy of General Pratt's subsequent career in India and the Crimea gives weight to the opinion formed thus early of Cleburne's soldierly qualities and capabilities.

Notwithstanding this advice, however, Cleburne, at the age of twenty-one, advised with his brothers and sister, arranged plans to obtain what means he could from his father's estate and his mother's fortune, purchased his discharge and prepared to take leave of home and country and seek his fortune in foreign lands. In company with these relatives he sailed from the harbor of Queenstown, November 11, 1849, in the bark *Bridgetown.* The voyage in a slow sailing vessel was monotonous but not devoid of pleasure. It was Christmas Day when the vessel entered the mouth of the Mississippi.

Sir Thomas Tobin, manager of the Ballincolleg Powder Mill, had furnished the family with a letter of introduction to Geo. Currie Duncan, at that time president of the Carrolton Railroad, and a prominent citizen of New Orleans. This letter was indirectly influential in deciding the future destiny of the strangers. Cleburne, impatient of introductions and acting on the principle of his life, that a man should depend on himself and not on others, declined to wait the result of the letter, pushed on to Cincinnati, followed two days later by his elder brother and sister. There he found employment in the drug store of a Mr. Salter on Broadway, with whom he remained about six months, when, receiving more remunerative offers, he removed to Helena, Arkansas.

From the time Cleburne went to Helena he seemed to feel he had found a congenial home. The rich soil, the diversified landscape, and the noble river flowing in majestic tides of wealth and power at its base offered inducements both to the man seeking his fortune and to the lover of nature. People who were open and frank in nature, cordial in manners, and full of courage and enterprise gave the young Irishman society which echoed his own sympathy. He easily won his way into fellowship and popularity, and early laid the foundation of that popularity he wielded at a later day.

Entering the drug store of Grant & Nash as a prescription clerk, he devoted himself assiduously to his profession till 1852, when he purchased Grant's interest in the business, and the firm was known as Nash & Cleburne. He was a hard student, both in his profession and in general literature. He joined and took great interest in a debating society formed by the young men of the place. Among these were Hon. John J. Horner, J. M. Hanks, Gen. J. C. Tappan, and the late Mark W. Alexander, men who afterwards became prominent in affairs and achieved distinction in their several walks in life. With such associates and competitors Cleburne held an honorable record. He was a ready and effective debater. Oratory charmed him and he devoted himself diligently to its pursuit. He soon became conspicuous for his oratorical abilities. In 1854 he was chosen orator at a celebration held by the Masonic fraternity of which he was already a bright member, and acquitted himself with such credit as to win general mention and applause. About this time he was persuaded by friends, especially by Dr. Grant, his former employer, to study law, and, selling out his interest in the drug business, he became a law student in the law office of the late Hon. T. B. Hanly. In 1856 he formed a law partnership with Mark W. Alexander, under the name of Alexander & Cleburne. In 1859 Alexander was elected circuit judge. The partnership of Cleburne, Scaife & Mangum was then formed.

While Cleburne was not a brilliant lawyer he had all the elements of success and distinction in this profession. His reading was careful and extensive, his application constant, his judgment clear, and his earnestness, always a marked characteristic of the man, clothed him with real ability. He was scrupulously honest and upright, stood well among his brother lawyers, and commanded not only a good practice but a wide and deep respect among the people. He dealt largely in lands, and at the beginning of the war was himself a large land owner. While he was always alert and eager in his professional duties, he identified himself thoroughly with all the interests of his city and section. He was known as a public-spirited citizen, quick in sympathy, ready of hand, lover of his adopted home, charitable in every impulse of his soul, and a friend of the poor. At no time in his life did he display more heroism than in 1855 when Helena was visited with a terrible scourge of yellow fever. The public generally was stricken with a panic and all that were able to go were flying in every direction to save their families from the dread contagion. But Cleburne remained in the fever-smitten place, going in daily rounds among the sick and helpless, nursing them, and soothing as far as possible the grief of the living and the last hours of the dying. His unselfish devotion at this time greatly endeared him to many hearts.

When Cleburne came to Helena he was an ardent Whig, a regular reader of Prentice's *Louisville Journal* and the old *National Intelligencer*. His best friends were in the habit of ridiculing the idea of one of his nationality being a defender of federalism and railing at him as the "Irish Whig." He met these tilts with perfect good humor, but always gave shot for shot. The discussions that passed in these days in the offices and along the streets of Helena when political discussion became warm would afford interesting reading to those who survive, and with whom those times have now passed into history. With the organization of the Know Nothing party the stubborn defender of Whig politics laid down his arms. He became a Democrat and remained steadfast in that allegiance to the day of his death. In religious faith he was an Episcopalian. For a succession of years he was chosen vestryman in St. John's Church, Helena.

Physically General Cleburne was of a striking appearance, although he would not come in the category of "handsome men." He was six feet in height, of spare build, with broad shoulders and erect carriage. In his large gray eyes the gleam of sympathy and the sparkle of humor were most often seen and they grew dark and stern in danger or battle. He was a man of great activity and of great powers of endurance. He was not a graceful man. In general society his manners would frequently be pronounced awkward or stiff. He was naturally modest in his own opinion of himself, and this often lent an appearance of diffidence and embarrassment to his actions. Very sensitive to the opinion of the world, his inborn pride rebelled against the admission or manifestation of it. This shyness was never more apparent than when in the company of the gentler sex, yet no man ever loved woman's society more or held woman's name in greater reverence. He was not a good conversationalist except when in the company of congenial friends whose intimacy freed him from all shackles of embarrassment. He was much given to fits of absentmindedness, his dreamy, poetic nature seeming often to beckon him away from present surroundings and realities. Yet, with all this, when duty pressed his faculties seemed tireless, unsleeping. And when the earnestness of the moment obliterated all thought of self and the occasion demanded dignity, no one showed more conspicuously than did Patrick Cleburne that nobility of nature which makes nobility of manners.

The most pronounced characteristic of the man, to those who knew him best and saw him in all the aspects of life, was his courage. He had, indeed, the lion's heart. He was absolutely indifferent to danger and was as cool when exposed to it as in the most peaceful moments of his life. He never grew noisy or furious, never exhibited the slightest form of bravado, and he never quailed before odds or difficulties. He went where duty called, calm and determined. He performed the behests of duty without question or fear, and in the performance of it his mind and his arm acted with the rapidity and force of lightning. In all the relations of private life he was what he afterwards showed himself to be in tent and field.

Thus the opening of war days found Pat Cleburne, days when the blackest cloud that ever loomed on a nation's vision gathered on his horizon and that of his fellow-countrymen, days when every young man buckled on his armor with fierce and eager delight and rushed forth to meet its baptism of fire and death. Cleburne was not a laggard then. Among the first he stepped to the front, and from the first he took prominent rank. During the summer of 1860 a military company was formed in Helena, composed of the flower of the young men in the city and county adjacent. It was called the Yell Rifles, in honor of Colonel Archibald Yell, who fell at the head of his regiment at the battle of Buena Vista, Mexico. Cleburne was chosen captain, with L. O. Bidwell, E. H. Cowley, and James Blackburn as lieutenants. A fellow-countryman of Cleburne's, named Calvert, who had been a sergeant in the United States Army, was employed as drillmaster. Calvert was a fine and thoroughly disciplined soldier, afterwards rising to prominence as a major of artillery, and under his efficient instruction the Rifles became a splendidly trained body of troops. It was one of the first to offer its services to the State in 1861, but before going into service was reorganized with Cleburne still as captain, E. H. Cowley, first lieutenant; L. E. Polk (afterwards brigadier general), second lieutenant, and James F. Langford, third lieutenant.

The Yell Rifles thus officered were, with other companies, ordered by the Governor of the State to rendezvous at Mound City, Crittenden County. At Mound City, in May, 1861, was organized the first Arkansas regiment of State troops. Through some confusion the Confederate records show two Arkansas regiments called the Fifteenth,* but this first regiment of State troops was the Fifteenth Arkansas of the Western Army. The

*Colonel James Gee's Camden regiment was given the same name and number, Fifteenth Arkansas.

following companies formed this regiment: Yell Rifles, Captain Cleburne; Jefferson Guards, Captain Carleton; Rector Guards, Captain Glenn; Harris Guards, Captain Harris; Phillips Guards, Captain Otey; Monroe Blues, Captain Baldwin; Napoleon Grays, Captain Green; Tyronza Rebels, Captain Harden. In the organization of this regiment Cleburne was chosen colonel; Patton, lieutenant colonel; Harris, major, and Dr. H. Blackburn, surgeon, * * *

L. H. Mangum was appointed adjutant of this regiment.

In describing Cleburne's personal appearance one writer says:

> In person he was about five feet nine or ten inches in height, slender in form, with a wiry, active appearance. His forehead was high and broad, high cheek bones, cheeks rather hollow and face diminishing towards the chin, the upper part being more massive than the lower. His hair, originally black, became tinged with gray, as was his delicate moustache and imperial. Eyes of clear steel gray in color, were cold and abstracted usually, but it needed only the flame of battle to kindle them in intensity, to stir the depths of his strong nature and show forth a soldier for stoutness of heart, for stubbornness of fight, for shining valor and forgetfulness of self, rarely to be matched.[3]

Though a member of the Episcopal Church he seldom talked of religion, always respecting it, whether as an institution or a personal opinion. In his diary, January 1, 1862, he wrote: "My God! whom I believe in and adore, make Thy laws plainer to my erring judgment, that I may more faithfully observe them, and not dread to look into my past." While not a fanatic on the subject, he abstained from the use of tobacco and liquor, and by precept and example tried to impress upon others his reasons. These reasons were that during the war he felt responsible for the lives of his men, and feared the possible effect of intoxicants, for the proper discharge of his duties. He also said that a single glass of wine would disturb the steadiness of his hand in use of the pistol, and effect his calculations in playing chess, a game in which he was an adept.

---

3. Archer Anderson, "The Campaign and Battle of Chickamauga," *Southern Historical Society Papers,* IX, 390. Henceforth cited *SHSP.*

Of firm convictions, strong personality, and unswerving loyalty and devotion to his friends, this last trait came near causing an early termination of Cleburne's career. One of his associates became engaged in a controversy with a man bearing the reputation of a "dangerous man." Cleburne had no interest at stake, but, Irishman-like espoused the cause of his friend "in a quarrel not his own," drawing upon himself the wrath of the desperado, who publicly swore vengeance against Cleburne. Cleburne was well known to be quick and expert with the pistol and it was equally well recognized that a front attack upon him would be extremely dangerous. While Cleburne was walking the street of Helena, without warning a dastardly attempt to assassinate him was made. A shot was fired from a door-way he was passing, the bullet entering his back and going entirely through his body. Desperately wounded as he was, his will power enabled him to draw his pistol and kill his assailant before he himself fell to the side-walk. His recovery was despaired of, but his indomitable will to live greatly, if not entirely, tended to his recovery, after months of confinement to his bed.

From the time of Mr. Lincoln's election Cleburne felt convinced as to the dissolution of the Union, but advocated secession through the united and concerted action of the slave-holding States in convention. He regarded the impending war as a struggle on the part of the South for liberty and freedom to control their own domestic affairs, as he believed was provided for under the Constitution.

CHAPTER TWO

War — First Services — Shiloh

In January, 1861, Patrick Cleburne was one among the citizens of Helena that tendered their services to Governor Rector to capture the United States arsenal at Little Rock, and he was present on the occasion of its surrender by Captain James Totten, U. S. Army. Cleburne was then serving as a private in the company organized for that purpose, called the "Yell Rifles." Upon the call of the Arkansas Military Board for troops to resist invasion of the Southern States, the Yell Rifles, 115 strong, entered the State service, with Cleburne in command, he having been elected from private to captain.

As before stated, after the organization of the Fifteenth Arkansas Regiment it had been ordered to rendezvous at Mound City, on the opposite side of the Mississippi River, above Memphis, Tennessee. From here it was ordered to Bearsfield Point, and from there it went to what was afterwards known as Fort Randolph, at that time held by General Pillow. It was here that Cleburne threw up the first entrenchments at that point. These works were originally called by the troops "Fort Cleburne" but later they were officially named Fort Randolph. Here, with his own regiment and one company of field artillery,—the advance post in that region,—Cleburne remained until July, in which month he was ordered to Pitman's Ferry in northern Arkansas on the Missouri State line. At this point General Hardee was in command of about six thousand men of all arms.

Here the Fifteenth Arkansas Regiment was drilled by its colonel, under the eye of that accomplished soldier and rigid disciplinarian, Gen. Wm. J. Hardee, who even at this time saw and recognized Cleburne's military ability, as he afterwards recognized his sleepless vigilance, his devotion to duty and his invincible courage; and Hardee's reliance upon him, coupled with his personal friendship, was never misplaced and was broken only by death. On August 31, Hardee's force, as reported, was composed of the infantry regiments of Cleburne, Hindman, Cross, Lyon, and Shaver, Shoup's battalion of artillery, Roberts's battery, and Bourland's and Phifer's cavalry.

In July, 1861, Generals Pillow and M. Jeff. Thompson were projecting movements from New Madrid upon the Federal forces at Bird's Point, Cape Girardeau, and St. Louis, and solicited General Hardee to cooperate with them. Informed that the Federals had left Ironton, for Greenville, Missouri, Hardee advanced to the latter place early in August, with 1,000 infantry, 250 cavalry and a battery of artillery to meet them; but learning of his approach the enemy fell back to Ironton. Hardee planned to attack that point, but the failure of General Thompson to cooperate prevented. Hardee decided to hold his position in Missouri, in which determination he was sustained by his superior, Maj.-Gen. Leonidas Polk, who had charge of military operations in Arkansas and Missouri. But on August 26, under orders of General Polk, Hardee retired to the Mississippi River at Point Pleasant and by September 1 had returned with his command to Pitman's Ferry. On the 17th of September Cleburne was despatched with his regiment to repair the road to Point Pleasant, which duty he performed in a manner so satisfactory as to gain the commendation of his commander. He, with the Fifteenth Arkansas, accompanied Hardee on the expedition into Missouri.

At Greenville there were some prisoners confined in the courthouse, and constant reports were rife as to attack by rescue or raiding parties of the enemy, and every one was on the alert. There was a citizen present with the troops, and quartered in the same building with Cleburne. This gentleman had the infirmity of somnambulism, which he, unfortunately, failed to make known. Influenced perhaps in his dreams by the above named rumors, one night in his sleep he forced his way into Cleburne's room, knocked down his clerk, who had jumped up to confront him, and approached Cleburne, who had been awakened by the noise. Supposing this person to be one of a raiding party or an escaping prisoner, Cleburne arose, pistol in hand, and fired, mortally wounding the man. Though fully exonerated from all blame by his victim before his death, the accident caused Cleburne deep distress and colored his whole life. He never referred to it but that it rendered him moody and abstracted.

On September 17 General Hardee was directed to move his command to the Mississippi River, which he did via the Point Pleasant road, his last detachment leaving Pitman's Ferry on September 24. From Point Pleasant the troops were transported by steamer to Columbus, Kentucky, and from there marched to Bowling Green, Kentucky, where he reported to Gen. Albert Sidney Johnston, commanding Department No. 2, on October 11. Soon after Hardee's command was thrown in advance to Cave City. On November 9 General Johnston ordered Hardee to send a force of 1,200 men, 1 howitzer, and a squadron of cavalry "under an intelligent officer" to Jamestown and Tompkinsville. The order read:

> Go to Jamestown and if the enemy are there, and not in too great force, attack and destroy them. Proceed to Tompkinsville and do the same thing, * * * return to this place as soon as these orders are executed, or it is apparent they cannot be. Create the impression in the country that this force is only an advance guard.[1]

The selection of Cleburne for this duty is evidence of the confidence Hardee had in his intelligence, ability, and discretion. This command reached Jamestown on the evening of November 11. They found no enemy, but had positive information that probably a small force was concealed in the vicinity of the Confederate camp. The Union sentiment was strong and the people were found to be "bitterly hostile" to the Confederate cause. The command arrived at Tompkinsville on the evening of November 13. In his report Cleburne says:

---

1. A. S. Johnston to W. J. Hardee, Nov. 9, 1861, *Official Records of the War of the Rebellion,* IV, 531. Henceforth cited as *O.R.*

We did not find a friend along the whole road from Jamestown here [Tompkinsville]; houses were closed and country apparently deserted. We saw a few women and children, but in almost every instance they were surprised and tried to run and conceal themselves at our approach, they having been told, and evidently believed, that we were burning, killing, and destroying as we advanced. One old woman met us with an open Bible in her hands; said she was prepared and ready to die, and could not be convinced that we meant her no harm. * * * We got nearly to the center of the town, when I was astonished at the utter silence and desertion, not having seen a human being, but two, who both fled. I merely mention this as an illustration of the feeling existing among the people here. Today, November 13, most of the women and children have returned, but all the men (a half dozen perhaps excepted) are absent in Grider's Federal camp at Columbia. * * * This is the nearest camp to us. There are two regiments of Kentucky volunteers there, and hundreds (inhabitants) have fled there, in front of our advance. * * * Did my instructions permit an advance on their camp I would not hesitate to make it. I made it my special business and used every effort to convince the people we were friends. * * * I think on the whole we have succeeded. No insult or injury to the person of any one has come to my notice. I am sorry to state that on yesterday for the first time the same respect was not paid to property. Our teamsters' rearguard * * * and individuals who fell back under pretense of being sick, stole some poultry and other things, along the road * * * and it only came to my knowledge now, when too late to repair it.[2]

In his report of November 16 he says:

I have paid out of my own pocket for the articles stolen by our men. * * * Confidence is restored, all the houses open, and families returned. Trunks and other articles found by our flankers, in the woods, I had carried to the houses and labelled, "Returned by Southern Soldiers."[3]

Thus early Cleburne, in his first independent command, manifested his conscientiousness and sense of justice, and gave practical evidence as to his views of conducting the war on civilized principles

---

2. *O.R.*, III, 545.
3. *Ibid*, 558.

—not upon women and children and non-combatants, but only upon bodies of armed men. His sense of justice was always one of his strongest characteristics.

The object of the expedition to Jamestown having been accomplished, the command returned to Bowling Green. A few days after Cleburne went to Nashville, where he met Governor Isham G. Harris, with whom he formed a strong friendship and who, impressed by the management of the Jamestown affair, showed him special attention. Cleburne thus gives his impression of the Governor: "I found the Governor more active-minded than any one else I met; more fully alive to the exigencies of the hour, and bending every energy he could command for the advancement of the cause."

The winter of '61 and spring of '62, spent at Bowling Green, were without special military interest. Hardee having been promoted major-general, as senior colonel, Cleburne commanded the second brigade of the first division, and gave his time and attention to drilling and disciplining it, and took an active part in all the movements prior to the fall of Fort Donelson. And his untiring energy was well demonstrated in superintending the moving of army supplies from Bowling Green. In a conference held at the latter place between Generals A. S. Johnston and Beauregard, on February 7, 1862, it was decided that, as Fort Henry on the Tennessee River had fallen on February 6, giving General Grant control of that river, cutting off Columbus, and separating Bowling Green from Nashville, it was imperative that the entire Confederate army in Kentucky fall back to another line to protect Memphis; and preparations were made to this end, by quietly moving all ordnance, quartermaster, and commissary stores southward. On February 11 the troops commenced their march, and on the 16th the last of them reached Nashville.

Meanwhile, Fort Donelson on the Cumberland River having fallen on February 16, Nashville was rendered incapable of being defended, from its position, and from the forces advancing from Bowling Green and up the Cumberland River from Donelson, and it was therefore evacuated, and Hardee's command moved to Murfreesboro, where it was hoped to assemble an army sufficient in strength to offer battle. But this was impossible, and the troops, with the escaped remnant from Fort Donelson, were marched south and crossed the Tennessee River at Decatur, Alabama, so as to cooperate, or unite with General Beauregard's force at Corinth, Mississippi; Columbus, Kentucky, having been evacuated, and the troops assembled at or near Corinth.

Cleburne having been made brigadier-general on March 4, was, with his brigade, two regiments of cavalry and battalion of artillery, left at Shelbyville, Tennessee, to forward supplies, after which he moved for and reached Tuscumbia, Alabama, early in the month. His promotion was inspired by the field officers of the brigade, and Hardee procured it, having discovered, in his good judgment of men, that beneath the rugged exterior of Cleburne resided the qualities of an efficient and admirable general officer.

In the latter part of March the forces of Generals Johnston, Beauregard, and Bragg having united, were concentrated along the Mobile & Ohio Railroad from Bethel to Corinth, Mississippi; and on the Memphis & Charleston Railroad from Corinth to Iuka, Mississippi. The main Federal army, under General Grant, was at this time at Pittsburg, on the Tennessee River, some twenty miles north of Corinth. It was determined between Generals Johnston and Beauregard to attempt to surprise, capture, or destroy Grant's army before it could be reinforced by the five divisions of the Army of the Ohio, 37,000 strong, under General Buell, then known to be advancing for that purpose by rapid marches from Nashville. On April 3 orders were issued directing that the four corps, constituting the Army of Mississippi (Johnston's) be put in motion, and march by their several designated routes towards Shiloh, a small log church near Pittsburg, around which Grant's forces were encamped. It was calculated and expected that the attack would be made on Saturday, April 5, but owing to unexpected bad conditions of the roads, and the difficulty of marching the raw troops that had been hastily sent by the governors of several States in response to an appeal of General Beauregard, some of whom marched direct from the railroad trains to the battlefield, the concentration in the vicinity of Shiloh did not occur until the evening of Saturday. Thus a delay of twenty-four hours was necessary, postponing the attack to Sunday, the 6th, and rendered all the more critical (and afterwards proving fatal) by the known proximity of Buell's reinforcing column. Hardee's corps, to which Cleburne's brigade belonged, was the first of the two parallel lines as arranged for battle. This brigade consisted of the Twenty-third, Twenty-fourth, Fifth, and Second Tennessee, Sixth Mississippi, and Fifteenth Arkansas regiments, with Calvert's and Trigg's batteries—an effective total of 2,750. A portion of this command had on the afternoon of April 4 engaged the cavalry of the enemy, repulsing it quickly, and capturing some prisoners.

Two streams, Lick and Owl creeks, flow easterly, parallel to each other, and empty into the Tennessee River, about four miles apart, but at a point about one and a half miles from Shiloh Church the two streams approach most nearly. The distance between them here is a little more than three miles. It was here that Hardee's corps was deployed, its right extending towards Lick, and its left being near Owl Creek. Gladden's brigade, of Bragg's corps, was attached to Hardee's, to fill the interval between its right and Lick Creek. Cleburne's brigade, the extreme left of the army, rested its left near Owl Creek, and was formed as follows, from right to left: Twenty-third Tennessee, Sixth Mississippi, Fifth Tennessee, Twenty-Fourth Tennessee regiments on the left; Fifteenth Arkansas deployed as skirmishers in front of the line, with their reserves near the left, and the Second Tennessee *en échelon* 500 yards in rear of the left flank, with a strong line of skirmishers covering the interval between its left and that of the Twenty-fourth Tennessee. With the corps the brigade was ordered to advance at daylight on Sunday, April 6, which it did soon after, keeping proper distance from and regulating its movements by those of General Wood's brigade, on Cleburne's right. Trigg's battery followed near the right, but was under control of the chief of artillery, and left the brigade after the first encounter.

The advance for some distance through the woods was without opposition. The enemy first showed his forces about 400 yards off towards the left flank, upon which Cleburne ordered Captain Trigg to send a howitzer in that direction and throw a few shells into them. Moving forward, the Fifteenth Arkansas engaged the enemy's skirmishers, and drove them back on their first line of battle, and the skirmishers of the Fifteenth Arkansas then fell back on their reserves. The brigade, advancing, was soon in sight of the enemy's encampments, behind the first of which he had formed his line of battle, very advantageously posted and overlapping Cleburne's left flank by at least half a brigade front. His line was lying down behind the rising ground on which his tents were pitched, and opposite the brigade's right he had made a breastwork of logs and bales of hay. From these deadly volleys were poured upon the men as they advanced. Everywhere musketry and artillery swept the open spaces between the tents, threatening destruction to every living thing that would dare to cross them.

An almost impassable morass covered the front of and impeded the advance of the center, and finally caused a wide opening in the line. The Fifth Tennessee and the regiments on its left swung to the left of this swamp, and the Sixth Mississippi and Twenty-third Tennessee advanced on its right. Cleburne's horse bogged down in it, throwing him, and he got out with difficulty. Trigg's battery, posted on the high grounds of the woods, in rear, opened over the heads of the men, but the leaves were so thick he could only see in one direction, while the enemy was firing upon him from several directions. Thus he was unable to accomplish much, and was ordered to a new position, and Cleburne had no artillery under his command from that time. The Sixth Mississippi and Twenty-third Tennessee charged through the enemy's encampment. The line was necessarily broken by the standing tents, and under the terrific fire from the serried ranks in front much confusion ensued, and a quick and bloody repulse was the consequence. The Twenty-third Tennessee was with difficulty rallied about 100 yards in the rear. Again and again the Sixth Mississippi, unaided, charged the enemy's line, and it was only when it had lost 300 men, killed and wounded, out of an aggregate of 425, or nearly seventy-three per cent., that it yielded, and retreated over its own dead and dying. Colonel Thornton and Major Lowry of the regiment were both wounded.

The left, which, after a desperate fight and heavy loss, caused chiefly by the fact that the enemy flanked the brigade on the left, had driven the Federals back at all points, was now in possession of his first line of encampments. Here the Second Tennessee, coming up on the left, charged through a murderous crossfire. Its gallant major, Wm. R. Doak, fell mortally wounded, and Col. Wm. B. Bate had his leg broken by a rifle ball. At this point the Twenty-fourth Tennessee won character for steady valor, and the Fifteenth Arkansas inflicted heavy loss upon the enemy, and lost many good men and officers, among the latter Maj. J. T. Harris, who was shot dead while firing upon the Federals with his revolver.

For the present the left of the brigade was unemployed. Of the right, about half of the Twenty-third Tennessee and 60 men of the Sixth Mississippi had reformed. These advanced directly to the front, through the enemy's encampment, they having retreated as soon as the Confederate left had broken their right. The Eighth Arkansas, of Wood's brigade, connected with the two regiments of Cleburne's brigade, and remained fighting with them until about 12 or 1 o'clock. At this time the fragment of the Sixth Mississippi marched to the rear. Its fearful losses in the morning, of all the field and most of the company officers, had completely disorganized and unfitted it for further service that day. Shortly after noon the Twenty-third Tennessee was ordered to the rear, there to reunite with other portions of the regiment which had become separated from it in the repulse of the morning. Cleburne was thus left without a command on that part of the field, and was proceeding along the rear to join his left wing, when meeting General Hardee he was ordered to collect and bring into the fight a large body of stragglers from different commands who were swarming the encampments in the rear. After great exertion he was partially successful in doing this, but finding that this kind of a force would not stand anything approaching a heavy fire, he determined to rejoin his own command on the left, which he did about 2 o'clock. The Fifth and Twenty-fourth Tennessee and Fifteenth Arkansas had halted under the brow of an abrupt hill. The Second Tennessee had suffered so severely in the morning's fight that it had to be moved back to reform, and did not rejoin the command again during the battle.

Upon arriving at his left Cleburne ordered an immediate advance, which was delayed by a Confederate battery firing across the line of intended attack. As soon as their fire could be stopped skirmishers were thrown out and pushed directly forward. The Twenty-third Tennessee came up at this juncture, and advanced with the brigade which had moved forward about half a mile when it was fired on by the enemy. The skirmishers were driven in, and soon the main body, with the exception of the Fifteenth Arkansas, was heavily engaged. This lasted about half an hour, when the Federals gave way. Owing to the nature of the ground the ordnance wagons could not follow the troops, and the men were now out of ammunition, and a strong detail was sent back to the wagons and brought boxes of cartridges on their shoulders, up and down the steep hills for over a mile.

As soon as the troops were supplied with ammunition an advance was made and continued until checked by a heavy fire from the enemy's field artillery and gunboats near Pittsburg Landing. When this firing ceased the advance was continued, until halted by a staff officer from General Beauregard, who informed Cleburne that he was not to approach nearer to the Tennessee River. It being now dark, the brigade returned and bivouacked in one of the enemy's abandoned encampments, close to the Bark road. During the night it rained heavily. Every fifteen minutes two shells were thrown from the gunboats, some of which exploded close around the troops, but fell chiefly among the Federal wounded, who were strewn thickly between Cleburne's camp and the river.

Soon after daybreak, Monday, April 7, notice was received that the enemy was pushing forward and driving the Confederate cavalry pickets. It was now plain that Buell's command had made a junction with Grant's, and that a fresh army of 37,000 had to be reckoned with. In a few moments General Hardee ordered Cleburne to advance on the Bark road. The brigade was sorely reduced; of the 2,700 taken into the fight, but 800 remained on the morning of the 7th. Two regiments, the Second Tennessee and Sixth Mississippi, were absent. Hundreds of its best men were dead or in hospitals. With the gallant few remaining an advance of a mile was made, to a point where there was a line of battle, which proved to be a part of General Breckinridge's command, and the brigade formed on the left of it, halted, and the men were ordered to lie down. The enemy's line was in plain view in front, stretching beyond Cleburne's brigade as far as the eye could see. The Washington Battery, of six guns, came up in rear of the brigade and offered its assistance. About half a mile to the left, in a neck of woods, could be seen troops moving from the direction of the enemy and passing far in rear of Cleburne's line, and soon heavy firing was heard in that quarter.

All endeavors to discover the character of this force failed, until Colonel Kelly, of the Eighth Arkansas, found them to be Federals and reported the fact. The Washington Battery opened on their flank and rapidly drove them from the woods. In reply to an order from General Breckinridge to move forward and attack the forces in his front, Cleburne stated that he was completely without support and outflanked on his left, and would be destroyed if he advanced. He received for answer that the order was from General Bragg; that it was positive and must be obeyed immediately, which was done; but the troops had not gone far before a battery on the left of Breckinridge's line commenced firing across Cleburne's front, compelling a halt. The Federals soon replied to this artillery fire with rifled guns, and the duel was carried on diagonally across the proposed line of advance. The brigade was then moved forward into a small valley, which separated it from the enemy, so as to permit the Washington Battery to take part in the fight, by firing over the heads of the men. The enemy then brought up another battery, and for half an hour a fierce artillery fight raged. The entire line of infantry on Cleburne's right had halted, and were merely spectators of the fight. Here the brigade had some men killed by limbs cut from trees by the Confederate guns.

It soon became apparent that the Confederate artillery was overmatched, and firing ceased, upon which the whole line of infantry charged. A very thick undergrowth of young trees obstructed their view, yet offered them no protection from the hurricane of rifle bullets, grape and canister shot that swept through this thicket. It was impossible to see what was going on, either to the right or left, but men were dropping all around under the fire of an unseen foe. It was here that the gallant Capt. E. H. Cowley, acting major of the Fifteenth Arkansas, was shot through the head and the brave Lieutenant-Col. James F. Neill of the Twenty-third Tennessee, through the body. The brigade was repulsed and almost routed in this unfortunate attack. As far as known, the Fifteenth Arkansas was the only regiment rallied anywhere near the scene of disaster. In the face of a deadly fire and exultant foe it was reformed, and fell back in order, behind a ridge, from where—some reinforcements coming up—Cleburne in person led them in a charge on the advancing enemy, who speedily fled. In this charge Lieut.-Col. A. K. Patton, the sole remaining field officer of the Fifteenth Arkansas, was shot dead. The regiment continued to pursue until out of ammunition, when 58 men, all that remained, fell back to replenish. The brigade was now completely scattered and disorganized. Many of the officers and men continued fighting in the ranks of other commands, or on their own responsibility, but not again in any organization which their general could command. Cleburne devoted himself personally to rallying stragglers, forming such as he could in line and doing all in his power to secure safe retreat for the army. He remained on such of the field as was still in Confederate possession, destroying property which could not be removed, and giving succor to the wounded until after sun-set, when, by General Hardee's orders, he left for Corinth.

On the morning of April 6, including Trigg's and Calvert's batteries, the brigade numbered 2,750, out of which 1,000—or over 36 per cent.—were killed and wounded, and 32 missing. It led the advance of the army on Shiloh, engaged and repulsed the Federal cavalry on Friday before the battle, fought in the front line both days, and, save at night, the brigade was never rested or relieved for a moment. It took many stands of colors, and assisted in the capture on the left at about 4 o'clock, of General Prentiss and the greater portion of his division. This was the first pitched battle in which the men or their commander had ever engaged, and their conduct gave eminent forecast of the future brilliant records of both. At the moment of recall on the evening of the 6th the brigade was pressing on to within 400 yards of Pittsburg Landing, beneath the bluffs of which cowered the demoralized masses of hopeless and helpless fugitives.

In his official report General Hardee says:

> During the action Brigadier-General Cleburne conducted his command with persevering valor. No repulse discouraged him, but after many bloody struggles he assembled the remnants of his brigade and was conspicuous for his gallantry to the end of the battle.

And later he wrote of Cleburne and his command:

> The enemy were steadily driven for 3 miles, through their encampments, past rich spoils * * * and over the heaps of their dead and dying, until the broken and demoralized masses sought the shelter of the river's bank and the cover of their gun-boats. * * * in this battle [Shiloh] Cleburne's brigade sustained a heavier loss in killed and wounded than any other in the army.[5]

On the Federal side much controversy and acrimonious discussion arose regarding this, the first great battle of the Western Army, as to whether or not the attack was a surprise to them. The fact that their cavalry was repulsed by infantry on the afternoon of Friday, April 4, should have put them on the alert, as it surely would have been the case a few months later. But there was an additional fact that on Sunday morning, the 6th, when the attack was made soon after daylight, the Federals had no advanced skir-

---

4. *O.R.*, X, part 1, 570.
5. *Ibid*, 569.

mishers, no line of battle formed and quite a large part of Sherman's men of the front line were found utterly unprepared—aroused from their slumbers by the fire of the attacking force. Many were surprised and captured in their tents, and the army caught, so to speak, *in flagrante delicto*—truly in their sin of omission. In view of this one simple fact it is hard for any unprejudiced or impartial reader of official history not to be convinced but that it was a surprise.

If further evidence is required as to its being so, it may be found in the language of the commander of the reinforcing army, General Buell, when he says:

> An army comprising seventy regiments of infantry, twenty batteries of artillery and a sufficiency of cavalry, lay for two weeks and more in isolated camps, with a river in its rear and a hostile army claimed to be superior in numbers twenty miles distant in its front, while the commander (Grant) made his headquarters and passed his nights nine miles away on the opposite side of the river. It had no line or order of battle, no defensive works of any sort, no outposts, properly speaking, to give warning or check the advance of an enemy, and no recognized head during the absence of the regular commander. On Saturday the hostile force arrived and formed in order of battle, without detection or hindrance, within a mile and a half of the unguarded army, advanced upon it the next morning, penetrated its disconnected lines, assaulted its camps in front and flank, drove its disjointed members successively from position to position, capturing some and routing others * * * and steadily drew near the landing and depot of its supplies in the pocket between the river and an impassable creek.[6]

Sherman wrote Grant on afternoon of April 5, "I do not apprehend anything like an attack upon our position";[7] and on the same date Grant wrote his superior, Halleck, "I have scarcely the faintest idea of an attack upon us."[8]

On the Confederate side the controversy was, first, as to whether the battle was fought as planned by General Johnston or as directed

6. D. C. Buell, "Shiloh Reviewed," *Battles and Leaders,* I, 487.
7. *O.R.,* X, part 2, 94.
8. *Ibid.*

in the orders of General Beauregard. This is of minor importance to another question, viz: as to the halting of the troops on Sunday evening, after having captured Prentiss's command, and forcing back the Federal army to the Tennessee River, with seemingly easy and assured victory in reach. The advance was kept up until within short musket range of the Landing, the Confederate line extending from Owl Creek on the left to the bottom-lands of the Tennessee River on the right. Between 5 and 6 o'clock P. M. orders were received from General Beauregard—who succeeded to the command of the army upon the fall of General Johnston—directing that the pursuit should be stopped. Much has been said and written, pro and con, as to this order, General Beauregard's adherents claiming that it was necessary and proper, while those of General Johnston assert that it was a fatal blunder. General Bragg, who was chief of staff to General Johnston, and also commanded the second line of battle, says in a letter to Col. Wm. Preston Johnston:

> In spite of opposition and prediction of failure, Johnston * * * ordered and led the attack * * * and notwithstanding the faulty arrangement of troops was eminently successful up to the moment of his fall. The *victory was won.* How lost the official reports will show and history has recorded.[9]

Colonel Lockett, of Bragg's staff, quotes the latter as saying when the order reached him: "My God! was a victory ever sufficiently complete?"[10] Of the same circumstance, Col. Wm. Preston Johnston writes:

> When Beauregard's staff officer gave Bragg this order, he said, "Have you promulgated this order to the commands?" The officer replied, "I have." General Bragg then said, "If you had not, I would not obey it. *The battle is lost.*"[11]

General Albert Sidney Johnston received his fatal wound about 2:30 P. M., while directing an attack by Statham's brigade of

9. W. P. Johnston, "Albert Sidney Johnston at Shiloh," *Battles and Leaders,* I, 553.

10. S. H. Lockett, "Surprise and Withdrawal at Shiloh," *Battles and Leaders,* I, 605.

11. W. P. Johnston, "Albert Sidney Johnston at Shiloh," *Battles and Leaders,* I, 568.

Breckinridge's corps. He was a graduate of West Point, served in the Black Hawk war, won distinction in Texas, and was placed in chief command of the army of the young Republic, and was afterwards its Secretary of War; he served under General Taylor in Mexico, commanded the expedition to Utah in 1857, and when he resigned from the United States Army in 1861 was colonel of the Second Cavalry. His joining the Confederate Army was hailed with loud acclamations by the public, and President Davis, who had an intimate knowledge of the officers of the United States Army, rated his accession as equal to 10,000 men. That the Federal Government appreciated his ability is evidenced by the fact that in its efforts to retain him, through his former adjutant, afterwards Maj.-Gen. Fitz-John Porter, it offered to place him in command of the Federal Army, immediately next to General Scott.[12]

The circumstances of General Johnston's wounding and death are thus related by his son, Col. Wm. Preston Johnston:

> General Johnston had passed through the ordeal seemingly unhurt. His horse was shot in four places; his clothes were pierced by missiles; his boot sole was cut and torn by a Minie; but if he himself had received any serious wound he did not know it. At this moment Governor Harris rode up from the right. After a few words, General Johnston sent him with an order to Colonel Statham, which having delivered, he speedily returned. In the meantime knots and groups of Federal soldiers kept up a desultory fire as they retreated upon their supports, and their last line, now yielding, delivered volley after volley as they sullenly retired. By the chance of war, a Minie ball from one of these did its fatal work. As he sat there, after his wound, Captain Wickham says that Colonel O'Hara, of his staff, rode up, and General Johnston said to him, "We must go to the left, where the firing is heaviest," and then gave him an order, which O'Hara rode off to obey. Governor Harris returned, and finding him very pale, asked him, "General, are you wounded?" He answered in a very deliberate and emphatic tone: "Yes, and I fear seriously." These were his last words. Harris and

12. Fitz John Porter, in footnote to W. P. Johnston, "Albert Sidney Johnston at Shiloh," *Battles and Leaders,* I, 541 fn.

Wickham led his horse back under cover of the hill, and lifted him from it. They searched at random for the wound, which had cut an artery in his leg, the blood flowing into his boot. When his brother-in-law, Preston, lifted his head, and addressed him with passionate grief, he smiled faintly, but uttered no word. His life rapidly ebbed away, and in a few moments he was dead. His wound was not necessarily fatal. General Johnston's own knowledge of military surgery was adequate for its control by an extemporized tourniquet had he been aware or regardful of its nature. Dr. D. W. Yandell, his surgeon, had attended his person during most of the morning; but, finding a large number of wounded men, including many Federals, at one point, General Johnston had ordered Yandell to stop there, establish a hospital, and give them his services. He said to Yandell: "These men were our enemies a moment ago; they are our prisoners now. Take care of them." Yandell remonstrated against leaving him, but he was peremptory. Had Yandell remained with him, he would have had little difficulty with the wound.[13]

The people and press, not knowing of the total inadequacy of Johnston's forces for the protection of his long line, reaching from Cumberland Gap on the right to Columbus, his left, manifested much discontent at his seeming inactivity in the fall and winter of 1861, and when the mishaps befell his command in the early spring of '62 these mutterings broke into open expressions of abuse and vituperation. Charges of incapacity and even disloyalty were heard, and demands for his removal made on Richmond. In reply to a delegation of Congressmen calling upon Mr. Davis, requesting Johnston's removal, Davis sadly replied, "If Sidney Johnston is not a general, I have none to give you."[14] It was not until after his death, when the true conditions were understood, that Johnston's vindication as a consummate general came. It is not too much to assert that his fall was the greatest calamity in the loss of an officer which the Confederacy suffered—Stonewall Jackson not excepted. The cir-

13. W. P. Johnston, "Albert Sidney Johnston at Shiloh," *Battles and Leaders,* I, 564.

14. Jefferson Davis quoted in *Ibid,* I, 541 fn.

cumstances of their wounding were singularly similar. Both fell at the crisis of battle, when, with their lives, easy victory seemed certain; for it is believed by those best qualified to judge, that had Jackson lived Hooker's army would have been captured or driven into the Rappahannock River, as would Grant's have been captured or driven into the Tennessee River had Johnston been spared a few hours longer. While victory over Hooker would have been as great a disaster to the Federals, as it would have been of incalculable benefit to the Confederates, at the period of Shiloh, in the spring of '62, a victory was more needed than at Chancellorsville, in 1863, for the reason that the appalling disasters of Fishing Creek, Forts Henry and Donelson, retreat from Kentucky, evacuation of Nashville and Columbus, and withdrawal of the army to Alabama had caused a despondency and disheartening among the people of the Mississippi Valley which threatened the integrity of the Government, and from which nothing short of a great success of arms could arouse them.

The first day's battle, up to 5 o'clock, was a victory, and although the full fruits were not gathered, it served to restore confidence and hope. Again the Federals were being forced into a *cul de sac,* in the narrow space formed by Snake Creek on their right and Lick Creek on their left, with the Tennessee River at their backs, where, if defeated, escape was impossible and destruction inevitable. If further pursuit was possible the failure to make it was not only an egregious blunder, but a crime. Prisoners from Nelson's division of Buell's army had been captured, and it was plain that the remainder of his reinforcing column was close at hand, and would cross to the west side of the river during the night. These, with the additional 5,000 men of Gen. Lew Wallace's division, then arriving upon the field from Crump's Landing, would give a fresh force of 23,000 men for the greatly reduced Confederate Army to meet on Monday, the 7th. If by a forward movement the cowering army could have been captured or driven into the river that night, as it appears almost certain would have been the case, that portion of Buell's army on the east would not have crossed to the west side of the river. General Buell speaks thus of the posture of affairs at about 6 P. M.:

> He [the Confederate commander] believed the victory to have been substantially won and that the fruits would certainly be gathered the following day. His confidence in that respect was shared in the fullest manner by his entire army, backed by a particularly able body of high officers. All demanded to be led against the last position; not one doubted the result. We can imagine the effort such an army would put forth when animated by such a spirit.[15]

With the addition of Van Dorn's force, between 15,000 and 20,000 men, which had been ordered from Arkansas to Corinth, where it arrived two days after the battle, the Confederate forces could have taken the initiative, forced Buell into retreat, reclaimed the lost territory abandoned by the withdrawal from Bowling Green, transferred the field of operations to Kentucky soil, thus threatening Louisville and possibly the country north of the Ohio River. But this was among one of the first of the several "lost opportunities" for the South to have gained so decisive a victory as to have changed entirely the result of the war, and Appomattox would never have been written—but *L'homme propose, et Dieu dispose.*

---

15. D. C. Buell, "Shiloh Reviewed," *Battles and Leaders,* I, 530.

CHAPTER THREE

Invasion of Kentucky — Battle of Richmond

THE TROOPS having been withdrawn in good order from Shiloh, within the defenses of Corinth, General Beauregard took immediate steps to meet or resist the inevitable advance of General Halleck, who had assumed personal command of the Federal army. Thirty thousand of the remainder of the Confederate force which had fought at Shiloh were reported for duty on April 9. Van Dorn, from the Trans-Mississippi Department, hastened to join these with 20,000 men. By the latter part of May Halleck had assembled an army of 110,000. In the interim between the battle of Shiloh and the latter date it was hoped that the Federal army would in its advancing expose itself to attack, but none was offered, save that of the small affair at Farmington on May 9, when Van Dorn was ordered to attack Pope's corps, only one division of which being in position was driven across Seven Mile Creek, and the bridge was burned. Obstructions of swamps, thickets, and ravines prevented Van Dorn's right flank from reaching the Hamburg road in time to cut off the enemy's retreat, as was intended.

Profiting by the lesson taught Grant at Shiloh, Halleck moved with extreme caution, covering his army with intrenchments as he advanced. General Beauregard's army, suffering from the bad climate, and worse water, was greatly reduced by sickness—18,000 being in hospital by the middle of May—made a change to a more healthy location an absolute necessity. Beauregard, however, determined to hold on at Corinth to the last moment consistent with safety. By the 25th of May Halleck had advanced his main line to within four miles of Corinth, and on his advance position, having mounted heavy siege artillery, was about ready to open with them upon a portion of the Confederate outer defenses, less than three-quarters of a mile distant. General Beauregard, watching and fully advised of these movements, had made his preparations for evacuation with the utmost secrecy. The sick were sent to the rear and all military stores safely removed, and before daylight on May 30 all troops except the cavalry had been withdrawn from Corinth. To that date Halleck, utterly deceived, believed that Beauregard was being heavily reinforced, and his successful retreat was as complete a surprise as it was a chagrin to Halleck, and equivalent to a defeat to him in upsetting his calculations as to his campaign. Beauregard, almost unmolested, and with insignificant loss of men or material, retired behind Tuscumbia Creek. Maj.-Gen. John Pope (afterwards of "Headquarters in the Saddle" fame) was put in charge of the pursuing column, and made this masterly escape of Beauregard from the net spread to entrap him the occasion of the following dispatch to his chief, Halleck, on June 4:

> They [the Confederates] have lost by desertion * * * near 20,000 men since they left Corinth. A farmer says that when Beauregard learned that Colonel Elliott had cut the railroad on his line of retreat he became frantic, and told his men to save themselves the best they could.[1]

At the time these dispatches were written Beauregard was within 27 miles of Corinth and by no means heavily pressed, and, far from being "frantic" with alarm and despair, he assumed such a threatening attitude that Halleck, at Pope's request ordered Buell to the front by forced marches, with 20,000 men to reinforce him. This doughty general, Pope, gave a striking illustration of the adage that the "pen is mightier than the sword," as he did with the former that which he failed to do with the latter—in causing discomfiture to Beauregard; and by these and similar exaggerated and untruthful official reports earned for himself from the English press the appellation of "Major-General of Liars." Despite the

1. John Pope to H. W. Halleck, June 4, 1862, *O.R.*, X, part 1, 774.

energetic pursuits and disasters reported, as to Beauregard, he leisurely marched without hindrance to his chosen position to Tupelo, 52 miles from Corinth, where he arrived June 9. Here, becoming satisfied that no attack was intended, General Beauregard, on June 17, went to Bladen Springs, Alabama, within the limits of his department, to recuperate his health, which had become seriously impaired. Command of the army and department was turned over to General Bragg temporarily, which a few days later was made permanent by the President.

After the occupation of Corinth, Halleck determined upon sending the Army of the Ohio, under Buell, into Middle Tennessee, with Chattanooga as its first objective, and General Thomas's division, which had been detached during the Shiloh-Corinth campaign, was ordered to join him. All of this was in conformity with the wishes of President Lincoln "not to do anything which would force * * * to give up or weaken, or delay the expedition against Chattanooga. To take and hold the railroad at or east of Cleveland in East Tennessee is * * * fully important as the taking and holding of Richmond."[2] The Confederate Government was fully sensible of the vital importance of Chattanooga as the gateway to the railroad center of Atlanta, which was the heart of Georgia, Alabama and Mississippi.

By the improvement in health of the troops, returns from hospitals, and from other causes, since its arrival at Tupelo, the effective strength of the army had increased, and it was determined to transfer it to Chattanooga; to assume the initiative before Buell was prepared to oppose; to push boldly through Tennessee into Kentucky, and by accessions to the ranks, recruited in these States, to drive the enemy beyond the Ohio River. Accordingly, on July 21, Bragg's army started from Tupelo, the infantry by rail via Mobile, and the artillery and trains moving across the country by the most direct practicable routes through north Alabama, and the bulk of it reaching Chattanooga early in August. At this time Cleburne's

2. Abraham Lincoln to H. W. Halleck, June 30, 1862, *O.R.*, XVI, part 2, 75.

brigade was composed of the Fifteenth Arkansas, Second, Fifth and Twenty-fourth Tennessee, and Calvert's battery.

General Bragg's troops crossed the Tennessee River at Chattanooga on August 28, and moved north, via Pikesville, Sparta, and Carthage, Tennessee, leaving Nashville to his left, and crossing the Kentucky line near Tompkinsville. General Buell at Murfreesboro, on September 7, learning of Bragg's whereabouts, and that Nashville had been flanked, and satisfied that no attack was contemplated on that place, but that Louisville was the objective of Bragg, determined to race with him for that point. The latter had the advantage of being 25 miles nearer to Louisville than Buell, but this was more than counter-balanced by Buell having a bridge by which to cross the Cumberland River, and the help of the railroad to assist movement of his troops.

While General Bragg was making this invasion on the left, Gen. Kirby Smith was commanding the Confederate forces in East Tennessee, with headquarters at Knoxville. He met General Bragg at Chattanooga on July 31, and agreed to cooperate with him by advancing into Middle Tennessee. Smith's first design was to cut off the supplies, and thus force the surrender of the Federal division occupying Cumberland Gap, commanded by Gen. Geo. W. Morgan; but learning the position was amply provisioned for a siege, and realizing the difficulty of feeding his own troops and animals in that barren region, he decided to push rapidly on to the rich blue-grass region of central Kentucky. General Bragg was advised of this determination and directed his march towards Lexington, Kentucky. On August 5 General Bragg had sent to Knoxville two brigades—Cleburne's commanded by the senior colonel, B. J. Hill, and Colonel Preston Smith's, both under command of General Cleburne. General Kirby Smith advanced from Knoxville, crossing the Cumberland Mountains through Big Creek Gap, turning the Federal position on the right at Cumberland Gap, and moved via Barboursville and Crab Orchard, reaching the vicinity of Richmond, Kentucky, August 29, on which day the cavalry, under Col. John S. Scott, found the enemy at Kingston, 5 miles south of Richmond, and the force displayed and resistance offered indicated that they intended to dispute the further advance of the Confederates. General Smith wisely decided to attack immediately, correctly believing that a bold initiative gave the best assurance of success. On the morning of August 29 Cleburne had been ordered to move on the Richmond road, and to be the infantry advance of the army. At 5 o'clock P. M. cannonading was heard, and he learned that Scott's cavalry were being driven. Soon this artillery fire ceased, and Cleburne was informed by Colonel Scott that the cavalry was encamped in his front, the whole of which was well picketed, and the enemy not advancing. Notwithstanding this assurance, Cleburne felt uneasy as to an unknown force confronting, and as a matter of wise precaution formed his command in battle line, facing the supposed direction of the enemy. It was after dark before the arrangements were completed. Regimental commanders had been instructed that at the first alarm they were to bring their men to the positions designated as theirs in the line of battle. Scarcely had these dispositions been made, when firing and yelling were heard in front, and a multitude of stragglers, wagons, etc., from a portion of Scott's cavalry, which had been stampeded, came flying through the infantry line, closely pursued by the Federal horse. Cleburne's line was quickly reformed, and when the enemy was within 25 steps, two companies of the Forty-eighth Tennessee Regiment fired on and checked the advance. A few sharpshooters were pushed forward, causing the enemy's retreat. Thirty prisoners, 100 stands of arms, and several horses were captured by the Confederates, with the loss of but one man wounded on their side. At daylight on the 30th Cleburne's division commenced a forward movement, his brigade, under command of Col. B. J. Hill, and Douglas's battery leading, followed, at a distance of a quarter of a mile, by Preston Smith's brigade and Martin's battery. The Buckner Guards (cavalry company) were sent in front to develop the enemy, which they did, finding his advance half a mile north of the village of Kingston, and soon after, discovering their main line of battle within 500 or 600 yards of this advance guard. Their first line was distinctly visible, facing the Confederates, and at right angles to the Richmond road, near which they had a battery masked. Hill's (Cleburne's) brigade was placed in line, behind the crest of a low hill, which ran parallel to the enemy and some 500 yards from them. Douglas's guns were placed on the summit of the crest, near the center. Smith's brigade formed within supporting distance, behind the top of a second ridge in rear of the first. Douglas's battery fired on a squad of cavalry, which quickly disappeared, unmasking the Federal battery, which opened up a rapid fire. Skirmishers were sent out towards the right flank and the line extended towards the left across the Richmond pike, with a strong company of skirmishers. The latter held a regiment of the enemy's infantry in check during the first of the fight and effectually protected the left flank. A good position having been found for another battery, Martin's, of Preston Smith's brigade, was sent to the front and placed on the hill near the right of Hill's brigade, and opened fire on the enemy. Just then Cleburne was ordered to avoid a general engagement until Churchill's division, of Kirby Smith's army, arrived upon the field. Accordingly, the artillery was directed to fire very slowly, and not to waste ammunition. After this the battle was a mere artillery and skirmish fight for over two hours, at which time the enemy commenced to move towards the Confederate right flank, driving in their skirmishers. The one hundred and fifty-fourth Tennessee Regiment of Smith's brigade was ordered forward and placed in line on the right of Hill's brigade. Here a close fire soon began, becoming so heavy that it was found necessary to strengthen further that flank. The Thirteenth and Fifteenth Arkansas regiments, under command of Colonel Lucius E. Polk, were detached to its support. A galling musketry fight resulted, and the enemy was found to be strongly concentrating against the right. Cleburne, satisfied that General Churchill must now be within supporting distance, ordered Col. Preston Smith, of the second line, to move immediately the three remaining regiments of his brigade, and place them on the right of the line already engaged, and he was instructed that if his line overlapped that of the enemy to swing around their left flank. It was now evident that the enemy had staked everything on turning the Confederate right flank and had weakened their center for this purpose. Cleburne decided that the moment he heard Preston Smith's musketry on the Federal left he would order Hill's brigade to attack their center, and he galloped to the right to see if Smith was getting into position, and he was found rapidly moving in admirable order. Cleburne then rode back to give personal attention to the advance of Hill's brigade and the two batteries of Douglas and Martin. Stopping to reply to a question of Colonel Polk's, who, wounded, was being carried to the rear, a rifle ball entered Cleburne's left cheek, carrying away his teeth on that side, and emerging through his mouth, which, fortunately, happened to be open in speaking to Polk. In a few moments this wound deprived him of the power of speech, and his service on the field was rendered useless. When informed of the disabling of Cleburne, Colonel Preston Smith assumed command.

The movements ordered by Cleburne, just prior to his being wounded, proved a complete success. The division, under command of Colonel Smith, moved forward on the right of the road towards Richmond, General Churchill's having been previously advanced on the left, and engaged the enemy soon after Cleburne's was put in motion. While the engagement was spirited and hotly contested by the enemy on the left of the road, shelling the division as it advanced through the open fields, being heavily pressed by Churchill's command, they fled. A scanty supply of much-needed water for the troops having been obtained, the division again pressed on, and soon came in sight of the enemy, posted on the south edge of the town of Richmond. An immediate attack was made upon them, and after half an hour's stubborn resistance the enemy was routed, with ranks so thinned, broken, and scattered that it was impossible for him again to rally. The town of Richmond, with its stores, was abandoned to the Confederates, and after an ineffectual pursuit three miles beyond that point, the division went into camp, after twelve hours of continual hard marching and fighting. In this engagement Cleburne commanded on the field, organized and directed the attack which broke the Federal line, and had practically won the battle before he was disabled. The victory was complete. Gen. H. G. Wright, commanding Department of Ohio (Federal), wrote from Cincinnati on August 31:

> Nelson has been badly beaten, I fear * * * his forces, being as he says, hopelessly broken and scattered * * * at any rate his force has been routed.[3]

And again from Louisville, on September 2, dispatches Halleck, at Washington:

> The force engaged in the battle in front of Richmond was utterly broken up, and after all the exertion to collect stragglers only some 800 or 900 could be found. The remainder were killed, captured, or scattered over the country.[4]

The total loss of Gen. Kirby Smith's army, in killed and wounded, was about 400. Of these, 27 killed and 194 wounded, or a total of 221, were from Cleburne's brigade. Besides Cleburne, Col. Lucius E. Polk, Col. G. H. Nixon, Colonel Hill, commanding the brigade, were wounded (the latter had two horses shot under him), and the gallant Lt.-Col. J. A. Butler of the Second Tennessee regiment was killed. The enemy lost in killed and wounded 1,050; captured, 4,303—total 5,383; besides 9 pieces of artillery, 10,000 stands of small-arms, and a large quantity of army supplies. Major-General Nelson,* commander of the Federal forces, was wounded, and his second in command, General Manson and his staff, captured.

---

3. H. G. Wright to H. W. Halleck, Aug. 31, 1862, *O.R.*, XVI, part 2, 464.

4. Same to same, Sept. 2, 1862, *O.R.*, XVI, part 2, 471-72.

*Maj. Gen. William Nelson had been an officer in the U. S. Navy. He was a brave man and meritorious soldier, but a rigid disciplinarian, blunt and rough in manner and speech. This won for him from his troops, who disliked him, the sobriquet of "Bull." General Cleburne, in speaking of the battle of Richmond, said, "His army was broken up, and 'Bull' Nelson sent 'howling' back to Louisville with a bullet through his leg." On September 29, 1862, General Nelson had a difficulty in the Galt House, Louisville, with Gen. Jefferson C. Davis, U. S. A., during which he slapped the latter's face, whereupon Davis inflicted a pistol wound in Nelson's breast, causing his death in less than an hour. Davis was immediately arrested and a court-martial requested. Instead of this being ordered, he was released ostensibly that his case might be turned over to the civil authorities, which was not done. Davis was restored to duty, and the slaughter of Nelson never investigated by either a civil or military tribunal.

This battle, which has had little place in history, was of importance as showing Cleburne's ability as commander on the field, in which his admirable dispositions, and tactics, won the fight, and cleared the way for Gen. Kirby Smith to march without further opposition to Lexington, and establish an outpost at Covington, opposite Cincinnati, and threatening that point. In his official report Gen. Kirby Smith said: "General Cleburne was badly wounded in the face, and thus at a critical moment I was deprived of the services of one of the most gallant, zealous, and intelligent officers of my army." The Confederate Congress passed a vote of thanks to Cleburne "for gallant and meritorious service" at Richmond, Kentucky.

General Bragg's design was to unite with General Smith at Frankfort and make a dash for Louisville before Buell reached that point. But the brave, unfortunate, and useless attack by General Chalmers on Munfordsville caused loss of time which enabled Buell to win the race to Louisville, and thus was lost to the Confederates a prize worth a score of the one gained—Munfordsville.

About September 26 General Buell had an available force of 137,000 with which to confront Bragg, who had, including Kirby Smith's and Humphrey Marshall's commands (the latter had joined from southwest Virginia) an effective total of 48,776.

After the capture of Munfordsville, Bragg's army was moved to Bardstown, from which point the General went in person on September 28, to confer with General Smith at Lexington, and after an agreement as to cooperation and plan of campaign, General Bragg proceeded to Frankfort, to be present and assist at the inauguration of Hon. Richard Hawes as Provisional Confederate Governor of Kentucky. These ceremonies were brought to a hasty conclusion by the sound of the artillery of Buell's advance force from the direction of Louisville.

CHAPTER FOUR

Battle of Perryville — Withdrawal Into Tennessee

On October 1 Buell commenced his march from Louisville, upon Bragg at Bardstown. Two of his divisions under Generals Sill and Dumont moved direct towards Frankfort to threaten Kirby Smith, and the latter's purpose was to meet them, and on October 2 General Bragg ordered Lieut.-Gen Polk, commanding army in Bragg's absence at Frankfort, to move the entire army from Bardstown via Bloomfield, towards Frankfort, and to strike Sill's column in flank, while Smith's met it in front. This order was not complied with, but on the approach of Buell, Polk marched via Perryville towards Harrodsburg, where he expected concentration of the whole army. Exaggerated reports reached Bragg as to the strength of the force moving upon Frankfort, and he was led to believe that the one approaching Polk was not so large as represented; accordingly, on October 7, the latter was directed to form his cavalry and the divisions of Cheatham, Buckner, and Patton Anderson at Perryville and vigorously attack the enemy. Since the commencement of Buell's movement on October 1 the cavalry, under General Wheeler, had engaged continually, and resisted the advance of Buell's two foremost columns.

After he was wounded at Richmond, Cleburne was taken to the home of a citizen near the field, and so well cared for as to be able early in October to rejoin his brigade, which meanwhile had been returned from Kirby Smith's army to its proper command—Buckner's division, Hardee's corps. This, consisting of Maj.-Gen. Buckner's and Brig.-Gen. Patton Anderson's divisions, constituted the left wing of the army. Each division consisted of four brigades, with a battery attached to each. Thinned by battle and reduced by long and arduous service, Hardee's effective force did not exceed 10,000 men, while that of the enemy, from reports of prisoners captured from five of their divisions, it is estimated displayed at that time not less than 35,000 troops, commanded by Major-Generals McCook, Rousseau, Jackson, and other able generals.

The country near Perryville is boldly undulating. Chaplin's Fork of Salt River flows northward through the town, and between four or five miles beyond it is a small stream known as Doctor's Fork (Creek), which empties into Chaplin some miles northwest of Perryville. The space between the two streams, from east to west, is about one and a half miles. A road running a little south of east from Mackville to Perryville crosses Doctor's Creek, and a turnpike from Springfield running nearly east and west, passes through Perryville to Danville. Another pike traverses the town from the south, in a northwardly direction towards Harrodsburg and Lexington, and another southwardly, in the direction of Lebanon. The key to the enemy's position was a point where the Macksville road crosses Doctor's Fork, about one and one-half miles from Perryville, near a white house on the hill west of the creek, which was almost dry, only pools of water being found here and there along its bed. The general direction of Hardee's line was originally nearly north and south, the left resting near the town, west of Chaplin's Fork, and the right extending down the stream. This line was subsequently advanced about noon, by order of General Bragg, so as to take position on the space between the two streams on the west of the town, extending across the Mackville road, with its left towards the Springfield pike. An interval between the left and the Springfield road was protected by a battery of 12-pounders, under Captain H. C. Semple, posted on Seminary Hill, near the eastern side of the village. General Patton Anderson's division covered the extreme left on the Springfield road to protect communications with

Danville and Harrodsburg. The enemy occupied the western or left bank of Doctor's Fork, extending across both sides of the Mackville, and across the Springfield road. His left, north of the former road, was thrown back in a northwesterly direction, forming an obtuse angle, along broken heights from their center and right, the angle being near the point where the Mackville road crosses Doctor's Fork. About 1 o'clock in the afternoon Cheatham's division crossed this Fork on the extreme right and engaged the enemy's left on the heights with great vigor, upon which Buckner's division was ordered to advance and attack the salient angle of the enemy's line where the Mackville road crosses Doctor's Fork. The position was very strong. The enemy was posted behind a natural parapet afforded by the character of the ground and some stone fences, which were enfiladed by their artillery on the right and swept by another strong battery posted in their rear. The brigade of Gen. Bushrod Johnson gallantly led the advance, with Cleburne's in support and Liddell's held as a reserve. The two latter continued to advance, keeping within supporting distance of Johnson. Cheatham becoming hotly engaged, the brigades of Johnson and Cleburne attacked the angle of the enemy's line with great impetuosity. A destructive fire was kept up on Johnson's brigade, which was endeavoring to ascend the ridge. Cleburne advanced down the open ground into the creek bottom, exposed to a heavy fire of both small-arms and artillery. The brigade moved in double time and was soon in the bed of the stream, and so immediately under the enemy that the latter's fire passed harmlessly over. While Johnson's brigade on the hillside, in Cleburne's front, was exchanging a rapid fire with the enemy, Cleburne moved the Fifteenth Arkansas Regiment a short distance to the right of his line, and making change of front, placed it on the hill at right angles to Johnson and the enemy, and opened a flank fire on the latter's left, without, however, exposing this regiment. A battery was gotten into such position on Johnson's left as to enfilade the stone wall from behind which the enemy was firing. Johnson's brigade having exhausted ammunition, it was retired to the creek bed, and simultaneous with this withdrawal Cleburne's brigade moved forward and filled the position vacated by Johnson.

The Federals had now been driven back from the stone wall near the summit of the ridge, and were sheltering behind this crest. The Fifteenth Arkansas was ordered back to its position on the right of the brigade, and skirmishers sent forward preparatory to the advance of Cleburne's main line. Captain G. Dixon of the Fifteenth Arkansas went ahead alone to within thirty steps of the enemy, and report of his observation caused an immediate forward movement of Cleburne's command, the skirmishers ten paces in front and carrying the battle-flag of the regiments. As the brigade ascended the hill it was fired into by its own artillery from the rear, and several men killed and wounded, and the line compelled to fall back. This fatal blunder can be accounted for only from the fact that the majority of the men had on blue pants and no doubt were mistaken for Federals. As soon as this artillery fire could be stopped the brigade moved forward in the same order as before. The moment the flags carried by the skirmishers appeared above the crest of the ridge the enemy supposing the skirmishers to be the main line, emptied their guns at them. Before they could be reloaded the true line was upon them, and they broke and fled under a deadly fire, and the salient angle was taken. Colonel Lytle, their commanding officer, rallied about one hundred of the enemy, but these were routed in a moment, with heavy loss. Cleburne's advance was continued through a cornfield, but the command became so scattered in the pursuit it was necessary to halt the brigade and reform the line, which was done, with its left resting on the Mackville road, and the line at right angles to it. Another advance was made until within seventy-five yards of the position known as the White House, where a fresh line of the enemy was strongly posted, with artillery protecting their flank. At this juncture the brigade was without artillery or supporting force on its left. A few sharpshooters were sent to watch this point. A regiment posted in the valley, upon the brigade's right, gave way, and most of them, despite entreaties and commands, fled to the rear, leaving Cleburne's small brigade of not over eight hundred men in the center of the battle, unsupported on both flanks. A furious cannonade between the Confederate artillery posted on the hill first taken by Cleburne, on the right of the Mackville road, and the Federal batteries located on the right of the White House, was carried on over the brigade line. This, coupled with the fact that the troops had exhausted their ammunition, prevented further advance. The position taken was held until night closed, when the enemy, flanked and surprised by General Liddell's brigade, retired entirely from this part of the field. Cleburne collected his wounded, and by permission of General Leonidas Polk, went into camp on the Harrodsburg road.

General Buell, commanding the army of the Ohio, states his forces on the 7th and 8th of October advanced upon Perryville, numbering 61,000, of which it is estimated about 40,000 took actual part in the battle, as prisoners were captured from five Federal divisions. Buell's loss, in killed, wounded and missing, amounted to 4,281, and 15 pieces of artillery. Among his killed was Gen. James S. Jackson, commanding division, Gen. William R. Terrill, and Colonel Webster, commanding brigades, and Col. William H. Lytle, commanding the brigade, wounded and captured. Major-General Polk, commanding the Confederate forces on the field, reports his whole force, including all arms, not to have exceeded 15,000, and his total loss, killed, wounded and missing, as 3,396. Of these, 1,930 belonged to Hardee's corps. No separate report can be found of Cleburne's brigade loss, but attacking as it did the salient and stone wall it must have been heavy. While Cleburne was leading a charge his horse was killed by a cannon shot, and the same ball wounded the General in the leg, but he remained in command until the close of the day. Lieutenant Seay of his staff was killed at Cleburne's side, and his aide, Lieutenant Mangum, by one volley from behind the stone wall received seven wounds, none of which, strange to say touched a vital spot.

Night closed with the entire battlefield in possession of the Confederates. The troops which had been engaged were jubilant, feeling that they had won a victory, and confidently expected to reap its full benefit by being led against the enemy the next morning. This feeling was shared by their officers, but they were ignorant of the fact that during the progress of the battle the left flank had been exposed to a fresh Federal corps, advancing from the direction of Lebanon. This accession to the already large preponderance of the enemy was too hazardous to justify any hope of success in renewing the conflict the following day. Accordingly, the line which rested on the field until midnight was at that hour retired to Perryville, and at dawn, from that point, commenced to march to Harrodsburg, and General Kirby Smith, at Lawrenceburg, was instructed to march his command and form a junction with Bragg, at the former place, which he did, arriving on the 10th. Buell advanced slowly and declined Bragg's offer of battle at Harrodsburg. Two days elapsing and the Federal general manifesting no disposition to attack, the Confederate army retired on the 11th to Bryantsville. Here again the enemy declined battle. General Bragg having decided to retreat, the troops, in two columns, under Major-Generals Polk and Smith, were on October 13th put in motion via Cumberland Gap for Knoxville, which point was reached on October 24th.

An important factor in causing General Bragg to make the Kentucky campaign was the reasonable belief that the people of that State would flock to his standard in multitudes. But such expectation was doomed to disappointment, as General Bragg wrote to his Government on September 24th: "I regret to say we are sadly disappointed in the want of action by our friends in Kentucky. We have so far received no accessions to this army. General Smith has secured about a brigade—not half our losses by casualties of different kinds. Unless a change occurs soon, we must abandon the garden spot of Kentucky." This was from no want of sympathy or desire to aid from the majority of the people, but knowing the immense disparity in forces, they apprehended an early withdrawal of the Confederate troops. Had a great victory been won on Kentucky soil, or sufficient time of occupation been given, the reverse of this seeming apathy would have occurred, and more recruits obtained than could have been armed. It is easily seen why the interception and defeat of Buell, which seemed in easy reach between Munfordsville and Louisville, or a decisive battle in favor of the Confederates at Frankfort or Perryville was of such vital importance. The failure to accomplish this at Perryville was attributed by General Bragg to disobedience of orders by a subordinate temporarily commanding the army. The controversy as to where the true responsibility rested has never been settled to the satisfaction of the supporters of the two generals. This is an apt illustration of Napoleon's maxim that "one bad general is better than two good ones" commanding on the same field.

While the loss of men in this campaign was heavy, the capture of the greatly needed army supplies was enormous. On the retreat the number of wagons was nearly four thousand, these with their contents being almost entirely from captures. In saving this immense train Cleburne was largely instrumental. Its slow movement, barely averaging five miles a day, greatly impeded the progress of the troops, while the enemy was energetically pressing the rear, and only kept in check by the superb efforts of General Wheeler, who had been appointed chief of cavalry, and in charge of the rear-guard, with authority to give orders in the name of the commanding general. So strong'was this pressure, that in spite of the resistance of the cavalry, and with the train almost at a standstill near a most difficult point known as Big Hill, to save it seemed impossible. General Kirby Smith on October 15th wrote General Bragg: "I have little hope of saving any of the trains, and fear much of the artillery will be lost";[1] and subsequently orders were issued to destroy them. Cleburne, who was disabled and off duty in consequence of his wound, hearing of these orders, asked for authority to use such means as he deemed best to extricate the train, and the desired permission was given. By stationing guards he arrested every straggler —officer or private—passing, thus collecting a large force, which he organized into fatigue parties along the road, and by doubling

---

1. E. Kirby Smith to Braxton Bragg, Oct. 15, 1862, *O.R.*, XVI, part 2, 949.

teams and the men assisting at the wheels, carried the wagons over the hill and to safety.*

The result of this campaign was of great value to the South. It cost the Federals a loss, in killed, wounded and missing, of 26,530 men, 35 cannon, 16,000 small-arms, millions of rounds of ammunition, 1,700 mules, 2,000 horses, and the huge wagon-train before mentioned. The South also recovered Cumberland Gap which had been evacuated by Federals under General Geo. W. Morgan, on September 17, and redeemed East and Middle Tennessee and north Alabama. The first success at Richmond, Kentucky, and the advance into the heart of Kentucky, and so close to Louisville, had raised high hopes in the breasts of the Southern people, and a want of understanding as to the reasons of General Bragg's withdrawal from the State drew down upon him a storm of popular denunciation and condemnation. This feeling, however, was not shared by the Richmond, Virginia, authorities, who being better advised, their confidence in the commanding general was not shaken. On the other hand, Buell, by the Northern people and his Government, was with better reason even more bitterly assailed for not destroying or so crippling Bragg as to have prevented his subsequently transferring his army to Middle Tennessee. Buell was removed from command of the Department of the Cumberland, and his conduct of the Kentucky campaign made the subject of a congressional investigation and Military Commission inquiry on five specifications. The opinion of this Commission was rather in the nature of a Scotch verdict—"not proven."

*While in Kentucky some whiskey was captured, over which Cleburne ordered a guard to be placed. Inadvertently this was detailed from an Irish company. Passing a few hours later, the General found one of the barrels *empty* and the guard and most of their company *full.* Placing them in arrest, he turned, incensed, to his provost-marshal and said, "*Lieutinint,* I thought you had more *sinse* than to put an Irishman to guard whiskey." Ordinarily, Cleburne had very little of the "brogue," but it was very pronounced when he became excited or angry.

CHAPTER FIVE

Battle of Murfreesboro — Withdrawal to Tullahoma — Promotion

FOLLOWING the rest necessary to troops after an arduous campaign of two months, under orders of Lieutenant-General Polk, commanding in absence of General Bragg at Richmond, Virginia, the army, on October 30, was directed to move towards Middle Tennessee. The infantry travelled by rail and the trains, under guard of Wheeler's cavalry, marched across the country, fording Clinch River above Kingston, thence down the Tennessee Valley to Smith's Cross-Roads, and from there across Walden's Ridge into Sequatchie Valley; thence via Jasper to Winchester and from there to Tullahoma, where the first concentration was made, and later to Murfreesboro, 30 miles southeast of Nashville, where army headquarters were established on November 26, with outposts in the direction of Nashville.

On December 12, 1862, Cleburne was promoted to major-general* and assigned to the division lately commanded by General Buckner. This embraced Cleburne's old brigade, now commanded by Lucius E. Polk, promoted brigadier-general; Liddell's Arkansas, Bushrod Johnson's Tennessee, and S. A. M. Wood's Alabama and Mississippi brigades, with Key's (Arkansas), and Swett's (Mississippi), Darden's (Mississippi), and Semple's (Alabama) batteries.

---

*In recommending Cleburne for promotion to major-general, General Bragg wrote to the War Department: "Cleburne is young, ardent, exceedingly gallant, but sufficiently prudent. Is a fine drill officer, and the admiration of his command, as a soldier and a gentleman." *O.R.*, XX, part 2, 508.

In front of Murfreesboro, Hardee's corps, consisting of Breckinridge's and Cleburne's divisions, with Wheeler's cavalry, held the left of the army at Triune and Eaglesville. Cleburne's division was stationed near College Grove about twenty miles west of Murfreesboro.

General Rosecrans, who succeeded Buell in command of the Federal forces, began his advance from Nashville on December 26. General Bragg decided to accept battle at Murfreesboro, at which point Stone's River flows northward about two miles west of the town. On December 28 Hardee's corps was withdrawn to Murfreesboro, and placed on the extreme right, his left resting on the east banks of the river and forming the right wing. Lieutenant-General Polk's corps formed the left wing, his right resting on the west bank of the stream, and his left extending in the direction of the Triune road. Thus it will be seen that Stone River separated the two wings of the army, and was by a bend, horse-shoe shaped near General Polk's center. The bend of the "shoe" being in direction of the town, or to the east. Hardee's formation was Breckinridge's division as the first line, and Cleburne's the second, which was posted 800 yards in rear of and parallel to Breckinridge. Both army commanders employed the intervening time in making preparations until the 30th, when heavy skirmishing occurred between Rosecrans's right and Polk's left, indicating a serious attempt of the former in that quarter. In the afternoon of the 30th, Hardee was directed to proceed to the left, take command of McCown's division, to place it in position, and to move Cleburne's division from the right to left of the army on the west side of the river. Breckinridge's division was left in its original position in the front line on the right. Hardee placed McCown's division in the front line, and it was the extreme left of the infantry. Cleburne's division was placed as a second line 500 yards in rear of McCown's. The commanding general during the night determined to assail the enemy, and Hardee was directed to attack the next morning at dawn, with McCown's and Cleburne's divisions, and Wharton's cavalry—2,000 strong—which had been ordered to report to him. It was not clear daylight when Cleburne formed line and advanced Polk's brigade with Calvert's battery (commanded by Lieut. T. J. Key), on the right of Johnson's brigade, with Darden's battery, in the center, and Liddell's brigade, with Swett's battery (Lieut. H. Shannon), on the left. Wood's brigade was placed a short distance in rear of Polk's. This brigade had no battery, as Semple's belonging to it, had been detached for service with Breckinridge's division. So close were the opposing lines that skirmishing opened immediately upon their advance, and the main line quickly engaged. McCown and Cleburne were directed to swing by a continuous change of direction to the right, pivoting on Polk's left. This was done by Cleburne, but not so promptly executed by McCown, who continued westwardly and far to the Confederate left, leaving a gap between his right and General Polk's left. This interval was filled by Cleburne's division, which thus became front line, instead of being second, supporting McCown, whose line had disappeared from Cleburne's front. The latter's line was now a single one, without support. After firing a few volleys it charged and drove McCook's corps (the right of Rosecrans's) with great carnage. This early attack caught the enemy totally unprepared—not in line and cooking their breakfasts. McCook was steadily driven and doubled back upon the Federal center. Three miles of ground had been gained by the Confederate left wing. That fought over was in many places limestone ridges and dense cedar thickets, with farm-houses and cleared fields interspersed. These cedars were so dense as frequently to form an impenetrable screen rendering it impossible to see but a short distance in front, and the continuous roar of musketry and artillery made it difficult to hear orders given by voice, and the direction of movements were on both sides at times by the bugle. Brigadier-General Polk while moving through one of these cedar thickets heard a bugle sound from the troops confronting him. Inquiring of his bugler the meaning of it, he was informed that it was an order to move by the right flank. He at once directed his brigade to move by the left flank, and as it emerged from the cedars the heads of the two commands met, and a bloody struggle followed.

The continuous din of battle from dawn until noon so alarmed and dazed the denizens of the rocks and cedars that they lost all fear of men—their natural enemies—and the poor, frightened creatures —owls, hawks, partridges and rabbits—sought refuge in the ranks of the troops, flying and running to their feet, and so close and deadly was the fire that in cleared fields and near houses, dogs, horses, cattle and other domestic animals were killed.

A detailed account of the parts taken by the brigades and batteries of the division will be found in Cleburne's official report at the close of this chapter.

On the morning of December 31 General Rosecrans's intention had been to attack the Confederate left, but Bragg's early movement snatched the initiative from Rosecrans, and forced him to accept battle on the defensive, and the driving back and defeat of his right wing deprived him of the advantage of the offensive movements designed. It was not until nightfall that the battle ceased. With pickets well to the front the division bivouacked in line of battle, which was the extreme infantry left of the army, and at right angles to and three miles in advance of its starting point.

Except for a reconnaissance by Wood's, Liddell's, and a part of Johnson's brigades to ascertain the state of affairs in their fronts, the division made no move on January 1. The enemy was found in force, and a sharp fight ensued, in which several hundred men were killed, wounded and captured. This loss fell chiefly upon Wood's brigade. On Friday, the 2d, the day passed without special incident on the left, but about 11 P. M. the enemy made a reconnaissance in force in Cleburne's front, but were driven back by skirmishers. General Bragg, anticipating an attack on the right, east of Stone's River, late in the night ordered the withdrawal of Cleburne's and McCown's divisions from the left, and that they be placed in the position on the right from which Cleburne had been moved on the 30th—the latter in rear of Breckinridge's line and McCown in reserve. These divisions did not reach their designed positions until after mid-night. Semple's battery, which had been detached to Breckinridge's division on December 30, rejoined Cleburne's on January 1, but on the following day Cleburne was ordered to send back four of its guns to support an attack about to be made by General Breckinridge. As its commander, Captain Semple, was acting chief of artillery of the division, four 12-pounder Napoleons were sent under command of Lieut. E. J. Fitzpatrick. In the desperate conflict on the afternoon of the 2d this battery was conspicuous for its services. Of its 45 officers and men, 20 were killed and wounded, among the latter the brave Lieut. Jos. Pollard, who was shot through both arm and leg. One gun was lost. Breckinridge's division, after a bloody struggle of forty minutes, was repulsed with heavy loss, at least 1,200 being killed and wounded. Saturday, January 3, was cold and a drenching rain set in.

Having received information that the enemy was being largely reinforced, General Bragg, in view of his reduced numbers, and the exhausted, worn condition of his troops from battle and hardships of their winter bivouacks, determined to retire. Near midnight on January 3, through a storm of sleet and rain, the division commenced its march to Tullahoma, via the Manchester road.

The strength of the Federal army at Murfreesboro was 43,400. Its total loss, 8,778, or 20 per cent.; Confederate strength, 37,712, and loss 10,266, or 27 per cent. Cleburne carried into the action 6,045 and lost 2,081 or 32¾ per cent. The heaviest loss of any one of the brigades was in Liddell's, or 607, while that of Johnson's was 606. Among the killed on the Confederate side were Brigadier-Generals James E. Rains and Roger W. Hanson. On the Federal side there were killed Brigadier-Generals Joshua W. Sill, Edward N. Kirk, and the accomplished Lieutenant-Colonel Julius P. Garesché, chief of staff of the army, whose head was carried off by a cannon ball while he was at General Rosecrans's side. Semple's battery, of Cleburne's division, fired this fatal shot, which was directed, from a mile away, at the figures riding along the pike.

In his official report General Bragg says:

> Major-Generals J. M. Withers and P. R. Cleburne, commanding divisions, are especially commended to the Govern-

ment for the valor, skill, and ability displayed by them throughout the engagement.[1]

In addition to those named in Cleburne's report, the following are mentioned by their respective brigade commanders as having been conspicuous for gallant service:

Polk's brigade.—Col. W. D. Robinson and Lieut.-Col. W. J. Hale, Second Tennessee; Captains William A. King, and Hugh S. Otey, of the staff.

Liddell's brigade.—Col. John H. Kelly, Eighth Arkansas (wounded); Col. Samuel G. Smith and Lieut.-Col. F. J. Cameron, Sixth Arkansas (both wounded); Lieut. H. Shannon, Swett's battery; William R. Liddell, aide; Lieut. W. R. Young (wounded), ordnance officer; Surgeon W. R. Kibler (wounded); Capt. George A. Williams, A. A. G.; Lieut. J. L. Bostick, aide; Lieut. J. M. Dulin, inspector; "and my brave bugler, Jake Schlosser, wounded, and taken from the field" (Liddell's report).

Johnson's brigade.—Lieut.-Col. R. H. Keeble, Twenty-Third Tennessee; Col. John S. Fulton and Lieut.-Col. John L. McEwen, Forty-fourth Tennessee; Capt. Put. Darden, commanding battery; Capt. Robert B. Snowden (wounded), A. A. G.; Capt. William T. Blakemore, John Overton and Jos. H. Vanleer, aides; Lieut. Geo. H. Smith, (wounded).

Wood's brigade.—Capt. O. S. Palmer, A. A. G.; Lieut. J. Percy Walker, inspector; Capt. William Simpson, Joshua Sledge, D. Coleman, and George D. Shorter, aides (the latter wounded.)

During the first day's fight Liddell halted his brigade to replenish the cartridge boxes, and sent Lieut. J. M. Dulin, of his staff, to bring up ammunition. The brigade, facing an open field overgrown with high weeds, was moved by the flanks to another position. Dulin came up with two ordnance wagons at a gallop. Supposing the brigade had continued its forward movement he called to the drivers, "come on!" and plunged into this field. The rush of the teams, the crashing and cracking of the dry stalks, spread terror into a skirmish line of the enemy hidden in the dense growth. Seeing wagons coming

1. *O.R.*, XX, part 1, 664.

down upon them, they broke cover and took to their heels, doubtless thinking it was no safe place where a Rebel ordnance train could venture unsupported. They were not more astonished than Dulin, who was never known to claim the distinction of being the only officer on record to charge a skirmish line with two ordnance wagons.

The giving up of Murfreesboro had a depressing effect upon the army. As at Perryville, the troops felt that they had won a victory, the fruits of which had been lost from no fault of theirs, and the retrograde or retreat caused deep dissatisfaction, which extended to many officers of high rank. The murmurs of discontent were not long in reaching General Bragg. The widespread impression was that his removal would ensue appears to have been shared in by himself, as is indicated in a remarkable circular letter addressed by him to his corps and division commanders. But notwithstanding the unconcealed loss of confidence of the majority of the rank and file, he was not relieved from command. The relations between the corps commanders and their commanding general became so unharmonious and strained that seldom did any of them visit army headquarters except officially.

Gen. Thomas L. Crittenden, who commanded the Federal left wing, very tersely and correctly states the case, as to failure to complete the battle already practically won, when he says:

> Every time the right [Federal] was driven in I thought (and now think) that nothing but a most extraordinary blunder on the part of a soldier of the experience of Bragg, hindered him from breaking Rosecrans's army in two, and leaving me standing with my troops looking at Murfreesboro. It is a pretty well-established maxim in military tactics that you should always press your advantage. Bragg had the advantage: all he had to do (it seems to me) was to pursue it and leave me alone with my success. Instead of that he attempted to drive the left; but he could not drive us, and meanwhile our right was reorganized. * * * I did not know on the 31st when they would come right up our rear.[2]

---

2. T. L. Crittenden, "The Union left at Stone's River," *Battles and Leaders*, III, 633.

CHAPTER SIX

From Tullahoma to Chattanooga

THE RETREAT of the Confederate army from Murfreesboro was slow, due to the muddy condition of the roads, and a blinding rain and sleet which prevailed from midnight until after daybreak on January 4, but it was almost unmolested, as the enemy had been too badly crippled to make energetic pursuit, and their feeble efforts were easily checked by the rearguard of cavalry.

The army assembled between the 5th and 6th, at Tullahoma, behind Duck River, and 18 miles southeast of Murfreesboro, the latter being Rosecrans's secondary base. General Bragg commenced immediately to strengthen his position by a chain of entrenchments on the north and west sides. These, protected by abatis of felled trees, rendered them formidable against a front attack. Hardee's corps was advanced across Duck River, and formed the right wing of the army. On April 30 Cleburne established his headquarters at Wartrace and Hardee his near by at "Beechwood." Wartrace is immediately on the Nashville and Chattanooga Railroad, 15 miles north of Tullahoma. Liddell's brigade was on outpost at Bellbuckle, 5 miles north of Wartrace. General Liddell was instructed to picket strongly the two gaps in his front, which had good roads leading to his position at Bellbuckle, viz: the railroad gap via New Fosterville and Liberty Gap to the east. The former 4 and the latter 3 miles from Bellbuckle. Early in June Liddell received additional orders to place two regiments and a section of artillery at Liberty Gap, which is a narrow defile about 300 yards in length, cutting the range of hills 2 miles east of New Fosterville. About 4 miles farther to the east and on Liddell's right flank the turnpike from Murfreesboro to Manchester passes through Hoover's Gap, which is an open gorge (or more properly the narrow valley of a small stream running northwestwardly into Stone's River) between ranges of high hills that skirt it on both sides for 4 miles nearly to the Garrison Fork of Duck River, where it begins. Both armies from the battle of Murfreesboro to the latter part of June occupied their time in fortifying their respective positions and recruiting their ranks. This rest was peculiarly acceptable to the Confederates after their hard marches and engagements since the preceding August. Depression disappeared, and the troops were in fine spirits and fighting trim. Who of the survivors of Liddell's command does not remember how, in the early spring at Wartrace, the brigade, armed only with sticks, would surround an old field, contract their lines, and drive the rabbits to a common center and kill them by hundreds? This afforded the men sport and at the same time a welcome and dainty addition to their not over abundant rations. Some of them will doubtless recollect, too, the gallant Capt. J. W. McDaniel, Thirteenth Arkansas, who, as officer of the day, at a later period ordered the lieutenant in command of the skirmishers to advance them, saying, "Charge them, boys. I am in need of a clean pair of socks." If he did not agree that "cleanliness is next to godliness," he certainly considered it worth the risk of life and limb. At this time one of the periodical religious revivals was in progress and meetings were held nightly, to attend which the men were given passes through the camp guards liberally. The chaplain's report of large attendance and "many being gathered to the fold" received rather a rude jar, as to the genuineness of some of the conversions, when the brigade commander wrote that since the revival set in he had received more complaints from citizens of hog stealing (capturing "mud larks," as the soldiers called it) than ever before, and recommended that the pass privilege be much restricted.

The fine brigade of Bushrod Johnson was here taken from Cleburne's and assigned to Stewart's division, and its place in Cleburne's filled by Churchill's Texas brigade. This command had just been exchanged from its capture at Arkansas Post in January. A portion of it was originally cavalry, but now dismounted and serving as infantry, which they did until the close of the war. By this change of arm of service the cavalry lost and the infantry gained as fine a body of soldiers, officers and men, as ever existed. The colonel of one of the regiments, Tenth Texas Infantry, R. Q. Mills, was afterwards the distinguished United States Senator from Texas, and author of the "Mills Tariff Bill."

While at Wartrace Cleburne had a visit from a distinguished British officer, Lieutenant-Colonel Fremantle, of the Cold Stream Guards. He accepted the tender of a review of Liddell's brigade at Bellbuckle, and while riding to that point General Cleburne discussed with him the difference in the drill and manual of arms between the American and British service, as Cleburne remembered the latter from his experience in the Forty-first English regiment, and asked many questions of his guest regarding his old command. After returning home Colonel Fremantle wrote an interesting narrative giving his impressions from observation, of both the Federal and Confederate armies, and in this narrative the above incident is mentioned. He served afterwards in the Soudan campaign, as major-general, and later was commandant of Malta. His fighting qualities may be judged from his troops having dubbed him "Hell-fire Jack."

During the spring a sergeant named Campbell deserted to the enemy from Colonel Govan's Second Arkansas regiment, to the surprise of many who knew him to be a most excellent soldier, and one that had served with credit through every battle in which the regiment had been engaged. This circumstance is mentioned for the reason that it was afterwards proved by his own confession that he fired the shot which killed Gen. John H. Morgan at Greenville, Tennessee, on September 4, 1864. (See Appendix B.)

At Wartrace Cleburne, appreciating the value of the sharpshooters he first organized at Corinth, determined to improve their efficiency. He first directed that each commander should send him names of a certain number of the best marksmen in their regiments. From out of these, making the highest practice score, the required number was selected, detached from their regiments, and placed under command of a lieutenant. Major Benham, of the division staff, instructed them first in the exact working of every part of the rifle, then in marksmanship, and to judge distance by the eye (no range finders were in use) by marching them to ground of different topographical features. An object would be pointed out, and distance to it estimated, after which the actual distance would be measured. By constant practice the men became quite expert in doing this, over hills and across ravines or level ground. Out of this body grew his famous "Whitworth Sharpshooters," of whom mention will be made later on. Personally, Cleburne devoted his time to drilling, inspecting and generally improving his command. While he was a rigid disciplinarian, and punishment swiftly and surely followed any detected breach of military rule, he would never allow the infliction of a punishment such as would humiliate and disgrace the offender, such as "bucking and gagging," barrel shirt, stocks, and rail carrying. He rightly contended that such lessened or destroyed self-respect, without which no man could be a good soldier. His method was for minor offenses, military work—extra guard duty, cleaning guns and accouterments, or withdrawing for a time any privileges enjoyed in the way of short leaves of absence from camp. For graver matters the case went before a court martial. On one occasion he found a soldier "marking time" before his quarters. Upon inquiring he found this was by order of his chief of artillery as punishment for some trivial breach of rule, and after ordering the man to his company, he sharply reprimanded the officer, reminding him that his headquarters was not a guard-house, and his disapproval of such mode of punishment—recommending instead the ones as above stated. Another time one of his men was arrested and confined to the provost guard-house for drunkenness and becoming boisterous, and he was "bucked," and whipped with the buckle end of a waist belt by the officer of the guard, who did not belong to his command. When Cleburne heard of this it put him in a towering rage. Vowing that none of his men could with impunity be maltreated and disgraced by corporeal infliction, he preferred charges against this officer, used all his influence, and never gave up pursuit until he was broken of his commission. It has been said that such a division as he commanded would have made the reputation of any general. This is granted, for better material never existed; but it must be considered and admitted that it was Cleburne's master hand that forged, tempered, and welded them into the superb fighting weapon they became. During the spring of '63 his old regiment, the Fifteenth Arkansas, gave him a surprise, and testimonial of their affectionate regard by presenting him with a sword, paid for by subscription of every officer and man of the regiment. Secrecy of the intention was required of the subscribers and was strictly observed. The sword was ordered and came through the blockade from Bermuda,—a fine Damascus blade in a plain polished steel scabbard, the hilt bearing the device of a shamrock, and the belt rings and bands being solid gold, as was a plate, on the scabbard, surmounted by the "Harp of Erin," upon which was the simple inscription, "To Major-General P. R. Cleburne, from his old regiment, Fifteenth Arkansas."[1]

So highly did Cleburne prize this token that it was never worn in battle, but always sent to the rear for safety, and he gave particular direction as to this before going on his last campaign. All trace of this sword has been lost since its removal from the public library in Atlanta where it was kept for a number of years. Its

---

1. There is uncertainty as to what became of Cleburne's personal belongings after his death. His pocketbook and diary were never found. His uniform cap is in the Tennessee Historical Society Museum, and his uniform coat, which he may have been wearing at the time of his death, is in the Confederate Memorial Museum in Richmond. The fate of Cleburne's sword is unknown. At one time, as Captain Buck says, it was in the Atlanta Public Library. Another report is that it was placed in "The Historical Building of Centennial Park" in Nashville in 1918.

proper place is in the same glass case where his uniform coat is, at the Confederate Museum, Richmond, Virginia.

At Wartrace new flags were ordered to be issued, but when the troops of the division learned that their old battle-flag—blue and white—was to be displaced by the newly adopted regulation one a hurricane of protests was heard, and also demands that they should retain their old ones or have new facsimiles of them. Their requests were heeded and they were allowed to retain their distinctive colors. General Hardee is authority for the statement that this was the only command in the Confederate service permitted to carry into action other than the national flag. This was a high compliment, but like all luxuries it was costly and carried with it penalties, for the enemy had learned to whom that flag belonged, and where it appeared there was concentrated their heaviest fire.

In the late spring of 1863 General Grant was threatening Vicksburg with a force largely superior to General Pemberton's, and this same condition existed as to Rosecrans and Bragg, in Tennessee. General Joseph E. Johnston, who commanded the two departments, pointed out to the Richmond authorities the impossibility of holding both, and that a choice should be made between Mississippi and Tennessee, advising selection of the latter, which, as he felicitously expressed it, was "the shield of the South." He further predicted that an attempt to hold the two would inevitably result in the loss of both, while by giving up one a quick concentration of the forces from it would save the other. Notwithstanding this warning, on May 23 General Breckinridge, with 6,000 men, was detached from Bragg and sent to Mississippi. The force was too small to be of avail against Grant and too greatly weakened Bragg to enable him to cope with Rosecrans's advance, then impending. On the evening of June 24 General Hardee informed Cleburne that the enemy in force had advanced simultaneously on Liberty and Hoover's Gaps, and carried both positions. On the morning of the 26th Wood's brigade was advanced to Bellbuckle. Liddell was found still guarding the approaches via Liberty Gap and New Fosterville, and was holding two wooded hills a mile south of Liberty Gap. On the evening of the 25th Liddell, supposing the enemy retiring, advanced on the gap, but after some hard fighting, in which he inflicted a heavy loss on the enemy, and suffered little himself, he fell back to his former position. It was now apparent that the Federals were still in force at Liberty Gap, and that he had there at least a division of infantry, besides cavalry and artillery. Three regiments of Wood's brigade and a section of Semple's battery were ordered to Liddell's support. One regiment each of Wood's and Liddell's brigades, with the other section of Semple's battery, were guarding the approach via New Fosterville. On the morning of the 26th this section of artillery and the two regiments rejoined their respective commands in front of Liberty Gap, and were replaced by a regiment of Churchill's brigade which had reached Bellbuckle at that time. The remaining two regiments of this brigade were moved up as a reserve to the forces in front of Liberty Gap. The enemy kept up a constant firing all day, and moved forward twice with a double line of skirmishers, which were driven back, and at night both parties held their former positions. There being no ammunition to spare, no reply was made to the continual fire of the enemy, except with five Whitworth rifles, which did good service in keeping down fire from the batteries. Mounted men were struck by these sharpshooters at distances ranging from 700 to 1,300 yards. During this day, the 26th, the enemy, advancing in overwhelming force through Hoover's Gap, forced back Stewart's division almost to Fairfield, thus threatening to turn Cleburne's right flank and cut him off from Wartrace. At night orders were received to withdraw to Tullahoma, via Schoefner's bridge over Duck River between Normandy and Shelbyville, at daylight of the 27th, which was done without loss, although the men were much wearied by the watching and fighting in front of the gaps, and it rained incessantly most of the time. The troops had no change of clothing, no tents, and could not even light fires to dry their clothing. Many had no shoes, and others left theirs buried in the deep mire of the roads. The entire loss of the division in the several engagements in front of the gaps amounted to 121.

The rear of the division at 7 P. M. on the 27th arrived and went into bivouac at Tullahoma.

From continuous rain the roads seemed bottomless. A mule had been known to fall and suffocate in the mud of the town streets. The question being asked as to the derivation of the name of Tullahoma a witty officer of General Hardee's staff replied that it was from two Greek words—"Tulla," which meant mud, and "Homa," which meant *more* mud.

The strategic and military worth of this point may best be judged by the following letter of General Hardee to General Bragg, January 26, 1863:

> It will be seen by the map I send you that this position [Tullahoma] offers few, if any advantages for defense. It can be turned, not only by the direct road leading from Manchester to Dechard and Winchester, but from the nature of the country, our flanks can be turned at this point. I see no advantage in this position which can compensate for superiority of numbers.[2]

It had been the hope and expectation of the army that Rosecrans, flushed with success in pushing Bragg back to that point, would attack him in the chosen position he had taken up and made preparation to defend; but these expectations were doomed to disappointment, and on the 30th of June the troops reluctantly turned their faces southward. General Bragg gives his reason for this in a letter to General Joseph E. Johnston, under date of July 3:

> My last advices to the department represented the enemy advancing upon us in heavy force. We were immediately ready to receive him, and offered him battle but he declined, and while holding a strong position, which we could not successfully attack, threw a force to our right and rear, by which he successfully assailed our communications. No adequate force could be placed at these several points along the line without too much reducing our main body. I accordingly withdrew to Tullahoma, and reached there just in time to prevent an attack upon its feeble garrison. The enemy established himself again in strong position on the defensive, and moved another heavy column against our bridges over Elk River, now swollen by

2. *O.R.*, XXIII, part 2, 617.

> heavy rains. By making a rapid march and using the railroad successfully we saved our supplies and crossed the Elk just before a heavy column appeared at the upper bridge. We were now back against the mountains [near Dechard and Cowan] in a country affording us nothing, with a long line of railroad to protect, and half a dozen passes on the right and left by which our rear could be gained. In this position it was perfectly practicable for the enemy to destroy our means of crossing the Tennessee, and thus secure our ultimate destruction without a battle. Having failed to bring him to that issue, so much desired by myself and troops, I reluctantly yielded to the necessity imposed by my position and inferior strength, and put the arm in motion for the Tennessee River. Should we succeed in crossing successfully, the Tennessee will be taken as our line.[3]

Cleburne's division crossed Elk River at Bethpage bridge, ascended the mountain on the road leading by University place (now Sewanee College), and on the night of July 4 bivouacked on the broad plateau of the Cumberland Mountain. Although it was midsummer, at this altitude the nights are chilly, and in the morning numerous rattlesnakes and copperheads, attracted by the warmth, were found around the smouldering fires, but fortunately none of the men were bitten. On the 5th the command descended, and via Jasper reached the Tennessee River, where it remained for a few days, and then crossed on pontoons to the south side at Shell Mound.

Vicksburg surrendered with its garrison on the 4th of July, and the fall of Port Hudson, a few days later, opened up to Federal navigation the Mississippi River from source to mouth, severing the Confederacy in twain. Arkansas, Louisiana, and Texas were thus entirely cut off from the States east. General Bragg had been maneuvered out of Middle Tennessee to within a few miles of the Georgia State line. Thus General Johnston's warning and prediction had been verified and both Mississippi and Tennessee were practically lost, never to be regained.

---

3. *O.R.* XXIII, part 1, 584.

CHAPTER SEVEN

Maneuvering in the Mountains

THE DIVISION passed through Chattanooga and camped at Tyner's station, on the Knoxville Railroad, a few miles to the east. Lieutenant-General Hardee having been assigned to duty in Alabama, on July 24 Lieut.-Gen. D. H. Hill succeeded him in command of the corps, which consisted of Cleburne's and Stewart's divisions. Brigadier-General Churchill having been sent to the Trans-Mississippi Department, Col. James Deshler, promoted brigadier, succeeded to command of the Texas brigade of Cleburne's division. Wood's brigade was sent to Harrison's Landing on the Tennessee River, northeast of Chattanooga, to guard the fords in that vicinity. On August 21 the enemy appeared on the opposite banks of the river and threw some shells into Chattanooga, thus showing his close approach. It was known to be his design to interpose a column between Knoxville and Chattanooga, and thereby isolate General Buckner at the former place. To prevent his crossing the Tennessee River the remainder of Cleburne's division was ordered to Harrison's Landing, and distributed so as to guard every ford and ferry from the mouth of the Chickamauga on the southwest to that of the Hiwassie, at Blythe's Ferry, on the northeast. These detachments were strengthened by rifle-pits, and at some points with artillery. The Federal general, Crittenden, whose corps was in Sequatchie Valley, after attempting all the crossings unsuccessfully, was withdrawn, with the exception of two brigades of infantry and some cavalry, down the valley in the direction of Bridgeport. It was learned on August 30 that McCook's corps had crossed and Thomas's was in the act of crossing the Tennessee at Caperton's Ferry, 35 miles below Chattanooga, and later it was ascertained that the latter, immediately after passing the river, had occupied Wills Valley, between Sand and Lookout Mountains, and established his headquarters at Trenton, threatening Bragg's rear, while at the same time his movements were screened by Lookout Mountain. By September 7 McCook had crossed Lookout Mountain, at Winston's Gap, and Thomas at Stevens's and Cooper's Gaps. Winston's is 46 miles and Cooper's about 25 miles from Chattanooga. McCook was directed to occupy Alpine, farther south, and east of Pigeon Mountain, and Thomas to take possession of McLemore's Cove on the east, a narrow valley between Lookout and Pigeon Mountains. The latter is parallel to Lookout, but not so high and rugged, nor does it extend so far north, ending 8 miles south of Chattanooga. Crittenden, who had by this time also crossed the river at Caperton's Ferry, was left with his corps in Will's Valley to watch Chattanooga. Here Bragg had some works strong enough to have been held against a superior force by a single division. By holding Chattanooga in that way Crittenden's corps would have been neutralized, and a junction with Rosecrans by Burnside impossible.

Burnside had, in the last week of August, advanced from Kentucky, towards Knoxville, with a force of 25,000, whereupon General Buckner, whose total strength, including infantry, artillery, and cavalry, did not exceed 5,000, evacuated, and Burnside occupied Knoxville. General Bragg, disovering that the enemy had penetrated so far south and to his rear, abandoned Chattanooga on September 8, marching south, Cleburne's division leading and halting at LaFayette, 22 miles from and almost due south of Chattanooga. Liddell's brigade had been temporarily detached, and with Walthall's formed a division in Walker's Reserve Corps—Liddell, commanding this division of two brigades, and Colonel Govan, in command of Liddell's brigade. Thus Cleburne's division was reduced to three brigades. These were sent to hold three gaps in Pigeon Mountain—Catlett's on the north by Deshler's; Dug, in the center by Wood's, and Blue Bird, on the south, by Polk's. Cleburne established his headquarters in a bivouac by the road leading to Dug Gap.*

Rosecrans's objective of the campaign was accomplished when Crittenden's corps, unopposed, marched into Chattanooga on the 9th. But Rosecrans made no attempt to concentrate his army there, but persisted in scattering it by pushing two of his corps—McCook's and Thomas's—to the Confederate left and rear. The lack of information on the part of the commanders of both armies as to the movements and dispositions of the other now seems incredible, but the mountains intervening between the two forces well veiled operations of both sides, or as General Bragg aptly remarked pointing to the Cumberland range across the river: "It is said to be easy to defend a mountainous country, but mountains hide your foe from you, while they are full of gaps through which he can pounce upon you at any time. A mountain is like the walls of a house full of rat-holes. The rat lies hidden at his hole, ready to pop out when no one is watching. Who can tell what lies hidden behind that wall?"[1]

After the occupation of Chattanooga by Crittenden, General Rosecrans labored under the delusion—and he should have known better—that Bragg was in rapid retreat to escape him, and pressed on his columns to intercept the supposed fugitives, and thus exposed himself to an attack in detail, by a wide separation of his corps, neither of the three being within a day's march of the other. Such an opportunity as was afforded Bragg to crush his opponent comes to a commander but seldom, giving him, as it did, the choice of utterly overwhelming and annihilating one of the two corps within reach: that of Crittenden on the Federal left at Ringgold, or Thomas, the center, in McLemore's Cove. With either of these destroyed, the

*Here Cleburne had a narrow escape from death. Sleeping on the ground he was wrapped in his blanket, which, upon arising one morning, he shook, and a large rattlesnake dropped out. Seeking warmth it had crawled into his blanket and coiled at his feet. Its semi-torpid condition probably prevented it stinging the General, but even this would not have saved him had he disturbed the reptile by a touch of his foot.

1. D. H. Hill, "Chickamauga—The Great Battle of the West," *Battles and Leaders*, III, 641 fn.

other two were easy prey. Herewith is quoted the events of the next few days, as described in a series of admirable articles written for the *Kennesaw Gazette* by Major Calhoun Benham, a member of Cleburne's staff during these operations:[2]

> The movements of the two armies during the few days prior to the battle of Chickamauga were of critical importance. To understand them it is indispensable to know the topographical features of the region. These are very remarkable. The Tennessee River may be regarded as the northern boundary of the general scene of these operations, beginning at Chattanooga on its left bank and following to Bridgeport about 28 miles below in a direction a little west of south. From a point on the left bank, about a mile below the center of Chattanooga, makes off in a direction a little west of south the celebrated Lookout Mountain. It is an isolated ridge upwards of 30 miles long, about 1,800 feet high above the waters of the river, with a plateau on the top of irregular width. From its base to within 100 feet of the plateau-top of the mountain, its sides steep, yet sloping, are covered with huge masses of rock, fallen from above, and are barely practicable of ascent for infantry. The remaining distance to the edge of the plateau above are sheer cliffs,—a precipice like the palisades of the Hudson River, breaking the plateau edge around the whole mountain,—only a few rude and difficult roads ascending to the top. From the easterly side of the mountain, at a point about 30 miles south of Chattanooga, a large spur breaks off, and, bending sharply around to the north, runs some 10 or 12 miles in an almost unbroken ridge, parallel with Lookout. This last ridge is known as Pigeon Mountain. The valley between Lookout Mountain and Pigeon Mountain is a cul-de-sac, a blind alley, with sides impracticable even for infantry, except at a few points, about 6 miles wide, and chiefly cultivated farms and here and there clumps of forest trees. It is known as McLemore's Cove. This valley is for the most part level, perfectly practicable for field evolutions, though perhaps somewhat embarrassed by the west branch of Chickamauga Creek (river it is called), and by Chattanooga Creek, which drains it.

---

2. Calhoun Benham, "Sketch of P. R. Cleburne," in *Kennesaw Gazette,* March 15, 1889.

When Bragg evacuated Chattanooga, Rosecrans (having information he confided in, to the effect that Bragg's army was in an entirely demoralized condition and retreating in a disorderly and precipitate manner) divided his forces. He sent Crittenden towards Ringgold, McCook to Alpine and Thomas into McLemore's Cove—the three detachments occupying the three angles of a triangle, not less than a day's march from the other. Bragg lay between them and close upon Thomas. Thomas had about 12,000 men. As he lay in the cove, Bragg lay just east of him across Pigeon Mountain—his whole army in hand, in fine condition, a morale of eager enthusiasm and fitness. The only passes over Pigeon Mountain were obstructed by felled trees and held by advanced guards from Bragg's army. These gaps were three: Catlett's Gap, held by Breckinridge* with his division, Dug Gap and Blue Bird Gap, held by Cleburne with his division, both in the corps of Lieut.-Gen. D. H. Hill. This was the 11th of September, 1863. During the day Hindman, with about 23,000 men, Buckner second in command, moved into McLemore's Cove by its mouth [via Davis Cross-Roads, on the road from La Fayette to Stevens's Gap.—I. A. B.] and confronted Thomas. D. H. Hill, with his corps, was holding himself in readiness to aid Hindman.

Thomas's situation was critical—indeed he was lost. Crittenden's nearest body of men was 15 miles away—a division of them 20 miles distant at Ringgold, with disposable forces in Bragg's hands to delay him if he undertook to come up. McCook was at Alpine, upwards of 10 miles away, and Bragg perfectly able to keep him off. Gordon Granger, with the reserve, was 20 miles away at Chattanooga. The only retreat open to Thomas was a narrow defile road through Stevens's Gap—*perhaps* one through Cooper Gap to the top of Lookout Mountain. Thomas formed across the cove, his left resting about Stevens's Gap, his right on Dug Gap, pointing towards Chattanooga. Hindman was coming in that quarter, and was expected to attack at daylight.

At half after 1 o'clock at night—it was September 11—Cleburne was ordered to cut out before day the obstructions

*This is an error. All three Gaps—Catlett's, Dug, and Blue Bird—were held by Cleburne's division. Walker's corps did on the morning of the 11th, follow Cleburne's to Dug Gap.—I. A. B.

which had been placed in Dug Gap and hold himself ready to strike Thomas in his rear when he should be engaged with Hindman; Breckinridge, who lay on the front and right of Thomas, to be ready to co-operate in the battle. Cleburne, on receipt of his orders, having not a moment to lose, set Wood, who actually occupied Dug Gap with his brigade, to work, and had the obstructions removed from it some time before day; and to secure his debouchment into the cove and avoid the effect of shells the enemy might throw into his column while he went massed down the defile of the gap he threw two brigades into the cove and deployed them at the foot of the ridge, before it was light. His orders instructed him to select his own time for striking the enemy. He then despatched an officer with a number of couriers along the ridge of Pigeon Mountain in Catlett's Gap to send him instant intelligence of Hindman's first gun, whether artillery or small-arms. The officer went several miles to the direction indicated, and waited until the morning was far advanced, when having heard no sound of an engagement between Hindman and the enemy, he returned to Cleburne at Dug Gap. Bragg and Hill were with Cleburne when he got back.* At this time the enemy was in plain view in the valley. He had been since it was light enough to see him.

The day advanced—no guns of Hindman's. Soon after noon, Cleburne having found a way little more than practicable for a chamois, conducted Polk's brigade into the valley, and formed it into a line behind the right of the enemy's rear, securing the junction of its right with the left of the two brigades already in the valley—Major Dixon, his inspector-general, making a daring reconnaissance under a long line of fire for this purpose. These dispositions made, Hill's command stood in eager but fading expectation of Hindman's attack. At length an hour or two by sun, certainly very late in the afternoon, a partial attack was made, seemingly from the right of Hindman's right wing. It was too late; the blow fell full upon the last of Thomas's rear-guard as it was entering the defile of Stevens's Gap. His main body was safe on Lookout

---

*I well remember seeing General Bragg at this time. His impatience at not hearing Hindman's guns was manifested by his restless walking back and forth on the top of the hill overlooking the enemy in the Cove, and occasionally he would stop and irritably dig his spurs in the ground.—I. A. B.

Mountain. He had been hours retreating—a movement he contrived to conceal, or the occasional intervening clumps of forest trees had concealed him from Bragg and Hill on Pigeon Mountain.

Hill's corps, every man of which had realized the enemy's situation the day through, was in ecstasies of grief. Men and officers swore, some were almost in tears, many were in despair. The opportunity of their deliverance had been lost—an opportunity such as a general making as many campaigns as Napoleon could never reasonably expect to meet with; a golden opportunity—manifest and simple as it was beautiful, perfect in reason. Rosecrans had better fortune than Wurmser, better than Alvinczi. If Hindman had attacked in front at daylight, or even much later, Breckinridge striking the right front, and Cleburne the right flank and rear on the reverberation of Hindman's first gun, Thomas must have laid down his arms instanter, or McLemore's Cove would have seen the slaughter of Roncesvalles pass. The first blow would have driven Thomas's left from Stevens's Gap and his more than doubly outnumbered force would have had no mode of escape, as it had no hope of succor. Behind him no road led out of the cove, or, if so, it was neither within accessible distance nor available under his conditions if it *had* been. The accepted information at the time was that there was no such road.

Whose was the fault? It boots little to inquire. Hindman was arrested. He justified his course, demanded inquiry. Bragg ordered no court. Bragg alleged he had given Hindman an order to attack at daybreak. Hindman produced the order, and challenged observation that it was permissive not peremptory. Certainly the fact that Hindman was all this time accessible to Bragg's couriers, and within one or two hours' ride, would seem not to dispense with Bragg's giving peremptory orders when he saw Hindman did not attack at daylight; while Hindman was yet far enough away from Bragg to have permitted, perhaps *exacted,* an attack on his own responsibility. General Bragg, in a communication to the authorities at Richmond, * * * states that he sent out repeated couriers to Hindman during the day, ordering him to engage. Whether the couriers delivered these orders or not I do not know. What General Hindman says as to receiving them I do not know. That officer read me a paper

> he had prepared, touching the issue between him and General Bragg, but I have no recollection of any thing in it relative to such order. Certain it is, between the two stools, the Confederacy that day fell to the ground, at least for that campaign. Had Thomas been captured Crittenden must have fallen next. He could not have joined either McCook or Granger. In their turn McCook and Granger, too far in the south to have ever got away must have surrendered also.

Major Benham is correct as to the effect of an attack by Hindman at daylight, or even some hours later on the 11th. As Generals Bragg and Hill were both with Cleburne, at Dug Gap, by sunrise, it may well be asked why an advance by Cleburne and Walker was not ordered. The answer is, that momentarily expecting to hear Hindman's guns, which was to be the signal for the advance from Dug Gap, it was apprehended that if such advance was made before hearing this signal Thomas would take the alarm and withdraw through Stevens's Gap before Hindman was in position to join in the attack and thus render victory less decisive than intended to be.

About noon General Hill was directed to move with Cleburne and Walker's commands and make a front attack. Hawkins's sharpshooters of Wood's brigade advanced, driving in the Federal skirmishers and pickets, and Cleburne's whole force was moving forward on their main line of battle, when it was halted by an order from General Bragg. The reason for this, as supposed, was to wait until Hindman got in the Federal rear. About an hour before sunset Hill was again ordered to advance, but the enemy was now rapidly retiring into the defile. His rearguard was attacked by a company of cavalry, and made a stand on the other side of Chickamauga Creek, under cover of a battery. Semple's battery of Cleburne's division was ordered up, and in a short time silenced the Federal fire, with heavy loss to them, and the rout was complete. This last attack was all too late to accomplish its purpose—the quarry had reached its haven of safety on Lookout Mountain, Thomas having taken the alarm and retired through Stevens's Gap.

On September 12 Rosecrans awoke to a full realization of his great peril, finding that Bragg had concentrated in front of his center, and was not retreating in the hot haste supposed, he made almost superhuman efforts to rectify his error in so widely separating his corps. At midnight on the 13th McCook, on his extreme right, at Alpine, 57 miles distant from him, was ordered to close in on Thomas, which he did, at Stevens's Gap on the 17th, by marching day and night through Lookout Valley. During these four days Rosecrans was in extreme danger. This corps (McCook's) was completely beyond the reach of affording succor to Thomas's or the latter to it, and during some of this time Crittenden's corps was separated from Thomas by an interval of from 10 to 12 miles. On the night of the 12th, from Ringgold Crittenden crossed to the west side of Chickamauga River, at Gordon's Mills, with the two divisions of Van Cleve and Palmer, which here joined the third one of the corps, Thos. J. Wood's, which had been isolated and unsupported for two or three days. The whole of this period Bragg's army was concentrated, well in hand, and had Wood's division at his mercy. Gen. D. H. Hill speaks thus of Crittenden's peril:[3]

> Surely in the annals of warfare there is no parallel to the coolness and nonchalance with which General Crittenden marched and countermarched for a week with a delightful unconsciousness that he was in the presence of a force of superior strength. On the 11th we find him with two divisions (Van Cleve's and Palmer's) at Ringgold, 20 miles from Chattanooga, and with his third (Thos. J. Wood's) 10 miles from Ringgold, at Lee and Gordon's Mills, where it remained alone and unsupported until late in the day of the 12th.

Lieutenant-General Hill was notified that Lieutenant-General Polk had been ordered to attack Crittenden at Lee and Gordon's Mills, on the 13th, and also that the reserve artillery and army trains were specially put under the care of his (Hill's) corps, at La Fayette. Breckinridge guarded the roads leading south from that point, and Cleburne, the gaps in Pigeon Mountain. No attack was made by Polk on Crittenden, as ordered. Another golden opportunity lost.

---

3. D. H. Hill, "Chickamauga—The Great Battle of the West," *Battles and Leaders*, III, 643.

CHAPTER EIGHT

Battle of Chickamauga

BY THE NIGHT of September 17 Rosecrans had concentrated his scattered command and formed a line some 11 miles in length, extending from Lee and Gordon's Mills to Stevens's Gap, and running in a direction east to southwest. He became apprehensive on the night of the 17th that an attempt would be made to seize the Chattanooga road on his left, and to prevent this he abandoned the aggressive and determined to act on the defensive. He said that on the 17th he was satisfied that Bragg would try to obtain possession of the Dry Valley and Rossville roads—the first on the west and the latter on the east of Missionary Ridge. Thus Rosecrans had divined Bragg's plan before the issuance of the latter's orders on the night of the 17th, which were to strike the enemy's left, with his right, force it back up the Chickamauga, towards Lee and Gordon's Mills, driving it farther away from Chattanooga. It was intended that the attack should be made at 6 o'clock A. M. on the 18th, by his extreme right at Reed's Bridge; but the execution of the order was found to be impossible and the movement proposed for that day did not begin until the 19th.

This delay of a day and a night was all to the advantage of Rosecrans, in affording him time for marching troops to extend his left. Thomas marched all night, the head of his columns reaching Rosecrans's headquarters on the Chattanooga—La Fayette road (Widow Glenn's)—at dawn on the 19th. On that morning the Federal battle line ran nearly parallel to the road above mentioned.

Learning that only a small force had crossed the Chickamauga at Reed's bridge, the evening before, and that the bridge had afterwards been burned behind them, Thomas, hoping to surprise and capture this force, threw forward two brigades, under General Brannan. This movement took away the initiative from Bragg and forced upon him the defense of his right flank. These two brigades of Brannan's were subsequently reinforced by the divisions of Baird and R. W. Johnson. The fighting through the day was in the nature of partial engagements from right to left and was desultory on the part of the Confederates, but none the less desperate. The respective lines would first on one side and then on the other drive back their opponents, only to be driven back in turn. The tide of battle ebbed and flowed as each side was reinforced, until at noon these fresh troops amounted to six divisions to the Federals and three to the Confederates, and the latter were compelled to withdraw a short distance to a line of low ridges.

At 3 o'clock P. M. General Hill received orders to leave Breckinridge's division at Lee and Gordon's Mills, and to send Cleburne's to report to the commander-in-chief at Tedford's Ford. This march was 6 miles over a road much obstructed by trains and artillery. From thence Cleburne was sent to Lieutenant-General Polk, on the right, who directed him to form as a second line, in rear of the one already in position, which was the extreme right of the infantry. About sunset this was done, the line being some 300 yards in rear of the first, with its right resting at Jay's steam sawmill. Polk's brigade, with Calvert's battery, was on the right; Wood's brigade, with Semple's battery, the center, and Deshler's brigade, with Douglas's battery, the left. As soon as these dispositions were completed, orders to advance, pass over the line in front, and drive back the Federal left were given, and the forward movement promptly made. The line in front was that of Walker's corps, which had been repulsed, and was laying down, to which Liddell's brigade was attached. The division was recognized and cheered as it passed over them. The enemy's line was encountered about 200 yards to the front, and from behind some hastily constructed works opened upon Polk and Wood a hot fire of musketry and artillery, of which Cleburne said, "For half an hour it was the heaviest I ever heard."

It was now night, and the darkness was intensified by the woods through which the advance was being made, and the heavy pall of smoke so obscured objects as to make accurate shooting impossible. The only break in the woods was a small enclosed clearing in front of Wood's brigade. Under cover of darkness Semple's and Calvert's batteries were run forward to this field, within 60 yards of the enemy, and opened a rapid fire. Polk at the same moment pressed forward. This combined attack caused the enemy to fall back quickly, and the pursuit was kept up to a point one mile beyond the starting point, when the advance of night, the difficulty of moving artillery through the woods in the dark and some entanglement with the command on the left (Cheatham's) rendered a farther advance hazardous. The division was halted and bivouacked in line with skirmishers thrown out 400 yards in front. Cleburne and his staff lay upon the ground without fires, a short distance in rear of the troops. Darkness prevented any opportunity of selection. Daylight revealed the fact that it was the spot where during the day the Eighth Arkansas regiment, of Govan's brigade, had captured Loomis's Michigan battery. Lying close around where they had slept were dead horses and artillerymen, among the latter Lieutenant Van Pelt, who had commanded the battery.*

The result of this night's engagement was that Cleburne had pushed back the enemy for over a mile, captured 3 pieces of artillery, 200 or 300 prisoners, and the colors of the Seventy-seventh Indiana and of the Seventy-ninth Pennsylvania regiments. At points the

---

*Riding through the dark woods a member of the staff came upon an abandoned Federal caisson on which were piled several sacks. Putting his hand upon the top one he discovered that it contained coffee. Calling a prowling "Reb," he informed him of this and asked that he fill his—the officer's—holsters, telling the soldier that he might have the balance. Soon sounds of grains falling into the holsters was heard and the finder's dream that night was of the luxury of coffee for breakfast, but daylight showed only *corn.* The top sack was *coffee,* the balance *corn.* The ungrateful wretch, taking advantage of the darkness, had tricked his benefactor and appropriated the entire sack of coffee.

hostile lines were very close to each other. The darkness and confusion of commands intermingling made it both difficult and dangerous to locate regiments or brigades. Lieutenant Hanly, Cleburne's aide, actually rode into an Indiana regiment, but fortunately found out his mistake before he himself was discovered, and escaped capture under cover of darkness. He learned what regiment it was by hearing the commander call it by number and State in giving an order.

An early advance the next morning was confidently expected and eagerly awaited, as through the night the proximity of the enemy enabled the men to hear the sound of axes and falling trees, and they knew that a renewal of the battle was certain, and were veterans enough to understand that every hour's delay made more formidable the log breastworks they would be called upon to assault. In the adjustment of the division line on the morning of the 20th, it was found that Cheatham's right brigade was at right angles to Cleburne's left, and when adjusted Cheatham's division was found to be exactly behind Stewart's, and therefore had to be taken out after the battle was begun, and placed in reserve. Cleburne's alignment was rectified and the division impatiently awaited orders to advance, feeling confident of victory. General Hill says, "I witnessed some of the heaviest fighting on the afternoon of the 19th and saw but one deserter from Hood's ranks and not one from Cleburne's."[1]

Early in the night of the 19th, General Bragg directed General Breckinridge to move from Lee and Gordon's Mills on the left and report to Lieutenant-General Polk. This division crossed at Alexander's bridge, and between 10 and 11 o'clock P. M. arrived, and bivouacked at a point about one and a half miles in rear of the line of battle. General Polk directed Breckinridge to prolong the line upon the right of Cleburne, which point was reached soon after daybreak on the 20th. Some little time was necessary to make the proper readjustment, which when done made Breckinridge the

---

1. D. H. Hill, "Chickamauga—The Great Battle of the West," *Battles and Leaders*, III, 652.

extreme infantry right of the general line of battle, which was supposed to be parallel to the Chattanooga road.

General Longstreet, whose appearance was as much of a surprise to the Confederates as later on it was to the Federals, arrived at army headquarters about 11 P. M. of the 19th. At this late hour General Bragg changed the organization of his army by a hazardous experiment. Being within a few hours of attacking, or indeed during a lull in the fight, he divided his army into two wings. He had probably never heard of Mr. Lincoln's remark, "It is unsafe ever to swap horses while crossing a stream." To General Polk he assigned the right wing, embracing the two corps of Hill and Walker and the division of Cheatham—five divisions in all, a total of 18,794 infantry and artillery, with 3,500 cavalry under Forrest. To Longstreet was given the left wing, consisting of the corps of Buckner, Hood, and Hindman's divisions,—six divisions in all,—a total of 22,849 infantry and artillery, with 4,000 cavalry under Wheeler. One of Longstreet's divisions from Virginia, that of McLaws, commanded by General Kershaw, did not arrive on the field until the morning of the 20th.

At daylight of the 20th Rosecrans's line to cover the Chattanooga and Dry Valley roads began 400 yards east of the Chattanooga road, on a crest which was occupied from left to right, in the order named, by Baird's division (Thomas's corps), R. W. Johnson's division (McCook's corps), Palmer's division (Crittenden's corps), and Reynolds's division (Thomas's corps). These four divisions became isolated during the day. They lay behind substantial breastworks of logs, in a line running due south and bending back towards the road at each wing. According to a Federal newspaper account, "Next on the right of Reynolds was Brannan's division of Thomas's corps, then Negley's, of the same corps, its right making a crochet to the rear. The line across Missionary Ridge was completed by Sheridan's and Davis's [Jeff. C.] of McCook's Corps; Wood's [Thos. J.] and Van Cleve's divisions of Crittenden's corps were in reserve at a proper distance." At the commencement the Confederate line ran from north to south. Hill's corps on the right, next Stewart's division. Hood in reserve, then Bushrod Johnson; Hindman's on the extreme left, and Preston's in reserve. After the fighting actually began, Walker's and Cheatham's divisions and Kershaw's brigade were taken out and put in reserve. Bragg was confronted with eight Federal divisions, protected generally by breastworks.

Orders had been issued by General Bragg that the attack should begin at daybreak, commence on the extreme right, and be taken up successively to the left, the pivot to be on Longstreet's left, so as to turn Rosecrans's left, and cut him off from Chattanooga. From some unfortunate miscarriage or misunderstanding of this order the attack did not begin at daylight. Meanwhile the ringing of axes and other sounds plainly indicated that the enemy was strengthening his position by field works. General Hill reached Cleburne's bivouac about 7 o'clock, and in the absence of orders to move, directed that the troops be given their breakfast. Soon after, Lieutenant-General Polk came up and assented to this. Immediately after he left General Bragg rode up, about 8 o'clock, and inquired of General Hill why he had not begun the attack at daylight, as directed. Hill replied that he was then hearing for the first time of orders to that effect, and had not known whether the Confederates were to be the assailants or the assailed. He was then ordered to attack as quickly as possible.

When the final necessary preparations were completed Breckinridge moved at 9:30 and Cleburne 15 minutes later. The latter had gone but a short distance when Polk's brigade on the right, of Wood's in the center, were subjected to a terrific fire of both small-arms and artillery, which swept the line at short canister range, from behind a line of log breastworks in front, from an unseen enemy, opposite Cleburne's right and right-center. The rest of his line, left-center and left, Wood's and Deshler's brigades, stretched off to the south (left), received an oblique fire from this line of breastworks, which at a point opposite the center formed a retiring angle running off west towards the Chattanooga road behind. The right-center—Polk's brigade and Lowrey's Thirty-second and Forty-fifth Mississippi regiments (consolidated) of Wood's brigade—was checked within less than 200 yards of the works in its front. The remainder of Wood's brigade was moved forward, and Semple's battery opened on the enemy at same time. The portion of Wood's brigade, to the left of the retiring angle before mentioned, in its advance entered a cleared space bordering on the Chattanooga road, and made an effort to cross it, in face of a murderous fire from works in its front. Just before reaching the road the men were driven back by a heavy oblique fire of smallarms and artillery upon both its flanks, an enfilading one on the right coming from the south face of the westward retiring angle of the breastworks, which had been concealed from view by the thick growth of scrub oaks on the sides of the clearing. Five hundred men were placed *hors de combat* by this fire in a few minutes.

Upon this repulse the brigade was drawn back about 400 yards to reform behind the crest of a low ridge, Lowrey's regiment, meanwhile, having also been forced to retire. Semple's battery, having no suitable position, was ordered back to the brigade. Of this conflict Gen. D. H. Hill writes:

> The fierce fight on our right lasted until 10:30 A. M. It was an unequal contest of two small divisions against four full ones behind fortifications. Surely there were never nobler leaders than Breckinridge and Cleburne and surely never were nobler troops led on a more desperate "forlorn hope" against odds in number and superiority in position and equipment. But their unsurpassed valor was not thrown away. Before a single Confederate soldier had come to their relief, Rosecrans ordered up other troops to the aid of Thomas. * * * At 10:10 A. M. he ordered McCook to be ready at 10:30; Sheridan's division to support Thomas. * * * * This weakening of his right by Rosecrans to support his left was destined soon to be his ruin. So determined had been the assaults of Breckinridge and Cleburne, though repulsed and badly punished, they were not pursued by the enemy, who did not venture outside of his works.[2]

Col. Archer Anderson said:

> Cleburne * * * led his division forward and very soon encountered a furious storm of canister and musketry from the

2. *Ibid,* III, 656-57.

same line [the one Breckinridge had attacked] of breastworks extending southward. The wooded ground was such that Cleburne could not use artillery, but for an hour or more his determined infantry pressed their fierce attacks at short range. There were no braver troops than Cleburne's, there was no bolder leader than Cleburne, but they could not drive Baird's, Johnson's, and Palmer's divisions from the breastworks. * * * Cleburne about the same time [as Breckinridge] withdrew and reformed his division. * * * But neither of these withdrawals took place till enormous losses had been endured and the fury of the Confederate assault had made deep lodgment in the minds of the two men directing the battle on the Federal side. Thomas, within a few minutes, sent three pressing calls for help to Rosecrans. Rosecrans, impressed by the terrific roar of the battle on his left and by his own preconceived notion that Bragg was moving his whole army to that quarter, and under painful stress from Thomas's calls for help, now gave three orders which were worth to the Confederates all the precious blood Hill's corps seemed then to have uselessly poured out. * * * At ten minutes past 10 Rosecrans sent McCook an absolute order to make immediate dispositions to withdraw the right so as to spare as much force as possible to Thomas, then heavily pressed. At half past 10 he ordered McCook to send two brigades of Sheridan's division with all dispatch to Thomas, and the third as soon as it could be withdrawn, adding that they must march as rapidly as possible. About the same time he also ordered Crittenden to send two brigades of Van Cleve's division to Thomas. Surely the desperate assaults delivered by Hill's corps was then swaying the battle in a manner that ought to teach every soldier the supreme value of stout fighting, however adverse the immediate result may seem.

But Rosecrans gave another order then, not less unlucky. He conceived the notion that Wood's [Thos. J.] division of Crittenden's corps was improperly posted, and directed him to close on Reynolds [Thomas's corps]. Now Brannan's division was on Reynolds's right, and Wood was aligned on Brannan's right. Wood so interpreted this order as to put his division immediately in motion by the left flank in rear of Brannan's, thus leaving a great gap in the Federal line, which Davis [Jefferson C., of McCook's corps] vainly attempted to fill with

> his reserve brigade. Just at this auspicious moment burst the storm which Longstreet had been carefully preparing. Stewart's, Hood's, Kershaw's, Johnson's [B. R.], and Hindman's divisions dashed impetuously forward, supported by Preston. The Federal line was quickly turned, the right-center was pierced. Wood's division was struck in flank as it moved from position. Negley's two brigades were caught in air in their march to the left, Brannan was struck in flank, large parts of Sheridan's and Van Cleve's divisions moving to the left were swept as before a whirlwind, and several thousand prisoners, 40 guns, and numerous wagon-trains were abandoned to the Confederates. Never was an attack more brilliantly successful. The Federals had fought gallantly but to no purpose.[3]

General Longstreet's advance did not commence until noon. At 2:30 he was sent for by General Bragg, whom he found in rear of his lines, and told him of the steady and satisfactory progress of the battle, that 60 pieces of artillery had been reported captured, that many prisoners had been taken, and that all was going well. He then asked for additional troops to hold the ground gained, while he pursued the two broken corps (McCook's and Crittenden's) down the Dry Valley road and cut off the retreat of Thomas. Bragg replied that there was no more fight in the troops of Polk's wing; that he could give Longstreet no reinforcements; that Longstreet should remain in the position he then was, and concluded by saying, "General, *if anything happens,* communicate with me at Reed's Bridge." He seems not to have known that up to that time, 2:30 P. M., Cheatham's division and a part of Liddell's had not been in action that day.[4] Absence from the field and consequent lack of knowledge of the true conditions as to Polk's wing is the only way to account for this unjust and untrue aspersion upon the troops who by their magnificent fighting had so pressed the Federal left as to make the brilliant movement by Longstreet's wing the grand success it was. And the heroic fight they afterwards made, as will later be

3. Archer Anderson, "Campaign and Battle of Chickamauga," in *SHSP,* IX, 411-413.

4. D. H. Hill, "Chickamauga—The Great Battle of the West," *Battles and Leaders,* III, 659.

described, entirely disproves the commanding general's opinion that "there was no more fight in them."

The following is an extract copy of a letter from General Longstreet to Gen. D. H. Hill, dated July, 1884:

> It is my opinion that Bragg thought at 3 P. M. that the battle was lost, though he did not say so positively. I asked him at that time to reinforce me with a few troops that had not been so severely engaged as mine, and to allow me to go down the Dry Valley road, so as to interpose behind Thomas and cut off his retreat to Chattanooga, at the same time pursuing the troops I had beaten back from my front. His reply was that he had no troops except my own that had any fight left in them, and that I should remain in the position in which I then was. After telling me this, he left me, saying, "General, if anything happens communicate with me at Reed's bridge." * * * Rosecrans speaks particularly of his apprehension that I would move down the Dry Valley road.[5]

From this it would appear that of all that large body of gallant men their commander was the only one whipped.

After the repulse of Wood's brigade, of Cleburne's division, Deshler's brigade was moved by the right flank towards the right of the enemy's advanced works, but it was found impossible to get it beyond the crest of a low ridge from which Lowrey's regiment had been repulsed. It was therefore ordered to cover itself behind this ridge and hold the position as long as possible. This placed it *en échelon,* about 400 yards in front of the left of the rest of the division, which here rested for some hours. While making this disposition the brave Deshler was killed by a shell. Upon his fall Col. R. Q. Mills, of the Tenth Texas Regiment, was by seniority called to command of the brigade. At about 3:30 P. M. Cleburne received orders to advance, which he did with his center and right, driving in the enemy's skirmishers. His main line was found in rear of the works from which Polk and Wood had been repulsed that morning. Semple's and Douglas's batteries were placed within 200 yards of these works, and opened a destructive cannonade upon them,

5. *Ibid,* III, 659 fn.

silencing batteries which had been firing upon Cleburne's line. In conjunction with this artillery fire the right brigade—Polk's—charged and carried the northwestern angle of the enemy's works, taking in succession three lines. In this success Polk was greatly aided by Calvert's battery, Lieutenant Key, commanding, and near the close by Douglas's battery, which had been ordered to Cleburne's extreme right, and was run into position by hand, the range being so close that the use of horses was not possible.* Upon Polk's charge the enemy abandoned his strong works and hastily retired. A number of prisoners were captured at the third line of works, among them some from the Sixteenth U. S. Regulars, who recognized Col. J. A. Smith, Fifth Confederate regiment, Polk's brigade, who had been an officer of their company in the U. S. Army. Polk pursued to the Chattanooga road, where he captured another piece of artillery. By this time it was twilight and the left and right wings had approached in a semi-circle so close as to resemble the two points of a horseshoe, and shots from each were reaching the other, so a halt was ordered, and soon the troops of the two wings were joining hands, and cheers of victory, mutual congratulations, and rejoicings being exchanged between the veterans of Lee and those of the Army of Tennessee. The troops bivouacked where night found them.

Thus ended Chickamauga, justly styled "the great battle of the West," and fully justifying the meaning of the Indian name, which signifies "the river of death." Upon this field of carnage lay dead

---

In reference to the closeness of this artillery fight, Lieut. John H. Bingham, of Douglas's battery, writes as follows, under date of August 28, 1908, from McKinney, Texas: " * * And being back there (Chickamauga) on the dedication of the Park, I went over the ground of the night's fight [September 19] where the fearless Hotchkiss led the battery to within 100 yards of the enemy's line and opened the fight. * * * I rode with Hotchkiss till he was wounded, after which Douglas took his place. * * * I remained some time at the spot from which I fired on the enemy's breastworks [afternoon of September 20] and found it to be 72 steps to the Federal line. A little post-oak tree about 20 inches in diameter today shows the marks of 22 canister shots, from the ground to a height of 5 feet. How any one escaped is more than I can tell. The Federal guns and also ours were depressed so much as to set the woods on fire. You will remember how this fire and smoke handicapped us."

or wounded 27,016, of which the Federal killed and wounded were 11,081; of the Confederates, 15,935. The missing on the Federal side were 5,255; Confederate, 1,000, or a total combined loss of 33,271. As to the relative strength of the two armies, Col. Archer Anderson, chief of staff to General Hill, says:

> From an examination of the original returns in the War Department, I reckon, in round numbers, the Federal infantry and artillery on the field at 59,000 and Confederate infantry and artillery at 55,000. The Federal cavalry, about 10,000 strong, was outnumbered by the Confederates by 1,000 men. Thus speak the returns. Perhaps a deduction of 5,000 men from the reported strength of each army would more nearly represent the actual strength of the combatants. But in any case it is, I think, certain that Rosecrans was the stronger in infantry and artillery than Bragg by at least 4,000 men.[6]

This battle presented some unusual if not unparalleled features. The Federal commander-in-chief and two of his corps commanders—McCook and Crittenden—were swept off the field into Chattanooga, and made no further appearance upon it, leaving the third one,—that stout, sturdy, indomitable son of Virginia,—Gen. Geo. H. Thomas, to resist stubbornly the torrent of attack on Snodgrass Hill, a strong position on a spur of Missionary Ridge, and with all that remained of the wreck and remnant of the army, defend it successfully, until under the friendly cover of night he was enabled to withdraw towards Chattanooga. On the other side, the Confederate commander-in-chief, back at his headquarters near Reed's bridge, seemed not until the morning of the 21st to have been aware of that which was plain to every man on the front line at 9 o'clock P. M. of the 20th, that a glorious victory had been won. Truly, on both sides it was a battle by subordinates. On the Federal side was killed the poet-soldier Gen. W. H. Lytle (author of "I am dying, Egypt, dying"). The Confederates lost in killed Brigadier-Generals Preston Smith, James Deshler, and B. H. Helm. Major-General Hood lost a leg, and Brigadier-Generals Adams, Gregg,

6. Archer Anderson, "Campaign and Battle of Chickamauga," in *SHSP*, IX, 400-401

and John C. Brown were wounded. For fuller details of the part taken by Cleburne's division the General's official report is given (see appendix), and as Liddell's brigade really belonged to Cleburne's command, though not with it during this battle, it seems appropriate that the report of the commanding officer of that brigade, Col. D. C. Govan, be appended (see appendix).

The effective total of Cleburne's division on the morning of September 19 was 5,115, and its loss in the two days' battles, 1,749, or a little over 34 per cent.

The gallant Maj. Sidney Coolidge of the Sixteenth U. S. Regulars was killed, and his captured sword with his name engraved upon it, given to Colonel Govan, who had his name and date of its capture put upon it. This sword was captured with Govan a little less than a year later at Jonesboro.

CHAPTER NINE

Battle of Missionary Ridge — Cleburne's Defense

CHICKAMAUGA was the worst and most demoralizing defeat the Federal army had received, with the possible exception of the first Manassas, and it was even greater than that, considering the numbers engaged. The Federal Assistant Secretary of War, Dana, wired Secretary Stanton, from Chattanooga, at 4 P. M., September 20, as follows: "Chickamauga is as fatal a name in our history as Bull Run."[1] Had a prompt and energetic advance been made on the morning of the 21st the disgrace of Missionary Ridge would never have occurred, and the fair pages of Confederate history not soiled by such a blot. The troops, after their two days' fighting, had a good night's rest and early breakfast, and flushed with victory, strained like war-dogs at their leashes, impatient that they be allowed to complete the destruction of the fleeing foe. The ever-active and vigilant Forrest was early in pursuit with his cavalry, finding the road strewn with the debris of the panic-stricken enemy, giving unmistakable evidence of complete rout. He sent repeated messages to General Bragg, urging that an immediate forward movement be made, for, as he expressed it, "every hour was worth a thousand men."[2]

All of this was unheeded. In the light of after knowledge there can remain no shadow of doubt that had such pursuit been made

1. C. A. Dana to E. M. Stanton, 4 P.M., Sept. 20, 1863, XXX, part 1, 192.

2. N. B. Forrest to Braxton Bragg, Sept. 20, 1863, *O.R.*, XXX, part 4, 681; see also Thomas Jordan and J. P. Pryor, *The Campaigns of Lieut. Gen. N. B. Forrest and of Forrest's Cavalry* (New York, 1868), 351.

the Federal army, in its demoralized condition, would have fled across the Tennessee River, and Chattanooga been the prize of Bragg, for Rosecrans devoted the entire day and night of the 21st in rushing his trains out of the town and across the river. But nothing was done during the greater part of the day of the 21st, except bury the dead, attend to the wounded, and gather the captured stores.

This inertness on the part of the commander-in-chief was as marvelous as it was inexplicable. His action, or rather his *inaction,* was in sharp contrast to the closing words of his report of the battle of Shiloh—his service upon which field made the brightest page in his military career. This shows the difference between a theory and the application of the theory. As to Shiloh he used this significant language:

> In this result we have a valuable lesson by which we should profit—never on a battlefield to lose a moment's time; but, leaving the killed, wounded, and spoils to those whose special business it is to care for them, to press on with every available man, giving a panic-stricken and retreating foe no time to rally and reaping all the benefits of a success never complete until every enemy is killed, wounded, or captured.[3]

In a little less than eighteen months after penning this sound military proposition, he himself most flagrantly violated it.

It was not until the afternoon of the 21st that Cleburne received orders to move in the direction of Chattanooga and the division bivouacked at Red House Ford, about half-way, reaching its destination in front of Chattanooga about noon on the 22d. That night Cleburne's skirmishers were close up to the town, very nearly reaching the railroad station.

Longstreet's troops were not put in motion until the morning of the 22d, thirty-six hours after the close of the battle. This tardy advance allowing, as it did, breathing time for Rosecrans to recover his nerve, and the panic of his troops to subside, he decided to hold Chattanooga. The Confederate forces were withdrawn from their advanced position. Lookout Mountain on the west and left was

3. Bragg's report of battle of Shiloh, *O.R.,* XX, part 1, 470.

occupied, as was the crest of Missionary Ridge, east of and facing the town some 3 or 4 miles distant. Rifle-pits were constructed at the base of Missionary Ridge, but none on the crest, until a few days before the battle, and then so slight as scarcely to be worthy of the name.

By the occupation of Lookout Mountain, and thus the entire control of the railroad communication with Bridgeport, Rosecrans's nearest railroad base, the effect was to force him to supply his army with every essential by a long haul over the steep and rugged wagon roads across the lofty ranges of the Cumberland Mountains, which traverse the region due north of the Tennessee River, and hence his wagons would be greatly exposed to interruption by cavalry raids. Thus Bragg sat down to the investment of Chattanooga, with the firm conviction that the Federal army would be starved into surrender, or a disastrous defeat. Had these conditions been maintained this probably would have been the result. What it was will be seen later.

The lack of confidence in General Bragg started with the close of the Kentucky campaign, grew with the retreat from Murfreesboro and evacuation of Middle Tennessee, and was intensified after Chickamauga to an extent that on October 4 a petition couched in respectful but firm language was addressed to President Davis, asking that another commander than General Bragg be assigned to the army.[4] This was signed by a number of officers of high rank. On October 10 President Davis visited Missionary Ridge, and soon after called a meeting at General Bragg's headquarters, of these officers, and of each one in turn asked if he had signed such petition, and, if so, to give his reasons therefor. This was a curious meeting: the president calling to the presence of the commanding general subordinates who had asked his removal; but none flinched or denied his own signature or hesitated to state reasons frankly. The most pronounced in opinion and expression were the two ranking officers present, and of the army. As there were no written minutes of this

4. Petition to Richmond asking for Bragg's relief, dated Oct. 4, 1863, *O.R.*, XXX, part 2, 65-66.

meeting it is difficult to give the exact language of each one's opinion, so that memory of the hearsay at the time has to be relied upon, and inference drawn from communications afterwards exchanged between some of those who were present. Therefore the details may not be absolutely stated, but the concensus of or rather the unanimous opinion as expressed, and here given, can be depended upon as substantially correct, viz.: that a change of commander was absolutely essential. The recollection as to Cleburne's reply is distinct —that, while he esteemed General Bragg a good organizer, disciplinarian, and a skillful soldier, the non-success attending the Kentucky, Tennessee, and Chickamauga campaigns had totally lost him the confidence of the army, and that no matter what his real ability as a general might be, this fact alone destroyed his usefulness, and his conviction was that a change was absolutely necessary. Some others of the signers did not handle the matter with the same delicacy of expression.

Meanwhile, Lieutenant-General Polk and Major-General Buckner had been suspended from command, and on the 15th of October, a few days after this meeting, Lieutenant-General Hill was relieved from duty with the army, and subsequently General Longstreet detached and sent to East Tennessee. Thus the four ranking officers of the army—with the exception of Cheatham—were removed or elsewhere assigned. Despite these petitions and protests, General Bragg was kept in command. This retention may be likened to the opening of the fourth seal in Revelations, "and all hell followed him"—at Missionary Ridge.

From Tullahoma a similar paper had been sent to Richmond.[5] It was noted that those officers signing it afterwards received no promotion in rank or command, while those who refrained were more fortunate. This may have been merely a coincidence, still it was significant and remembered. When the petition of Missionary Ridge was being circulated, that gallant old soldier, Gen. William Preston,

5. So far as known, no petition was sent by officers of the Army of Tennessee from Tullahoma, Tenn. Captain Buck presumably refers to the period following the Kentucky campaign or after the battle of Murfreesboro.

of Kentucky, was asked if it were being signed in his command. His reply was, "We all over our way have very bad colds." Being asked to explain this, he said: "There is a fable that a rumor had gone abroad that the wolf, who was sovereign, had a foul breath. This reaching his ears, he summoned his subjects to verify or disprove the report. He opened his jaws, and called upon the rabbit to thrust in his head and take a sniff. The stupid animal complied, and replied that there certainly was a malodorous smell, whereupon his head was promptly snapped off. Such was the fate of several others. Meanwhile, the wily fox was taking notice, and, when called upon, thrust his head into the open mouth; but quickly withdrawing it, said, 'Your majesty, I have a bad cold and cannot smell anything.' "

Upon the relief of General Hill, General Hardee, to the delight of his old troops, was recalled from Alabama, and resumed command of the corps. In the division Col. M. P. Lowrey, of the Thirty-second Mississippi Regiment, was promoted brigadier, and placed in command of Wood's brigade, vice Wood resigned; Col. J. A. Smith, Third Confederate regiment, promoted brigadier, assigned to command of the Texas brigade, vice Deshler, killed. The Seventh Texas Regiment, Col. H. B. Granbury, was transferred from Gregg's to Smith's Texas brigade.

Missionary Ridge, or that portion of it here referred to, rises abruptly to a height of from 400 to 600 feet, and extends from McFarland's Gap, at Rossville, on the south, and runs in a northeasterly direction, to a distance of about 5 miles until it abuts close upon the main Chickamauga River, some 2 miles from where it empties into the Tennessee River, and lays east and southeast of Chattanooga, which is 3 or 4 miles distant. It is intersected at several points of greatest depression by wagon roads leading from Chattanooga to the railroad in the rear, and to the east. In front, or to the west, broken by occasional hills, or more properly speaking, knobs, with here and there some thin belts of timber, was a level plain, where the Federal army was encamped. The rising ground immediately about Chattanooga was dotted with strong earthworks. In the daytime from the crest of Missionary Ridge could be seen

Chattanooga, Lookout Mountain, and Moccasin Point in the bend of the Tennessee River, all spread out like a vast map. At night the camp-fires of both armies were visible. On the west side of Lookout Mountain is what is known as Wills Valley, drained by the stream of Lookout Creek. Through this valley comes a railroad leading from Bridgeport, 28 miles below Chattanooga, on the Tennessee River; and passing by a bridge over Lookout Creek and around the nose, or point, of Lookout Mountain, where its slope rests upon the river, it enters Chattanooga.

The strategic relation of Lookout Mountain to the general line of Bragg's investment of the Federal army was that the railroad from Bridgeport being the only source of supplies from the north, except by wagons over the long difficult country roads to the north of the Tennessee River, through a naturally sterile and also war-swept mountain region. As Lookout Mountain commanded this railroad, and no supplies could be brought by it into Chattanooga, the importance of it to both sides is apparent. General Bragg did not hesitate publicly to state that the sole object of holding Lookout Mountain was to deprive Rosecrans of his railroad communications and compel him to haul his supplies over the almost impracticable route before mentioned. From this it is plain that for General Bragg to succeed in his plan to starve out the Federal army he must hold on to the mountain and its western approaches. Unfortunately, these conditions were not maintained, for on October 27 two Federal corps, the Eleventh and Twelfth, sent from Virginia under General Hooker, advanced from Bridgeport through Wills Valley, drove the Confederates across Lookout Creek, and passed two or three miles down the river—which at this point makes a sharp bend to the north,—where the Federals had a pontoon bridge.

Having thus lost command of the railroad from Bridgeport, which the enemy could now use to within a very short distance of his bridges, Bragg ordered a night attack upon him in Wills Valley to recover it. This attack was made by Longstreet, on the night of October 28. It was short, bloody, and unsuccessful, the enemy being heavily entrenched at his bridgehead, and his position so strong as to give no hope of a second attempt to dislodge him succeeding. This holding of Wills Valley enabled the Federals by use of pontoons at Brown's Ferry to send with ease all necessary supplies into Chattanooga, and the starvation plan of Bragg was abortive. This loss of Wills Valley, and the consequent loss of the railroad control, so lessened the value of Lookout Mountain, in fact, rendering it worthless, that the wise course would have been its abandonment, and the troops necessary to hold it should have been withdrawn to strengthen the line on Missionary Ridge. Unfortunately, this was not done. Bragg still clung to Lookout Mountain, now of no earthly use to him.

Prior to these events Rosecrans had been relieved from command, and Grant placed in charge at Chattanooga, where he arrived on October 22. As before stated, two corps under Hooker had been sent to reinforce the Army of the Cumberland at Chattanooga, and it was well known to Bragg that Sherman with the Army of the Tennessee was approaching from Memphis for the same purpose and had crossed the Tennessee River, and was at Florence, Alabama, on November 1. Notwithstanding his knowledge as to this actual and prospective large addition to the force he was confronting, on November 4 Bragg detached Longstreet, with his corps of 15,000 men, to operate against Burnside at Knoxville. So, while the enemy was being heavily reinforced, the Confederates were depleting their force already numerically inferior, and soon further reduction of 4,000 more was made to reinforce Longstreet. From the time of its arrival from the field of Chickamauga Cleburne's division was encamped on the crest and eastern slope of Missionary Ridge. At midnight of November 22 Cleburne was ordered to go to Chickamauga station, assume command, in addition to his own, of Buckner's division (B. R. Johnson, commanding), and with both proceed by rail to East Tennessee, and report to General Longstreet. The division moved at dawn of the 23d. Johnson having preceded was the first to be put upon the train, and all but his last brigade—Reynolds's —got started about noon, when a dispatch was received from General Bragg, stating that his front had been attacked and that he was then heavily engaged, and directing Cleburne to move rapidly to army headquarters with such troops as had not already gone to East Tennessee. Placing Brigadier-General Polk in command of the division, Cleburne went ahead in person to General Bragg for further orders, which were to place his division as reserve in rear of the right center of the army.

It was afterwards ascertained that the enemy, seeing Johnson's wagon-train moving across the ridge, and understanding from information given by deserters that its meaning was reinforcements for Longstreet, attempted to prevent this by heavily demonstrating against Bragg, and opened artillery fire upon the train, soon following this by a strong advance of infantry, which drove the Confederate pickets to the rifle-pits at the foot of the hill. Grant's efforts to prevent the reinforcement of Longstreet were partially successful in causing Bragg to recall Cleburne's division to take part in the battle, now evidently impending.

General Hardee, who had three times been shifted from one extreme of the army to the other, as the exigencies required, was, on November 24, placed in command of the right, consisting, on the 25th,—the day of the battle,—of Cleburne's, Walker's, Cheatham's, and Stewart's divisions.

During the forenoon of the 24th Cleburne's division remained in reserve, in sight of Lookout Mountain, and within hearing of the battle there, which the volume of musketry and artillery indicated to be of serious character. The summit of the mountain was visible, but the base and middle were obscured by a thick mist, from which the enemy's shells emerged in graceful curves, bursting high above this veil, and throwing out white puffs of smoke against the dark background of the mountain, the whole constituting a battle-piece so grand and magnificent that anxiety as to the result was lost in admiration of the spectacle. This mythical and miscalled "Battle above the Clouds" had but little more foundation in fact than had "Barbara Frietchie." The apex and down to midway the mountain was obscured. The veil or curtain from thence to the base was a dense, and to sight, impenetrable fog, caused by the damp atmosphere rising from the Tennessee River at its base. However, it made Hooker's success possible by screening his men from the unerring riflemen in his front, until close enough to make a rush and by sheer weight of numbers overrun the thin opposing line. The beaten-back Confederates rallied, formed a new line, and held their position until night, when they were withdrawn from the plateau on the mountain. By the aid of good fortune, ably seconded, it is true, by the overwhelming confidence of his opponent, Hooker possessed the mountain, and forced Bragg to do that which he should have done before and of his own volition—abandon it. Bragg's position was now confined to Missionary Ridge alone, with both of his flanks exposed, the left to Hooker's advance from the direction of Lookout Mountain via Rossville, and the right from Sherman, who had marched his army east from Brown's Ferry, on the north side of the Tennessee River, to a point opposite the north end of Missionary Ridge, concealing his movement behind the foot-hills.

It was now evident that the enemy had determined to attack. Behind Bragg was a bad stream with deep bottom, separating him from his depot. The stream was bridged, it is true, and the bottom was corduroyed, but the passage over both difficult and insufficient in case of hurry. What motive Bragg had for remaining on the ridge is inscrutable.

Before Sherman reached his point of destination there had been prepared and concealed on North Chickamauga Creek, which empties into the Tennessee, some 7 or 8 miles east of Chattanooga, 116 pontoon boats, capable of carrying 30 men each. At 2 o'clock on the morning of November 24 these pontoons, manned, drifted quietly with the current until arrival near the mouth of South Chickamauga, which flows into the Tennessee, some four miles from their starting point. Here, some of the troops being landed, they surprised and captured the Confederate picket post. The greater part were disembarked lower down, where it was intended to start the bridge. Some of the pontoons and a steamer brought from Chattanooga were used for ferrying over as many as possible of Sherman's men from the north side. As fast as they landed they were instructed to entrench their position. Early in the afternoon all of his command was on the south side of the river, and Sherman moved forward.

Late in the morning Cleburne was informed of this crossing, both above and below the mouth of South Chickamauga, and was directed to send a brigade and battery to the East Tennessee and Georgia Railroad bridge over the Chickamauga, to guard that point. Brigadier-General Polk's brigade and Semple's battery were sent.

This information was direct from General Bragg, who also ordered that, at all hazards, this bridge should be held. Between 2 and 3 o'clock P. M. Cleburne was directed to proceed rapidly with his three remaining brigades and batteries, to the right, and take possession of the rising ground near the mouth of South Chickamauga. Considerable distance over the rugged ground had to be marched, and it was late before the command arrived at the indicated point, and not soon enough to occupy a detached hill on the right as was intended, for as the leading brigade—Smith's Texas—came up it was ordered to move quickly and try to get possession before the enemy could, but as it approached the foot it was fired upon from the hill top. The enemy had already crowned it, and Smith, under his orders, if he found such to be the case, formed line on the main ridge, his two left regiments facing the detached ridge, his right one thrown back in an easterly direction to protect his flanks. Scarcely time was allowed him to throw out his skirmishers before they were sharply attacked by those of the enemy, an attack easily repulsed. The failure to occupy this dominating hill made necessary the best immediate disposition possible. Not a moment was lost by Cleburne, who rode rapidly over the ground, carefully examined it, and quickly decided upon his line of defense. Lowrey's brigade had been placed south of the tunnel, and it was intended to put Govan's* (Liddell's) brigade on Lowrey's left, so as to complete connection with Walker's division, when the firing to the right made it evident that the enemy was attempting to turn the right flank, and get possession of the main ridge between it and the

*After Chickamauga this brigade had been returned to the division.

Chickamauga. If he was successful in this, Cleburne's connection with Polk and his line of retreat by the bridge he was guarding would be cut off, and the safety of the whole army endangered. Therefore, instead of putting Govan on Lowrey's left, on the main ridge, he was placed on that spur in rear of it which jutted out just north of the tunnel and covered a valley and road which led over the main ridge from direction of the enemy. General Hardee was soon on the ground and approved of these dispositions, and ordered the destruction of a bridge which crossed the Chickamauga close in rear of the right flank, and directed two regiments of Lowrey's brigade and some artillery into position in rear of the right flank. Between the left of Smith's brigade and Walker's division, a distance of nearly a mile, there were now but two regiments of Lowrey's brigade.

With darkness the fighting in front of Smith ceased. The artillery and ordnance train of the division had been halted on the opposite side of the river for the reason that, based upon the reduction of Bragg's forces by the detachments referred to, the increase of Grant's by reinforcements by Hooker and Sherman, coupled with the loss of Lookout Mountain and consequent exposure of his left flank, Cleburne was impressed with the belief that General Bragg, with his slim force, would fall back behind the Chickamauga, and not attempt to hold the extended line of Missionary Ridge.

About 9 P. M. Cleburne, unable longer to restrain his anxiety, said to one of his staff, "Go at once to General Hardee and ask what has been decided upon, and say that if we are to make a stand it is necessary that I should know, in order to get my artillery and ammunition trains in their proper place without delay." Upon reaching corps headquarters it was found that General Hardee had been called to a conference at General Bragg's, several miles farther up the ridge to the left. Declining the courteous invitation of Colonel Roy, Hardee's chief of staff, to await the General's return, this officer went on and reached army headquarters just as the meeting was breaking up. The first remarks of General Breckinridge as he came from the house, "I never felt more like fighting than when I saw those people shelling my troops off of Lookout today, and I mean to get even with them," indicated the result of the conference before General Hardee's reply to Cleburne's message. General Breckinridge had argued in favor of a stand, that it was too late to withdraw his troops from the eastern slope of Lookout Mountain before daylight would reveal and seriously endanger the movement. To the staff officer (I. A. Buck) General Hardee said, "Tell Cleburne we are to fight; that his division will undoubtedly be heavily attacked, and they must do their very best." The reply was, "The division has never yet failed to clear its front, and will do so again." No vain boast, as the morrow proved. As the party rode along the crest of the Ridge in the stillness of the night the sparse camp-fires showed how attenuated the line was—less than elbow to elbow, in single rank. This was remarked upon, and suggestion made that a bold dash by the enemy on the center might prove very serious, if not disastrous. General Hardee observed that the natural strength of the position would most probably deter such an attempt; that the enemy had all day been massing on the flanks, especially that of the Confederate right, where the heaviest attack was to be looked for.

It was near midnight when Cleburne received General Hardee's message, and he immediately ordered up his artillery and ordnance and made such other preparations as practicable in the night, now rendered abnormally dark and somber by an eclipse of the moon. General Hardee, who from its liability to be turned felt most solicitous as to Cleburne's position, came to that part of his line between 2 and 3 o'clock in the morning, and, in company with Cleburne, made careful inspection. A hill was found on the north bank of the Chickamauga, between the right and the railroad bridge, guarded by General Polk, which completely commanded the line of retreat. General Polk was ordered to occupy this hill at once with two regiments of infantry and a section of artillery. Appreciating the facility which it afforded for turning his extreme right, Cleburne determined to throw a line across the other east spur of Missionary Ridge which jutted out from the north point of the ridge, at the base of which flowed the Chickamauga. Here were placed the two regiments of

Lowrey's brigade which had been left near the tunnel. These later dispositions made necessary a readjustment of the first one, and finally this was done. Smith had thrown up some light defenses in his front, which at Cleburne's suggestion he abandoned, and took up a new line, viz.: his left resting on the crest of the main ridge about 150 yards north of the tunnel, and extending in the same direction for the length of one regiment, the Sixth, Tenth, and Fifteenth Texas (consolidated), Col. R. Q. Mills. The right of this regiment rested close under the summit of Tunnel Hill. On top of the latter a space was left clear of infantry, and Swett's battery of four Napoleon guns, commanded by Lieut. H. Shannon, was placed in it so as to sweep north in the direction of the position abandoned by Smith. Northwest of the detached ridge, or west into the Tennessee Valley, as occasion might require at a point about 60 yards northeast of the right of Mills's regiment, Smith's line recommenced, but in place of continuing north it bent slightly north of east, down the side of the hill for the length of two regiments—the Seventh Texas, Col. H. B. Granbury, and the Seventeenth, Eighteenth, Twenty-fourth and Twenty-fifth Texas (consolidated), Maj. W. A. Taylor. This formation made the angle on the apex of Tunnel Hill, where Swett's battery had been posted, which was the weak point in Smith's line, but it secured his flank by throwing his extreme right back to within 200 yards of Govan's left, bringing the latter's line nearly at right angles to his north front, thus enabling either line to aid the other if attacked. At a favorable point in Govan's line was Douglas's battery. Lieut. John H. Bingham, so placed as to enfilade any attempt to assault Smith's north front. Lowrey's position, the spur before mentioned, was *en échelon* about 200 paces in front of Govan. His whole brigade was ordered to occupy this position, and thus the line was completed from Tunnel Hill on the left to the Chickamauga on the right. Lowrey was without artillery, as the spur was too steep to allow guns to be brought up. Calvert's battery, Lieut. Thos. J. Key, was placed directly over the tunnel and between the tunnel and left of Smith's brigade were placed three regiments of Brown's brigade of Stevenson's division. The attempt to construct some slight works in front was greatly retarded by the darkness, and before much progress had been made the day broke hazy; but a little after the mists partly disappeared, and before the sun was fairly up, the troops were called to arms by picket firing, and soon by the line and artillery.

About 10 o'clock the conflict arose to the dignity of a general engagement. At first the enemy's artillery was directed towards Smith's working parties, and prevented the erection of any defenses in front of the battery on top of Tunnel Hill. At 10:30 he drove in Smith's skirmishers and obtained possession of the works Smith had abandoned in the morning. A heavy attack upon the tunnel and Smith's front was anticipated. General Hardee directed Cleburne to take position at the tunnel and charge of everything in that vicinity; both to right and left. Repeated and strong attempts were made to carry the position, and the assaulting columns were repulsed and hurled bleeding down the slope, only to reform and charge again, in gallant but vain effort. Cleburne seemed omnipresent, watching and guarding every point, and providing for any contingencies. Once or twice the slight works were jumped and sorties or counter-charges made by the Confederates, Cleburne leading or accompanying them. His veterans had found foeman worthy of their steel, in the seasoned ones of Vicksburg, and under personal command of Sherman, and those of the Army of the Potomac under Howard of Hooker's corps.

Almost the entire day was thus consumed. The enemy, met at every advance by a plunging artillery fire, followed when in range by a withering one of small-arms, were repulsed at all points, and slowly and stubbornly fell back. In some instances squads of them finding shelter behind obstructions afforded by the rugged sides of the hill, kept up annoying sharp-shooting, until they were dislodged by stones hurled down upon them by the Texans. Meanwhile the enemy had shown in force and made demonstrations at points farther to the left. Early in the forenoon they had occupied a farmhouse and outbuildings near to the left front of the tunnel, from which their sharp-shooters were beginning to do effective work. From this position they were driven by a charge directed by General Hardee and handsomely executed by the Twentieth Alabama Regiment, Lieutenant-Colonel Davis of Pettus's brigade, Stevenson's division, and the buildings destroyed.

About the middle of the afternoon a strong Federal brigade, Gen. J. Mason Loomis commanding, approached Cleburne's left front, through an open field under heavy fire of artillery and musketry. The Napoleon guns, posted over the tunnels, and rapidly served, were turned upon this brigade with deadly precision. Every discharge plowed huge gaps through the lines, which were promptly closed up as these brave troops moved forward with a steadiness and order which drew exclamations of admiration from those who witnessed it. This brigade advanced to an old fence row, where, planting their colors, and laying down, they opened and kept up a damaging fire and held their position with a tenacity which was proof against all efforts to dislodge them.

About the middle of the afternoon a staff officer was despatched to ascertain the condition of affairs on Lowrey's front. Finding all well there this officer returned by a detour made necessary by the conformation of the ground, which brought him in view of the flanks of the opposing forces. Attracted by the sound of heavy firing and the sight of the two lines in closer proximity than their former position justified, he moved towards the scene of action and discovered a considerable body of men in blue uniforms coming through the woods. Supposing the right flank had been turned, and an attack in rear about to be made, he galloped to Cleburne and made his report. He was met with the reply that the men seen were prisoners going to the rear. Such indeed was the fact. Seeing a column of assault advancing up the hill, Cleburne had placed himself at the head of the Texas Brigade, and leaping the works, met and repulsed the charge, returning with a number of prisoners and several stands of colors. Simultaneously with this assault upon Cleburne's left, General Hardee, from his post of observation near the tunnel, had opportunely directed an effective charge of a brigade, conducted by Brigadier-General Cumming (who had been sent to Cleburne from

Stevenson's division), against this attacking foe. At the same moment of Cumming's charging in front, the left of Mills's Texas regiment, it being the extreme left of the division, also with a yell charged the right flank. The enemy, completely surprised, fled down and were pursued by the Texas troops, beyond the foot of the hill and partly across the open ground in front. Immediately on his last repulse the enemy opened a fierce artillery fire on Tunnel Hill, under cover of which he went to work felling trees and fortifying his position, but no further attack was made upon Cleburne.

The sun was sinking, and General Hardee, being satisfied as to the security of his right, now proceeded up the ridge to his left, as the ringing cheers of victory raised by Cleburne's men were taken up and re-echoed by the entire line. Hardee reached the end of his command only to find that the left-center of the army had been pierced and carried by assault, and a force of Federal infantry was bearing down the crest of the ridge against his left flank. In the midst of the rejoicing of his men this appalling information was conveyed to Cleburne by General Hardee, who ordered him, in addition to his own, to take command of Walker's and Stevenson's divisions and form a line across the ridge, so as to be prepared to meet the attack which was expected would be made upon his flank; and he was further instructed to take every precaution for the safety of the right wing. General Gist, commanding Walker's division, was directed to form it across the ridge. All vehicles which could be spared were sent across the Chickamauga. Brigadier-General Polk was ordered to place a force at the Shallow Ford Bridge, over the Chickamauga, and to hold it at all hazards, and Govan's brigade was sent to dispute the enemy's advance on the road leading to this bridge.

After nightfall General Hardee charged Cleburne with the duty of covering the movements of and protecting the right wing of the army as it retreated to Chickamauga Station. Lowrey attacked and drove back the skirmishers in his front and then withdrew from his position. Cleburne strengthened his skirmish line and made all the display of force possible. At the proper time the artillery was withdrawn and started across the Chickamauga, then the infantry line in turn, Smith's brigade being the last. By 9 o'clock everything was safely across the river, except the pickets left under charge of a staff officer, who was instructed to withdraw them at a stated hour, which was successfully done without the loss of a man. Later the Chickamauga bridge was fired, and Cleburne's division—the rear-guard—took up its sorrowful march to the railroad, which was reached at a late hour. The scene of disorder at Chickamauga Station beggars description; it can only be appreciated by one who has seen a freshly beaten army. Regiments were separated from the brigades, the latter from divisions, and commanders from commands, and in great part army organization seemed lost. The staffs of the various commands spent the remainder of the night in endeavoring to bring some order out of chaos. It was difficult for those acquainted with the unflinching bravery of these same soldiers—tried and never found irresponsive to the call of duty upon every field of battle from Shiloh to Chickamauga—to realize, much less to understand, the unaccountable, shameful panic which seized them, and for which no apology could be found. Troops may be defeated without their morale being destroyed, so long as they have the consciousness that it was only the fortune of war and not from bad conduct on their part, or even that it was through mistakes of their leaders; but if the contrary, the sting of disgrace is so keen as to destroy the *elan* and self-respect and create a sullen, dangerous demoralization. This was much the condition of the beaten troops of the left wing on the night after the battle. Both General Smith and Colonel Mills of the Texas Brigade were wounded.

In 1867 General Hardee wrote of this battle:

> Cleburne's position on the right was most insecure from its liability to be turned. He maintained it with his accustomed ability, and upon the repulse of the last assault, directed in person a counter-charge which effected the capture of a large number of prisoners and several stands of colors. The assailants gave up the contest and withdrew from our front. But while the cheers of victory raised on the right were extending down the line, the left of the army had been carried by assault and the day was lost. All that now remained to the victorious right

was to cover the retreat of the army. This it did successfully. If the right instead of the left had been carried it would have given the enemy possession of the only line of retreat, and no organized body of the Confederate army could have escaped. In the gloom of nightfall Cleburne's division, the last to retire, sadly withdrew from the ground it had held so gallantly, and brought up the rear of the retiring army.[6]

In his official report General Bragg says:

> Major-General Cleburne, whose command defeated the enemy in every assault on the 25th [Missionary Ridge], and who eventually charged and routed him on that day, capturing several stands of colors and several hundred prisoners, and who afterwards brought up our rear with great success, again charging and routing the pursuing column at Ringgold on the 27th, is commended to the special notice of the Government.[7]

---

6. W. J. Hardee, "Sketch of P. R. Cleburne," dated at Selma, Alabama, May 1, 1867, in J. F. Maguire, *The Irish in America* (New York and Montreal, 1867), 654.

7. Bragg's report of battle of Missionary Ridge in *O.R.*, XXXI, part 2, 664.

CHAPTER TEN

Defense at Ringgold Gap

ANTICIPATING that Grant would pursue vigorously, Bragg, by the dawn of the 26th, put the infantry in motion towards Dalton, leaving the trains and artillery to follow, in charge of Cleburne's division, with a detachment under General Breckinridge as the rear-guard. The trains were toiling along over a single narrow road, wheels cutting into the mud in many places up to the hubs, stalling frequently, and stopping all teams behind them. These delays exposed the rear-guard, under Breckinridge, to great peril of being overwhelmed by numbers. The last vehicle was still in sight of Chickamauga Station when the enemy, eager, and flushed with success, pressed forward and opened upon troops and trains with shells. Showing his men at all prominent points to create impression of large force, Cleburne gradually pressed on towards Graysville. He had progressed but a few miles when a strange young officer rode up and said to Cleburne that General Hardee (who had been called forward to confer with General Bragg) directed that he at once push forward his infantry towards Graysville. Surprised at such an order and hearing no sound of battle in front to indicate that the column of march had been intercepted, Cleburne hesitated an instant, turned to the bearer of the alleged order and asked if he had written instructions. Upon receiving a negative answer, Cleburne then asked him if he realized that its import and effect was the abandonment and loss of the artillery and transportation of the whole army? The officer evidently had not, and he was greatly confused, explaining that he had been without rest for two nights, and might have misunderstood his instructions. So suspicious was this message that Major Dixon, of the division staff, suggested that the bearer might be an emissary of the enemy and advised his arrest. But he was finally identified as a volunteer aide who had been on General Hardee's staff but a few days, and after this occurrence was never seen with it again. Cleburne decided to disregard this order until he could communicate with General Hardee, to whom he immediately despatched an officer, and soon learned that no such instructions had been given, that abandonment of the train had not for an instant been contemplated, and that the actual order had been entirely misunderstood.*

The great apprehension was that an attack in flank would be made at Graysville by Hooker's command, which had the day before passed around Bragg's left at Rossville, and had a road from there crossing the West Chickamauga at Red House Ford, which by three forks, close to each other, from that point led to the road by which Cleburne must pass. Fortunately, owing to a delay in crossing at Red House Ford, the stream being swollen, Hooker had not been able to push forward fast enough to make the intended interception effective, as at Graysville. After sundown the division crossed to the west bank of the Chickamauga, quickly following which the enemy's cavalry made a dash, but were easily repulsed by Govan's brigade, and without further molestation the weary and hungry troops at 10 o'clock P. M. reached the west bank of the river on the side opposite the town of Ringgold; and Cleburne was ordered to cross his command and bivouac it on the other bank, and thus put the river, which at that point was wide and deep, between the pursuing enemy and the division, which, all the balance of the troops having passed, was the rear-guard. He was further directed to move at 4 o'clock

---

*I had not supposed that any one besides myself had remembered this incident, but at the Richmond Reunion in 1907 I met Gen. George M. Helm, of Mississippi, former engineer officer for General Hardee. In talking over our war experiences, quite incidentally he mentioned this one, saying that he was present at the time of its occurrence, and confirmed, in every particular, my recollection of it.—I. A. B.

A. M. the following day, still as rear-guard. The night was freezing cold and the wind cut keenly. Cleburne said that if his men waded the stream waist deep and slept in their wet clothing he would lose more men by rheumatism and pneumonia than he would if attacked, and he decided upon camping where he was, and starting an hour earlier (3 o'clock) the next morning when the exercise of marching might be relied upon to prevent evil effects of wading. Thus twice in one day did Cleburne disregard orders which he was satisfied were wrong, and had this proved disastrous he could have been charged with gross disobedience; but he was not the man ever to shirk responsibility no matter how grave. A few hours later, under different conditions, he promptly obeyed an order which appeared vastly more threatening to the safety of his command than either of the two orders referred to.

About midnight an officer from General Bragg reached Cleburne, bearing him a verbal order that he take position in a pass of the hills a short distance in rear of Ringgold, and to hold it at all costs up to a stated hour the next day. Cleburne had less than 200 men in excess of 4,000, and knowing the great numerical superiority of the pursuing foe, and that he would be totally without support, stated these facts to the officer, and also his apprehension that it would mean the destruction of his division; but he added that he was accustomed to obey orders rigidly, though as a protection to himself in case of disaster he requested that the messenger put the order in writing, which was done. At 3 o'clock A. M. of the 27th, in addition to the order from the staff officer he received the following in writing:

Major-General CLEBURNE.

GENERAL: The General [Bragg] desires that you will take strong position in the gorge of the mountain and attempt to check pursuit of enemy. He must be punished until our trains and the rear of our troops get well advanced. The reports from the rear are meager and the General is not thoroughly advised of the state of things there. Will you be good enough to report fully?

Respectfully,

GEORGE WILLIAM BRENT,
Assistant Adjutant-General.[1]

The troops were put in motion and staff-officers left to conduct them across the river and to the designated position, while Cleburne rode ahead, to see as well as he could, in the darkness, the ground he was to occupy and to form a plan of defense, at the same time sending an officer to General Bragg, with information as to starting of troops, and asking more specific instructions—this after the hasty examination he was able to make. General Bragg was found at Catoosa Station, and his instructions were: "Tell General Cleburne to hold his position at all hazards, and keep back the enemy, until the artillery and transportation of the army is secure, the salvation of which depends upon him."* Such was the brief but comprehensive order in pursuance of which Cleburne with 4,157 effectives was to confront Hooker's confident veterans, and to do battle and risk sacrifice for the safety of the army.

In regard to the orders given Cleburne the following is an extract from a letter of General Bragg, to Maj. E. T. Sykes:

---

1. (Braxton Bragg) G. W. Brent to P. R. Cleburne, 3 A.M., Nov. 27, 1863, *O.R.*, XXXI, part 2, 754.

*I was the officer sent by Cleburne to Bragg, and a trivial incident impressed me of the nervous anxiety the latter was under at the time. Army headquarters, in the large freight room at the station, was reached about 4 o'clock. A single candle only intensified the darkness of the room beyond the reach of its feeble rays. Upon announcing myself I was recognized by Colonel Brent, A. A. Gen., who had been major of my old regiment in Virginia. Before our greeting was over a voice from the gloom inquired who it was. "Captain Buck of General Cleburne's staff," said Brent. Any one at all acquainted with General Bragg will remember that he was far from emotional, and not at all "gushing" in his nature, and the younger officers stood in considerable awe of him. At Colonel Brent's reply, footsteps were heard advancing, and to my surprise, I may say embarrassment, he extended his hands, and grasping my right one in both of his gave the order above quoted. He exhibited more excitement than I supposed possible for him. He had evidently not rested during the night. This was the last time I ever met—I will not say saw—him as it was too dark to see.—I. A. B.

In our retreat from Missionary Ridge the enemy could make but a feeble pursuit for want of artillery horses (Grant's report). At the mountain gorge near Ringgold I believed he could be successfully repulsed and the army quickly withdrawn. General Cleburne, one of the best and truest soldiers in our cause, was placed at that point, in command of the rear-guard. Late at night, hours after all the army was at rest, my information being all in, I called for a reliable staff officer, and gave him verbal directions to ride immediately to Cleburne, about three miles in my rear, at this mountain gorge, *and give him my positive orders to hold his position up to a named hour the next day,* and if attacked to defend the pass at every hazard. The message was delivered at Cleburne's camp-fire. He heard it with surprise and expressed his apprehension that it would result in the loss of his command, as his information differed from mine, and he believed the enemy would turn his position and cut him off. "But," said he, true soldier as he was, "I always obey orders," and only asked as a protection, in case of disaster, that you "put the order in writing." This was done, as soon as materials could be found, and the staff officer returned and reported the result of his mission. He had not reached me, however, before the attack, *in front,* as I expected, was made. Cleburne gallantly met it, defeated the enemy under Hooker, drove him back, and then quietly followed the army without further molestation. Mark the difference in conduct and results. A good soldier, by obedience, without substituting his own crude notions, defeats the enemy and saves an army from disaster. And mark the credit he gets for it. The Confederate Congress passed a vote of thanks to the gallant Cleburne and his command for saving Bragg's army. Not to this day has it ever been known that he did it in obedience to orders, and against his judgment, which does not detract from, but adds to his fame. Captain Samuel A. Harris, assistant adjutant-general, of Montgomery, Alabama, was the officer who delivered the order. He is now an Episcopal clergyman, with the largest congregation in New Orleans, and has recently repeated the whole matter to me as distinctly as if it had occurred yesterday.[2]

General Bragg in the foregoing made two small errors: First, when he says that his staff officer, upon his return, had not "reached

2. Braxton Bragg to E. T. Sykes, Feb. 8, 1873, in *SHSP,* XII, 46.

me * * * before the attack in front * * * was made," for he states that this officer "late at night" was sent. The distance from the gap to his headquarters was only three miles, and it surely did not require until 8 o'clock, about the time the fight opened, to cover this space. Besides, the officer sent by Cleburne to Bragg, after the former had arrived in person at his designated position, had reached General Bragg and left while it was yet dark, and reported back to Cleburne at least an hour before firing commenced. Second, he is mistaken when he says: "Not to this day [February, 1873] has it ever been known that he [Cleburne] did it in obedience to orders," etc., for as shown after delivery of the verbal order by and departure of Captain Harris, a written order to hold the gap from General Bragg's assistant adjutant-general was received at 3 A. M. and later Cleburne despatched an officer of his staff, who received from General Bragg verbal orders, thus making three orders—two verbal ones and one written of the same tenor. Certainly to the two staff officers who bore the verbal orders this must have been known, and the publication of Cleburne's official report, in which was a copy of the written order, must have given publicity to the fact which General Bragg thought confined to himself. Cleburne certainly never claimed that he made the stand without orders, or disclaimed that he considered the duty one of extreme peril, but as usual he did his best, which was amply sufficient

Taylor's Ridge rises abruptly just east of the town of Ringgold and runs nearly due north and south, and is divided by a gap of just sufficient width of level ground for the passage of the Western and Atlantic Railroad, a wagon road, and a large branch of the East Chickamauga River. The gap is about half a mile in length. The creek in its winding was bridged at three points within the first half mile of the road leading to the rear or east entrance from Dalton, thus rendering the position hazardous in case of the turning of either flank. The western mouth of the gap widens out some towards the north. The ridge on the right or north of the gap facing the town rises gradually, while on the left or south it is abrupt and precipitous. On the latter was placed the Sixteenth Alabama Regiment of

Lowrey's brigade,—Maj. T. A. Ashford,—to protect the left flank, while in front of the hill were posted three companies of the Sixth and Seventh Arkansas (consolidated) of Govan's brigade, under charge of Lieutenant Dulin of his staff. For defense of the gap were placed the remainder of Govan's brigade—the Fifth and Thirteenth Arkansas (consolidated), Colonel John E. Murray—formed across the gap's mouth; from the north side to the railroad embankment the Eighth and Nineteenth Arkansas (consolidated), Lieut.-Col. A. S. Hutchison, 50 paces in rear of the first line; the Sixth and Seventh Arkansas (consolidated), Col. Peter Snyder, about the same distance behind the second line, and the Second, Fifteenth and Twenty-fourth Arkansas (consolidated), Col. E. Warfield, a like distance in rear of the third line. The narrowness of the gap allowed four short lines across it. Connecting with Govan's right and behind a fringe of young trees at the base of the hill were placed two regiments of Smith's brigade (Col. H. B. Granbury, commanding in absence of General Smith from wound received at Missionary Ridge) ; the Sixth, Tenth and Fifteenth Texas, Capt. John R. Kennard (Colonel Mills having also been wounded at Missionary Ridge) on the left, and the Seventeenth, Eighteenth, Twenty-fourth and Twenty-fifth Texas (consolidated), Maj. W. A. Taylor, on the right. The other regiment of this brigade, the Seventh Texas, Capt. C. E. Talley, was posted on the crest of the ridge to guard the right flank of the brigade at its base. The Thirty-second and Forty-fifth Mississippi regiments (consolidated) of Lowrey's brigade, Col. A. B. Hardcastle; the Thirty-third Alabama, Col. Samuel Adams, and the Forty-fifth Alabama, Lieut.-Col. H. D. Lampley, which constituted the remainder of the brigade, were held in reserve in the center of the gap. Only a portion of Polk's brigade was with the division, consisting of the First Arkansas, Col. J. W. Colquitt, the Second Tennessee, Col. W. D. Robinson, and Third and Fifth Confederate (consolidated), Lieut.-Col. J. C. Cole, was placed at the rear or eastern outlet of the gap. Shirmishers from Govan's command were thrown out in front of his line, and upon his front line was posted a section of Semple's battery,—two Napoleon guns,—commanded by Lieut. Richard W. Goldthwaite. These pieces were charged, one with canister and the other with shell, and both screened with bushes. The artillerymen were ordered to shelter themselves in a ravine close by. All of the other troops were directed to keep concealed from view. The few cavalrymen at Cleburne's disposal had been instructed to watch the crossing of the river, and as soon as the enemy appeared to fire upon him at long range, and retreat in haste through the town and gap to make the impression that only a weak force of cavalry confronted them.

These dispositions, hastily made, were barely completed when the cavalry discharged their guns, and in seeming panic rushed into the gap, followed soon after about 8 o'clock by the Federals marching in column of fours down the railroad, with skirmishers in front and on the flanks, but completely deceived, and unsuspicious of the infantry and artillery concealed and awaiting them. Cleburne, on foot, was on Govan's front line near Goldthwaite's section. The approaching column was allowed to come within short range, when Cleburne gave the order to Goldthwaite to throw down the mask of brush and open with both guns. This fire, striking the head of the column, caused it to stagger and recoil, and being kept up rapidly, and that of the infantry joined, forced the column to seek shelter under the railroad embankment from the flank fire which the conformation of Cleburne's line enabled him to deliver on their right. Notwithstanding the suddenness and surprise of the attack, the confusion in the enemy's ranks was but brief, and with admirable steadiness they deployed in front of the gap and opened a heavy fire, at the same time moving a force and making a vigorous attack upon the right of Cleburne's line at the foot of the ridge. Major Taylor's command directed upon them a deadly fire, but did not at once succeed in checking their advance. Colonel Granbury, being apprised of this, sent two companies from his left to strengthen his right. Major Taylor had previously placed skirmishers up the hill at right angles to his line, and now, with three companies, he charged this flanking force, and routed it, capturing 100 prisoners and the colors of the Twenty-ninth Missouri Regiment. Another body of the enemy moved beyond Cleburne's right to ascend the ridge. Information of this movement was sent to General Polk, in rear of the gap, with orders to meet and check it. General Polk had learned of it, and with good judgment and discretion had anticipated these instructions by sending to the proper point the First Arkansas Regiment, which encountered the enemy's skirmishers near the crest of the ridge, and with the assistance of the Seventh Texas Regiment drove them back after a stubborn fight, in which the officers used their pistols, and in some instances both officers and men used rocks, and so close was the fight that a number of the enemy were knocked down with these and captured.

Large masses were now seen passing to the Confederate right, and General Lowrey was moved up to strengthen Polk, and prolong the right along the top of the ridge. Moving rapidly ahead of his men Lowrey found the First Arkansas heavily engaged, but holding its own against great odds. Assuring them that support was near at hand he encouraged them to renewed efforts. The Thirty-second and Forty-fifth Mississippi, being brought up at double quick and thrown into the fight at the critical moment, the enemy gave way and went down the hill in great confusion. The two other regiments of Lowrey's brigade were now brought up, as were the two remaining ones of Polk's. Constantly reinforcing, the enemy made another attempt to carry the hill at a point farther to the right. Favored by some ravines or depressions of the slope, he concentrated a heavy column in one of these. General Polk, assisted by General Lowrey, rapidly formed a double line opposite this force and at the same time the Second Tennessee was placed so as to enfilade the flank of any troops debouching from it. Again defeated in his attack, the enemy was sent fleeing down with loss of many killed, some prisoners, and the flag of the Seventy-sixth Ohio Regiment.

Meanwhile, a force of the enemy, sent to menace the extreme left, was checked by the skirmishers of Ashford and Dulin on the hill, and those of Govan on the bank of the stream and to left of the railroad. During all this time Govan's men at the gap had been subjected to a heavy and continuous fire, which was replied to with spirit and effect, and under the voice and eye of their intrepid commander the men felt themselves equal to any emergncy. Cleburne, with Govan, remained on the front line in the mouth of the gap and watched every movement.

The enemy effected a lodgment in some buildings near the line, from which he kept up a well-directed and annoying fire of sharpshooters. Finally concentrating a force under cover of these buildings they charged Govan's skirmishers, but were repulsed by canister from Goldthwaite's guns, which afterwards shelled the houses with such good effect that in a great measure the annoyance from that quarter was abated. In this charge upon Govan's skirmishers a stand of colors was left lying upon the ground within 50 yards of the line, and Captain McGehee, of the Second Arkansas, begged permission to charge with a squad and secure it. But Cleburne refused, saying he would not have a single one of his brave men killed or disabled for the honor of its capture, so the flag remained temptingly under the covetous eyes of the gallant McGehee, who could with difficulty be restrained from making the attempt alone, notwithstanding the General's prohibition.

It was now past noon, and for nearly five hours Cleburne had been battling against odds increasing every moment. Large masses of the enemy at this time in full view justified the belief that a great part of Grant's army was now at Ringgold or near there preparing to precipitate itself upon the flanks of the single small opposing division. Between 12 and 1 o'clock a dispatch was received from General Hardee to the effect that as the trains had now reached a safe distance Cleburne was at liberty to withdraw when, in his judgment, it was advisable. Up to 12:30 o'clock the enemy's fire had been exclusively of small-arms, but getting some guns up he now opened a rapid and heavy artillery fire, but did not again advance his infantry.

About 1 o'clock P. M. Goldthwaite's guns were remasked by brush and now run back by hand, without loss, followed soon after by the main line of infantry, and only skirmishers were left along the front. These were withdrawn about 2 o'clock and the bridges across the creek fired. All of this was barely accomplished when the enemy advanced simultaneously over the ridge on the right and through the gap. Cleburne took up a position on a wooded hill about a mile in rear of the eastern mouth of the gap known as "Dick's Ridge," where some slight works were thrown up and preparations made for another contest; but the enemy declined further battle, and not advancing beyond the eastern outlet of the gap, abandoned the pursuit. The division carried into action 4,157 bayonets, and its loss in killed, wounded, and missing—there were only 11 of the latter—was 221. With exception of the few cavalrymen before mentioned, who took no part in the actual battle, it was fought by this division alone. For 6 hours it held at bay a large force of Grant's army. For this engagement and this splendid defense, Cleburne, his officers, and men received a vote of thanks from Congress. The General's official report will be found in the appendix, see pages 346-51, but it seems proper to quote one clause of it here, viz:

> The conduct of officers and men in this fight needs no comment. Every man, as far as I know, did his whole duty. To Brigadier-Generals Polk and Lowrey and Colonels Govan and Granbury I must return my thanks. Four better officers are not in the service of the Confederacy. Lieutenant Goldthwaite, of the artillery, proved himself a brave and skillful officer.

Never was praise more worthily bestowed, nor given by one more competent to bestow it. Remaining in undisturbed possession of "Dick's Ridge" until after dark, Cleburne, in obedience to orders, marched to Tunnel Hill, arriving about midnight, when the weary men had their first regular ration since the 25th.

Of Cleburne's troops it need only be said that they were worthy of their commander—a man of lofty courage and pure patriotism, unerring in his military instincts, quick and resolute in the execution of his plans, which when once matured, never miscarried. As with Stonewall Jackson, Cleburne's officers and men, alike, had implicit confidence in him, and hence his orders were obeyed promptly and unquestioned. This was one of the elements of his success, a success so uniform that at length friend and foe learned to note the position in battle of his distinctive blue and white battle-flag. Just one year and three days after his brilliant service at Ringgold, on the fatal field of Franklin, Cleburne gave up his life.

Christopher Cleburne, a youth not out of his teens, came to his brother at Missionary Ridge. The General said to him, "I can give you a position on my staff, but my advice is that you enlist as a private, and if worthy of it you will win promotion. If not worthy, I do not want you around my quarters." This advice was acted upon, and he became a member of Polk's brigade and served with it, in the ranks, until offered a commission in Gen. John H. Morgan's cavalry, and as captain, leading his company, he was mortally wounded at Dublin, Virginia, where there is over his grave a monument erected by the ladies of that vicinity.

At Ringgold Gap, when ammunition ran low, the men, remembering how effective it had been two days before at Missionary Ridge, resorted to hurling stones down the hill upon the enemy. General Cleburne was much diverted and pleased when told that one of the prisoners, an Irishman, who was disabled by one of these missiles, upon seeing Christopher ("Kit," as his comrades called him), said, "Ah, you are the little divil who smashed me jaw with a rock!"

CHAPTER ELEVEN

In Winter Quarters — Cleburne Advocates Arming of the Slaves

THE BULK OF THE ARMY went into winter quarters at Dalton, Georgia, but Cleburne's division was ordered to remain on outpost at Tunnel Hill 9 or 10 miles north of that point. On November 30 General Bragg at his own request was relieved from command of the army and was succeeded by General Hardee.

Just here let it be said that if in this narrative any seemingly harsh or carping criticisms have been made of General Bragg, such criticisms have not been intentional or made in a spirit of vindictiveness, but are merely statements which are of official record. To say the least, Bragg was not a fortunate commander. His patriotic devotion to the South, his ability to plan and fight a battle successfully (if the benefits were not reaped), and his bravery are beyond question, and these characteristics were never more conspicuously displayed than at Shiloh. But suffering as he was from a chronic bodily malady, he was physically incapacitated to give the close oversight in battle so necessary for the head of an army and he was frequently in the saddle when the more appropriate place for him would have been the bed. This infirmity caused him to be irritable, often harsh, and this alienated from him the affection and enthusiasm of his troops, and he was never without serious friction with some, and at times all, of his corps commanders. Some historian has said that an attack of indigestion caused Napoleon to lose the battle of Leipzig.

It was at Tunnel Hill that Cleburne asked and received his first and only leave of absence, to act as "best man" at the marriage of

General Hardee, and it was upon this occasion that Cleburne met, in Mobile, Alabama, the beautiful and accomplished lady to whom he became betrothed. General Hardee having declined permanent command of the army, Gen. Joseph E. Johnston was appointed to it on December 16, 1863. This assignment was hailed with delight by rank and file, or as one writer says, "The coming of General Johnston to take command of the Army of Tennessee instantly restored confidence, and the accession of a single man was as welcome as a reinforcement of 10,000 soldiers."[1] As the army was likely to remain in winter quarters for several months, Cleburne, ever alive to the necessity of improving the discipline and efficiency of his command, caused to be erected a log hut, and used it for a school of daily instruction in the art of war to his brigade commanders, they, in turn, instructing their regimental commanders, and these, their company commanders, each chief hearing the recitations, and by such system this was imparted from brigade to company officers.

It was known that General Sherman, who had succeeded Grant in command, was gathering a large army and making extensive preparations for a vigorous campaign in the spring, and it became a question of paramount importance for the Confederate authorities to consider how best to prepare to meet this problem. Despite the fact that appeals were made with success, especially in Cleburne's division, for the reenlistment of those troops whose terms of three years were on the eve of expiring, the utmost efforts to recruit the ranks from those not in service (the latter source already well-nigh exhausted of material), the able-bodied on detailed service, the morning reports showed a steady diminution of effective force—the numbers obtained from the above sources not balancing the loss from death, and discharge from disability. The time was critical and some means must be adopted promptly to reduce the disproportion of number between the two armies. Cleburne fully realized this and the absolute necessity for recruiting the exhausted ranks. He pointed out the surest, if not the only means left, in a paper dated January 1,

1. Archer Anderson, "Campaign and Battle of Chickamauga," *SHSP*, IX, 392.

1864, addressed to the generals and regimental commands, advocating enlistment of slaves. This paper was suppressed by the Richmond authorities, and save to those to whom it was read at the time, and to the War Department, was only known by hearsay to the public, as it was not printed until 32 years after. As it was in many respects one of the most remarkable documents of the war, it is of interest to know its history, which follows, it being a copy of a letter which accompanied this paper when given to the *Richmond Times-Despatch* in January, 1896, or before its publication in the Official Records in 1898,[2] viz.:

> Some time ago [Spring of 1897] I had a letter from the War Department at Washington, asking me to authenticate a document in the files of the Confederate Record office. Considering this paper of the first interest and value, I send herewith a copy and will give your readers the circumstances surrounding it, viz: After the disgraceful defeat of the Confederate army at the battle of Missionary Ridge, in front of Chattanooga on November 25, 1863, the bulk of it retreated to Dalton, Georgia. Cleburne's division, * * * retired under orders to Tunnel Hill, some 10 miles north of Dalton, where it remained on outpost. In December, following, I noticed that General Cleburne was for several days deeply preoccupied and engaged in writing. Finally he handed me his manuscript, upon reading which I found it to be in advocacy of freeing the negroes and enlisting them in the military service. In reply to his inquiry, I said that while fully concurring in his opinion as to the absolute necessity of some such step to recruit the army, and as fully recognizing the force of his arguments, still I doubted the expediency, at the time of formulating those views. First: That the slaveholders were sensitive as to such property, and totally unprepared to consider such a radical measure, and many not being in service could not properly appreciate that it had become a matter of self-preservation that our ranks should be filled to meet in some degree the heavy numerical superiority of the enemy, consequently it would raise a storm of indignation against him. Second: That one of the corps of our army was without a lieutenant-general; that he, General Cleburne, had lately achieved a signal success at Ring-

2. *SHSP,* XXXI, 215-218.

gold, for which he had received the thanks of Congress, and stood in reputation first among the major-generals, and might justly expect to be advanced to this vacancy; that I felt assured the publication of this paper would be used detrimentally, and his chances for promotion destroyed. To this he answered, that a crisis was upon the South, the dangers of which he was convinced would most quickly be averted in the way outlined, and feeling it to be his duty to bring this before the authorities, he would do so irrespective of any result to himself. To my question as to whether or not negroes would make efficient soldiers, he said that with reasonable and careful drilling, he had no doubt as to this, and as deep as was his attachment to his present command, that he would cheerfully undertake that of a negro division in this emergency. Under his instruction I made from his draft a plain copy of the document which was read to, and free criticisms invited from, members of his staff. One of them, Maj. Calhoun Benham, strongly dissented, and asked for a copy with the purpose of writing a reply in opposition. The division brigadiers were then called together, and my recollection is that their endorsement was unanimous, namely, Polk, Lowrey, Govan and Granbury. Later a meeting of the general officers of the army, including its commander, Gen. Joseph E. Johnston, was called at General Hardee's headquarters and the paper submitted. It was received with disapproval by several, and before this assembly Major Benham read his letter of protest. Not having been present, I am unable to state the individual sentiment of the higher officers, but my impression is that Generals Hardee and Johnston were favorably disposed, though the latter declined to forward it to the War Department, on the ground that it was more political than military in tenor.

This was a sore disappointment to Cleburne, who supposed his opportunity of bringing the matter before the President was lost, and he was too good a soldier and strict disciplinarian to think of sending it over the head of his superior. The day following, Maj.-Gen. W. H. T. Walker addressed him a note, stating that this paper was of such dangerous (I think he said "incendiary") character that he felt it his duty to report it to the President, and asking if General Cleburne would furnish him a copy and avow himself the author. Both requests were promptly complied with, Cleburne remarking that General

Walker had done him an unintentional service in accomplishing his desire that this matter be brought to the attention of the Confederate authorities. Communication with Richmond was then very slow and uncertain. General Cleburne naturally felt somewhat anxious as to the outcome of this affair, though feeling no regrets, and in discussing the matter and probabilities said that the most disastrous result personally could only be a court martial and cashiering and if such occurred he would immediately enlist as a private in his old regiment, the Fifteenth Arkansas, then in his division; that if not permitted to command, he could at least do his duty in the ranks. After a lapse of some weeks the paper was returned endorsed by President Davis, substantially, if not verbatim, as follows: "While recognizing the patriotic motives of its distinguished author, I deem it inexpedient, at this time, to give publicity to this paper and request that it be suppressed.—J. D." Upon receipt of this General Cleburne directed me to destroy all copies except the one returned from Richmond. This was filed in my office desk, which was subsequently captured and burned with its contents by the Federal cavalry during the Atlanta campaign.

After the war I was several times solicited by both Confederate and Federal soldiers to furnish copies, which was impossible, as I was sure that the only one retained had been destroyed, as before stated, and that no other existed. A few years ago Major Benham died in California, and, to my surprise and delight, a copy—the one supplied him at Tunnel Hill—was found among his papers. This was forwarded to Lieutenant Mangum, who sent it to me to identify, which I readily did, recognizing it at once. Mangum afterwards placed it in the hands of Gen. Marcus J. Wright, agent of the War Department, for collection of Confederate records, and it was this paper I was called upon to authenticate, the reason for which being that as it was a copy, and not an original, official certification was desired.

A short while before the death of Cleburne * * he had the gratification of knowing that a bill embodying exactly his proposition was advocated upon the floor of the Confederate Congress. This was subsequently passed, and became a law by executive approval. It is scarcely a matter of speculation to tell what the result of this measure would have been had it been promptly put into effect early in the spring of 1864. General Hood, whose opinion is entitled to weight, probably states it correctly in his book "Advance and Retreat," when, referring to Cleburne, he says: "He was a man of equally quick perception and strong character, and was in one respect in advance of our people. He possessed the boldness and wisdom to earnestly advocate at an early (?) period of the war the freedom of the negro and enrollment of the young and able-bodied men of that race. This stroke of policy and additional source of strength to our armies would, in my opinion, have given us our independence."

IRVING A. BUCK.

Here is the document referred to:*

January 2, 1864.

COMMANDING GENERAL, THE CORPS, DIVISION, BRIGADE AND REGIMENTAL COMMANDERS, OF THE ARMY OF TENNESSEE.

GENERAL: Moved by the exigency in which our country is now placed, we take the liberty of laying before you, unofficially, our views of the present state of affairs. The subject is so grave, and our views so new, we feel it a duty both to you and the cause that before going further we should submit them for your judgment and receive your suggestions in regard to them. We therefore respectfully ask you to give us an expression of your views in the premises. We have now been fighting for nearly three years, have spilled much of our best blood, and lost, consumed or thrown to the flames an amount of property equal in value to the specie currency of the world. Through some lack in our system the fruits of our struggles and sacrifices have invariably slipped away from us and left us nothing but long lists of dead and mangled. Instead of standing defiantly on the borders of our territory or harrassing those of the enemy, we are hemmed in to-day in less than two-thirds of it, and still the enemy menacingly confronts us at every point with superior forces. Our soldiers can see no end to this state of affairs except in our own exhaustion; hence, instead of rising to the occasion, they are sinking into a fatal apathy, growing weary of hardships

*It was not until publication, in 1898, of Vol. LII of Official Records that I ever saw the correspondence between General Walker and the President, which will be found in Appendix C of this book.—I. A. B. See *O.R.*, LII, part 2, 586-93.

and slaughter which promises no results. In this state of things it is easy to understand why there is a growing belief that some black catastrophe is not far ahead of us, and that unless some extraordinary change is soon made in our condition we must overtake it. The consequences of this condition are showing themselves more plainly every day; restlessness of morals spreading everywhere, manifesting itself in the army in a growing disregard for private rights; desertion spreading to a class of soldiers it never dared to tamper with before; military commissions sinking in the estimation of the soldier; our supplies failing; our firesides in ruins. If this state continues much longer we must be subjugated. Every man should endeavor to understand the meaning of subjugation before it is too late. We can give but a faint idea when we say it means the loss of all we now hold most sacred—slaves and all other personal property, lands, homesteads, liberty, justice, safety, pride, manhood. It means that the history of this heroic struggle will be written by the enemy; that our youth will be trained by Northern school teachers; will learn from Northern school books their version of the war; will be impressed by all the influences of history and education to regard our gallant dead as traitors, our maimed veterans as fit objects for derision. It means the crushing of Southern manhood, the hatred of our former slaves, who will, on a spy system, be our secret police. The conqueror's policy is to divide the conquered into factions and stir up animosity among them, and in training an army of negroes the North no doubt holds this thought in perspective. We can see three great causes operating to destroy us: First, the inferiority of our armies to those of the enemy in point of numbers; Second, the poverty of our single source of supply in comparison with his several sources; Third, the fact that slavery, from being one of our chief sources of strength at the commencement of the war, has now become, in a military point of view, one of our chief sources of weakness.

The enemy already opposes us at every point with superior numbers, and is endeavoring to make the preponderance irresistible. President Davis, in his recent message, says the enemy "has recently ordered a large conscription and made a subsequent call for volunteers, to be followed, if ineffectual, by a still further draft." In addition, the President of the United States announces that "he has already in training an army of 100,000 negroes as good as any troops," and every fresh raid he makes and new slice of territory he wrests from us will add to this force. Every soldier in our army already knows and feels our numerical inferiority to the enemy. Want of men in the field has prevented him from reaping the fruits of his victories, and has prevented him from having the furlough he expected after the last reorganization; and when he turns from the wasting armies in the field to look at the source of supply, he finds nothing in the prospect to encourage him, our single source of supply is that portion of our white men fit for duty and not now in the ranks. The enemy has three sources of supply: First, his own motley population; Secondly, our slaves; and thirdly, Europeans whose hearts are fired into a crusade against us by fictitious pictures of the atrocities of slavery, and who meet no hindrance from their governments in such enterprise, because these governments are equally antagonistic to the institution. In touching the third cause, the fact that slavery has become a military weakness, we may rouse prejudice and passion, but the time has come when it would be madness not to look at our danger from every point of view, and to probe it to the bottom. Apart from the assistance that home and foreign prejudice against slavery has given to the North, slavery is a source of great strength to the enemy in a purely military point of view, by supplying him with an army from our granaries; but it is our most vulnerable point, a continued embarrassment, and in some respects an insidious weakness. Wherever slavery is once seriously disturbed, whether by actual presence of the approach of the enemy, or even by a cavalry raid, the whites can no longer with safety to their property openly sympathize with our cause. The fear of their slaves is continually haunting them, and from silence and apprehension many of these soon learn to wish the war stopped on any terms. The next stage is to take the oath to save property, and they become dead to us, if not open enemies. To prevent raids we are forced to scatter our forces, and are not free to move and strike like the enemy; his vulnerable points are carefully selected and fortified depots. Ours are found in every point where there is a slave to set free. All along the lines slavery is comparatively valueless to us for labor, but of great and increasing worth to the enemy for information. It is an omnipresent spy system, pointing out our valuable men to the enemy, revealing our positions, purposes, and resources, and yet acting so safely and secretly that there is no means to guard against it. Even in the heart of our own country, where our hold upon this secret espionage is firmest, it waits but the opening fire of the enemy's battle line to wake it, like a torpid serpent, into venomous activity.

In view of the state of affairs what does our country propose to do? In the words of President Davis, "no effort must be spared to add largely to our effective forces as promptly as possible. The sources of supply are to be found in restoring to the army all who are improperly absent, putting an end to substitution, modifying the exemption in law, restricting details, and placing in the ranks such of the able-bodied men now employed as wagoners, nurses, cooks, and other employees, as are doing service for which the negroes may be found competent." Most of the men improperly absent, together with many of the exempts and men having substitutes, are now without the Confederate lines and cannot be calculated on. If all the exempts capable of bearing arms were enrolled, it will give us the boys below eighteen, the men above forty-five, and those persons who are left at home to meet the wants of the country and the army; but this modification of the exemption law will remove from the fields and manufactories most of the skill that directs agriculture and mechanical labor, and, as stated by the President, "details will have to be made to meet the wants of the country," thus sending many of the men to be derived from this source back to their homes again. Independently of this, experience proves that striplings, and men above conscript age, break down and swell the sick lists more than they do the ranks. The portion now in our lines of the class who have substitutes is not on the whole a hopeful element, for the motives that created it must have been stronger than patriotism, and these motives, added to what many of them will call breach of faith, will cause some to be not forthcoming, and others to be unwilling and discontented soldiers. The remaining sources mentioned by the President have been so closely pruned in the Army of Tennessee that they will be found not to yield largely. The supply from all these sources, together with what we now have in the field, will exhaust the white race, and though it should greatly exceed expectations and put us on an equality with the enemy, or even give us temporary advantages, still we have no reserve to meet unexpected disaster or to supply a protracted struggle.

Like past years, 1864 will diminish our ranks by the casualties of war, and what source of repair is there left us? We therefore see in the recommendation of the President only a temporary expedient, which at best will leave us twelve months hence in the same predicament we are in now. The President attempts to meet only one of the depressing causes mentioned; for the other two he has proposed no remedy. They remain to generate lack of confidence in our final success, and to keep us moving down hill as heretofore. Adequately to meet the causes which are now threatening ruin to our country, we propose, in addition to a modification of the President's plans, that we retain in service for the war all troops now in service, and that we immediately commence training a large reserve of the most courageous of our slaves, and further that we guarantee freedom within a reasonable time to every slave in the South who shall remain true to the Confederacy in this war. As between the loss of independence and the loss of slavery, we assume that every patriot will freely give up the latter—give up the negro slaves rather than be a slave himself. If we are correct in this assumption it only remains to show how this great national sacrifice is, in all human probabilities, to change the current of success and sweep the invaders from our country.

Our country has already some friends in England and France, and there are strong motives to induce these nations to recognize and assist us, but they cannot assist without keeping slavery, and to do this would be in conflict with their policy for the last quarter of a century. England has paid hundreds of millions to emancipate her West Indies slaves and break up the slave trade. Could she now consistently spend her treasure to reinstate slavery in this country? But this barrier once removed, the sympathy and the interests of these and other nations will accord with our own, and we may expect from them both moral support and material aid. One thing is certain, as soon as the great sacrifice to independence is made and known in foreign countries there will be a complete change of front in our favor of the sympathies of the world. This measure will deprive the North of the moral and material aid which it now derives from the bitter prejudices with which foreigners view the institution, and its war, if continued, will henceforth be so despicable in their eyes that the source of recruiting will be dried up. It will leave the enemy's negro army no motive to fight for, and will exhaust the source from which it has been recruited. The idea that it is their special mission to war against slavery has held growing sway over Northern people for many years, and has at length ripened into an armed and bloody crusade against it. This baleful superstition has so far supplied them with a courage and constancy not their own. It is the most powerful and honestly entertained plank in their war platform. Knock this away and what is left? A bloody ambition for more territory, a pretended veneration for the Union, which one of their own most distinguished orators (Doctor Beecher in his Liverpool speech) openly avowed was only used as a stimulus to stir up the anti-slavery crusade, and lastly the poisonous and selfish interests which are the fungus growth of war itself. Mankind may fancy it a great duty to destroy slavery, but what interest can mankind have in upholding this remainder of the Northern war platform? Their interests and feelings will be diametrically opposed to it. The measure we propose will strike dead all John Brown fanaticism, and will compel the enemy to draw off altogether, or in the eyes of the world to swallow the Declaration of Independence without the sauce and disguise of philanthropy. This delusion of fanaticism at an end, thousands of Northern people will have leisure to look at home and to see the gulf of despotism into which they themselves are rushing.

The measure will at one blow strip the enemy of foreign sympathy and assistance, and transfer them to the South; it will dry up two of his three sources of recruiting; it will take from his negro army the only motive it could have to fight against the South, and will probably cause much of it to desert over to us; it will deprive his cause of the powerful stimulus of fanaticism, and will enable him to see the rock on which his so-called friends are now piloting him. The immediate effect of the emancipation and enrollment of negroes on the military strength of the South would be: To enable us to have armies numerically superior to those of the North, and a reserve of any size we might think necessary; to take the offensive, move forward, and forage on the enemy. It would open to us in prospective another and almost untouched source of supply, and furnish us with the means of preventing temporary disaster, and carrying on a protracted struggle. It would instantly remove all the vulnerability, embarrassments, and inherent weakness which no longer find every household surrounded by spies; the fear that sealed the master's lips and the avarice that has, in many cases, tempted him practically to desert us would alike be removed. There would be no recruits awaiting the enemy with open arms, no complete history of every neighborhood with ready guides, no fear of insurrection in the rear, or anxieties for the fate of loved ones when our armies moved forward. The chronic irritation of hope deferred would be joyfully ended with the negro, and the sympathies of his whole race would be due to his native South. It would restore confidence in an early termination of the war with all its inspiring consequences, and even if contrary to all expectations the enemy should succeed in overrunning the South, instead of finding a cheap, ready-made means of holding it down, he would find a common hatred and thirst for vengeance, which would break into acts at every favorable opportunity, would prevent him from settling on our lands, and render the South a very unprofitable conquest. It would remove forever all selfish taint from our cause and place independence above every question of property. The very magnitude of the sacrifice itself, such as no nation has ever voluntarily made before, would appall our enemies, destroy his spirit and his finances, and fill our hearts with a pride and singleness of purpose which would clothe us with new strength in battle. Apart from all other aspects of the question, the necessity for more fighting men is upon us. We can only get a sufficiency by making the negro share the danger and hardships of the war. If we arm and train him and make him fight for the country in her hour of dire distress, every consideration of principle and policy demand that we should set him and his whole race who side with us free.

It is a first principle with mankind that he who offers his life in defense of the State should receive from her in return his freedom and his happiness, and we believe in the acknowledgement of this principle. The Constitution of the Southern States has reserved to their respective governments the power to free slaves for meritorious service to the State. It is politic besides. For many years, ever since the agitation of the subject of slavery commenced, the negro has been dreaming of freedom, and his vivid imagination has surrounded that condition with so many gratifications that it has become the paradise of his hopes. To attain it he will tempt dangers and difficulties not exceeded by the bravest soldiers in the field. The hope of freedom is perhaps the only moral incentive that can be applied to him in his present condition. It would be preposterous then to expect him to fight against it with any degree of enthusiasm, therefore we must bind him to our cause by no doubtful bonds; we must leave no possible loophole for treachery to creep in. The slaves are dangerous now, but armed, trained, and collected in an army they would be a thousand fold more dangerous; therefore, when we make soldiers of them we make free men of them beyond all question, and thus enlist their sympathies also. We can do this more effectually than the North can now do, for we can give the negro not only his own freedom, but that of his wife and child, and can secure it to him in his old home. To do this we must immediately make his marriage and parental relation sacred in the eyes of the law and forbid their sale. The past legislation of the South concedes that a large free middle class of negro blood, between the master and slave, must sooner or later destroy the institution. If, then, we touch the institution at all, we would do best to make the most of it, and by emancipating the whole race upon reasonable terms and within such reasonable time as will prepare both races for the change, secure to ourselves all the advantages, and to our enemies all the disadvantages that can arise, both at home and abroad, from such a sacrifice. Satisfy the negro that if he faithfully adheres to our standard during the war he shall receive his freedom and that of his race. Give him as an earnest of our intentions such immediate immunities as will impress him with our sincerity and be in keeping with his new condition, enroll a portion of his class as soldiers of the Confederacy, and we change the race from a dreaded weakness to a position of strength.

Will the slaves fight? The helots of Sparta stood their masters good stead in battle. In the great sea fight of Lepanto where the Christians checked forever the spread of Mohammedanism over Europe, the galley slaves of portions of the fleet were promised freedom, and called on to fight at a critical moment of the battle. They fought well, and civilization owes much to those brave galley slaves. The negro slaves of Saint Domingo, fighting for freedom, defeated their white masters and the French troops sent against them. The negro slaves of Jamaica revolted, and under the name of Maroons held the mountains against their masters for 150 years, and the experience of this war has been so far that half-trained negroes have fought as bravely as many other half-trained Yankees. If, contrary to the training of a lifetime, they can be made to face and fight bravely against their former masters, how much more probable is it that with the allurement of a higher reward, and led by those masters, they would submit to discipline and face dangers.

We will briefly notice a few arguments against this course. It is said republicanism cannot exist without the institution. Even were this true, we prefer any form of government of which the Southern people may have the moulding, to one forced upon us by a conqueror. It is said the white man cannot perform agricultural labor in the South. The experience of this army during the heat of summer from Bowling Green, Kentucky, to Tupelo, Mississippi, is that the white man is healthier when doing reasonable work in the open field than at any other time. It is said an army of negroes cannot be spared from the fields. A sufficient number of slaves is now administering to luxury alone to supply the place of all we need, and we believe it would be better to take half the able-bodied men off a plantation than to take the one master mind that economically regulates its operations. Leave some of the skill at home and take some of the muscle to fight with. It is said slaves will not work after they are freed. We think necessity and a wise legislation will compel them to labor for a living. It is said it will cause terrible excitement and some disaffection from our cause. Excitement is far preferable to the apathy which now exists, and disaffection will not be among the fighting men. It is said slavery is all we are fighting for, and if to give it up we give up all. Even if this were true, which we deny, slavery is not all our enemies are fighting for. It is merely the pretense to establish sectional superiority and a more centralized form of government, and to deprive us of our rights and liberties. We have now briefly proposed a plan which we believe will save our country. It may be imperfect, but in all human probability it would give us our independence. No objection ought to outweigh it which is not weightier than independence. If it is worthy of being put in practice it ought to be mooted quickly before the people and urged earnestly by every man who believes in its efficiency. Negroes will require much training; training will require time, and there is danger that this concession to common sense may come too late.

P. R. CLEBURNE, Major-General Commanding Division;
D. C. GOVAN, Brigadier-General;
JOHN E. MURRAY, Colonel 5th Arkansas;
G. F. BAUCUM, Colonel 8th Arkansas;
PETER SNYDER, Lt. Col., Commanding 6th and 7th Arkansas;
E. WARFIELD, Lt. Col. 2nd Arkansas;
A. B. HARDCASTLE, Colonel 32d and 45th Mississippi;
M. P. LOWREY, Brigadier-General;
F. A. ASHFORD, Major 16th Alabama;
JOHN W. COLQUITT, Colonel 1st Arkansas;
RICH J. PERSON, Major 3rd and 5th Confederate;
G. S. DEAKINS, Major 3rd and 8th Tennessee;
J. H. COLLETT, Captain Commanding 7th Texas;
J. H. KELLY, Brigadier-General Commanding Cavalry Division.

CHAPTER TWELVE

Opening of the Atlanta Campaign

IN FEBRUARY the sharpshooters referred to at Wartrace were more thoroughly organized. The Ordnance Department received through the blockade a shipment from England of fine Whitworth and Kerr rifles, of beautiful finish and workmanship — both long range, but the former superior to the latter in this respect. The Whitworth was fitted with telescopic sights, and had accurate range of 2,000 yards. Of these guns Cleburne received 20 Whitworth and 10 Kerr—more than was given any other division. These were placed in the hands of the marksmen already composing the body, which was added to by fresh details. It was an *elite* corps, and while the service was dangerous it was exciting and had immunity from the drudgery of camp and guard duty, and a place in it was eagerly sought. It had its own wagon, reported to division headquarters, and received orders direct from division headquarters near which it habitually camped. The sharpshooters were placed under command of Lieut. A. B. Schell, detached from Company I, Second Tennessee Regiment, an officer who had been mentioned for courage and intelligence in numerous engagements, and his name given in the "Honor Roll" of Chickamauga. Under his management the company became most efficient, and its service was rated as equal to a light battery; for if one of the enemy's batteries was especially annoying, the Whitworths were put to work on it, and the effect was immediately apparent, as they rarely if ever failed to silence or reduce the fire. Of its original members was Walter L. Bragg, of Alabama, afterwards one of the first Inter-State Commerce Commissioners. In addition to the regular sharpshooters there was attached to them two scouts for special service, armed with a short heavy rifle, of 400 yards range. In the Georgia campaign this command was of special value. During this campaign Lieutenant Schell was twice wounded, and the casualties amounted to 60 per cent. of its members; but vacancies were quickly filled, as each brigade kept a waiting list of good men, anxious to be transferred to this service.

The division remained at Tunnel Hill until near the last of February. Sherman had gone in person to Mississippi, and was moving against Lieutenant-General Polk's command, after the capture of Meridian. On February 22 Cleburne's division was marched to Dalton, and the following morning placed on train with orders to go to the assistance of Lieutenant-General Polk, and help to repel Sherman. It reached West Point, Georgia, where telegraphic orders were received directing its return to Dalton. General Thomas, who was left in command at Chattanooga, in Sherman's absence, learning that troops had been detached to Mississippi on the 23d, advanced, drove in the Confederate outposts on the 24th, and on the 25th appeared before Mill Creek Gap, near Dalton, where skirmishing was kept up all day. This advance was really a reconnaissance, for the double purpose of ascertaining conditions in his front, to see if Dalton was being evacuated, and if not, by this move to stop further reinforcements being sent to General Polk. These attacks which were successfully met, both in Mill Creek Gap and Crow Valley, east of Rocky Face Ridge, satisfied him that Johnston was still holding on to Dalton, and he accordingly withdrew. This movement was the cause of the recall of Cleburne's division, which left West Point after dark, arriving in Atlanta at midnight, where it remained until the following evening. The cause of this halt was the information of Thomas's withdrawal from in front of Dalton and the probability of the division being ordered to resume its trip to Mississippi.

Early in the morning, Cleburne, thinking it likely that his command would go into action immediately upon reaching Dalton, and not wishing his men delayed for want of food, prudently drew from the post commissary two days' rations, which the ladies of Atlanta volunteered to cook. About nightfall word was received that Sherman was withdrawing towards his base at Vicksburg, and the division was directed to proceed to Dalton that night by rail. A Federal brigade had driven away the Confederate guards and occupied Dug Gap, which is a pass in Rocky Face Ridge, five miles southwest of Dalton. Granbury's brigade being the first of the division to reach Dalton, upon its return was ordered to march to the foot of the mountain on the night of the 25th, to attack next morning the force occupying, and to retake the gap, which was promptly accomplished soon after sunrise of the 26th. The enemy having entirely retired from his front on the night of the 26th, Granbury the following day rejoined the division, which instead of returning to outpost duty at Tunnel Hill was entrenched upon Mill Creek on the Middle Spring Place road, some 3 miles east of Dalton, where it remained for over two months. Colonel D. C. Govan, and Colonel H. B. Granbury had been promoted brigadiers. The former was assigned to the Arkansas brigade, vice Liddell, relieved at his own request for service elsewhere, and the latter to the Texas brigade, vice Smith, absent on account of a severe wound.

While encamped on the Spring Place road the first and only military execution in the division occurred, that of a member of the First Arkansas Regiment, condemned by court martial for persistent desertion. In March, a heavy snow having fallen, the memorable snowball battle was arranged between Polk's and Govan's brigades. General Polk being sick, Cleburne led his old brigade, but was captured and paroled. Later, the battle waxing hotter, and Polk's men getting the worst of it, Cleburne could not stand this, and violating his parole again took a hand. His command being routed, Govan's men chased its leader to his quarters, with (merry) threats of a drumhead court martial and punishment by ducking him in the creek nearby; but they finally agreed to pardon him, on the plea that it was the first time they had ever known him to break his word to them. It was by such sport that these Trans-Mississippians, cut off from all communication with home, relieved the tedium of camp routine.

A young Marylander, Aubrey Pearre, taking advantage of Lee's invasion to escape, crossed the Potomac, to give his services to the South, sought and found at Tullahoma a friend who had left Baltimore earlier in the war, and was then occupying a staff position at Division headquarters. Pearre enlisted in Semple's Alabama battery and was immediately detailed to a clerkship in his friend's office. After a few days he expressed his appreciation of this kind invitation to a safe and easy berth, and added that he was fully sensible that he was not actually needed as a clerk, that he could not conscientiously accept pay and allowance without giving adequate return, and requested to be ordered back to his command. His intelligence and unremitting devotion to duty quickly gained his first promotion as ordnance sergeant of his battery, and soon thereafter, assignment as acting, and afterwards permanent, ordnance officer of Liddell's brigade, in which position his ability attracted the attention of General Cleburne and won his entire confidence.

Every survivor of the command will remember that most efficient but irascible old Prussian, Colonel Oladowski, chief of ordnance of the army. He had been in that department of the old service, and some one facetiously said that General Bragg captured him along with the rest of the ordnance stores at Pensacola. If such was the fact, he was not the least valuable prize, as no better man could have been found for his position. He worshipped but two idols—General Bragg and ordnance supplies. What the spending of a dollar is to the miser, the wasting of a cartridge was to Oladowski, and it rent his very soul in agony. This ammunition penuriousness brought him in frequent conflict with his subordinates, even where mutual appreciation existed.

At Dalton, Pearre, with a requisition for supplies, also made certain suggestions. The first suggestion carried with it an extravagance, and the latter a presumption, in the mind of the irate Colonel, not to be tolerated, and he returned the papers with a pungent endorsement, administering a sharp rap over Pearre's knuckles. Cleburne took up the matter, and in a counter endorsement sustained the young officer and won the case for him. The Colonel ever afterwards referred to him, as "that d—d Frenchman, *Pir-ee.*" Perhaps this appellation was suggested by the name and hereditary animosity of the Teuton for the Gaul, but Pearre was of pure American blood. It must be said to the credit of the Colonel that he did not allow his personal grievance to be at variance with the good of his beloved idol —the ordnance department; for a short while after this occurrence when recommendations were called for from Richmond for confirmations of temporary assignments or advance of rank, Captain Hill, the division ordnance officer, said to Oladowski, "Are you going to send up Pearre's name?" his reply was, "I would be one great [only *great* was not the word used] fool if I did *not* recommend *Piree.*" During the Atlanta campaign General Forrest wrote Cleburne requesting his consent to have Lieutenant Pearre transferred to his command. Cleburne asked Pearre if such would carry promotion with it, and unless it did he would decline to allow him to go out of his division, as he needed good officers as much as did General Forrest or any one else.* These two incidents are mentioned to show that, in the first, Cleburne would sustain to the last his subordinate officers when they were in the right, and he was one more prone to administer rebuke for the slightest dereliction of duty than to express in *words* praise for faithful service, as he considered this only the *duty* of a soldier, but in *acts* he was ever their champion. In the second case, while he would not stand in the way of promotion not in his power to bestow, at the same time, without this, he did not propose to allow his command to be deprived of its best material.

The late winter and spring months were employed by both Federal and Confederate commanders in preparing for the campaign to follow soon as the weather and the roads would permit. This actually opened on May the 4 by advance of the Federal Army to Ringgold, and on the afternoon of the 7th, after driving the Confederate cavalry from Tunnel Hill, took position a mile south of the

*It is a coincidence that after Cleburne's death General Hood made Pearre field ordnance officer of the army during the Tennessee campaign, and as such he had supervision of Forrest's ordnance during these movements and the retreat to Corinth. At the surrender at Greensboro, North Carolina, he turned over to the Federals the entire ordnance supplies of Hardee's corps, acting as the chief of that department with the rank of captain.

railroad gap in Rocky Face Ridge, and in front of Dalton. On April 30 the morning reports of Johnston's army showed the following totals: Infantry, 37,652; artillery, 2,812, with 112 guns; and cavalry, 2,392—a total of all arms of 42,856. The infantry was divided into two corps commanded by General Hardee and Hood, the latter having recently been promoted to lieutenant-general. The cavalry was under Major-General Wheeler. In his official report General Johnston says: "I commenced this campaign with Bragg's army of Missionary Ridge, with one brigade added (Mercer's) and two taken away (Baldwin's and Quarles's), and also on 2d (May) Brigadier-General Mercer's command arrived—about 1,400 affective infantry * * * The effective artillery and infantry of the army of Tennessee after the arrival of Mercer's brigade amounted to 40,900—the effective cavalry to about 4,000"—or a grand total of all arms of 44,900. Lieutenant-General Polk, with Cantey's and Loring's divisions, reached Resaca on May 11, and French's division joined Polk's corps at Cassville on the 18th, and Jackson's division of cavalry at Adairsville on the 17th. Quarles's brigade of infantry joined Polk's corps at New Hope Church on the 26th. These reinforcements by Polk's corps amounted to 14,200 infantry and artillery and 3,900 cavalry—a total of 18,100, which added to the force stated above, at the opening of the campaign, of 44,900, gives the entire strength, after reinforcement by Polk, of 63,000. These were all which were received during the campaign to the Chattahoochee River, and upon reaching there they were joined by about 1,500 Georgia State troops, under Maj.-Gen. G. W. Smith, and used in the defense of Atlanta.

General Sherman states that he had at the opening of the campaign a total of all arms of 98,797, but he failed to say that 8,168 men of the army of the Tennessee (Federal) had not joined at that time, as they did later at Resaca on May 11th. Sherman's field return for April 30th gives the total of all arms as 110,123, and that of May 31, a few days after crossing the Etowah River, a total of all arms of 112,819. Taking the first return of 110,123, deduct from Johnston's 63,000 Quarles's brigade of 2,200, which did not join until May 26th at New Hope Church, will make Johnston's forces to the Etowah

River 60,800, which deducted from 110,123, leaves 49,323 as Sherman's excess over Johnston. The Federal force with Sherman in chief command was divided into three armies—that of the Cumberland, Gen. Geo. H. Thomas; that of the Tennessee, Gen. James B. McPherson; that of the Ohio, Gen. John M. Schofield.

On May 8 Grigsby's brigade of Kentucky cavalry was placed near Dug Gap, 5 miles southwest of Dalton in the direction of Resaca, and also two regiments of Reynolds's infantry brigade, of Cantey's division, were guarding that point. About 4 o'clock in the afternoon of that day Geary's division of Hooker's corps attacked these two regiments, which were soon joined by Grigsby's men fighting on foot, and held the enemy in check, until the arrival of Cleburne in person with Lowrey's and Granbury's brigades, with which he had been ordered to the assistance of Grigsby and Reynolds, all being under command of General Hardee, who had been sent to that point by General Johnston. A rapid march was made, and upon arrival at the foot of the ridge Cleburne found some cavalry horses, upon which he mounted two men each of Granbury's brigade, and hurried them to the crest. Such as could not be mounted marched as speedily as their fatigue and the steepness of the road would allow. With the reinforcement of the mounted men of Granbury's the assailants were put to flight, and driven back down the slope, and no further attempt made by them. On the morning of the 9th, Cleburne, now in command,—Hardee having returned the night before to Dalton,—advanced to the western base of the ridge. On its rugged sides many dead, some wounded, and a number of small-arms were found. No attack was made during the day, but a few prisoners were captured by the skirmishers.

Snake Creek Gap is well described by General Cox as follows:

> Snake Creek is an insignificant branch of the Oostanaula, running south between high and rugged ridges, which on the east are nearly continuous with Rocky Face, and are known by the general name of Chattooga Mountains. On the west the parallel range is called Horn Mountains. A watershed half way from Tunnel Hill to Oostanaula separates the sources of Mill Creek

from those of Snake Creek, and this divide is properly the gap. The whole pass, however, is known by the name, and is a wild and picturesque defile, five or six miles long.[1]

This gap is at the southern end of Rocky Face Ridge, and its eastern debouchment is only 5 miles north of Resaca, and the entire length of 6 miles was practicable for infantry, cavalry, and artillery, and the possession of which, if held by the enemy, completely flanked Johnston and would have rendered his position at Dalton untenable, opening as it did upon his rear. While easy to be obstructed, for some reason never satisfactorily explained, this was not done. It was stated at the time by General Mackall, Johnston's chief of staff, that it was the result of a flagrant disobedience of orders (by whom he did not say) that this back door was left wide open and totally undefended by works, and with only a weak force to watch it.

At 1 o'clock A. M. of the 10th Cleburne was ordered to move to the junction of the Sugar Valley and Dug Gap roads. Upon arriving at that point additional orders were received to move towards Resaca. Leaving Colonel Williamson with his Arkansas troops in Dug Gap (Grigsby having previously been sent to Snake Creek Gap), Cleburne, with the brigades of Lowrey and Granbury, moved to within a mile of Resaca, where he remained for three hours, when, under orders, he returned to the Dug Gap road, arriving about sundown. Here the other two brigades of the division joined it. This movement was caused by General McPherson advancing on the 9th from Villanow on the west, and finding it unoccupied he pushed the head of his column through the eastern mouth of Snake Creek Gap. In the Confederate Army McPherson was known to be a bold and enterprising officer, and rated as equal, if not superior, to Sherman in military ability, and it was confidently expected that he would make an energetic dash upon Resaca, which was but slimly garrisoned. But to the utter surprise of the Confederates, after a sharp fight with two brigades of General Cantey's command, in which he was repulsed, McPherson withdrew at dark

1. J. D. Cox, *Atlanta* (New York, 1882), 35.

and took up a position between Sugar Valley and the eastern entrance of the gap. General Sherman, when advised of this, was both disappointed and vexed, and in his Memoirs says:

> McPherson * * * had not done the full measure of his work. He had in hand 23,000 of the best men of the army and could have walked into Resaca (then held only by a small brigade), or he could have placed his whole force astride the railroad above Resaca, and there have easily withstood the attack of Johnston's army, with the knowledge that Thomas and Schofield were on his heels. * * * Such an opportunity does not come twice in a single life, but at the critical moment McPherson seems to have been a little timid. Still he was perfectly justified by his orders, and fell back, and assumed a defensive position in Sugar Valley, on the Resaca side of Snake Creek Gap. As soon as I was informed of this, I determined to pass the whole army through Snake Creek Gap, and move on Resaca with the main army.[2]

But McPherson's course was prudent, as he was aware that Hooker had failed to carry Dug Gap on the previous day, and therefore the road from Dalton to Resaca was open for a column to move upon, and while he was attacking Resaca, Johnston could quickly, and without difficulty, throw a force upon his rear and cut off his retreat through the gap. This exact move was made on the 10th when Hood with three divisions—one of which was Cleburne's—marched from the Dug Gap road.

On this march Cleburne had a very narrow escape from capture. He was riding with two of his staff some half a mile ahead of his men, and a Federal scouting party passed between, and picked up a couple of cavalrymen a short distance in rear of the General. General Sherman, upon learning on the 10th that General McPherson was holding a strong position in the east mouth of the gap, and that the way through it was unobstructed, directed that the rest of his command, except Howard's Fourth Corps, should move through Snake Creek Gap. Howard was left in front of Dalton to threaten

---

2. W. T. Sherman, *Memoirs of Gen. W. T. Sherman* (New York, 1891), II, 34.

it and thus hold Johnston there. These movements were screened by the mountains, but on the night of the 11th information from scouts reported a general movement of the Federal army to its right; a reconnaissace by General Wheeler confirmed this on the morning of the 12th. Under orders received the night before, Cleburne at 7 o'oclock on the morning of the 11th started on the Sugar Valley road in the direction of Resaca. After proceeding a few miles the division halted for several hours and then resumed the march in the afternoon, and a halt was made about sunset, at a point where a new military road debouched into the Sugar Valley road, 10 miles south of Dalton. A line of battle was selected before camping. On the morning of the 12th cavalry skirmishers, in advance on the Sugar Valley road, having been driven in, some slight breastworks were thrown up as promptly as possible. The enemy was reported to be advancing in battle order, but no attack was made. General Sherman was confident that Johnston would fall back to Resaca so soon as he learned of the general movement of the Federals in the direction of Snake Creek Gap; but Johnston was in no hurry, as he had the shorter and direct road unobstructed, and was fully aware that it would require considerable time for Sherman to pass his large army through the gap, six miles long, and while the road was good it was narrow, so he remained at Dalton until the night of the 12th, when he withdrew his infantry and artillery, and the cavalry on the following day, without loss, or as the Federal General Howard states it, "he made off in one of his clean retreats."[3]

The army went into position at Resaca, to the west of the Western and Atlantic Railroad—Polk's corps on the left, its left resting on the Oostenaula River; Hardee in the center, Hood on the right, with his extreme right bent back to the railroad at, or near, the Connasauga River. The general direction of the line was north and south, and with the two wings bent back was somewhat semi-circular in formation. Cleburne's position was in the center of the corps, Bate's division on his right, and Cheatham's on his left. Such

3. O. O. Howard, "The Struggle for Atlanta," *Battles and Leaders,* IV, 209.

breastworks as could be were constructed on the crest of the hill across which the troops were placed. In front was a valley several hundred yards wide, on the west side of which ran Camp Creek, a small stream, at the base of a hill opposite to Hardee's corps, and separated from it by this valley and creek.

Early in the morning of the 14th Cleburne, on foot reconnoitered the ground in his front, going across the valley to the edge of the stream, a hazardous and imprudent thing, as the hill beyond the stream was heavily wooded, and soon afterwards occupied by the enemy, who immediately opened upon Cleburne's command a heavy fire. In the afternoon they made several attempts to charge across the open level ground, but uniformly without success, notwithstanding one of their commanders was heard to appeal to his men and incite them by saying, "You are the men who scaled Missionary Ridge, and you can carry this!" But all to no effect, for they were then confronting the men who had repelled every assault upon the part of the line held by them in that battle. His men would advance a short distance into the open, and quickly recoil under the fire of Cleburne's veterans. On both sides firing subsided towards nightfall. Upon returning to a small building used for division headquarters, a short distance in rear of the line, a solid shot from the enemy's artillery was found to have entered and rolled itself up in the blankets spread on the floor.

During the 15th heavy artillery firing was heard to the right and left of the division, but along its front the attack was by musketry alone, which gradually slackened until it became an affair of sharpshooters. This was quite annoying, as the left of the division ran across a bare hill protected by a low rifle-pit, not of sufficient height to shelter a man standing; and so accurate was this fire that the men had to lay prone upon the ground, and the raising of a head or even a hand was almost sure to be followed by death or wound. A staff officer in carrying an order had to crawl over the bodies of the men until this point was passed. The position of Resaca was with two deep and difficult streams—the Connasauga, and Oostenaula in rear—and it was impregnable from a front attack. This fact was recognized by General Sherman after two days' trial, when he resorted to the method pursued during the entire campaign, of holding an equal or superior force in front, with an amply large one to do the flanking. Accordingly a Federal division crossed the Oostenaula at Lay's Ferry, on a pontoon bridge. Lay's Ferry is immediately in rear of Resaca, and about half way between that point and Calhoun. This, with the fact that Polk's corps, on the left, had lost a position which commanded the bridges on the line of retreat, compelled the evacuation of Resaca.

About 10 o'clock P. M. on the 15th, Cleburne's division crossed the river on the trestle bridge, expecting every moment that the enemy would discover the movement and open on them with artillery. The command halted at midnight, a few miles from Calhoun. About sunrise the division went into line, its right stretching near to the railroad where it enters the town, and the left resting on a wagon road to the south. At 11 o'clock orders were given to move to the left and rear, to meet a detachment advancing from that direction. Polk's brigade was thrown forward, with Granbury as a second line and Govan placed *en échelon* on Polk's right, while Lowrey was located on a hill in the angle between Oothkaloga Creek and the Oostenaula River. Four rifled cannon were posted on the hill so as to enfilade the main line of the enemy in General Walker's division front to the right. Polk had gone but a little distance until he was briskly engaged with the Federal skirmishers. The rifle pieces on the hill opened upon the enemy's right, enfilading it; and as this was entirely unexpected, it seemed to create great confusion, and would no doubt have proved very effective, but, unfortunately, before time was allowed to fire but a few rounds, information was received that the enemy was advancing upon Calhoun and driving the cavalry before him. In view of the exposure of his rear to this force, Cleburne was ordered to withdraw and pass the creek. This was about 5 P. M., and preliminary dispositions made. Granbury was posted on a small wooded hill on the creek's bank, which commanded the approach to the bridge and ford over the creek, with Polk on his right along the stream's bottom. Rifle-pits were constructed, and upon the hill earthworks for a battery. Govan and Lowrey were moved some 2 miles south, upon the Adairsville road. Skirmishers were thrown well out on the Calhoun side of the creek, and a strong force placed so as to hold a position on that bank of the stream, which it was feared the enemy, now swinging to the right and feeling for Polk, who had withdrawn from their front, might occupy. Such a position would have given the enemy command of Walker's flank and rear, but he did not come on. In this affair the opposing force to Cleburne was the division of that gallant one-armed Irishman, General Thos. W. Sweeny, who later, by flag of truce, sent a message to Cleburne that after the war was over they both would raise a Fenian army and liberate Ireland. Cleburne's answer was that after this war closed he thought both would have had fighting enough to satisfy them for the rest of their lives. It was the fortune of these two generals to be pitted against each other on several occasions, and Cleburne is reported to have said that Sweeny gave him the hardest fight he ever had. This may be doubted, but whenever two Irish commands met there was invariably tough work. It was indeed "claw for claw," as Conan said to the Devil.

Soon after dark of the 16th orders were received directing the march towards Adairsville, about 8 miles south of Calhoun. Granbury was left to draw in the pickets, when all the balance of the division had gotten away. This he did, and rejoined the division, which moved at 1 o'clock A. M. on the 17th, arriving and halting 2 miles north of Adairsville near daylight. About 3 P. M. the enemy appeared in considerable force on the railroad leading from Calhoun. Cheatham's division was placed in position on the crest of a ridge immediately facing the enemy, his line crossing the railroad at right angles. Cleburne's division was drawn up on the left of the road in two lines, about 800 yards in rear of Cheatham—Polk and Granbury in the first, and Govan and Lowrey in the second line. An open field traversed by a creek with swampy banks intervened between these two divisions and on Cleburne's left ran Oothkaloga Creek, a considerable stream. This flank and also the two lines were strengthened by rifle pits. One of Lowrey's regiments was thrown across the creek for a further protection to the left, which was the most assailable point. This regiment was subsequently withdrawn and gave place to Bate's command. Cheatham repulsed an attack, but Cleburne was not engaged.

From maps General Johnston had been led to believe the valley in which the railroad ran was sufficiently narrow for his army to form across, and allow a force to occupy the heights on each side; but the breadth of it far exceeded the front of his army in line of battle, and would leave exposed one or both flanks, and he therefore decided to retire to Kingston and orders to this effect were given. Cheatham was to lead the corps, Bate to follow in half an hour, Walker next after the same interval of time, and Cleburne to bring up the rear as soon as the road was clear of the above named three divisions. Skirmishers were left in position with instructions not to retire until the corps had gotten well on the road; but by some misunderstanding they were withdrawn at 2 o'clock, and came in before Cleburne had filed into the road, and nothing was left between his command and the enemy. Great confusion and delay was occasioned by a fog so thick and impenetrable that it was impossible to distinguish objects at 10 paces. But after the brigades were gotten upon the road this fog proved fortunate for them, as it completely concealed the movement. The division reached Kingston in the early morning of the 18th and was halted for several hours, then moved and marched until near 4 o'clock P. M. with three brigades to within 2 miles of Cassville. Polk's brigade was left as rear-guard at Kingston.

The next morning, the 19th, Polk having rejoined Cleburne, held the left of the army, his line crossing the railroad at right angles. Walker's division was on Cleburne's right. The enemy had followed promptly and opened a heavy artillery fire on the line. About 3 P. M. orders were received to send ambulances and ordnance trains to the rear of Cass Station. This was preparatory to withdrawing the whole corps line, a most delegate movement in the presence of the foe, and almost in contact with it, but rendered imperatively necessary by the heavy artillery fire on Walker's line, which was unavoidably exposed in an open field to the east of the railroad and resting on it. The command was ordered to fall back in line of battle, and this was successfully done, the Federals not daring to press while the corps was in this formation. A new line was taken up 2 miles farther back, east of, and covering Cass Station—Hardee's corps on the left, Polk's the center, and Hood's the right. The right and center were upon a ridge, while Hardee was on low ground, his left extending to the railroad. Cleburne's division immediately proceeded to strengthen its position by industriously fortifying. The troops were in the best of spirits and very confident, and lustily cheered General Johnston when he rode along the line a little before sunset. The following address from him had just been read to them, showing his intentions:

HEADQUARTERS ARMY OF TENNESSEE,
CASSVILLE, GEO., *May 19, 1864.*

General Order No.—

SOLDIERS OF THE ARMY OF TENNESSEE: You have displayed the highest qualities of the soldier—firmness in combat, patience under toil. By your courage and skill you have repulsed every assault of the enemy. By marches by day and marches by night, you have defeated every attempt upon your communications. Your communications are secure. You will now turn and march to meet his advancing columns. Fully confiding in the conduct of the officers, the courage of the soldiers, I lead you to battle. We may confidently trust that the Almighty Father will still reward the patriot's toils and bless the patriot's banners. Cheered by the success of our brothers in Virginia and beyond the Mississippi our efforts will equal theirs. Strengthened by His support these efforts will be crowned with like glories.

J. E. JOHNSTON,
*General.**

At 12:30 A. M., May 20th, orders were received to put the command in motion on the road to Cartersville. To General Hardee, Cleburne expressed his disappointment and surprise, as the troops

---

*I have in my possession the original of this order sent to Cleburne. —I. A. B. See *O.R.*, XXXVIII, part 3, 728.

were eager to be led to battle and confidently expected it, and that he could not understand why, after the order read to the troops, General Johnston should have changed his plan. Hardee replied that at a conference between the commanding general and two of his corps commanders, Lieutenant-Generals Polk and Hood had stated that they could not hold their positions for an hour after the Federal artillery should open upon them; that General Johnston said with this lack of confidence of two in three of his corps commanders, he felt it would be too great a hazard to risk battle under such conditions. In reference to this, General Johnston says:

> As I rode along the line while the troops were forming, General Shoup, chief of artillery, pointed out to me a space of 150 or 200 yards which he thought might be enfiladed by artillery on a hill a half mile beyond Hood's right and in front of the prolongation of our line if the enemy should clear away the thick wood that covered it, and establish batteries. He was desired to point out to the officer who might command there, some narrow ravines, very near, in which his men could be sheltered from such artillery fire, and to remind him that while artillery was playing upon his position no attack would be made upon it by infantry.
>
> The enemy got into position soon after our troops were formed and skirmished until dark, using their field-pieces freely. During the evening Lieutenant-Generals Polk and Hood, the latter being spokesman, asserted that a part of their lines would be so enfiladed next morning by the Federal batteries established on the hill before mentioned that they would be unable to hold their ground an hour after fire was opened upon them, and therefore urged me to abandon the position at once. They expressed the conviction that early the next morning batteries would open upon them from a hill *then thickly covered with wood and out of range of brass field-pieces.* The matter was discussed perhaps an hour, in which time I became apprehensive that as the commanders of two-thirds of the army thought the position untenable, the opinion would be adopted by their troops which would make it so. Therefore I yielded. General Hardee, whose ground was least strong, was full of confidence. Mr. Davis says ("Rise and Fall") that "General Hood asserts, in his report and in a book, that the two corps were on ground

commanded and enfiladed by the enemy's batteries." On the contrary they were on a hill, and the enemy were in a valley, where their batteries were completely commanded by ours.[4]

In his book, "Advance and Retreat," General Hood says:

> * * * The truth is, General Shoup reported to General Johnston that a larger portion of the ridge he proposed to occupy in rear of Cassville would be enfiladed by the Federal artillery; in other words, that the position of the line subsequently occupied by Polk and myself would be so enfiladed. * * * After our lines had been enfiladed for one or two hours before sunset, as General Shoup had pre-admonished General Johnston, Polk and I decided upon consultation, to see the commanding general and apprise him of our real condition; to state also that whilst our position was as good as we could desire to move forward from and engage the enemy in pitched battle, the line we held was unsuited for defense; and if he did not intend to assume the offensive the next morning, we would advise him to change his position. This is the sum and substance of our suggestion, or recommendation, to the commander of that army, viz.: that if he did not intend to fight a pitched battle we would advise him to change our position for one better suited for defense.[5]

Lieutenant-General Polk was killed in less than a month after these occurrences, and left no written statement of the affair, but his son, Dr. W. M. Polk, now of New York (at the time a member of his father's staff), wrote General Hood on June 17, 1874, confirming Hood's version as given above. General Johnston in his official report in reference to this withdrawal said, "It was a step I have regretted ever since."

4. J. E. Johnston, "Opposing Sherman's Advance to Atlanta," *Battles and Leaders,* IV, 268.

5. J. B. Hood, *Advance and Retreat* (New Orleans, 1880), 105-106.

CHAPTER THIRTEEN

Battle of Pickett's Mill

CLEBURNE'S DIVISION moved over the Etowah River by a bridge near the railroad-crossing, and marched with the corps to Willford's Mill on Pumpkin-Vine Creek, where it remained until May 23, when it was moved by Dyer's Tan-yard and Tanners to the Dallas road, 6 miles distant, and camped. On the 24th it was moved via New Hope Church to Powder Springs and from thence on the 25th at 3 A. M. the march of the day before was retraced to Lysters, when it turned to the right at that point, going a mile or two through the woods to Darby's. It remained here under orders to be ready to move at a moment's notice. Orders were received accordingly about dark to go to New Hope Church where General Hood's corps had been fighting for several hours. The intense darkness of the night, added to by the woods, made it impossible to distinguish the road; besides, its movements were impeded by the rear of Walker's column, so the division was halted and instructions asked for from corps commander. About 10:30 P. M. orders were received to bivouac until 4 o'clock A. M. on the 26th, and then to move to Mauldin on the Dallas-Atlanta road, which point was reached at 6:30 in the morning of the 26th. Later in the day it was ordered to the support of General Hindman, who was at that time the extreme infantry right of the army. Cleburne was now reporting to Lieutenant-General Hood.

Polk's brigade was placed on the right of Hindman. Hotchkiss's artillery of the division, consisting of four Napoleons, four Parrotts, and four howitzers, was placed on the right of Polk, but later the four Napoleons were sent farther to the right, leaving the Parrotts and howitzers under command of Capt. Thomas J. Key. On the right of the artillery, to support it, was placed one of Govan's regiments. The remainder of this brigade and that of Granbury's and Lowrey's were placed in a second line to support Hindman's right brigade and Cleburne's first line. Rifle-pits were constructed for the first line on the afternoon of the 26th and morning of the 27th. At 7 o'clock on the morning of the 27th Govan was sent with his brigade to reconnoiter. He from time to time reported that the enemy was moving in force to the Confederate right. At 10 o'clock Govan was directed to leave out skirmishers three-quarters of a mile to the front, and to return with the remainder of his brigade to the main line, where he was placed on the right of the artillery, and entrenched. In inspecting his line Cleburne discovered that works in which the artillery was placed had been so constructed as to give only a direct front range to the guns. He ordered the tearing away of these works so as to secure a flank fire, which was most fortunate, as during the progress of the battle the howitzers were used with deadly effect by an oblique fire upon the masses of the enemy, several lines deep, as they advanced up a depression to the right of this battery. The attacking force, the whole of the Fourth and one division of the Fourteenth Corps, about 4 o'clock, having driven in the infantry,—skirmishers were pressing back the cavalry,—Granbury was ordered from the second line to prolong Govan's right, but so sudden and vigorous was the rush of the Federals that Granbury was barely in time to prevent Govan's flank from being turned—his men firing by file as they came into line. In front of the right of Granbury's line was a field. The enemy, driving back some cavalry at that point, crossed this field and passed some 40 or 50 yards in rear, where they were met by the Eighth and Nineteenth (consolidated) Arkansas Regiment hastily sent by Govan, upon Granbury's request. In a sweeping charge this regiment drove the enemy back across the field. The impetuosity of this charge was all the more irresistible from the fact that Gen. John H. Kelly, of the cavalry, the former colonel of the Eighth Arkansas, coming up at this moment was recognized and received with lusty cheers by his old command, and, with Col. Geo. F. Baucum, led them. When this charge was about to be made, Lowrey's brigade had been ordered up, and, like Granbury's, fired by file as they wheeled into line on Baucum's right, which the enemy were beginning to pour around. Neither Granbury nor Lowrey had any protection or intrenchment.

The battle lulled with nightfall, the enemy having been badly punished and repulsed at all points, with severe loss, his dead numbering fully 700. Among the killed in the division were Capt. J. T. Hearn, the brave and accomplished assistant adjutant-general of Granbury's brigade. General Johnston writes of this battle:

> On the 27th, however, the fighting rose above the grade of skirmishing, especially in the afternoon, when at half-past 5 o'clock the Fourth Corps (Howard's) and a division of the Fourteenth (Palmer's) attempted to turn our right; but the movement, after being impeded by the cavalry, was met by two regiments of our right division (Cleburne's) and the two brigades of his second line brought up on the right of the first. The Federal formation was so deep that its front did not equal that of our two brigades; consequently, those troops were greatly exposed to our musketry—all but the leading troops being on a hillside facing us. They advanced until their first line was within 25 or 30 paces of ours, and fell back only after at least 700 men had fallen dead in their places. When the leading Federal troops paused in their advance a color-bearer came on and planted his colors 8 or 10 feet in front of his regiment, but was killed in the act. A soldier who sprang forward to hold up or bear off the colors was shot dead as he seized the staff. Two others who followed successively fell like him, but the fourth bore back the noble emblem. Some time after nightfall the Confederates captured above 200 prisoners in the hollow before them.[1]

For Cleburne's official report see appendix (p. 352-55). The original of this, in my handwriting, but bearing Cleburne's signature,

1. J. E. Johnston, "Opposing Sherman's Advance to Atlanta," *Battles and Leaders,* IV, 279.

is now in my possession. It was the last battle report made by him, as after this continual movements offered no opportunity to do so, as he had intended. Saved from my office files, I now have the original reports of his brigade commanders, never used by him, covering the operations around Kennesaw Mountain, in front of Atlanta, including Jonesboro.

CHAPTER FOURTEEN

Kennesaw Mountain—Death of General Polk

On the morning of May 29 Cleburne's division was moved from the right, and rejoined Hardee's corps on the extreme left in front of Dallas. During the day the Sabbath was undisturbed, except by occasional picket skirmishes, but about midnight a sudden and furious artillery fire broke out from the enemy's line combing the bare hill upon which Cleburne's line rested; but owing to the darkness it did but little damage, beyond disturbing the sleep of the troops, who were aroused to repel a possible attack under cover of this artillery. It was ascertained later that a false rumor of the Confederates advancing caused this firing which was not replied to.

On June 1 Cleburne was taken out of the front line and held as reserve in rear of New Hope Church as the Federals were withdrawing their right, and extending their left in the direction of the railroad, making about a mile a day and entrenching as they advanced, and the Confederates making corresponding movements to their left to confront these extensions. By the 8th the Federals had reached the railroad, and were massing on it between Ackworth and Big Shanty. Cleburne's division was on the 5th placed at Gilgal Church on the Lost Mountain line, to the northeast of Kennesaw Mountain. On June 13, contrary to his habit of not leaving his command, General Cleburne, with a single staff officer, rode to the summit of Pine Mountain, a detached hill, not on, but a short distance north of his line. It is a lofty peak, and commanded a fine view of the valley occupied by the Federals. It was crowned by two batteries in redoubts—that of the Fifth Company Washington Artillery of New Orleans, and Beauregard's battery commanded by a son of the famous general of that name. The artillerymen, who were sheltering themselves from sight a short distance in rear of the crest, warned Cleburne that a battery of Parrott rifled guns, about half a mile to the front, had been firing at any group appearing, and had the range so accurately as to make such exposure exceedingly dangerous. The General determined to have a look, and scarcely had begun to peer over the logs when a shell whistled over, and a second one quickly followed, passing only a few feet overhead. This satisfied his curiosity, and turning he remarked to his companion, "Let's get out of this. I have seldom known one to go where he had no business but that he got hurt." The staff officer heartily concurring in this opinion, gladly followed his chief down the mountain.

The following day, June 14, General Johnston, Lieutenant-Generals Polk and Hardee, and Maj.-Gen. W. H. Jackson, of the cavalry, with their staffs, rode to the top of Pine Mountain, where the same caution was given them as had been given Cleburne. General Johnston mounted Beauregard's works and turned his field-glasses to the left, when a shot directed at him came directly from the front. He immediately turned his glasses upon the battery firing, at the same time directing the staff and escort to disperse. General Polk moved off by himself, walking thoughtfully along, his hands folded behind his back, his left side towards the enemy, when a second came, then a third, the last of which—a Parrott shell—struck him, entering his left arm, passing through his body, emerging from his right arm, then struck a tree and exploded. As he was falling Generals Johnston and Hardee ran to him, the former catching him in his arms. His body was placed on a stretcher, and tenderly borne down the mountain by his sorrowing staff. Thus perished this gallant patriot and noble Christian soldier.* In his pocket were found his

*This account of General Polk's death is an extract of a letter dated January 29, 1908, from Rev. Philip D. Stephenson, at the time of the occurrence a member of the 5th Company Washington Artillery. He is now a distinguished clergyman, in charge of the Presbyterian Church at Woodstock, Virginia.

prayer-book and four copies of the Rev. C. T. Quintard's little work entitled, "Balm for the Weary and Wounded." Upon the fly leaves of each of these, indicating for whom they were intended, were inscribed the names of Gen. Joseph E. Johnston, Lieutenant-General Hardee and Lieutenant-General Hood, with the "Compliments of Lieut.-Gen. Leonidas Polk, June 12, 1864." Within the fourth volume was inscribed his own name. All were saturated with blood from his death-wound.

Major-General Loring succeeded to and commanded Polk's corps until the promotion of Maj.-Gen. A. P. Stewart to lieutenant-general a short time afterwards.

On the 16th Cleburne was moved back to high ground east of Mud Creek, and faced west. During this change the division was subjected to a heavy artillery fire, and while the casualties were few in number, one was sustained which was never repaired. Brig.-Gen. Lucius E. Polk, the senior brigade commander, had his horse killed, and the same shell tore away the greater part of the calf of his leg, incapacitating him for field service during the rest of the war. He was an able, intelligent young officer, who had served with marked distinction in all the battles in which the division had been engaged.

On the 19th the army was moved to the Kennesaw Mountain line, Hood's corps the extreme right, two of Loring's (Polk's corps) divisions being on Hood's left, and the other two divisions of this corps occupied the crest of Kennesaw from end to end. Hardee's corps was the extreme left, and located on level ground. Cleburne's division was in the center of the corps, with Cheatham on his right, both strongly entrenched, covered by rifle-pits surmounted by head logs. On the 24th Hardee's entire skirmish line was unsuccessfully attacked, and the assailants quickly repulsed. On the 27th, after a furious cannonade of several hours by the enemy, he made a general advance in heavy columns, but was repulsed at all points with great loss. Their assault, in seven lines deep, was vigorous and persistent on Cheatham's and Cleburne's divisions of Hardee's corps, and French's and Featherstone's of Loring's corps. The Confederates being covered by strong rifle-pits, which could not be carried by front attack, coolly and rapidly poured a murderous fire into the massed Federals, causing losses to them entirely out of proportion to those inflicted upon the Confederates. This is substantiated by the report of General Hardee, which states that the loss in Cleburne's division was only 11, and that of the enemy in his front 1,000.

After the repulse of the second desperate assault the dry leaves and undergrowth in the forest before Cleburne's entrenchments were set on fire by the shells and gunwadding, and began burning rapidly around the Federal wounded—exposing them to a horrible death. This danger was observed by the Confederates, who were ordered instantly to cease firing, and Lieut.-Col. W. H. Martin, First Arkansas Regiment, of Cleburne's division, called to the Federals that, as an act of humanity, his men would suspend further battle until the assailants could carry off their wounded, who were liable to be burned alive. This offer was accepted, and in this work of mercy the Federals were joined by the Confederates, who leaped their head-logs and aided in rescuing the enemy's wounded from the awful fate threatening them—an occurrence perhaps unparalleled in the annals of the war. This unofficial truce, be it said to the credit of both sides, was rigidly respected, and during its continuance no prisoners were taken. When all the wounded were removed the combat was renewed by the two sides with the most determined zeal. In the mean time, along the entire line for miles, to the right and left of Cleburne, there was maintained between both armies a tremendous fire of artillery and musketry.

In this great struggle the Federal army numbered about or over 100,000 men; the Confederates had about 55,000 present; the Confederate loss, in killed, wounded and missing, was 808 men; that of the Federals has never been exactly reported, but it is conceded that it went into the thousands. Sherman's generals, after some three hours, withdrew their shattered battalions from nearly all of the points of assault, and for one time there was a confessed failure of a great move in the campaign.

Among the killed on the Federal side were Generals Daniel McCook, Charles G. Harker, and Colonel Harman, commanding brigades. This assault ended Sherman's attack upon entrenched lines. On June 29 he wired General Halleck in reference to this, "I am accumulating stores that will enable me to cut loose from the railroad for a time and avoid the Kennesaw Hill, which gives the enemy too much advantage"[1]—in accordance with which he resorted to the safer mode of flanking by an extension towards his right and the Chattahoochee River. To meet this movement, Cleburne, on the night of July 2, was withdrawn to Smyrna Camp Ground, 10 miles south of Marietta, where it remained until the morning of the 5th, when it was transferred nearer the river, on high ground previously prepared by General Shoup, chief of artillery of the army, with a novel and peculiar line of redoubts. These consisted of detached works, protected by sharpened stakes driven through holes in a center log, forming a formidable *chevaux-de-frise,* somewhat resembling a farmer's rack for cattle feeding, and very effective to a front attack, which Sherman had not the slightest idea of making. Instead of which, on the 8th and 9th, he extended to, and part of his command crossed the Chattahoochee River at Rosswell, Soap Creek, Power, and Pace's Ferries, 10 to 15 miles above Johnston at the railroad bridge crossing. This brought him nearer to Atlanta than was Johnston in the position he occupied on the 5th, and caused him, on the night of the 9th, to cross to the south bank of the river. Cleburne's division crossed on pontoons below the railroad bridge. It halted north of and between Atlanta and Peach Tree Creek, where it bivouacked and entrenched.

This ended the Dalton campaign to the Chattahoochee.

---

1. W. T. Sherman to H. W. Halleck, June 29, 1864, *O.R.,* XXXVIII, part 4, 635.

CHAPTER FIFTEEN

Johnston Relieved — Battle of Atlanta

NOTWITHSTANDING the fact that the army had retired before General Sherman's from Dalton, there was no demoralization or depression. The troops were in splendid spirits and fighting trim. The intelligent soldiers felt that though under seeming defeat they were actual victors. It had required the Federal commander 74 days to bear back this inferior force over the 100 miles intervening. They did not feel that they had been beaten—only out-flanked, as every front attack had been met and invariably repulsed, no matter as to odds. Each successive position taken up had been held until the numerical superiority of the enemy enabled him to place in front at least an equal number to the whole of Johnston's, and to move upon either flank with a column almost as great. The men were ready to respond to any call made upon them. After retiring from one, another defensive line would be taken up a few miles in rear, without hurry or confusion, necessitating days, and sometimes weeks, of reconnoitering and partial attacks upon the Confederates, covered by entrenchments, before their flanks could be located and the turning movement repeated by Sherman. By this species of Fabian tactics the loss to the latter was so much greater than to Johnston, that the numerical superiority was being daily neutralized, and the Confederates would have been wholly successful but for the reinforcements continually received by Sherman. At this time, Johnston, while nearing his base, was drawing Sherman farther from his, and lengthening and exposing his railroad communications to cavalry raids. In no instance during the campaign did an attack by the enemy result in success. The ones at Resaca, New Hope Church, Pickett's Settlement and Kennesaw Mountain, and especially the latter, were disastrous failures. The Confederates were regularly and well fed, always ready to meet the foe, and though in retreat, confidence in their leader was unbounded. Hence the *morale* of the army was better when it reached the Chattahoochee than when it left Dalton. No material was lost save four pieces of artillery which were abandoned by General Hood, in an exposed angle at Resaca. During this campaign the engagements of Dug Gap, Resaca, New Hope Church, Dallas, Pickett's Settlement, and Kennesaw Moutain occurred, and daily heavy skirmishing which amounted, in many instances, to the dignity of battle.

General Johnston, having drawn the Federal army far into the interior, with a broad river—the Chattahoochee—in its rear, arranged to deliver a decisive battle. His line was formed along the southern bank of Peach Tree Creek, which is a tributary to the Chattahoochee, and flowing in a westerly course, and emptying into it near the railroad bridge. This stream was of difficult passage, and admirable for defense, owing to its broad and muddy channel and steep banks. Johnston's plan was to attack Sherman in his attempt to cross, rightly anticipating that in making the movement upon Atlanta there would be left a gap between Thomas, the Federal right, and Schofield, the center, into which Johnston proposed to push one or two corps, with every chance in his favor of defeating and crushing in detail the Armies of the Cumberland and Ohio, respectively commanded by the above-named generals. This would leave only the Army of the Tennessee, under McPherson,—the Federal left,—easy prey after defeat or repulse of the other two. Be it remembered that General Sherman's command was composed of three armies: that of the Cumberland (Thomas, formerly Rosecrans), that of the Ohio (Schofield, formerly Buell), and that of the Tennessee (McPherson, late Sherman), sent from Mississippi. These embraced all the troops west of Virginia and east of the Mississippi River, except those in the Department of Louisiana. Truly a vast host.

Late in the night of July 17 General Johnston was relieved from command and directed to turn over the command of the army to General Hood, who had been promoted to temporary rank of General. This order was received with depression by the Confederate troops, as great as was the elation of the Federals upon learning of it. This feeling of the enemy is reflected by Gen. O. O. Howard when he says:

> Much to our comfort and his surprise, Johnston was removed, and Hood placed in command of the Confederate army. Johnston had planned to attack Sherman at Peach Tree Creek, expecting just such a division between our wings as we made.[1]

And General Sherman writes of this:

> At this critical moment the Confederate Government rendered us a most valuable service. Being dissatisfied with the Fabian policy of General Johnston, it relieved him, and General Hood was substituted to command the Confederate army. Hood was known to us to be a "fighter." * * * The character of a leader is a large factor in the game of war, and I confess I was pleased at this change, of which I had early notice. * * * I was willing to meet the enemy in the open country, but not behind well-constructed parapets. * * * These three sallies (July 20, 22, and 28) convinced him (Hood) that his predecessor had not erred in standing on the defensive. Hereafter the Confederate army in Atlanta clung to its parapets. I never intended to assault them, but gradually worked to the right, to reach and destroy his line of supplies.[2]

Both Lieutenant-Generals Hardee and Stewart, two of the three commanders, joined with General Hood in a telegram to President Davis asking that this change of commanders be suspended, at least for a few days, but without avail. Hood's accession to command was the beginning of an Iliad of woes. The apprehension this change caused was not without good foundation, as events quickly demonstrated. He immediately reversed the wise and efficient policy of his predecessor, and instead of receiving attacks in chosen positions and

---

1. O. O. Howard, "The Struggle for Atlanta," *Battles and Leaders,* IV, 313.
2. W. T. Sherman, "The Grand Strategy of the Last Year of the War," *Battles and Leaders,* IV, 253.

fortifications, threw his troops against those of the enemy's, with the inevitable result of losses too great for the already small army of the Confederates to afford. This was a grand display of gallantry and courage upon the part of the troops, but it was not war, or the proper course for a general in Hood's condition to pursue. To illustrate: In reply to a question to the assistant adjutant-general of the army, Colonel Kinloch Falconer, after the battle of Ezra Church, July 28, he stated that in the 11 days since change of commanders casualties had been greater than in the previous 74, and with no material advantage. In speaking of the supersedure of General Johnston, Lieut.-Gen. Richard Taylor, brother-in-law of President Davis, wrote: "Certainly no more egregious blunder was possible than that of relieving him from command in front of Atlanta."[3]

During the operations of the following 10 days Cleburne had only three brigades. Polk's brigade had been so reduced that, after he was wounded at Mud Creek, his command was broken up and the remnants of the regiments distributed as follows: The First and Fifteenth Arkansas to Govan's, and the Fifth Confederate to Smith's brigade of Cleburne's division; the Second Tennessee to Tyler's brigade of Bate's division, and the Forty-eighth Tennessee to Quarles's brigade of Walthall's division.

On July 20 the relative positions of the opposing armies were substantially as follows: That of the Confederates being in line of battle, running east and west, covering Atlanta, and south of Peach Tree Creek, while the Federals were north of that stream, and between it and the Chattahoochee River. Of the latter, the Army of the Cumberland, under Thomas, on their right, and that of the Ohio (Schofield) next, with an interval of some 2 miles between them; while that of the Tennessee (McPherson) on their left, and moving to strike the Augusta Railroad at or near Decatur, 6 miles in a direct line east of Atlanta. The armies of the Cumberland and Ohio were in the act of crossing Peach Tree Creek, and General Hood attempted to carry out the plan (decided upon and communicated to him by

3. Richard Taylor, *Destruction and Reconstruction,* 44.

General Johnston) of attacking them while executing this movement. Accordingly, Stewart's corps was placed on the left, facing Thomas; Hardee in the center and Cheatham, commanding Hood's corps, upon the right, with Wheeler's cavalry prolonging the line, and facing Decatur, on the east. The hour for this movement by the Confederates was fixed for 1 o'clock P. M. of July 20, but from some delay—about which, since, much acrimonious controversy has taken place—did not occur until near 4 o'clock. So much time—3 hours—had been lost between the *intended* and *actual* hour of advance, that the attack proposed, upon unprotected troops while crossing the creek, was converted into an assault upon a strongly entrenched position, the enemy in this interval having crossed to the south side, which was covered by powerful artillery on the north side, and the assault failed.

Stewart first came in contact with the enemy, and carried some advance works. Hardee's left division—Walker's—was badly cut up and forced to retire before the fire from the massed batteries which Thomas had established on the opposite bank of the creek. Cleburne's division had been placed as a reserve to the corps, and after the repulse of Walker was ordered to replace this command in the front line and to renew the attack. An incident showing the proximity of the opposing forces was when Generals Hardee and Cleburne, with their staffs and escorts, met upon a road running through the line, and rode together forward over a slight rise of ground. Soon a puff of smoke arose, and a shell passed over the group. Hardee was of the opinion that one of the Confederate batteries was between this party and the Federals, and drawing their fire, and continued to ride onward. It was not until the second discharge that it was discovered the fire was point-blank from the enemy's guns at the party, and the third shot, quickly following, killed Sergeant Marshall, of Cleburne's escort, immediately in rear of Cleburne. The sound of axes felling trees to strengthen their works could be distinctly heard from the Federal side, and Cleburne, who had been ordered to replace Walker, had only to rise to the crest of the wooded ridge, not 200 yards away, to encounter the enemy thus prepared. Preliminary orders for the assault by the division had been given, and Cleburne had selected staff officers to send to each of his brigade commanders with orders to advance, when an officer galloped up, announcing that McPherson was approaching Atlanta from the east, pressing back the cavalry, and had gained a position near the exterior line of the city, and that General Hood directed that a division from Hardee be sent with all haste to meet this movement, and Cleburne, being in reserve, was naturally the one to go. Five minutes more would have been too late, and would have found this command heavily engaged. This withdrawal of Cleburne, and the approach of night, prevented any further attack by Hardee.

The division was marched back through Atlanta, Cleburne and staff riding ahead to ascertain position, which was found to be some 2 miles east of the city limits, the left of the division resting on the Augusta Railroad. In locating the troops it was found they were replacing cavalry, and that the enemy's line gradually on the left inclined towards the one being taken up by Cleburne, until it approached very close to his right. The officer placing the men was notified by the one he was relieving to do this quietly, as he would be fired upon if making any noise. This caution was extended to the brigade commanders, with advice to construct noislessly such defenses as they could. The first brigade, Govan's, arrived about midnight, and was placed as the left of the division, its left resting on the railroad, the other two being upon his right in the order of their coming up, Lowrey in center and Smith the right. It was extremely dark, and the cavalry line so slight that there was great difficulty in tracing it. Skirmishing opened, and the pressure from the front began at dawn. Before sunrise one of the best colonels of the division—Col. Samuel Adams, of the Thirty-third Alabama Regiment—was killed by a sharpshooter. He was walking in rear of the ditch inspecting his command, when a Minie ball struck him in the breast. Clasping his hands over the wound he sank at the foot of a small tree and in a few moments expired. Daylight revealed the fact that the line, of which there was no choice, thus taken up in the night, and with reference to the enemy's position, was weak, ill protected, commanded by higher ground in front, and badly enfiladed by the enemy's artillery on the left. But for the timely arrival of Cleburne, and these dispositions, McPherson's infantry could easily have brushed aside the thin screen of cavalry confronting him, and entered the works defending Atlanta. General Wheeler, commanding the Confederate cavalry, thus refers to the situation on the night of July 20, after McPherson had pressed him back to a point near the city:

> I finally reached a strong position which I had fortified with some care, and held it against a spirited assault of two lines of battle. It was during these operations that Generals Hardee and Stewart were attacking General Thomas some 4 or 5 miles northwest of my position. From the line of works occupied by my troops they could see masses of the enemy, fully 20,000 strong, all aligned and ready to attack. I felt that any respectable effort upon their part could easily dislodge my force and leave nothing between McPherson and the interior works which had been erected for the final defense of Atlanta.[4]

At 7:15 P. M., July 20, this dispatch was sent to General Wheeler:

> General Hood directs me to say that Cleburne's division is moving to your support. Communicate this to the men, and *urge them to hold on.*[5]
>
> A. P. MASON,
> *A. A. G.*

To quote from Col. T. B. Roy, Hardee's chief-of-staff, "And by a combination of good luck, audacity, and hard fighting, Wheeler did '*hold on*' until Cleburne relieved him and enabled him to move farther to the right to confront the extending lines of the enemy."[6]

This day's fighting—July 21—was spoken of by Cleburne as "the bitterest" of his life. Surely it was one of the most trying ordeals that men can be subjected to. Unable to advance, from the nature of the ground, outclassed in artillery, and occupied in repel-

---

4. Wheeler's Report, Battle of Atlanta, *O.R.*, XXXVIII, part 3, 952.
5. Hood to Wheeler, 7:15 P.M., July 20, 1864, *O.R.*, XXXVIII, part 5, 893.
6. T. B. Roy, "General Hardee's Military Operations about Atlanta," *SHSP,* VIII, 353.

ling charges without the opportunity of making counter ones, forced strictly to act upon the defensive, they had to endure the whole day, not only the harassing and deadly fire of small-arms from commanding ground, but also that of the enfilade and reverse of powerful artillery, especially that of De Grass's First Illinois Battery of 20-pound Parrotts. To give some idea of how destructive this was, in his report Gen. J. A. Smith, commanding the Texas brigade of Cleburne's division, says:

> I have never before witnessed such accurate and destructive cannonading. In a few minutes 40 men were killed and over 100 wounded by this battery alone. In the Eighteenth Texas Cavalry, dismounted, 17 out of the 18 men composing one company were placed *hors de combat by one shot alone*.[7]

To add to the discomforts, the day was fearfully hot, and it truly seemed that a modern Joshua had appeared and commanded the sun to stand still. Never was its sinking more gladly hailed. Night came, but with it no relief as to fatigue. General Hood had conceived a move worthy of Stonewall Jackson, in attempting to strike and crush Sherman's left wing by a flank movement. After dark of the 21st, Stewart and Cheatham—the former on the left—were ordered to take position, and construct works to defend the city from the east front, and the artillery was massed upon Cheatham's right. Hardee's corps was drawn out of line and directed to march through Atlanta, and by a detour, first south and then east, to cross Entrenchment Creek at Cobb's Mill, face north along the old McDonough road, and turn McPherson's left—his army being to the left of Sherman as he faced Atlanta. Wheeler's cavalry was directed to move to Hardee's right, and both attack at daylight. So soon as McPherson was forced back, Cheatham, from the Atlanta front, was to move by his right, continuing to drive the enemy from the Confederate right to left, down Peach Tree Creek, and Stewart was to take up the movement in turn, so soon as the engagement became general; these movements to be concerted and simultaneous.

---

7. J. A. Smith's Report, battle of Atlanta, *O.R.*, XXXVIII, part 3, 766.

Several contingencies, which were not properly considered and provided against, proved fatal to entire success; first as to the actual distance to be traversed by Hardee, in order to attack at or near the hour designated, daylight. While the distance in a direct line from Atlanta due east to Decatur by railroad is only 6 miles, that by the detour necessary in making this flank march is at the least 15 miles. The troops, wearied by two days' fighting and one night's total loss of sleep, moving upon a single narrow road, hampered and impeded by passing cavalry and artillery, could not, despite every effort, reach the projected point until somewhere near 12:30 P. M. of the 22d. The ground for the last two miles of the advance was covered with such a dense thicket of trees and undergrowth that it was difficult to see 50 yards in any direction, to the front or flanks, making it utterly impossible to keep distance or connections, necessitating frequent halts to adjust the alignment.*

The second contingency not counted upon, that instead of catching the Federal flank "in air" unprotected,—as did Jackson at Chancellorsville,—during the night it had been bent back at an angle facing south, and earthworks erected, covered in front by saplings cut partly through and forming a formidable abatis. Cleburne's division was formed with Govan's brigade's left resting upon the east side of the McDonough road—Smith's brigade (Texas) upon Govan's right, Lowrey's brigade 500 yards in rear as a reserve. Walker's and Bate's divisions of the corps were upon the right of Cleburne, in the order named, from left to right, with orders to conform their movements to his, which was the column of direction. In this order the division advanced to the attack between 12:30 and 1 o'clock P. M. General Govan in his report says:

> The enemy opened a section of Napoleon guns from the

*At Cobb's Mill General Hardee interrogated a farmer as to the proposed line of advance. In reply to a question he stated that besides the thick woods and undergrowth there was no obstacle to marching troops, but upon closer questioning he said there was a mill pond, wide, and half a mile long and ten feet deep, which would have to be crossed. This was rather a novel idea, as to that which in the mind of the "granger" constituted a military "obstacle"—unless the men were web-footed!

McDonough road but without effect. * * * The engagement began at 1 o'clock P. M. * * * The entrenchments of the enemy facing Atlanta extended along the road (McDonough) upon which we advanced. Contrary to our expectations and information, we encountered other works almost perpendicular to these, and designed to protect him from the very movement we were then making. These consisted of two lines of breastworks—the first about 200 yards in length, the second, in its rear and reaching farther to our right, each having in front an almost impassable abatis formed by cutting down the thick undergrowth of small oaks. A line of battle occupied the ground in front of my right, upon the extension of the line of works. The two Napoleon guns before alluded to were upon the right of the first works and swept the road and woods upon either side. My left came full upon these formidable entrenchments. The men charged to within 30 paces of them and sustained for 15 or 20 minutes the withering fire which was poured upon them, at the same time making their way through the abatis to the enemy. At length the enemy ceased firing and called upon my men to stop also, saying they surrendered, while some of them aimed their guns and were only prevented from firing by their comrades, who preferred to end the fighting. At this juncture a portion of the Second and Twenty-fourth Arkansas advanced to the works to receive the surrender, when the Federals, who filled the trenches, seeing the fewness of their numbers, took them prisoners. The enemy made a dash upon my center, and for a few moments checked the advance, when the Fifth Arkansas gallantly charged them back. Meanwhile the right * * * had advanced beyond the flank of the enemy's works and driven before it the line there opposed * * * and captured a battery of six Napoleon guns, which before that time had been vigorously used against us.

Perceiving that the right had passed on, and that the work was not yet done upon the left, where my small force was liable to be overpowered by the large number whom they thought to capture, I directed the right to change direction to the left in order to take them in flank and rear. This was promptly and opportunely done, and compelled the immediate surrender of all who did not take flight in the confusion. This timely success rescued those of the Second and Twenty-fourth

Arkansas who had been entrapped, and the officers of this command now received the swords of their late captors. * * * The First and Fifteenth Arkansas took the two guns which were placed upon the road. * * * I can scarcely conceive how the left, being a very attenuated line, succeeded in gaining the works under the murderous fire to which they were exposed in passing the abatis. In some places the enemy were bayonetted in their trenches, so stubbornly did they resist my little band. With a single unsupported line the work was done—a largely superior force, protected by formidable lines of entrenchments, had been routed and many hundred prisoners taken.

The success was great and signal, but it was accomplished at a fearful cost. * * * The regiments, much reduced, were drawn up along the enemy's second work. At about 5 P. M. the major-general commanding directed me to move forward again. The order was given, and the men passed the works and moved with alacrity, notwithstanding their thinned ranks and exhausted condition. Passing through the woods for about 500 yards, the command reached an open field sloping upward and forward, on the west side of which extended the continuation of the works that had been carried. We were now in rear of them as they fronted Atlanta, but the enemy had faced about and constructed a second and parallel line alongside of the former, being thus protected both in flank and rear. He had also thrown up a work at an angle with this, with its left thrown back, which commanded the field above referred to, and from which he kept up a heavy and constant flank fire upon my men. * * * My command charged across the open field, changing direction to the left, on which flank the enemy was nearest, and carried the entrenchments. * * * We now held the most advanced position of the works that had been carried, with our right extending away towards the enemy, and within 25 or 30 yards of him, and having our front, rear, and flank exposed to an unintermitting fire. Operations ceased with the approach of night, and my troops lay in this exposed position under fire until about 2 o'clock next morning, when upon my representing that it would be extremely hazardous to attempt to remain there after daylight, I was directed to retire my command to the second works taken from the enemy. * * * My men carried three distinct works, without being once repulsed, and held the ground gained until ordered to back from the last position, being unsupported. When the command took possession of the first works these were filled with the enemy, all of whom we captured, except such as fled in the confusion. * * * I think we captured about 700 prisoners at the first charge. * * * We brought off 8 pieces of artillery, several wagons loaded with ammunition and entrenching tools, and 10 or 15 mules and artillery horses.*

The artillery captured, as referred to by Govan, were 2 guns of the Second Illinois battery, and 6 pieces of Company F, Second Regular U. S. Artillery, and taken with the latter was its commander, Lieut. Joseph C. Breckinridge, afterwards brigadier, and Inspector-General, U. S. Army. Among the prisoners captured by Govan was the Sixteenth Iowa regiment entire, and its gallant commander, Lieut.-Col. Sanders. It is but just to state that there was a contention between the Arkansas and Texas brigades as to which actually captured the 6 pieces of regular artillery.

During Govan's operations, Smith's Texas brigade, upon his right, had promptly advanced and was soon heavily engaged. In his report General Smith says:

After advancing in line for about a mile and a half we struck the enemy, who fled in confusion, abandoning his artillery, ordnance, tool wagons, and ambulances * * * owing to the rapidity of the pursuit, the ungovernable enthusiasm of the men, and a most impassable morass through the brigade passed it became much lengthened, and thereby weakened, presenting a front scarcely more formidable than a strong skirmish line. The pursuit was, however, continued with great spirit and vigor, until we had carried three lines of their temporary works, when we came upon them in heavy force and strongly entrenched in an open field. Finding that my brigade was far in advance of the troops on my right and left and that the position was insecure, I despatched an officer to the major-general with the

*At the time of this writing there is before me the *original* report of Captain George A. Williams, A. A. G. of Govan's brigade, giving effective strength and casualties in this battle, viz: Effective total, 772; killed, 86; wounded, 322; missing, 91—Total, 499, or nearly 53 per cent. loss in killed and wounded alone. *O.R.*, XXXVIII, part 3, 783.

request that reinforcements be sent. In the meantime, the enemy opening a cross-fire on us, I found the position untenable and ordered the brigade to fall back a short distance.[8]

In this engagement General Smith was wounded, and all of his regimental commanders save one were killed, captured, or wounded. Among the latter was Col. R. Q. Mills, Tenth Texas, and the command of the brigade devolved upon Lieut.-Col. R. B. Young, Tenth Texas, he being the ranking officer not disabled. General Smith says:

> Owing to the fact that every regimental commander was either killed, wounded, or captured, reports are meager and imperfect. The list of casualties therefore are only approximate and is as follows: Killed, 23; wounded, 100; captured and missing, 75—total, 198.[9]

Among the captured by Smith's brigade was Col. Robert K. Scott,* Sixty-eighth Ohio regiment, but then commanding a brigade in the Seventeenth Army Corps. He was afterwards promoted to brigadier-general, and became military Governor of South Carolina in the days of reconstruction.

Govan's losses had been so severe in his first attack, as described, that it was deemed necessary, to enable him to carry the second line of works, that Lowrey's reserve brigade should be brought up to support him. A staff officer was sent by Cleburne with instructions to this effect. While in performance of this the officer ascertained that owing to the thick woods and impossibility of keeping alignment, the division of Walker, to Cleburne's right, had swung away to the east, and that an interval of about a brigade front existed. Not having time to apprise the division commander of this, the order as sent was delivered to General Lowrey, and at the same time he was notified of this gap, and it was suggested to him to fill it, instead of obeying the order to support Govan, which was given in ignorance of this break; and at the same time assurance was given that Cleburne would approve his action, as he afterwards did. This gallant

---

8. J. A. Smith's Report, *O.R.*, XXXVIII, part 3, 738.
9. *Ibid*, 747.

*I now (1908) have the sabre which Colonel Scott turned over to me on the field of July 22, 1864.—I. A. B.

preacher-soldier, appreciating the danger, unhesitatingly assumed the responsibility and hurried his command to this vital point, which was most opportune, as he was fiercely met by the head of the Federal column just penetrating this space. Lowrey made a gallant charge upon the Iowa brigade of the Seventeenth Army Corps, and checked the movement, which, if it had been successful, would have separated and imperiled one or both of the two divisions of Walker and Cleburne. In this fight that brave and able old soldier of three wars, Maj.-Gen. W. H. T. Walker, lost his life. Lowrey's report says:

> Taking the brigade altogether, I never saw a greater display of gallantry, but they failed to take the works, simply because the thing attempted was impossible for a thin line of exhausted men to accomplish. It was a direct attack by exhausted men against double their numbers, behind strong breastworks. I lost in killed, wounded and captured about one half the men that were in the charge. * * * To add to the difficulties, my men had had neither sleep nor rest for two days and nights * * * and under the oppressive heat many good men fell completely exhausted and could go no farther.[10]

Five color-bearers were shot down in this brigade. General Lowrey reports his loss in killed, wounded, and missing as 578. So near were the men led to the enemy's entrenchments that Col. H. D. Lampley, of the Forty-fifth Alabama regiment was wounded in the ditch and pulled over the parapet of the works by Col. W. W. Belknap, of the Fifteenth Iowa regiment. The colors of this regiment were captured, and are now in the State House, at Des Moines, Iowa. Maj. George C. Freeman, of the Forty-fifth Alabama, lost a leg and was captured, and Colonel Lampley's wound proved fatal in a few days.

Just at the juncture of these attacks of Govan, Smith, and Lowrey, the third contingency, and the one most potent, arose. By contraction of McPherson's line in its approach towards Atlanta, the evening previous, General Dodge's Sixteenth Army Corps had been crowded out, and placed in reserve, and at the time of Hardee's

---

10. M. P. Lowrey's report, *O.R.*, XXXVIII, part 2, 732.

attack was in the act of marching to strengthen the left of the Seventeenth Corps. Hood's flank movement was a complete surprise to Sherman, but had he been aware of it this accidental position of the Sixteenth Corps could not have been better arranged to meet the crisis. It was fresh and had only to face to the left to be in line and ready for action, and by hindering Walker's and Bate's divisions (Bate was on the right of Walker) from closing in and enveloping McPherson's rear in the extension of his line southward, and as stated by Gen. Frank Blair, who commanded the left corps of McPherson's army, "prevented the full force of the blow from falling where it was intended."[11] The only reasonable hope of the success contemplated was that so soon as Hardee's attack upon the Federal left flank from the south developed, Cheatham and Stewart should attack from the west, upon Sherman's front facing towards Atlanta. But strange to say that while the assault by Hardee was made, works captured, and the Federal left wing driven between 1 and 2 o'clock, this concert of action was not made, and Cheatham did not advance until 3 o'clock (according to General Hood's report), while Sherman, in his, fixes the hour at 4 o'clock. Meanwhile, reinforcements were actually withdrawn from the Fifteenth Federal Corps, confronting Cheatham, and hurried to the support of the Sixteenth and Seventeenth Corps, on the retired Federal left; and Hardee had been sharply checked and was being heavily pressed by this concentration of forces, before Cheatham was ordered to advance, which, when made, these same men were afterwards marched back and used in meeting Cheatham's attack. The Confederates had violated the well-established military maxim of not to fight "masses with fractions."

Night closed the battle, and Hardee's left, facing north, rested at right angles to and within a short distance of where his right had faced east the evening before. He held the ground gained, and while all the results hoped for were not realized, a stop was put to further attempts in that direction upon Hood's railroad communications with Macon and West Point.

11. Blair's report, battle of Atlanta, *O.R.*, XXXVIII, part 3, 544.

In a few days Sherman withdrew his left, and with it extended his right, fortifying as he made each successive move, until on September 1, six weeks later, he planted his army upon the railroad at Jonesboro, south of Atlanta, and compelled its evacuation. It must be kept in mind that Hardee was in sole charge of this flank movement and had swung entirely away from the remainder of the army, and was now too far away to receive quick orders from General Hood, who remained with Cheatham's and Stewart's corps to direct their movements from the east front of Atlanta. This move—as before stated, was admirably conceived and the strategy good, but the tactics bad. Had the conditions on the morning of the 22d been the same as at dark of the 21st, an opportunity, not only possible, but reasonably probable, would have been presented to inflict a crushing blow upon Sherman, as on the night of the 21st his left flank was naked and unprotected, while on the following morning it was found bent back and strongly fortified.

In the first event, while Cleburne was fighting on the left, and driving the enemy's flank, Walker and Bate (center and right of corps) would have made a left wheel, catching the Federals in rear, while Cheatham and Stewart, attacking in front, would have either captured or pressed them back upon Peach Tree Creek. How Bate was foiled in this has been shown by the unexpected position of the Sixteenth Corps, and it is this that General Blair referred to when he wrote "* * * prevented the full force of the blow from falling where it was intended."[12] The bad tactics consisted in Hood's failure to attack with Cheatham's corps and the massed artillery simultaneously with Hardee, and have thus made it impossible for the enemy to reinforce his hard-pressed flank from his front,—as was done,—and in turn to use these same troops in repelling Cheatham when he did move, Hardee being too much crippled to do more than hold that which he had gained. It is difficult to estimate the result which the full fruition of this move would have wrought. The Federal General Belknap, who greatly distinguished himself in this battle, won his promotion, and was afterwards Secretary of War in President

12. Blair's report, *Ibid.*

Grant's Cabinet, and well competent to judge, said, "It would have rolled up the Army of the Tennessee like a scroll." Had this been the case it would have been pressed back into the angle formed by the junction of the Chattahoochee and Peach Tree Creek, a *cul de sac* from which escape would have been impossible and defeat inevitable.

This day was the most disastrous as to casualties in the career of the division, not excepting Murfreesboro and Chickamauga—not so much as to loss of numbers, but that of officers, which was exceptionally heavy, and irreparable, amounting to 30 general, field, and acting field officers alone, not to count company commanders. The loss of the Federals, by their own admission, at least equalled that of the Confederates in numbers, and exceeded it in one respect —in the death of that able and chivalrous young soldier, Maj.-Gen. James B. McPherson, commander of the Army of the Tennessee, who fell before the skirmishers of Govan's brigade. Without doubt he was the ablest of Sherman's lieutenants, and his death was lamented by the Federal army as Stonewall Jackson's was by the Confederates. He was well known to many of the latter officers, who had been with him at West Point or served with him in the old army, and while they felt that a tower of strength to his side had fallen, they sincerely regretted that so noble a sacrifice was made. The circumstances of his death were as follows: At the time of Hardee's attack McPherson was conferring with General Sherman, when upon hearing the firing he mounted his horse and started in the direction of the sound. Attended by a single orderly he rode into the woods, where but a short time before he had left his line resting. This, without his knowledge, had been driven back, and he found himself confronted by the skirmishers of Cleburne's division,*

*At the time it was understood that the skirmishers before whom General McPherson fell were those of the Third Confederate regiment, commanded by Captain Beard of Govan's brigade; but since a detailed account has been given which states that the fatal shot was fired by Robert D. Compton, Company I, Twenty-fourth Texas regiment of Smith's brigade. The right of Govan and left of Smith were so commingled that discrepancies as to incidents of the battle are not unnatural.

who called upon him to surrender. Lifting his hat in graceful salute, he turned his horse and attempted to escape, but was instantly shot dead. For a few minutes his body was in possession of the Confederates, but a charge of his troops, forcing back the skirmishers, soon recovered it. His brilliant career was thus cut short in his thirty-seventh year.

The distinguished General Giles A. Smith, commanding a Federal division opposing Cleburne, says in his official report:

> Regimental commanders with such men as would follow them [he might better have said "with such men as they *had* to follow them."—I. A. B.] were not infrequently occupying one side of the works and our men the other. * * * The flags of two opposing regiments would meet on the opposite side of the same works and would be flaunted by their respective bearers in each other's faces. Men were frequently bayonetted across the works and officers with their swords fought hand to hand with men with their bayonets.[13]

* * * * * *

The same writer says:

> The battle of Atlanta was a warfare of giants. In the impetuosity, splendid abandon, and reckless disregard of danger with which the Rebel masses rushed against our line of fire, of iron and cold steel, there has been no parallel during the war.[14]

Lt. Col. Strong, on General McPherson's staff, says:

> It seemed to us that every mounted officer of the attacking column was riding at the front of or on the right or left of the first line of battle. The battle from half past three was desperate and bloody in the extreme, and the result was extremely doubtful until late in the day. Our lines were broken and pierced in several places, and batteries and regimental colors were lost and won again and again.[15]

General Hood, deeply chagrined by the failure of his plan, sought to place the blame upon General Hardee for not making

---

13. Giles A. Smith's report, Battle of Atlanta, *O.R.*, XXXVIII, part 3, 582-83.
14. *Ibid.*
15. W. E. Strong, Asst. Ins. Gen., McPherson's staff in *Proceedings*, The Army of Tennessee, 1878, 118.

the attack at daylight, and for not having entirely turned McPherson's flank. The first charge is unjust, as it has been shown that its accomplishment was a physical impossibility—the time of starting and distance to go being miscalculated, the impeded condition of the one narrow road, and the thick woods and undergrowth through which the troops had to be marched in line not having been taken into consideration as to time required. The second charge is equally unfair, for the reason that an exposed flank was contemplated, while in fact the flank was found strongly entrenched and protected by abatis along the front of the Confederate advance; and last, and not least, the accidental position of the Sixteenth Corps was not, nor could have been, anticipated; but the fact remains that it was there, and effectually barred Walker and Bate from swinging forward to the left. Among the numerous killed or mortally wounded were Col. John E. Murray, Fifth Arkansas; Lieut.-Col. Anderson Watkins, Eighth Arkansas, and Lieut. J. L. Bostick, A. D. C. of Govan's brigade; Col. John C. Wilkinson, Eighth Mississippi; Col. Samuel Adams, Thirty-third Alabama, and Col. H. D. Lampley, Forty-fifth Alabama, of Lowrey's brigade.

General Lowrey claims that his brigade captured two stands of colors, and General Smith the same number. Among these was the flag of the Third Iowa Infantry. Referring to this regiment, the following is a quotation from L. D. Ingersoll's "Iowa and the Rebellion:"

> At the memorable battle of Atlanta, July 22, the Third Iowa Veteran Battalion literally fought itself out of existence. * * * A large portion of the command were killed, wounded, or captured. There was a desperate combat for the colors.[16]

It was thus afterwards described by a correspondent of the *Dubuque Times:*

> As the battle grew raging hot and desperate, a handful of our undaunted men gathered amidst the pelting showers of shot and shell, and there around our flag and banner they stood its guard in the most perilous moments. The color-bearer, the

16. L. D. Ingersoll, *Iowa and the Rebellion* (Philadelphia, 1867), 73.

> bravest of the brave, relinquished his hold by death alone. Still the masses stood there madly fighting for its defense. Their numbers fast decreasing by death, their hopes began to fail, and, as they surrendered themselves to the enemy they tore the emblem * * * into pieces and into shreds, which concealed, they proudly brought back to us, untouched and unsoiled by impious and traitorous hands.

The "reliable" correspondent makes a grievous error in this statement, as will be seen from the correspondence in the appendix to this book,* that this identical flag was returned to the State of Iowa, in 1883, by a lady who had kept it since it was given her by General Cleburne a few days after the battle.

On July 24 Mercer's Georgia brigade was transferred from Walker's to Cleburne's division.

---

*See Appendix D.

CHAPTER SIXTEEN

Evacuation of Atlanta

On July 27, Gen. Stephen D. Lee, having been promoted to lieutenant-general, was assigned to command of Hood's old corps, and about the same time General Granbury took command of the Texas brigade of Cleburne's division, in place of General Smith, wounded on the 22d. On the 27th, Sherman having begun to withdraw his left from the east, Cleburne's division was taken from the position it had occupied and placed in reserve behind the exterior works, about 2 miles from and due east of the city. A few hundred yards to the rear of the line division headquarters were established in a fine old stone house, located on a knoll covered with a grove of large oaks. The house was directly in line of Sherman's fire and had been abandoned after a rifle shell had shattered a partition wall and converted two rooms into one. This same battery was in the habit of throwing a few shells every day about noon. The second day after locating quarters, Colonel Hallonquist, Lee's chief of artillery, called and was invited to dine with Cleburne's mess, which consisted besides himself, of Maj. Calhoun Benham and another member of his staff. Several shots had passed over just before dinner was announced. Benham, whose courage was beyond doubt, was addicted to the vice usually ascribed to the Army of Flanders. As he approached the mess table he noticed that it had been placed without the protection the house afforded had it been situated a few yards in a different direction, and he remarked that while he was perfectly willing to take all legitimate risk of battle, he could not see the sense of unnecessary ones, especially when nothing was to be gained by it. Scarcely was the group seated before a shell exploded a few feet immediately above them, scattering fragments in every direction. Benham arose, staggering from his chair, with blood streaming down his face. A small jagged piece had struck him at the corner of his right eye, laying open the flesh back to his ear, but fortunately not penetrating the skull. So soon as he recovered from the shock he first swore fiercely at Stiefel, the cook, next called for a drink of whisky, and then exclaimed, pointing to his wound, "This is 'not as deep as a well, or wide as a church door,' but is good for thirty days' leave of absence."*

Benham was an original character. Graduating in law, he opened an office in Louisville, Kentucky, and married the sister of George D. Prentice, editor of the then famous *Louisville Courier*. His wife lived only a year or more, when Benham, as one of the "Forty-niners," crossed the plains to San Francisco, California. Here he volunteered, in 1851, as counsel for one Burdue, a notorious criminal who was being tried by the vigilance committee, and succeeded in securing a disagreement of the jury and saving his client's life. He was second for Judge Terry in the celebrated Terry-Broderick duel, in which the latter lost his life. Afterwards Benham was U. S. District Attorney, which position he resigned to return to Kentucky upon the breaking out of the war. During his residence in California he met and was well acquainted with McPherson, Hooker, and other army officers who afterwards became distinguished. He resigned after the fall of Atlanta, and made his way to Mexico, to join his friend, former Senator Gwynn, of California, who had been created a duke by Maximilian. Upon the execution of the latter, Benham returned to San Francisco, where he died some fifteen years ago.[1]

---

*In December, 1906, the writer, one of the old mess group, sought and found this place, then several miles within the city limits; but the ground not having been built over, it was easily identified. Only the foundation of the house remained, but the fine old trees were still standing, and plainly showed the scars of the shells here spoken of.

1. Benham died in San Francisco, June 12, 1884. San Francisco *Call,* June 13, 1884.

On August 3 Cleburne's division was shifted from the east to the north front of the city, where the shells thrown by Sherman passed over in their flight into Atlanta. On the 7th the division was again transferred to the extreme left of the army, continuing day by day to move in that direction to meet a corresponding one of the enemy, and fortifying each position as it was taken up. Finally the left of the command, Lowrey's brigade, reached to within 2 miles of East Point, on the 9th, and on the 16th pushed near to that place. Except occasional picket skirmishing for the next 10 days, nothing of special military importance happened. One incident, however, is worthy of notice. While near East Point a fine-looking young officer, elegantly dressed, was brought in by Cleburne's scouts. He proved to be Lieut. James Coughlan, of the Sixth Kentucky Cavalry, and aide to Gen. Jacob D. Cox (afterwards Secretary of the Interior), commanding a division of the Twenty-third Federal Corps. When mess was ready he was asked to partake of it, such as it was, and treated with every courtesy. The next morning Cleborne learned that after the prisoner had been sent to the provost guard, in the rear, he was robbed of his hat, boots, and blanket. This greatly incensed the General, but being unable to detect the perpetrators or recover the property, he sent the victim an extra hat of his own, and one of the only pair of blankets he owned. This generous act later proved to be "bread cast upon the waters"—if not to Cleburne, at least to one of his military family.*

*Upon the surrender at Greensboro, North Carolina, the writer with several comrades separated from the bulk of the army, moving south, and had to cross the country to our homes in Virginia. We were destitute of money or subsistence. Learning that General Cox was in command, I rode to his quarters, and upon announcing my late position was most courteously received. When I referred to the capture of Lieutenant Coughlan the General said that after exchange the Lieutenant had spoken of the kind treatment received from Cleburne, and he further informed me that the young officer had been killed near the gin house at Franklin, Tennessee; which was close to the spot where Cleburne fell. Upon explaining my needs, General Cox directed his commissary to fill our wagon (we were fortunate enough to have secured one out of the army wreck) with hardtack, bacon, sugar and coffee. This afforded our party good living during the twelve days overland journey to our homes, as the sugar and coffee were current exchange for eggs, milk, and butter from the farm houses we passed.

On the morning of August 30 the division was shifted to the left, and several times during the day this movement was continued, after halts at short intervals. During one of these Cleburne received a letter from some ladies of Dublin, Virginia, announcing the death of his brother Christopher, and he started to dictate a reply of thanks for the care they had given. This was never sent, as before it was finished orders came to move, and the incomplete letter placed in the office desk, which was afterwards captured and burned with its contents. On the evening of the 30th General Hardee was ordered, with Lee's and his own corps, then resting near Rough-and-Ready, to go to Jonesboro, 26 miles south of Atlanta, and drive off the enemy in possession at that point—Cleburne in command of Hardee's corps, and Lowrey in command of Cleburne's division leading, with Lee's corps in rear. The command marched the entire night, and was expected to reach its destination before daylight, but Cleburne encountered the enemy upon the road he had been instructed to take, and he was compelled to cut out and open another involving a delay which caused the head of his column to reach Jonesboro and get into position about 9 o'clock. Lee did not get into position until about 11 o'clock. The troops were greatly fagged by the night march and loss of sleep. Three brigades of Lee's corps, which had been left on picket, did not arrive until 1:30 P.M. This was the condition of affairs in the forenoon of the 31st of August. The Federals had on the evening previous appeared near Jonesboro, and with their right flank resting on Flint River, which flows nearly parallel to, and distant between 1 and 2 miles from the Macon Railroad at Jonesboro. The Federal line faced east, with two corps entrenched in position, and the third in reserve. West, and across Flint River, was another line of works, supported by artillery. The Federals had also three other corps in supporting distance between Jonesboro and Rough-and-Ready. Sherman had left but one corps—Slocum's Twentieth, in front of Atlanta, while Hood had retained for its defense Stewart's corps and the Georgia State troops.

The Confederate line was formed with Granbury's Texas brigade on the left; Lowrey's—Col. John C. Weir, commanding—in the center; Mercer's—Col. C. H. Olmstead, commanding—on the right, and Govan's in reserve in rear of Granbury's. Brown's division was on the right next to Mercer's brigade and Lee's corps was on the right of Hardee's. The general line was slightly east of north, from left to right, in a northerly direction and facing west. On Lee's right the line inclined near the railroad to the north of Jonesboro. Granbury's left regiment was made the battalion of direction, and all regimental commanders were ordered to guide to the left and swing gradually to the right.

The division moved forward at 3:30 P.M., and soon encountered the enemy in an open field, and strongly posted behind rail breastworks, with four pieces of artillery. This force, from prisoners captured, was ascertained to be Kilpatrick's cavalry, dismounted. The advancing Confederate line was vigorously opened upon by both small-arms and artillery, but after a short contest the enemy fled in confusion. A portion of this force made a slight stand at a second line of works to hold their assailants in check, so as to enable the remainder of their men to cross Flint River; but this stand was brief, and this force soon followed the others to the west bank of the river, leaving in front of Lowrey's—the attacking brigade—2 pieces of artillery in a slough nearby. Contrary to orders, Granbury's brigade rushed across the river for the purpose of capturing a battery which was doing some damage to his line. Inspired by uncontrollable impetuosity, Lowrey's and Mercer's brigades followed Granbury's example, and the enemy were driven from another line of works beyond the river. General Lowrey immediately directed the return of these brigades and directed that they should form their lines on the side they had left. Observing that the division was far in advance, and that its connection with the troops on its right was broken, General Lowrey ordered Govan to change the direction of his line, unite with the forces on his right, and press the enemy's flank, if one could be found, and assurance given that the other three brigades of the division would join him in the movement as soon as it was possible.

In reconnoitering the right Lowrey found that the enemy was entrenched in good works, the right flank of which rested on the river, and that Cheatham's division, General Maney commanding, had come up and occupied the ground between Cleburne's division and the enemy's infantry works. General Lowrey, supposing that a charge would be made, was making all haste to get into position to join in it, when an order was received from General Cleburne, directing the division to return to position from which it had advanced. The reason for this was that General Lee, on the right, had been ordered by General Hardee to attack when he heard Cleburne opening it; but mistaking the sound of the skirmishers' guns for those of the main line, Lee began his movement before Cleburne had become seriously engaged, and encountered formidable entrenchments, which he was unable to carry, and after considerable loss was repulsed. In reply to inquiry from General Hardee, General Lee expressed the opinion that his corps was not in a condition to renew the attack in support of that which Cleburne's (Hardee's) corps was then preparing to make upon the enemy's works. Immediately afterwards, Hardee had information that the enemy was arranging to attack Lee, and Cleburne's division was ordered to go in haste to the right and report to General Lee, and it became necessary for the remainder of the corps to assume the defensive. But no attack was made upon Lee, and night closed operations. In this day's fight two batteries, under command of Capt. Thomas J. Key, advanced with the infantry and rendered as efficient service as the formation of the ground would permit.

On the night of the 31st General Hood directed General Hardee to withdraw Lee's corps at 2 o'clock A. M. of September 1st and start it back towards Atlanta. The dispatch said: "There are some indications that the enemy may make an attempt upon Atlanta tomorrow."[2] Lee's corps proceeded as ordered, and Hardee was left with his own corps and a body of cavalry under General Jackson. As will be seen from this order, Lee's corps was recalled to Atlanta to protect it from an apprehended attack by Sherman's army, which General Hood still believed to be in front of that city. In point of fact, as

2. Hood to Hardee, Aug. 31, 1864, *O.R.*, XXXVIII, part 5, 1008.

before stated, the Federal Twentieth Corps was the only one there, and to confront it were Stewart's corps and the Georgia State troops. It must be born in mind that Sherman's whole army, with exception of the Twentieth Corps, had been concentrated upon Jonesboro. The withdrawal of Lee's corps made it necessary that Hardee's corps should be strung out to fill the gap thus made, and to cover with one corps the ground which the day before had been occupied by two.

Accordingly, at 1:30 A. M., Cleburne's division was shifted to the right, the men in single rank—Mercer's brigade on the left of the division, his left uniting with Brown's division; Lowrey's brigade next to Mercer's, and next Granbury's with Govan on the right. The general direction was almost due north and south and parallel with the railroad, the right of Govan turning back into a skirt of woods near the railroad. Taking up the position occupied by Lee's corps, Mercer's, Lowrey's, and a part of Granbury's brigades found an inferior line of entrenchments, incomplete and on badly selected ground, and very close to the enemy. A portion of Granbury's brigade and the whole of Govan's brigade found no works at all, except a few fence rails scattered along a line that had been marked out. The troops went to work, and amid shelling and sharpshooting by the enemy soon had a fairly good line of breastworks.

Information having been received early in the afternoon that the enemy were moving to the Confederate right, General Hardee directed General Lowrey to select a line on the right of Govan for two other brigades that had been ordered to report to him. From a hasty examination it was found necessary to change a portion of Govan's line in order to get good ground, and the proper direction towards the railroad for the two brigades. The new line was hastily marked out and work commenced by a small detail from Govan, and that officer ordered to place his right regiment on the rear line, prepare new works, and destroy the old ones in his front, and expedition in these dispositions was impressed upon him. Brigadier-General Lewis's brigade, and Gist's—the latter commanded by Col. James McCullough—soon reported to Lowrey and were placed, Lewis's with his left connecting with Govan's right, and extending to the railroad; Gist's on the east side of the railroad, and his right turned back almost parallel to it. The change in Govan's line referred to formed a sharp salient where its left was connected with Granbury's right. In other words, its first direction was north, but the second one due east, but facing north, an unfortunate formation, but unavoidable under the exigencies of the situation.

About 3 P.M. the enemy drove in the skirmishers along Govan's entire front, and half an hour later advanced upon it and his flank. The abandoned works in his front prevented by heavy artillery fire from being destroyed, as ordered, afforded excellent shelter to the enemy and gave him great advantage over the men in the new and uncompleted works. The enemy's artillery fire was most severe, being front, cross, and on Govan's line, enfiladed, which cut down the wheels of his cannon, causing the pieces to fall to the ground. The first assault was repulsed, but the enemy advancing in three columns, all converging on the Arkansas brigade, broke its line near the center, capturing General Govan, his adjutant-general, Captain George A. Williams, and 600 of his command, also the 8 pieces of artillery from which the wheels had been shot away. Col. P. V. Green, Fifth Arkansas, reformed a portion of the brigade which had not been captured, and gallantly charged and retook a part of the works, but could not hold them, though checking the enemy's advance on the flank after this break.

General Granbury, seeing this capture of the works on his right, threw back his line and began to form another one perpendicular to his original one; but learning that assistance was close at hand, immediately reoccupied his first position, which was held until the close of the battle. Vaughan's brigade, commanded by Gen. Geo. W. Gordon, of Cheatham's division, reported to Cleburne about the time of the disaster to Govan's brigade, of which Cleburne was not aware, and he had directed one of his staff to place the reinforcing brigade in the line where it was "most needed," a difficult matter to determine. General Gordon, stating that his men had come from the extreme left of the army at double-quick, were much fatigued, and nearly breathless, asked to be allowed to rest them for a few minutes. The officer (I. A. Buck) who was to conduct the command requested permission to go ahead and ascertain where best to place it. Meeting Colonel Green near the angle, he was informed by him of Govan's capture and the break in the line. While talking with Green, the staff officer was struck in the leg by a Minie ball. Riding back he met General Cleburne leading Gordon's brigade, and advised him of the condition of affairs at the front. In reply to the question if he had been wounded, the officer said, "Yes, but not too severely as to prevent my carrying in the brigade." Cleburne said, "I will do it myself. You go to the rear."*

Gordon's brigade was directed to retake Govan's trenches. In advancing to the attack it was either obliqued to the left or was not placed in position far enough to the right. Three of the regiments went into Granbury's trenches, and only one confronted the enemy in Govan's, but this one drove them from the timber and threw them upon the defensive and confined them to Govan's captured works, and relieved Granbury's line to a great extent from the enfilading of musketry; but one of his batteries farther to the right continued its harassment, the fire coming obliquely from the rear. The Federal loss in front of Granbury's was heavy, and his repeated efforts to break that portion of the line were repulsed and the position held until the command was ordered to retire at 11 P. M. Semple's battery, commanded by Lieutenant Goldthwaite, was withdrawn about dusk by Granbury's order. Mercer's and Lowrey's brigades were not severely attacked, but both lost some men from artillery and skirmish fire.

The check given the enemy by aid of the reinforcements drawn from the left enabled Hardee to hold his position until night offered

---

*These were the last words General Cleburne ever addressed to me. I never saw him again, as he met his death before my return to duty. When this wound was received I was mounted. A man passing me at the moment was shot through the breast and instantly killed by the same ball that struck me. The force of the shot thus being broken no doubt saved my leg bone from being shattered.—I. A. B.

an opportunity to withdraw his troops, and the entire subsistence and ordnance train of the army—which were under his charge and protection—in the direction of Lovejoy Station, 4 miles south of Jonesboro, where the corps reunited with those of Stewart and Lee.

The impossibility of one corps preventing six (commanded by General Sherman in person) from obtaining lodgment on Hood's only remaining line of railroad communication, 26 miles south of it, forced the evacuation of Atlanta. Towards the close of the day of September 1 the fire from all arms was terrific, and the corps seemed to be in the center of a circle of hissing lead and hurtling iron. It was so surrounded that there was literally no rear, except in a comparatively small opening in the direction of Jonesboro, the passing through which may be likened to emerging between the points of a horse-shoe.

Colonel Roy, of Hardee's staff, writes:

> Two incidents occurred at Jonesboro, which illustrate the *esprit du corps* of Hardee's troops, which General Hood says were "the best troops in the army." When the salient occupied by Govan was carried, Granbury, who was in single rank on the left, found his position enfiladed and turned and began to draw back his right. Hardee, who was for the moment prevented by a screen of woods from seeing what had befallen Govan, now saw Granbury's right retiring under heavy fire, and thought the troops had given way. The situation must be desperate indeed if Granbury's Texans gave way and Hardee at once rode into the line to rally the troops, but soon learned the true state of affairs. Granbury was hurt at the supposition that his troops would under the circumstances give way, and although the fire at that point was so hot that explanation and vindication might well have been postponed, he needs must have it out then and there, and said, with feeling and a just pride, "General, my men never fall back unless ordered back." And they justified their commander's confidence in them a moment later, by the coolness and intrepidity with which, co-operating with troops farther to the right, they retook and held the line from which they had been withdrawn. And it was next morning that the remainder of Govan's Arkansans sent a solemn delegation

to Granbury's Texans to ascertain whether the latter had lost confidence in them. It is needless to add that the answer was satisfactory.[3]

The loss of the division in the two days' fight was 83 killed, 344 wounded, and 659 missing; total, 1,086.

---

3. T. B. Roy, "General Hardee and Military Operations about Atlanta," *SHSP,* VIII, 374-75.

CHAPTER SEVENTEEN

The Advance into Tennessee—Spring Hill

THE DIVISION quietly withdrew from Jonesboro at 11 P. M. on September 1, and, unmolested, reached Lovejoy Station early the following morning, where it was formed in line 1 mile east of this point, its general direction being east and west, and the men in single rank. Construction of breastworks was begun. Before these were finished the enemy advanced upon the Confederate pickets with a strong body of skirmishers, followed by two lines of battle, driving in the pickets, and made a charge upon the uncompleted works, getting within 250 yards, but were handsomely repulsed. Their second line was brought up, but with no better success than the first, after which they fell back in the direction of Jonesboro. In this affair the enemy's loss was considerable in killed, and among the wounded was 1 brigadier; 4 colonels and 1 lieutenant-colonel. The attack chiefly fell upon Lowrey's brigade, which was the center of the division. Soon after the enemy retired, Stewart's and Lee's corps joined Hardee's.

General Sherman, after the battle of Jonesboro and the capture of Atlanta, withdrew from the former to the latter, having ended the campaign, and for the purpose of giving his troops a rest and to prepare for his next move. General Hood also proceeded to reorganize and arrange his command for whatever contingency might arise. The immediate future movements of each depended somewhat upon that of the other, and each was closely watching that of his adversary. On September 9 a special exchange of 2,000 prisoners was agreed upon, by which means, among others, General Govan and his troops captured on the 1st, and who had only gotten as far as Nashville, were liberated, after less than two weeks' captivity. While negotiations for exchange of prisoners were pending, General Sherman issued his infamous order directing that the women and children, the infirm and sick, in fact the entire population of Atlanta go either north or south. He informed General Hood of this, saying that those who preferred going south would be sent to and delivered at Rough-and-Ready Station and proposed, if Hood consented to this, that a two days' truce be declared for this purpose. Having no alternative, General Hood accepted the proposal in a letter of protest to General Sherman, doing this in the following words:

> * * * Permit me to say that the unprecedented measure you propose transcends, in studied and ingenious cruelty, all acts ever before brought to my attention in the dark history of war. In the name of God and humanity I protest, believing that you will find that you are expelling from their homes and firesides the wives and children of a brave people.[1]

This arrangement was carried into effect, and concluded on the 13th. How, later on, Atlanta was wantonly burned, and the burning being followed by the vandalism, rape, robbery and rapine of his march to the sea, are matters of history, giving a "bad eminence" to General Sherman, an eminence not attained by any other commanding general on either side during the war.

On the 18th the Confederate army commenced to move west in the direction of the West Point Railroad, which it reached at Palmetto on the 19th, where lines of battle were formed, with right to the east of the railroad and left resting near the Chattahoochee River. At Palmetto the army was visited by President Davis to ascertain from personal observation its condition, and to confer with General Hood and the corps commanders as to the proposed impending campaign which was being considered by General Hood. It was well known that General Hardee, for reasons stated in his official report,

---

1. Hood to Sherman, quoted in Hood, *Advance and Retreat,* 230.

was unwilling to serve under General Hood. Immediately upon the assignment of the latter as commander-in-chief, Hardee applied to the War Department to be relieved from duty, and only consented to remain at the urgent request of President Davis, and after the battle of Jonesboro he tendered his resignation. Upon arrival of the President at Palmetto, Hardee renewed his application, and was relieved from his corps, by assignment to the larger command of the Department of South Carolina and Florida, with headquarters at Charleston, South Carolina. Of this transfer President Davis wrote:

> General Hardee had earnestly requested to be relieved; it had been the subject of correspondence between us before my visit to the army, and my objections to complying with his wishes were entirely complimentary to him. My assent to his persistent request to be relieved was finally given because of irreconcilable differences between himself and the officer commanding in chief.[2]

This removal of their loved commander—"Old Reliable," as they fondly called him—caused in his old corps a feeling paralleled by that of the army by Johnston's relief at Atlanta. But Cleburne was most of all grieved and distressed, as with brief exceptions he had served under Hardee since the spring of 1861, and he was heard to say in substance, that but for his affection for his division, now the only tie that bound him to the Army of Tennessee, he would apply for service in Hardee's new command, even if he had to resign his major-general's commission and accept a staff position with him. General Cheatham assumed command of Hardee's corps.

After the fall of Atlanta seldom has a more serious problem confronted a commander than was Hood's. Sherman's army at Atlanta, too large to be attacked as a unit, could be divided into two columns; either one larger than Hood's entire force, the one to overrun Georgia and the Carolinas, and the other could be sent to Tennessee, to do the same as to Alabama and Mississippi. And to embarrass Hood further he had to devise means to prevent the

---

2. Jefferson Davis to T. B. Roy, Feb. 29, 1880, quoted in T. B. Roy, "General Hardee and Military Operations about Atlanta," *SHSP,* VIII, 377.

liberation of the thousands of prisoners at Andersonville, by interposing between them and Sherman, until they could be removed or some arrangement made, outside of the main army, to defeat any attempted liberation. In homely parlance, Hood had "two large holes to cover with one small patch." He wisely decided upon the plan most promising of success, in fact, there was scarcely left him a choice. To stand still was sure disaster. He determined to move upon Sherman's communications, hoping to force him to divide his army, by sending a part of it to Tennessee, which would be most immediately threatened, and if he followed Hood with the portion remaining in Georgia the latter would seize any favorable opportunity to attack after such division.

This plan was only partially successful. Sherman did so divide his forces, but was too wary to expose himself so as to be taken at a disadvantage. These proposed operations were laid before President Davis and approved by him with some reluctance. Accordingly, on September 28th Hood put his army in motion, and on October 1 crossed the Chattahoochee, on pontoons, at Pumpkin Town and Phillip's Ferry, and bivouacked 8 miles north of Pray's Church.

Meanwhile, Sherman, on September 28, sent two divisions of his army to Tennessee, and the following day directed his now ablest lieutenant, Gen. George H. Thomas, back to Stevenson and Decherd to look after the defense of that section. On October 3 the main body of Confederates had reached to within 4 miles of Lost Mountain. The march having been made in a northeasterly direction, gradually approached the railroad. Lieutenant-General Stewart was ordered to move with his whole corps and take possession of Big Shanty, and then to detach a sufficient force to capture Ackworth, both of which were accomplished. On the 5th French's division of Stewart's Corps attacked Allatoona, which was strongly fortified. Though his loss was heavy a part of the works were captured; but General French, receiving information that he would be cut off by a large force of the enemy, then advancing upon his rear, if he remained longer to complete the reduction of the fort, withdrew and rejoined the army near Lost Mountain.*

On October 6 the troops moved to Dallas, and to Van Wert on the 7th, and on the 8th reached Cedartown, and on the 10th Coosaville, 10 miles southwest of Rome. On the 11th the army crossed Coosa River and marched in the direction of Resaca and Dalton. A demand for the surrender of the latter place was at first refused but afterwards complied with. No assault was made, but Cleburne's division was drawn up for that purpose in case one became necessary, and it was in front of this command that General Hood received the surrender. The railroad having been effectually destroyed between Tunnel Hill and Resaca, and thus temporarily breaking Sherman's communications with Atlanta, the Confederate army from Dalton marched towards Gadsden, Alabama, at which point it arrived on the 20th. During the march Cleburne's division on the 16th bivouacked in nearly the same position at La Fayette as it did in September, 1863, just prior to the battle of Chickamauga.

It was at this time Hood conceived the idea of invading Tennessee, by crossing the Tennessee River at Guntersville, and again destroying Sherman's communications at Stevenson and Bridgeport; and after doing that to move upon Thomas and Schofield and rout them before they could reach Nashville. This plan was approved by General Beauregard (commanding the department) upon his arrival at Gadsden, and by him its execution was authorized on the evening of October 21st, and on the following day the movement began in the direction of Guntersville, as far as Bennettsville, at which point it was learned that General Forrest, who was to accompany Hood in the campaign, was then at Jackson, West Tennessee, and could not reach the middle of the State on account of the swollen condition of the river, and that it would be impossible for him to join Hood at Guntersville. Therefore it was decided to move westward

*From Kennesaw Mountain Sherman signalled to General Corse, in command at Allatoona, the famous dispatch, "Hold the fort." To this incident the world is indebted for the beautiful hymn, "Hold the Fort, for I am Coming."

to meet, effect a junction, and cross the Tennessee River with Forrest at Florence, Alabama.

During the 27th and 28th army headquarters were near Decatur, which place was garrisoned by the Federals, and only a slight demonstration was made against it, to enable the troops to pass safely by and towards Tuscumbia, which was reached on October 31.

Sherman had followed Hood as far as Gaylesville, Alabama, up to that time uncertain as to the latter's intentions; but now being convinced that the Confederates were serious as to invading Tennessee, he at once ordered Stanley's Fourth Corps, numbering 12,000, to report to General Thomas. He also directed Schofield with the Twenty-third Corps, 10,000 men, to the same officer. These were in addition to the force previously sent him from Atlanta, and two divisions under command of Gen. A. J. Smith were ordered from St. Louis to Thomas, which was all the force the latter deemed necessary to repel any attempt of the Confederates. After these dispositions, and leaving Hood in the hands of Thomas, Sherman returned with the remainder of his army to Atlanta, preparatory to his wrecking "March to the Sea."

It had been Hood's intention, immediately upon his arrival at Tuscumbia, to cross the river, but he was disappointed upon finding that the railroad, upon which he depended for supplies, was in such wretched condition that it would require weeks before an amount sufficient to subsist his army until he reached Middle Tennessee could be accumulated. Nothing could be done but to wait, and it was not until November 13 that army headquarters were established at Florence, and the troops did not all cross the river until the 15th. Forrest arrived on the 14th. Continuous and heavy rains again delayed supplies, and rendered the railroad almost useless, and in spite of every exertion it was not until the 19th that the cavalry moved forward. The following day Lee's corps marched about 10 miles on the Chisholm road, between the Lawrenceburg and Waynesboro roads. The entire army had crossed and bivouacked several miles beyond the Tennessee River on the 20th. Stewart's corps followed Lee's on the Chisholm, and Cheatham marched on the

Waynesboro road. It was hoped to get in the rear of Schofield's force at Pulaski before they could reach Duck River. Army headquarters were on the night of the 20th established at Rawhide, on Waynesboro road, 12 miles north of Florence. The Federals at Pulaski were alarmed at Hood's rapid march, as it had placed a large force upon their flank, threatening to cut them off from and imperiling the railroad and turnpike bridges over Duck River at Columbia, and placing their only line of communication with Nashville in the hands of the Confederates. By forced marches, day and night, they escaped to Columbia, formed line of battle and entrenched, where they were confronted by Hood on the 27th, Lee's corps, with its right upon the Mount Pleasant pike, Stewart's on Lee's right, and Cheatham's with its left on the Pulaski pike, connecting with Stewart's right, his own right resting on Duck River. No attempt was made to assail the entrenchments, as it was both desired and anticipated that the enemy would, without being assaulted, retire to the north bank of the river, as they did on the night of the 27th. The reason for wishing this move was that General Hood rightly supposed that after having interposed the river between the two armies the enemy would feel secured by such obstacle, and remain in that position a sufficient length of time to allow Hood, by a feint at crossing and heavy demonstration in front, to throw, unsuspected, pontoons across the river 3 miles above Schofield's left flank, and gain his rear at Spring Hill, before he became aware of the movement, which was a complete success. Pontoons were laid during the night of the 28th, and at dawn of the morning of the 29th Cheatham's and Stewart's corps and Johnson's division of Lee's corps, crossed over this bridge—Lowrey's brigade of Cleburne's division leading, General Hood and staff riding at its head.* Forrest had crossed the evening before. Lieutenant-General Lee, with Stevenson's and Clayton's division, and most of the artillery, was left to make heavy demonstration and divert attention from the real move, and to follow Schofield should he discover it and attempt to retire; and well did Lee carry out his

*General Hood in his report and book erroneously states that Granbury's brigade was in the lead. *O.R.*, XLV, part 1, 656-57.

instructions. As a matter of wise precaution, Schofield had ordered Stanley with the divisions of Wagner and Kimball to go back to Spring Hill, taking with him the army trains and all of his reserve artillery. On reaching the point where Rutherford Creek crosses the Franklin pike, Kimball was halted and faced to the east to cover the crossing from a possible attack from that direction. Here he remained all day. With Wagner's division, Stanley pushed on to Spring Hill with the trains. As the head of his column was approaching that place about noon he was informed that Buford's division of Forrest's cavalry was coming from the east. The leading brigade of Wagner was double-quicked into town just in time to prevent the cavalry of Buford from occupying it. As the other brigades arrived they were deployed, stretching a thin line from the railroad station north of the village to a point some distance east, and to the pike below, forming a semi-circle within which the trains were parked. Bradley's brigade was placed upon a knoll, about three-quarters of a mile east, commanding all of the approaches from that direction. Most of the artillery was on a rise of ground south of the town.

Such is the Federal account of their position at Spring Hill, by Col. Henry Stone of General Thomas's staff.[3]

Cheatham's corps, Cleburne's division in advance, followed by Bate's, with John C. Brown's in rear, marched as rapidly as the condition of roads would allow and arrived at Rutherford Creek, one and a half miles east from Spring Hill, at about 3 P. M. General Hood, who was with it, ordered that Cleburne's division be gotten across the stream, march towards Spring Hill, communicate with General Forrest, who was near the village, ascertain from him the position of the enemy and attack immediately, while General Cheatham should remain at the creek until Bate's division got over, and then go with and put it in support of Cleburne, and General Hood would push forward Brown to join the other two divisions of the corps. The Federal force at Spring Hill was between 4,000 and 5,000, while the Confederates had there, or within supporting dis-

3. Henry Stone, "Repelling Hood's Invasion of Tennessee," *Battles and Leaders,* IV, 444-45.

tance, 16,000 infantry, and with Forrest's cavalry a total of at least 25,000.

Cleburne, who had three brigades,—the fourth one, Mercer's, under command of Gen. J. A. Smith, having been left behind at Florence to convoy a supply train,—promptly attacked and drove the enemy until, as General Cheatham states:

> I received a message from General Cleburne that his right brigade had been struck in the flank by the enemy and had suffered severely, and that he had been compelled to fall back and reform with a change of front. * * * Instead of advancing directly upon Spring Hill, his forward movement was a little south of west and almost parallel with the turnpike towards Columbia, instead of northwest upon the enemy's line south and east of the village. General Cleburne was killed in the assault upon Franklin the next day, and I had no opportunity to learn from him how it was that the error of direction occurred.[4]

General Lowrey commanded the right brigade, and his account conflicts with that of General Cheatham's, viz.:

> * * * After I made the attack my command was not struck in flank by the enemy as you [General Cheatham] seem to have understood from General Cleburne, and I only had to make a slight change of direction by swinging my left round, which was done without much confusion. As I drove the enemy from his rail protection, a command of the enemy was left in line on my right and I saw demonstrations by the officers which led me to believe they were attempting to charge me in flank. I reported this to General Cleburne, and he moved against them with Govan's Arkansas brigade. The only trouble I had with these fellows on my right was to give them a few shots from my right flank to keep them demoralized, and as their flank was to my flank they could not have charged us without changing front, and as I was in full view of them, I watched them. * * *[5]

This statement of General Lowrey is confirmed by General Govan's letter, which will follow later. In fact, after Govan and Lowrey had driven the enemy (Bradley's brigade), these two bri-

---

4. B. F. Cheatham, "The Failure at Spring Hill," *SHSP,* IX, 526-27.

5. M. P. Lowrey to B. F. Cheatham, Nov. 8, 1881, quoted in *Ibid,* IX, 536.

gades were halted to reform and the division was soon ready to advance again, Granbury on the pike and Lowrey and Govan on the new position taken up by the enemy,—Bradley and Lane,—whom they had driven back to the southern outskirts of the town; but just at this juncture Colonel [T. H.] Bostick, of Cheatham's staff, brought an order from that officer directing Cleburne not to move forward, but to remain where he was until further orders. No "further orders" to advance came, except that given to do so following the attack General Brown is alleged to have been directed to make, but which *never occurred.* From all the foregoing it is plain that Cleburne's division was not "compelled to fall back," but was ready and anxious to continue the battle. So soon as Bate arrived he was placed in position on the left of Cleburne's line of march, to the west of the Rally Hill pike, from whence he was directed by General Hood in person (Cheatham not being present, but upon another part of his line) to move westward, reach the pike (Columbia and Franklin), and swing south towards Columbia. He moved forward in line of battle for over a mile to the pike, a little north of Colonel Cheair's house, where he encountered the enemy, and attacked with Major Caswell's sharpshooters, followed by the rest of his division, and was quickly driving the enemy across the road when he received an order through Lieut. A. B. Schell from General Cheatham to move to the right, find out and form on Cleburne's left. As this was contrary to the one he had been given, direct from General Hood, General Bate was in doubt as to obeying, and did not do so until General Cheatham reiterated it. This order of Cheatham must have been given in ignorance of that of General Hood to Bate, as a continuation of the movement then in progress would have caught in flank the Federal column at that time moving on the pike, completely blocked the way, and stopped the passage through Spring Hill of Schofield's forces retreating from Columbia, and compelled them to form line and remain until morning in that position, with two corps and a division on his flank and front and Lee with two divisions on his flank and rear. What the result of this would have been is beyond question—surrender, destruction, or a disorganized flight.

When General Brown, with his division, came up he was ordered to the right to turn the range of hills over which Cleburne and Bate had crossed, to form a line of battle and attack to the right of Cleburne. After Brown had reached the position designated and formed line he sent word to General Cheatham that it would be certain disaster for him to attack, as the enemy's line extended beyond his right several hundred yards. Upon this, Cheatham sent him orders to throw back his right brigade, and attack, informing him, at the same time, that Stewart's corps was close at hand, under orders to go to Brown's right, and be placed across the pike. Stewart, however, did not cross the pike, the reason why being thus stated by General Hood:

> Guides were at once furnished to point out Cheatham's right to General Stewart, who was ordered to form thereon, with his right extending across the pike. Darkness, however, which was increased by large shade trees in the vicinity, soon closed upon us, and Stewart's corps, after much annoyance, went into bivouac for the night, near but not across the pike, at or about 11 or 12 o'clock.[6]

When Brown was ordered to throw back his right brigade, as before stated, he was at the same time ordered that as soon as they could connect their lines that he and Cleburne should attack. *Brown to begin it,* Cleburne to take it up as soon as Brown moved forward, and Bate following Cleburne. In other words, Brown's was the column of direction and his to be the signal for attack from right to left, taken up successively by Cleburne and Bate; but *no attack was made by Brown,* and of course under their orders, none by Cleburne and Bate. The troops were ready and eager to be led forward, and chafing and impatient at this delay. Finally orders were received to bivouac. General Cheatham says:

> I found General Stewart with General Hood, one and a fourth miles back on the road to Rutherford Creek. The commanding general there informed me that he had concluded to wait till morning, and directed me to hold my command in readiness to attack at daylight. I was never more astonished

6. Hood, *Advance and Retreat,* 286.

> than when General Hood informed me that he had concluded to postpone the attack till daylight. The road was still open, orders to remain quiet until morning, and nothing to prevent the enemy from marching to Franklin. * * * General Hood said to me repeatedly, when I met him between 4 and 6 o'clock in the afternoon, "Stewart will be here in a few minutes." Stewart's column did not come up until about dark. Stewart says he was at Rutherford Creek before General Brown's division crossed that stream. He also says that General Hood there ordered him to form line of battle on the south side of the creek, and that he was not allowed to move thence until dusk. If General Stewart had followed Brown he would have been in position on my right, across the turnpike, before dark. That he would have executed an order to make such a disposition of his command no one who knows that officer will doubt; and he would have done it in the darkness of midnight as surely and as certainly as in the day.[7]

By his demonstrations Lee had held Schofield at Columbia all day, and he, Schofield, reached Spring Hill with his leading troops about 7 P. M., and it was 11 P. M. before his rear column—Cox's—arrived. Just before midnight this command started from Spring Hill for Franklin. At 1 A. M. of the 30th he was on the road, and the train, over 5 miles long, was drawn out, and so difficult was the movement that it was 5 o'clock in the morning before the wagons were fairly under way, and near daybreak when the last one left Spring Hill. The head of the Federal column from Columbia, under General Cox, reached the outskirts of Franklin about the same hour that the rear-guard was leaving Spring Hill. Thus the troops and the immense train of the enemy were allowed to march, unmolested, along a road within less than half musket shot of the sleeping Confederates, and so close that it was said "the Yankees lit their pipes by the camp-fires of the Rebs," and not a shot fired into the passing troops or trains. In the whole annals of the war no such golden opportunity was offered on either side for the capture or utter annihilation of an enemy. Where the responsibility rests for this dismal failure and criminal neglect of the fundamental and simplest prin-

7. Cheatham, "The Failure at Spring Hill," *SHSP,* IX, 526-27.

ciples of the art of war has been a matter of controversy for over forty years, but it would seem that it has indisputably been settled in a recent publication by Judge Young in the *Confederate Veteran,* and letter of General Govan, as both of these writers arrive at the same conclusion.[8] General Govan is the only surviving general officer of Cleburne's division. He and his brigade belonged to it during its entire existence. The following is General Govan's letter, addressed to his former assistant adjutant-general:

SUMMIT, MISSISSIPPI, *June, 1906.*

CAPT. GEORGE A. WILLIAMS,
New Orleans.

MY DEAR CAPTAIN: Replying to your inquiry as to General Cleburne's alleged failure of duty at Spring Hill, Tennessee, will say: That, while hesitating to give my opinion as to fixing this responsibility, at the same time feel it to be my duty to put it where I believe it to belong, instead of allowing this imputation to rest where it should not. It is all the more incumbent upon me to do this from the fact that General Cleburne was killed the following day and had no time or opportunity to explain, or vindicate himself. The failure was that of not taking possession of the pike at Spring Hill, immediately in rear of General Schofield's army at Columbia, and on his main line of retreat to Nashville. Were I to speak entirely from personal knowledge, I would be limited to the part taken by my brigade and Cleburne's division; but there was not an officer or private present in Hood's army who could but understand that a culpable and inexcusable blunder had been made, and that a golden opportunity to deal the Federal army a crushing defeat with but slight loss to ourselves had been thrown away. This criminal failure seems to have, in his own opinion, justified General Hood in his mad, haphazard attempt the following day to accomplish an impossibility at Franklin, upon which fatal field the flower of our army was ruthlessly and needlessly sacrificed. Fortunately for the truth of history, Hon. J. P. Young, Judge of first Circuit Court of Shelby County, Tennessee, has devoted years since the war in clearing up the mystery which has hung over the movements of our army at Spring Hill, and I think

8. J. P. Young, "Hood's Failure at Spring Hill," *Confederate Veteran,* XVI (1908), 25-44.

has made it perfectly clear as to who was responsible. He has written in no partisan or partial spirit, but entirely that of fairness.

In order to have a clear understanding of the flank movement to Spring Hill it is best to refer to the situation of the two armies near Columbia on November 27, 1864, and I may be compelled to repeat facts as well known to you as to myself, both of us having been in that unfortunate campaign. General Schofield occupied the north side of Duck River, General Hood the south. Realizing the opportunity, the latter conceived the plan of moving by his right flank and intercepting Schofield on the pike at Spring Hill 16 miles north of Columbia and immediately across the only practicable line of his retreat. Official records show that the two armies numbered about 25,000 each. Instead of attempting to cross the river and make a direct front attack, General Hood adopted the plan of the flank movement in pursuance of which Gen. Stephen D. Lee was left in front of Columbia with the divisions of Stevenson and Clayton, and directed to demonstrate heavily against Schofield, to create the impression that a front attack would be made. Meanwhile, General Forrest, with 5,500 cavalry, on the 28th crossed Duck River and with his usual vigor attacked the Federal General Wilson's cavalry, driving it back as far north as Mount Carmel Church, 20 miles east of Spring Hill. So skilfully did he execute his orders as to completely deceive Wilson, who appeared to have been possessed with the idea, and so informed both Generals Thomas and Schofield, that Forrest was moving directly on Nashville; but the "Wizard of the Saddle" had other plans.

Leaving General Ross's small command to attack vigorously and thus keep up the delusion, Forrest turned sharply to the southwest with the balance of his command for Spring Hill, where he arrived a little after 12 o'clock M., at about the same time that Stanley's small Federal corps of infantry reached there. This numbered about 5,000 and was intended to protect the wagon and reserve artillery train of some 800 wagons and also half dozen or more batteries.

As soon as General Forrest arrived at Spring Hill he dismounted his men and proceeded to find out what force was before him. He directed General Chalmers with a regiment to charge Bradley's brigade, which had taken position on the crest of a hill and had commenced erecting breastworks. Forrest was in doubt as to whether the force was infantry or cavalry. Chalmers made the charge and was sharply repulsed, which satisfied Forrest that it was inexpedient to make serious attack with his cavalry alone, so he held his ground and eagerly awaited the arrival of our infantry.

Early on the morning of 29th General Hood crossed Duck River on pontoons, 3 miles above Columbia, in the following order: Hardee's old corps (Cheatham commanding), Stewart's corps, and Johnson's division of Lee's corps following. Cleburne's division of Cheatham's corps leading, Lowrey's brigade of Cleburne's division in front, Govan's next, and Granbury in rear. Lee with two divisions had been left at Columbia, with instructions to follow Schofield should he discover this flank movement and retire. Our orders were to attack immediately at Spring Hill any Federal forces found in our front without waiting for the whole command to come up. This order was promptly and gallantly executed, and the Federals rapidly driven from their works on the hill a little southeast from the town. Generals Forrest, Cleburne, and myself, as you will remember, rode in rear of my brigade to the top of the hill as the Federals were driven. Only Lowrey's and my brigades participated in this charge, as Granbury's, on our left, had but little or no opposition. The routed Federals retreated rapidly and in confusion across the pike, and took a position near their wagon-train and reserve artillery southwest of the town. Cleburne's division continued to advance down the slope of the hill from which the enemy had been driven, until we reached a point near the pike, where we were ordered to halt.

At about this time you will recall that a house near our lines was fired by a shell from east of the town and that you and myself helped to rescue the family, each of us taking a child in his arms and carrying it to a place of safety on the hill top. There was also saved a part of the household goods by volunteers from our brigade, who entered the burning building—a gallant act, as it was accomplished amid bursting shells from a furious cannonade opened by the Federal batteries southwest of the village. I regret not to remember the name of the party to whom this timely service was rendered, but the incident impressed me as a most pathetic object-lesson of the horrors of war.*

After rectifying our lines we were ready to again advance, but received no orders to do so after being halted, as above stated, up to which time everything had proved a complete success. Schofield was in blissful ignorance of his perilous position, and acted as though he still believed that Hood's whole army was in his front at Columbia. The *status* at Spring Hill at this hour (4 P. M.) was that we had present and in line of battle Cleburne's, Brown's, Bate's and Johnson's divisions, with Stewart's corps crossing Rutherford Creek in short supporting distance in our rear. In other words, we had available, including Forrest's command, near 25,000 men, confronting Stanley's corps of only 5,500, encumberd with the care of their wagon-train and reserve artillery. Had we not been halted and instead made a determined advance, we could in 20 minutes have captured or destroyed Stanley, together with 800 wagons and his artillery, and have planted our army firmly on the pike. With general Lee in his rear in retreat from Columbia and our two corps, Johnson's division and Forrest in his front directly across his line of retreat the escape of the remainder of Schofield's command would have been impossible and capture or destruction inevitable; but a fatal paralysis seemed to have seized those in command, and the Federals all through the night marched past our bivouacs near the pike, and so close that it was said that many of them "lit their pipes at our campfires." But not a shot was fired as they moved along our front and it was not until after 5 A. M. of the 30th that their rear-guard passed Spring Hill.

Now who was responsible for this criminal and fatal failure, which General Hood attempted to make the army

*Touching the rescue of this family the following is from the *Confederate Veteran* of February or March, 1901: * * * At Spring Hill, the day before the battle of Franklin, when Cleburne made his attack upon Thomas's (Schofield's) moving column, General Govan and his adjutant-general, Capt. Geo. A. Williams, rode up to the burning house, just after dark, while artillery was still playing upon it. The family (a young man, his wife, and two little children) were in the yard. All terror-stricken. General Govan and Captain Williams had the father pass the children over the fence, and each took one before him, while the parents followed, shrinking and dropping at every shell, until conveyed to a place of safety by these two officers.

atone for a few hours later at Franklin? General Hood was on the field and was supposed to and certainly should have known the exact conditions. I should say the blame must be his, as would have been the credit had the movement proven a success. Instead of remaining quietly at his headquarters, issuing orders which were not carried out, he should have mounted his horse, taken personal command and directed the advance himself (would this not have been the course of Lee, Jackson or Forrest?), for upon the success of this flank movement depended the fate of his campaign and also that of his army. He the following day censured General Cheatham, to whom he had directed the adjutant-general of the army, Colonel Mason, to send an order to attack. Governor Harris, who was a volunteer on Hood's staff, said that Colonel Mason told him he had never sent such order to Cheatham. This being communicated to General Hood, he wrote a note to General Cheatham stating that he held the latter blameless. Notwithstanding which, in his dispatches to Richmond, and in official report, he reiterates the charge of disobedience of orders by Cheatham. The latter had previously received a sort of general order to attack as soon as possible, which he attempted to do by directing Gen. John C. Brown to move forward, which General Brown failed to do, alleging to Cheatham that his right flank was threatened by a Federal force. General Cheatham sent him word to throw back his right brigade and make the attack, which was to be taken up by Cleburne, Bate and Johnson, from right to left in the order named. In other words, as Brown was on the right he was to initiate the movement to be taken up successively, as above indicated. Brown's division was the column of direction which the others were to follow: its failure to move caused the others not to do so. General Cheatham had ridden down the line to the left, and expressed his astonishment at not hearing Brown's guns, and after this strange delay, proceeded to General Hood's quarters, who told him that as the troops were wearied and it was getting late, he should bivouac his men and be prepared to advance the next morning early.

While these orders and counter-orders were being given, General Stewart arrived and reported with his corps to General Hood. He was furnished with a guide and directed to place his command across the pike north of Spring Hill. While in process of executing these instructions he was overtaken by an officer claiming to be from General Hood, who informed Stewart that he was moving on the wrong road and that General Hood wished him to form on General Brown's right. Amid this confusion of orders, Stewart rode to see Hood and asked if it was intended he should move as first directed to get across the pike north of the town, to which Hood replied it was; but these conflicting orders had caused loss of precious time, and as darkness was fast approaching, Stewart was directed to bivouac his men to the right of Brown, and move early in the morning.

Extensive correspondence by Judge Young with parties familiar with the facts, and careful examination of official records, sustain him in his statement, and while his yet unpublished MS.* does not say in so many words who was responsible for the failure to attack, the data which he has collected unerringly points it out. As many of the participants in this flank movement have passed away, and cannot give their side of the story, I desire to do them no injustice, and therefore wish you to distinguish between what I state of my own knowledge, and the data and evidence presented by Judge Young, which I am convinced is correct and unbiased. General Cheatham refused to make any statement relative to the affair, except so far as it affected himself, saying that General Brown was his friend, that the war was over, and he could see no good in reviving the question of responsibility. General Brown made an official report, of which his family have refused to furnish a copy or publish the original. The testimony of General Cheatham's staff all seems to concur in the opinion that General Brown disobeyed orders in not promptly initiating the attack, which was to be the signal for the other commands to join in the movement. Now if this disobedience of orders on General Brown's part is true (of which it appears there can be no doubt) this completely vindicates General Cleburne of the charge of failure, as his orders were to follow Brown's movements—if Brown made no advance, of course General Cleburne could not do so.

Again, any one knowing Cleburne would be slow to believe that he would ever have failed to carry out promptly any order to attack. If it is true that he failed in his duty on this occasion,

---

*Since the date of this letter Judge Young's paper has been published. See *Confederate Veteran* of January, 1908.

it was the only one of his military career. Reviewing all the circumstances of the failure to take possession of the pike at Spring Hill, the conclusion is, that, while General Brown hesitated to move forward in obedience to the orders of General Cheatham, which movement of General Brown was to initiate the attack which was to be taken up by Generals Cleburne, Bate, and Johnson [?] [Johnson's division belonged to Lee's corps. I. A. B.], the divisions of Cheatham's corps, and consequently no serious effort was made to take possession of the pike, which would have inevitably resulted in the capture or dispersion of Schofield's army, wagons, and artillery and rendered unnecessary the bloody battle of Franklin. General Hood himself, as he was on the field of battle at Spring Hill, must of course be held responsible for the failure or success of the movement; for his subordinate could not be held responsible for the failure to carry out his orders when he himself was present. So far as trying to attach any blame to General Cleburne, or his division, for failure to move forward, I can myself testify that his division was in line, ready to move forward whenever the division or troops on his right were ready to comply with the order to advance.

D. C. GOVAN.

The following is an extract from a letter of Lieut.-Gen. A. P. Stewart, published in *The Confederate Veteran,* September, 1907:

> * * * Was not the fault at Spring Hill General Hood's own? Was he not up with Cheatham? If there was any disobedience of orders, was not the remedy in his own hands? He was there in command of the army and could have put the troops in himself if necessary. I was kept west of Rutherford Creek until towards night; had no orders to attack; was not in position to attack; General Hood was responsible for the failure.[9]

From these letters it is apparent the responsibility was divided. Primarily, Hood's, as he was near the field, and should have seen that his orders were obeyed, and that his subordinates were not confused with conflicting orders; secondarily, Brown's, in not moving to the attack, as directed by General Cheatham to do, just as soon

---

9. A. P. Stewart, "Controversy Upon Hood's Campaign," *Confederate Veteran,* XVI (1907), 425.

as he reached the position assigned him. General Brown's fine record during the entire war forbids the suspicion that he would have ever failed to attack when ordered, and the only ground upon which to account for his alleged disobedience on this occasion is that he misunderstood the orders, said to have been given him by General Cheatham, to throw back his right brigade and make the attack. That such order was given has been disputed, and much evidence adduced on both sides; but the weight of it seems in favor of General Cheatham, especially in the absence of General Brown's unpublished report, referred to by General Govan.

General Brown writes thus of this affair, so far as it concerned Cleburne:

> On the march to Franklin, General Cleburne, with whom I had long enjoyed very close personal relations, sent a message to the head of my column requesting an interview. Allowing my column to pass on, I awaited his arrival. When he came up we rode apart from the column through the fields, and he told me with much feeling that he had heard that the commanding general was endeavoring to place upon him the responsibility of allowing the enemy to pass our position on the night previous. I replied to him that I had heard nothing on that subject, and that I hoped he was mistaken. He said, "No, I think not; my information comes through a very reliable channel," and said that he could not afford to rest under such an imputation; and that he should certainly have the matter investigated to the fullest extent, so soon as we were away from the immediate presence of the enemy. General Cleburne was quite angry, and evidently was deeply hurt, under the conviction that the commander-in-chief had censured him. I asked General Cleburne who was responsible for the escape of the enemy during the afternoon and night previous. In reply to that inquiry he indulged in some criticisms of a command occupying a position on the left, and concluded by saying that "of course the responsibility rests with the commander-in-chief, as he was upon the field during the afternoon and was fully advised during the night of the movement of the enemy." The conversation at this point was abruptly terminated by the arrival of orders for both of us from yourself (Cheatham) or the commanding general.

As he left he said, "We will resume this conversation at the first convenient moment"; but in less than three hours after that time this gallant soldier was a corpse upon the bloody field of Franklin.[10]

10. J. C. Brown to B. F. Cheatham, Oct. 24, 1881, quoted in Cheatham, "The Failure at Spring Hill," *SHSP,* IX, 538-39.

CHAPTER EIGHTEEN

Battle of Franklin

AT DAWN, November 30, the Confederate army was put in motion towards Franklin, 18 miles distant. Stewart's corps first, next Cheatham's, followed later by Lee, which had reached Spring Hill from Columbia at 9 o'clock A. M. of the 30th. The Federal troops had reached Franklin early that morning. The town is located on the south side and in a bend of the Big Harpeth River, which completely encircles it on three sides, crescent in shape. The Federal entrenchments extended from a point east to one north, in a sharp curve near the bridge of the Nashville and Decatur Railroad, thence to another curve west, both flanks resting on the river, their line crossing the neck of a peninsula. On the high ground north of the river was a strong redoubt, Fort Granger, for the protection of which and their train was stationed the Third Division of the Fourth Federal corps. Their entrenchments on the south side of the river were built in front of the now celebrated Carter house, a one-story brick dwelling, west of the Columbia pike, and a large gin house stood on the east side of it. This pike ran through the entrenchments, while to the east side of it was the railroad. On a slope half a mile in front of the main works two brigades of Wagner's Federal division had been halted, and proceeded to throw up breastworks. Schofield's cavalry, under General Wilson, was on his left, on the north bank, with a detachment under General Croxton on the south side of the Harpeth, and between it and the Lewisburg pike.

General Hood formed his line of battle behind Winstead's Hill about two and a half miles from Carter's Hill, the Federal position.

Cheatham's corps was the left and center. Stewart on the right and Lee's in reserve, and Forrest was directed to protect both flanks with his cavalry. Cheatham's formation was Bate on the extreme left of the army and corps, Brown commanding Cheatham's division, on the left, or west of the Columbia pike, with his right resting on it. Cleburne on right of this pike, his right on or near the railroad. Cleburne's division was formed with Lowrey on the right, Govan center, and Granbury on the left. Upon arrival General Cheatham had ridden to the top of Winstead's Hill to make observation of the Federal position, which he at once saw was very strong and well protected, and he knew that to try to dislodge them would be a desperate attempt. Going to General Hood he said, "I do not like the looks of this fight; the enemy has an excellent position and is well fortified." "I prefer to fight them here where they have had only eighteen hours to fortify, than to strike them at Nashville where they have been strengthening themselves for three years," replied Hood. General Forrest was also opposed to a front attack, advising that the enemy be flanked by moving to the right across the Harpeth River, which was fordable, and offered to attempt it with his cavalry if adequately supported by an infantry column.

On marching from Spring Hill Cleburne dismounted, and while waiting for the head of his column to come up he drew a checker-board in the sand and with different colored leaves for men, played several games with a member of his staff. The day before the battle of Franklin the road upon which Cleburne was marching ran by Ashwood, 6 miles from Columbia, where is located the church and burial ground of the Polk family. It was a romantic place. The beautiful little Episcopal church was in the purest Gothic style, its walls and sharp-pointed roof concealed by ivy, while the flowers and shrubbery looked fresh and green even on this bleak November day. Cleburne reined in his horse and lingered for a moment to admire a place of such singular beauty, and said to one of his staff that it was "almost worth dying for, to be buried in such a beautiful spot." How little he thought how soon his body would rest there, and that the flowers then blooming would fade and wither on his grave, and that the evergreens were then so nearly ready to lay upon his coffin lid!

Upon his arrival at Winstead's Hill, whilst awaiting the formation of his command, he ascended to the summit, rested his field-glasses upon a stump, and gazed long at the enemy's entrenchments. He simply remarked, "They are very formidable." Seating himself upon the stump, he wrote rapidly for a few minutes in a small blank-book, which he returned to his pocket. He had doubtless noted down his impressions as to the situation, and it would be interesting and valuable to know what these were, but after his death his body was robbed, and the book lost.

The ground over which the advance was to be made from the base of Winstead's Hill was a level plain, about two and a quarter miles across to Carter's Hill, and save for a hedge of osage orange on the knoll near the railroad cut, and a considerable thicket of locust trees, close to and in front of the Carter house, it was entirely unobstructed and fenceless, and every part of the advance in plain view of the Federals. Cleburne, anticipating the deadly fire from artillery,—the Confederates used little or none in reply,—and wishing to expose as small front as possible, requested and received permission to form his command in columns of brigades, explaining that from such formation he could without confusion deploy it into line of battle when within small-arms range of the enemy. The advance was begun between half-past three and four o'clock in the afternoon. A regiment was thrown out as skirmishers in advance of each division. There was no halt from the time of starting until the Confederates struck the Federal breastworks. The first was that of the two exposed brigades of Wagner's division in the detached works half a mile to the front of the main line. As has been stated, the whole Confederate advance was in plain sight of the enemy, not only from Carter's Hill, but also from Schofield's headquarters across the river, two miles in the rear of the front line, the latter being under command of General Cox, who said that Wagner had orders to withdraw within the rear entrenchments as soon as he saw that

Hood intended to advance in force, and that it was Wagner's mistake that his troops made a stand and opened fire, instead of retiring.

Be this as it may, a military maxim, as old as the art of war, was disregarded, viz: "A force large enough to obstruct should never be posted in front of a line awaiting attack." Scarcely a man was lost until within fifty yards of this advanced force of Wagner, which could make but feeble resistance to the overwhelming numbers pressing upon them, and when they gave way were so closely followed by the Confederates as to prevent fire from the Federal line in rear of this advanced position, which would have been as fatal to their own men as to the assailants. And this proved the salvation of the latter, for otherwise Cox's command with its artillery could have mown down Cheatham's and Stewart's men before they could have gotten within musket range of the Federal main line on Carter's Hill. Wagner's troops broke in confusion and fled to the protection of these works. For a long time there had existed a rivalry between Cheatham's (Brown's) and Cleburne's division, and as the line rushed forward, the former troops shouted to the latter, as the Federals scattered, "We will go into the works with them," and the two divisions were pushed so rapidly that on the right of the Franklin-Columbia pike Cleburne's reached the entrenchments almost as soon as did Wagner's demoralized men. To describe truly that which followed is beyond the power of tongue or pen. In the reckless disregard of life, and in tenacity of purpose displayed, the attack has rarely been equalled, never exceeded. The men fought like demons. Often the combatants were near enough to use clubbed muskets and the bayonet. The first desperate charge by Cheatham was repeated again and again, while Stewart, on his right, threw his force upon the Federals in their entrenchments and fought with the same daring and determination that Cheatham's men had shown. Inside the Federal works a new raw regiment broke and ran to the rear, and into the gap thus created Brown's and Cleburne's men rushed, but from losses they were too weak to hold the ground against the reinforcements of the seasoned and well-disciplined brigade of Gen. Emerson Opdyke. Besides, of their leaders the inspiring voice of Cleburne was already hushed in death, and Brown lay wounded on the field. The division were driven only to the ditch outside, into which they dropped fighting as they thus lay as opportunity offered to fire at any exposure by the troops defending the works; these in turn discharging their guns by inverting and holding them perpendicularly over the fortifications. Neither antagonist at the time was able to retreat without risk of certain death. It was by such inverted gun fire that, after being wounded, General Strahl was killed in the trench. Lieutenant Mangum, Cleburne's aide, in delivering an order, finding himself between the embrasures of two Federal batteries, found it safer to remain where he was with only the ditch separating him from the enemy, than to attempt to return until the simultaneous discharge of the guns to his right and left enabled him to ride back in safety.

In the assault upon the main line the heroic Granbury, cheering on his Texas brigade, was shot through the head and instantly killed, as was also Capt. O. S. Palmer, the gallant adjutant-general of Lowrey's brigade; while Capt. B. F. Phillips of the division staff lost his leg, and Capt. Geo. A. Williams, adjutant-general, and Lieut. Frank H. Govan, aide to General Govan, were wounded. Owing to the peculiar formation of the field, the left wing of Stewart's line was thrown upon the same ground with the right of Cleburne, and the two commands were much intermingled. While the infantry fight was in progress Forrest ordered Chalmers to the left, where his cavalry charged and dislodged the enemy from every position. Forrest also directed General Jackson's cavalry division to cross Harpeth River and drive the enemy from a hill from where he was firing upon the Confederate troops on the Lewisburg pike. General Buford's cavalry was dismounted and took position in line of battle to the right of Stewart's corps, covering the ground from the Lewisburg pike to Harpeth River. Skirmishing began at once, and Buford rapidly advanced, driving the enemy's infantry across the river, where it joined Federal General Wilson's cavalry. Jackson engaged this united force of infantry and cavalry and held them in check until night, when he threw forward his pickets, and drew back across the river to replenish his exhausted ammunition.

It would require vastly more space than can here be given to record the instances of individual gallantry displayed. The deepening shadows of the afternoon betokening the approach of night, brought no relief to the weary yet determined combatants. Darkness came, but the struggle continued. Flashes of the guns upon one side would furnish light by which a volley would be directed by the other. The opposing lines at points were within easy reach of each other, and kept up the fusillade until between 9 and 10 o'clock, when it abated, simply because both sides were actually worn out physically, and human endurance could bear no further strain. Between 11 o'clock and midnight the Federals took advantage of this cessation to slip away quietly in retreat towards Nashville.

Thus ended the battle of Franklin, and its needless and horrible butchery—it cannot truthfully be called less. The engagement was short but most desperate. The hardest part of it only embraced about two hours, though there were sharp assaults from both sides up to as late as 10 o'clock or after. The fiercest fighting had been confined within a radius of not over 50 yards front, excepting the cavalry on the north side of the river. In this narrow space lay killed or wounded 1,500 men—900 Confederates and 600 Federals. The loss of general officers on the Confederate side was unparalleled by that on either side in any single battle of the war. Killed: Maj.-Gen. P. R. Cleburne, Brigadier-Generals H. B. Granbury, S. R. Gist, John Adams, and O. F. Strahl; wounded, Maj.-Gen. John C. Brown, Brigadier-Generals John C. Carter (mortally), F. M. Cockrell, A. M. Manigault, William A. Quarles, and T. M. Scott; Captured, Brig.-Gen. Geo. W. Gordon—a loss of 5 killed, 1 mortally wounded, 5 wounded and 1 captured; total loss, 12 general officers. This speaks as to how the troops were led and how such assaults were met. The loss in Cleburne's division was heavy, but unfortunately, owing to the death of its chief and the loss of other commanders, no official record of its casualties is found, other than the general one of Gen. J. A. Smith, who was not at the battle of Franklin, but as senior officer assumed command of the division a few days afterwards. He says, "I found it [the division] much reduced in numbers, especially in officers, many having been killed and wounded in the battle of Franklin." Truly did General Hardee write of Cleburne's command: "Where this division defended, no odds broke its line; where it attacked, no numbers resisted its onslaught, save only once; and there is the grave of Cleburne and his heroic division." Capt. James Dinkins in an article published in the *New Orleans Picayune,* December 30, 1902, makes the following comparison between Gettysburg and Franklin:

> The Confederates actually engaged at Franklin were as follows: Stewart's corps, 7,877; Cheatham's corps, 9,783; or a grand total of 17,660 infantry, and a little less than 5,000 cavalry. Lee's corps of 7,852 men in reserve, with 2,405 artillerists, were not engaged. The Federal infantry was in all 23,116 muskets and 70 cannon. In addition, General Wilson's cavalry exceeded 7,000, making the total Federal force 30,116 * * * It has been the pleasure of old soldiers to refer to the Gettysburg affair as the great martial drama of the war. Yet an analysis will show that it yields in grandeur, in boldness, and in results when compared with the assault on Franklin. It is a singular fact that the two assaulting columns were evenly matched, as the following figures will show. The five divisions of Brown, Cleburne, French, Walthall and Loring, at Franklin, aggregated 15,551 bayonets. The strength of Pickett's division just before the battle of Gettysburg is given at 6,548; Heth's 6,149, and Pender's, 2,814; total of 15,511—a difference of only 40 men. At Gettysburg the assaulting column was totally repulsed, while at Franklin, Brown's division captured the trenches in their front and held them against all efforts to dislodge them. At Gettysburg there were no intrenchments, save a low stone wall along a part of the Federal line, and a rail fence which had been torn down and piled up. At Franklin the enemy was sheltered by earthworks of the strongest character, and in many places over five feet high, exclusive of the ditch. The loss at Gettysburg, as shown by official figures, was a total of 4,519. A part of this loss occurred on the first day's battle. The loss of Pickett's was about 21 per cent. The loss of the assaulting column at Franklin was 6,444, exclusive of prisoners,

or 36 per cent. of all the infantry engaged—vastly more bloody than the result at Gettysburg. From whatever point we view it, the charge at Franklin exceeds in interest and tragic and dramatic results any event in modern war. History will surely place it where it belongs, as the greatest drama in American history. * * * It has been said that war ever devours the best. At Franklin perished, unhappily and without profit, some of the choicest officers of the Confederate service. * * * The fearful onset of the Confederates was in vain, because under the circumstances no number of troops could have carried the position; but the display of superb valor in officers and men was as great as ever signalized a battlefield.

Col. Henry Stone, of General Thomas's staff, who participated in the battle, says:

On came the enemy as steady and resistless as a tidal wave. A couple of guns in the advance line gave them a shot and galloped back into the works. A volley was sent into their ranks, but without causing any delay in the array. A moment more, and with that wild "Rebel yell," which once heard is never forgotten, the great human wave swept along. We were struck by the resistless sweep of Cleburne's and Brown's divisions. In that wild rush, in which friend and foe were intermingled, and the piercing "Rebel yell" rose high above the "Yankee cheer," nearly 700 [Federals] were made prisoners. * * * With loud shouts of, "Let's go into the works with them!" the triumphant Confederates, now more like a wild howling mob than an organized army, swept on to the very works, with hardly a check from any quarter. So fierce was the rush that a number of the fleeing soldiers—officers and men—dropped exhausted into the ditch, and lay there while the terrific contest raged over their heads, till, under cover of darkness, they could crawl safely inside the entrenchments. * * * The tremendous onset, the wild yells, the whole infernal din of the strife were too much for such an undisciplined body. As they saw their comrades from the advance line rush to the rear they too turned and fled. The contagion spread, and in a few minutes a disorderly stream was pouring down the pike past the Carter house towards the town. The guns posted on each side of the Columbia pike were abandoned, and the works, for the space of more than a regimental front, both east and west of the pike were deserted. Into the gap thus made without an instant's delay, swarmed the jubilant Confederates, urged on by Cleburne and Brown, and took possession of both works and guns. * * * It is impossible to exaggerate the fierce energy with which the Confederate soldiers, that short November afternoon, threw themselves against our works, fighting with what seemed the very madness of despair.[1]

Capt. W. O. Dodd, of Louisville, Kentucky, says:

> Our loss was about 5,000 men, including 5 generals killed and 6 wounded. I could but feel that the lives of these men were a useless sacrifice. It seemed to me to be a rashness occasioned by a blunder of the day before. It was an attempt to make good by reckless daring the blunder which incapacity had occasioned the preceding day. * * * The next morning we *should* have buried our dead and those of the enemy, and retired from the State. While we held the battlefield, and the dead of our adversaries, we were disheartend and demoralized. We had witnessed on one day a brilliant flank movement terminated by lying down by the roadside in order to let the enemy pass by, and on the next day saw the army led out in a slaughter pen to be shot down like animals. * * * But instead of retreating at once and saving the remnant of a magnificent army, we moved up and formed around Nashville. Our little army, now about 23,000 strong, was stretched for miles around the city * * * and we were not strong enough to make a good picket line. The rout and retreat were inevitable. Thomas accumulated an army of 82,000. * * * It seemed then, as it looks now as we glance back over the scene, that a hand stronger than armies had decreed our overthrow.[2]

The following is an extract from a letter of Lieut.-Gen. A. P. Stewart in *The Confederate Veteran* of September, 1908, in reply to a recent publication regarding Spring Hill and Franklin.

> * * * Speaking of the battle of Franklin, he [the author of the publication referred to] says: "To assault was a terrible proposition to troops who, during Johnston's long retreat, had

1. Henry Stone, "Repelling Hood's Invasion of Tennessee," *Battles and Leaders,* IV, 451.
2. W. O. Dodd, "Reminiscences of Hood's Tennessee Campaign," *SHSP,* IX, 523.

been trained to avoid charging breastworks." What breastworks were in their way which it was necessary to charge? This writer has evidently accepted as true General Hood's claim that the Army of Tennessee was demoralized by General Johnston's conduct of the Atlanta campaign. There could not be a greater mistake. If anything could have demoralized that army, it would have been the removal of General Johnston from the command and the substitution of General Hood.

The truth is, the failure at Spring Hill was General Hood's own failure. He was at the front with the advanced troops, or could have been, and should have been; and if he gave "explicit orders for an immediate attack and occupation of the pike" and they were disobeyed, the remedy was entirely in his own hands. If it had been true that Cheatham and I disobeyed orders to make an immediate attack and absented ourselves from our commands that evening and Hood had overlooked such offenses, that would have demonstrated his incapacity for the chief command.

The author * * * excuses the attack on Franklin on the ground that Hood saw no alternative, since he had lost the one opportunity of the campaign at Spring Hill the night before. The loss at Spring Hill could have been fully retrieved at Franklin by crossing the Harpeth River by fords above Franklin and getting a strong position among the Brentwood hills in the rear of the enemy. * *[3]

3. A. P. Stewart, "A Critical Narrative," *Confederate Veteran,* XVI, (1908), 463.

CHAPTER NINETEEN

Death of Cleburne

THERE HAVE BEEN numerous sensational and dramatic accounts of Cleburne's death written, the most of them purely fanciful or imaginative, such as his horse being killed just when his fore feet were over the top of the Federal entrenchments, and the General himself falling "pierced by forty-nine balls." His favorite horse, "Stonewall," not being fit for service at Spring Hill he was riding his other, "Red Pepper," a large dark bay, which had been wounded by a shell in that engagement. So the General went into the Franklin fight mounted on a borrowed horse, which was killed under him, between the advance position of Wagner and the Federal main line. One of his couriers, James Brandon, of Mississippi, dismounted to give him his horse, which was killed by a cannon shot as the General was in the act of mounting, and at the same moment Brandon's thigh was shattered by a rifle ball. Not stopping to get another animal, Cleburne proceeded on foot to lead his men. In view of the conflicting statements as to Cleburne's death the writer spared no pains to get at the exact circumstances, which he believes he has accomplished in the following letter from General Govan, who was, as far as can be ascertained, the last officer to speak with General Cleburne, and any statement made by him can be relied upon as absolutely correct.

MAGNOLIA, MISSISSIPPI, *September 3, 1907.*

MY DEAR CAPTAIN:

I understand from your letter (August 20th) you simply desire a restatement of my version as made to you during the reunion at New Orleans, of the death of our heroic division commander. I shall confine myself, therefore, to the desperate charge of our division. General Hood, smarting under the charge of his failure at Spring Hill, determined to attack the enemy in his position at Franklin. His division (Cleburne's) was selected to attack the main line of the enemy, extending from the Spring Hill (Columbia) pike to the right, passing the old gin-house, which was the most strongly entrenched [part] of the Federal position. Our division occupied a position on Winstead's Hill from which we were expected to advance. General Cleburne had just returned from a consultation with General Hood and the other generals, all of whom were opposed to attacking [along] the main pike entering the town, as the enemy could have been flanked and compelled to abandon his strongly fortified position. General Hood had directed General Cleburne to call his brigade commanders together and give specific instructions as to the method of attack and the importance of breaking the Federal lines. If we took Franklin we would take Nashville, which was the key to the independence of the Southern Confederacy. We were directed to advance by the head of columns, and as soon as we came under fire, to fix bayonets, charge, and go over the breastworks and break the enemy's line at all hazards.

General Cleburne seemed to be more despondent than I ever saw him.* I was the last one to receive any instructions from him, and as I saluted and bade him good-bye I remarked, "Well, General, there will not be many of us that will get back to Arkansas," and he replied, "Well, Govan, if we are to die, let

*This statement as to "depression" is at variance with that of General Hood's (*Advance and Retreat,* p. 294): "About that time Cleburne returned, and expressing himself with an enthusiasm which he had never before in our intercourse, said, 'General, I am ready and have more hope in the final success of our cause than I have had at any time since the first gun was fired." It seems incredible that as clear headed, intelligent a soldier as Cleburne *could* have made such remarks at a time when any one above the degree of idiocy must have known that chances for final success of the Confederacy were desperate.—I. A. B.

us die like men." After receiving his final orders we were directed to advance, which was about 2 o'clock in the afternoon. We had to advance across an old open common, subjected to the heavy fire of the Federal forces. We met the enemy in a short space of time and carried the first line commanded by General Wagner. When that line was broken, General Cleburne's object seemed to be to run into the rear line with the fleeing Federals from Wagner's division. About that time General Cleburne's horse was killed. His courier brought him another, and as he was in the act of mounting, this horse was killed. He then disappeared in the smoke of battle, and that was the last time I ever saw him alive. I spoke to his aide-de-camp, Mangum, and told him I was sure the General would be killed, as I did not see how he could escape with his life under such terrific fire, and as he never again appeared in the lines, confirmed my opinion that he was dead. The above is the substance of what I am able to recall after a space of forty odd years.

Yours very sincerely,

D. C. Govan,

To Capt. Irving A. Buck.

In the article of Captain Dinkins, before referred to, he quotes from a letter of General Govan, as follows:

> General Cleburne was not killed while attempting to leap his horse over the Federal entrenchments, as some have said. The manner in which he met his death was about as follows, and from personal observation and credible statements of others I believe these to be about the facts of the matter: General Cleburne had two horses killed under him in the attack on Franklin. I was very near him when his first horse was killed. The impetus at which he was moving carried the horse forward after his death wound, and he fell almost in the ditch on the outside of the entrenchments. One of the couriers dismounted and gave him his horse, and while in the act of mounting, this second horse was killed by a cannon ball fired as well as I remember from the gin-house. General Cleburne then moved forward on foot, waving his cap, and I lost sight of him in the smoke and din of battle, and he must have met his death in a few seconds afterwards. All of this occurred near the intersec-

> tion of the pike, and his body was found within 20 yards of where I saw him last waving his cap and urging his command forward. Never in any attack during the war did troops display greater gallantry—not Pickett's division at Gettysburg, nor the Old Guard at Waterloo—than when the heroic commander of the Arkansas division fell, sword in hand, near the entrenchments in that desperate and ill-fated attack on Franklin.[1]

Cleburne was pierced through the heart with a single rifle ball and fell in front of the Federal trenches near the old gin-house. General Cheatham, pointing to the spot in 1883, said: "Here one of the best soldiers that ever drew sword gave up his life." Cleburne's absence from his line caused the uneasiness of his staff to increase as the hours went by, until the unwilling conviction was forced upon them that some disaster had befallen him, which was hoped not to be greater than wounding or capture. But all doubts were removed by the finding of his body, the best account of which is given by Mr. John McQuade, of Vicksburg, Mississippi:

> The terrible report that Cleburne was missing ran through our ranks that whole dreadful night, and our fears and anxieties were almost disheartening. We almost prayed that he might have been wounded only, or captured; but that was not to be. I and two others were the first to discover his dead body at early dawn the next morning. He was about 40 or 50 yards from the works. He lay flat upon his back as if asleep, his military cap partly over his eyes. He had on a new gray uniform, the coat of the sack or blouse pattern. It was unbuttoned and open; the lower part of his vest was unbuttoned and open. He wore a white linen shirt, which was stained with blood on the front part of the left side, or just left of the abdomen. This was the only sign of a wound I saw on him, and I believe it is the only one he had received. I have always been inclined to think that feeling his end was near, he had thus laid himself down to die, or that his body had been carried there during the night. He was in his sock feet, his boots having been stolen. His watch, sword belt and other valuables all gone, his body having been robbed during the night * * * Upon discovering Cleburne's body I went to some parties who had an ambulance up at the

1. James Dinkins in New Orleans *Picayune,* Dec. 30, 1902.

> breastworks and were picking up the wounded and the more distinguished of the dead officers. I found the ambulance to be in charge of Rev. Thomas Markham, the well-known Presbyterian minister of New Orleans. * * * He was chaplain of Featherston's Mississippi brigade, Loring's division. I pointed Cleburne's body out to him, and asked him to come with the ambulance and get it. The men at that moment were lifting up the body of Gen. John Adams * * *[2]

In corroboration of this statement an extract copy of letter to him from Dr. Markham is given:

NEW ORLEANS, *January 26, 1893.*

Mr. JOHN MCQUADE.

> DEAR FRIEND: * * Our brigade (Featherston's of which I was chaplain) ambulance was in my charge. It was just after daylight in the gray of the morning. The men were in the act of lifting General Adams's body into the ambulance, when you rode up and reported that General Cleburne's body lay on the field. The ambulance was at once driven to the spot indicated by you. His body was placed beside that of General Adams's and both taken to Colonel McGavock's residence. The two were placed together on the lower gallery, perfectly protected and cared for until their friends removed them. Your recollection of the position of their bodies on the field, when Cleburne was discovered by you, and Adams by me, agrees with mine in every particular.

THOMAS R. MARKHAM.[3]

The first interment of Cleburne was at Rose Hill, near Franklin; but mindful of his remark as he passed St. John's Church at Ashwood, a few days before the battle of Franklin, his remains were removed there, and by his side were buried his brave comrades, Generals Granbury and Strahl, who fell in the same action. Years afterwards Cleburne's remains were claimed by the State of Arkansas and removed to Helena and placed beneath an elegant monument erected by the Ladies' Memorial Association. Touching this removal,

---

2. John McQuade, *Battles and Leaders,* IV, 439.
3. *Ibid.*

I here quote from General Chalmers's address on "Forrest and his Campaigns":

> Poor Cleburne, he was a noble specimen of the Irish gentleman. I knew him as a promising young lawyer, and watched with interest his brilliant career in arms. He supplied my division with ammunition on the morning of Franklin, and we parted to meet no more. I shall never forget the solemn scene that occurred when his body passed through Memphis, after the surrender, to its final resting-place in his adopted State of Arkansas. Like the burial of Sir John Moore, it was a sad and silent scene as we laid him down on the steamer's deck. Around him stood Jefferson Davis, Isham G. Harris, and the few Confederate Generals then in Memphis. * * An Irishman approached, and in humble accents asked permission to kiss the coffin of his dead commander. Mr. Davis noded a silent assent. Kneeling and making the sign of the cross on his breast, the humble soldier lingered a moment in prayer, and then pressed his lips with fervor on the head of the coffin. Not a word was said; but each hat was involuntarily lifted from the head and silent tears stole down the manly cheeks of those who were present.[4]

A fanciful story gained credence and a poem was written based upon it, that Cleburne on the morning of the battle, noticing that one of his officers was barefooted, pulled off his boots, and insisted that the captain should put them on, remarking that "no Confederate soldier shall walk with naked feet while I ride fully shod." This story is pure fiction and absurd on its face. No doubt his generous impulses would have prompted him to this, but his sense of duty would have forbidden his so disqualifying himself for its performance. The only foundation for the alleged incident was that Cleburne's body was found in stocking feet, it having, as before stated, been robbed of boots.

The history of Cleburne and his command would be incomplete without giving quotations showing the estimate in which both were held by their associates and superiors. Gen. R. E. Lee spoke of him as

A meteor shining from a clouded sky.

---

4. J. R. Chalmers, "Forrest and His Campaigns," *SHSP,* VII, 481.

General Hardee wrote:

> Two continents now claim his name; eight millions of people revere his memory; two great communities raise monuments to his virtues, and history will take up his fame, and hand it down to time for exampling wherever a courage without stain, a manhood without blemish, and integrity that knew no compromise, and a patriotism that withheld no sacrifice are honored of mankind.[5]

General Buckner, speaking of Cleburne and his command, says:

> And particularly I recall the virtues of the Irish character, when a few short months ago I stood in the twilight hour over the grave of one of the noblest sons of Ireland. As I looked upon the plain board inscribed with his name in pencil lines, and upon the withered flowers which the fair hands of our countrywomen had strewn upon his grave, I wept tears to the glorious memory of General Patrick Cleburne. He commanded a brigade in my division, and afterwards succeeded me in the command of troops whom I cannot more praise than to say he was one of the few worthy to command such men. And conspicuous among such gallant men and worthy soldiers of such a glorious leader were Irishmen, who illustrated their high military virtues on so many fields and displayed on so many occasions their fidelity to the cause they had espoused.[6]

General Hood says:

> Major-General Cleburne had been distinguished for his admirable conduct upon many fields, and his loss at this moment was irreparable. * * * He was a man of equally quick perception and strong character, and was especially in one respect in advance of many of our people. He possessed the boldness and wisdom to earnestly advocate at an early period of the war the freedom of the negro and the enrollment of the young and able-bodied men of that race. This stroke of policy and additional source of strength to our armies would, in my opinion, have given us our independence.[7]

---

5. W. J. Hardee in J. F. Maguire, *The Irish in America,* 505.
6. S. B. Buckner in *Ibid,* 585.
7. J. B. Hood, *Advance and Retreat,* 296.

Colonel Henry Stone (Federal) says of Cleburne's division:

> A division unsurpassed for courage, energy, and endurance by any other in the Confederate Army.[8]

Maj.-Gen. (afterwards Governor and Senator) William B. Bate, of Tennessee, in an address delivered on the field of Franklin, October 5, 1889, spoke thus of Cleburne:

> Just to the left there fell Major-General Cleburne, whose name in history is circled with a halo as bright as the sun-burst on the green flag of his native Ireland.

President Jefferson Davis, writing of the battle of Franklin in his "Rise and Fall of the Confederate Government," pays the Arkansas chieftain a tribute which ranks him with Lee and Jackson as the third star in its galaxy of military leaders:

> Around Cleburne thickly lay the gallant men, who in his desperate assault followed him with implicit confidence that in another army was given Stonewall Jackson, and in the one case, as in the other, a vacancy was created which could never be filled.[9]

The editor of the *Houston Telegraph* draws a parallel between the Earl of Cardigan, who led the charge of the Light Brigade, in the Crimean war, and General Cleburne, and the following picture is given of him:

> The same reflections apply to that grand hero of the Confederate army of the west, Major-General Cleburne. He was as brave a man as the Earl of Cardigan. He was brave as any man the world ever saw. He was not brave as most brave men are, from the high moral qualities of the soul alone, but like the Earl of Cardigan he was physically brave. He had a contempt for fear: he disdained danger: he defied death. He was the most perfect specimen of a truly brave soldier—brave to perfection—that it was our good fortune to become acquainted with during the war. When commanding in battle, the hail of bullets and the tornado of all-destroying shells, so far from

---

8. Henry Stone, "Repelling Hood's Invasion of Tennessee," *Battles and Leaders,* IV, 444.

9. Jefferson Davis, *The Rise and Fall of the Confederate Government* (New York, 1881), II, 577.

impressing his mind, or relaxing the steel springs of his nerves, did not even attract his attention, except so far as his eagle eye watched the swaying fortunes of the fight. His courage, too, manifested a most rare combination. He was as ferocious as a tiger, and yet as cold-blooded as a fish, and as impassible as an owl. He fought his men so as to kill and destroy as many of the enemy as possible in the shortest space of time, and yet he smiled with a grim delight at the success of his measures for the destruction of human life, and cooly and nonchalantly reveled in the carnage of blood. Although he taught his men assiduously that the art of war was the art of killing, so that every soldier in his command soon became accustomed to fire in battle with the same coolness and precision as when shooting squirrels or deer, yet he was noted for teaching his men how to preserve themselves from the fire of the enemy, detecting with quickness of instinct every advantage of ground, natural or artificial, for such preservation, and teaching his men the same sagacity and true courage. His courage, though cool and calculating, was electric in its influence upon his men. There never was a time when his simple presence and voice would not reform and reinspire the most utterly routed and broken brigade or regiment. Men seemed to be afraid to *be* afraid where he was. He did nothing to win the popularity of his men, and yet they worshipped him. We are satisfied, even at this late day, that he was the most effective, reliable and able division commander we ever knew. The drill, discipline, and inspection of his whole division were as perfect as that of a single company, under a captain of similar qualities to his own.

Capt. W. O. Dodd, before quoted, says:

* * And just a little back the gallant old soldier, General Pat Cleburne, lay dead. He was the idol of his command, and a better soldier never died for any cause.[10]

Fulsome as these willing tributes may seem to the present reader, yet those who served with Cleburne will know that they are but just, and that "Prex-Chevalier" died, as he had lived, *"sans peur et sans reproche."*

10. W. O. Dodd, "Reminiscences of Hood's Tennessee Campaign," *SHSP,* IX, 523.

CHAPTER TWENTY

Advance to Nashville — Defeat and the End

ON THE 1ST OF DECEMBER the army was ordered forward in the direction of Nashville, Lee's corps in advance, followed by Stewart's and Cheatham's, and the troops bivouacked that night in the vicinity of Brentwood. On the morning of the 2d the march was resumed and line of battle formed in front of Nashville. Lee's corps was placed in the center, and across the Franklin pike; Stewart's occupied the left, and Cheatham's the right, their flanks extending as near the Cumberland River as they would reach, while Forrest's cavalry filled the gap between them and the river. Cleburne's division was the extreme infantry right of the army, its left, Govan's brigade, resting on the Nolensville pike, and the right, Lowrey's brigade, on the Nashville and Chattanooga Railroad cut, about two and a half miles from the city. Granbury's brigade was in reserve to support the other brigades, or check any movement of the enemy on the division's right flank. Mercer's brigade, Gen. J. A. Smith commanding, which had been detached at Florence, joined the division on December 6, and by seniority General Smith took command of the division. On December 7, Smith's (Mercer's) brigade, under command of Col. Chas. H. Olmstead, was again detached, and ordered to report to General Forrest, who was operating against a Federal force at Murfreesboro, in rear of the Confederate right. Thus, as at Chickamauga, Atlanta, Spring Hill and Franklin, the division had only three brigades. Why General Hood, after his losses at Franklin, should have elected to advance on Nashville is beyond comprehension. It is a well-established military maxim that a force investing a fortified position should be largely superior to the invested. Without reasonable hope of reinforcements, General Hood, with a little in excess of 23,000 men of all arms, formed line in front of Nashville, which had for three years been strengthened by the most elaborate and formidable works, while it was known that General Thomas's 82,000 men were being added to constantly. Granting that Hood could repel or defeat the attack of Thomas upon him, the latter could retire into his impregnable defenses, await further reinforcements, and, thus strengthened, make another attack upon Hood's first inferior force, which would have necessarily been reduced by the natural casualties of battle; meanwhile, the Federal cavalry could have operated in rear of and upon Hood's line of communication for supplying his army with subsistence, to meet which Forrest would have had to be withdrawn from the front of Nashville, and Hood's fighting force reduced to the extent of such detachment.

In the interval between his arrival and December 15 General Hood was engaged in strengthening his line of investment and making the best disposition practicable to resist assault. The attack was delayed by General Thomas, despite urgent orders from General Grant, until the abatement of the cold, rain and sleet permitted the movement of troops over the heretofore frozen ground. At daylight on the morning of the 15th he moved against Hood's right, not intended as a real attack, though it had that effect, while General Thomas's plan of battle was to demonstrate on the Confederate right, while his right should make a grand left wheel, with his entire right wing assaulting and, if possible, overlapping and enveloping the left of Hood. In his book, "Advance and Retreat," General Hood says:

> Throughout that day [December 15th] they were repulsed at all points of the general line with heavy loss, and only succeeded towards evening in capturing the infantry out-posts on our left, and with them the small force, together with the artillery, posted in these unfinished works. Finding that the

main movement of the Federals was directly against our left, the chief engineer was instructed to carefully select a line in prolongation of the left flank. Cheatham's corps was withdrawn from the right during the night of the 15th and posted on the left of Stewart—Cheatham's left flank resting near the Brentwood Hills. In this position the men were ordered to construct breastworks during that same night. The morning of the 16th found us with Lee's right on Overton Hill. At an early hour the enemy made a general attack along our front, and were again and again repulsed at all points with heavy loss, especially in Lee's front. About 3:30 P. M. the Federals concentrated a number of guns against a portion of our line, which passed over a mound to the left of our center, and which had been occupied during the night. This point was favorable for massing troops for an assault under cover of artillery. Accordingly, the enemy availed himself of the advantage presented, massed a body of men—apparently one division—at the base of this mound, and, under the fire of artillery, which prevented our men from raising their heads above the breastworks, made a sudden and gallant charge up to and over our entrenchments. Our line, thus pierced, gave way; soon thereafter it broke at all points, and I beheld for the first and only time a Confederate army abandon the field in confusion. * * * I was seated upon my horse not far in rear when the breach was effected, and soon discovered that all hope to rally the troops was vain. I did not, I might say, anticipate a break at that time, as our forces up to that moment had repulsed the Federals at every point, and were waving their colors in defiance, crying out to the enemy, "Come on, Come on!" * * * The day before the rout the artillery posted in the detached works had been captured; a number of guns in the main line were abandoned at the time of the disaster, for the reason that the horses could not be brought forward in time to remove them. Thus the total number of guns captured amounted to 54.[1]

In this engagement General Govan was wounded in the throat, and the command of the brigade devolved upon its senior colonel, P. V. Green, Fifth Arkansas. Upon the defeat of the Confederate forces they were withdrawn some 4 miles to Brentwood, where the

---

1. Hood, *Advance and Retreat,* 302.

troops were "somewhat collected and Lieutenant-General Lee took command of the rear-guard, camping for the night in the vicinity."

On the 17th the retreat was continued towards Columbia, and the army camped for the night at Spring Hill. During the day the Federal cavalry pressed with boldness and activity, charging the infantry repeatedly with the sabre, and at times penetrating the lines, and Lieutenant-General Lee, commanding the covering forces, was wounded. The retreat was continued across Duck River to Columbia, the corps alternating as rear-guards to the army. At this point, on the 21st, the army resumed its march for Pulaski, with protection of a rearguard under that indomitable and able leader, General Forrest, assisted by the skillful and no less gallant Major-General Walthall, with Ector's, Strahl's, Maney's, Granbury's and Palmer's infantry brigades. These met and held in check every assault of the victorious enemy. Contesting the ground inch by inch, making stand and fighting from every favorable point, and always with success, until the main army reached the Tennessee River at Bainbridge on the 25th, and completed its crossing on the 27th, without further molestation, and from this point by easy marches to Tupelo, Mississippi.

It is difficult to give an accurate description of the hardships endured by the troops in this retreat over frozen ground, with worn, and in many instances no shoes, their exposed feet bleeding from the laceration of the rough roads and sharp stones, and their tattered garments forming but scant protection against the cutting, wintry winds, and with such short rations as to add the pangs of hunger to their other miseries.

At his own request, on January 23d, General Hood was relieved from command, and Lieut.-Gen. Richard Taylor was assigned to command of the Army of Tennessee, or probably, to speak more correctly, he was appointed to assist at its funeral, for it was now plainly in death's rigor.

Far be it from the intention of this work to cast any imputation upon one so gallant and worthy as General Hood, or to attempt to pluck from his brow one laurel of the many so well earned in scores of battles. Personally as brave as Ney and as patriotic as Washington, he did not possess the great-mindedness of Lee to acknowledge the responsibility which justly belonged to him. The flank movements on July 22 at Atlanta, and that on Schofield at Spring Hill, were the inspiration of genius in conception, and were not entirely successful in results on account of his failure to see to the proper execution of details—again good strategy, but poor tactics. As a brigade and division commander he was seldom rivalled and never surpassed, but higher promotion seemed to have been beyond his capacity. As a corps commander he made no special reputation, and became captious and critical in his disposition, and impatient and restive under control, and, to quote Gen. "Dick" Taylor, "Unwillingness to obey is often interpreted by governments into capacity for command."[2] This may be the reason that after holding the rank of lieutenant-general for only six months he was placed in command of an army. Every failure or disaster he attributed to some subordinate. This was the case as to the able and reliable Hardee, whom he charged with the failure at Peach Tree Creek on July 20, and that of Atlanta two days later, and again at Jonesboro, Georgia, on September 1. It appears strange, and would seem effectually to refute the charges as to the first two, that if he failed on these occasions, that this officer should at Jonesboro, 6 weeks later, when the fate of Atlanta depended upon that point being held, be assigned to the command, 22 miles distant from army headquarters, and entrusted with two of the three corps, or over two-thirds of the army; and on July 28, when Stewart's and Lee's corps were engaged at Atlanta, General Hood called Hardee from his own command, on the extreme right of the army, to take command of these two corps on the extreme left, at a time of apprehended disaster. Such confidence would not seem to indicate that General Hood had any suspicion of Hardee's capacity or loyalty to his commander-in-chief, up to Jonesboro, whatever opinion he may have had after.

Again, upon that gallant old soldier of two wars, and a hundred battles, Gen. B. F. Cheatham, Hood placed the onus of the lost

2. Taylor, *Destruction and Reconstruction,* 217.

opportunity at Spring Hill, Tennessee, which first caused the frightful slaughter at Franklin and the subsequent defeat at Nashville. The charitable construction to place upon this disposition on Hood's part is perhaps as stated by General Taylor:

> The mistake [at Spring Hill] may be ascribed to Hood's want of physical activity, occasioned by severe wounds and amputations.[3]

This may probably give the key to his inclination to saddle upon others the responsibility which in part, at least, was really his own, for in his book "Advance and Retreat," in one of the instances before referred to, he claims that disaster would not have ensued had he been present on the field. He was on the field at Nashville, but the disaster there was not averted or checked.[4]

After the Tennessee campaign, from ill health, caused by long service and exposure, that able, faithful Christian soldier General Lowrey resigned. This left the division only two of its original four brigadiers,—J. A. Smith and D. C. Govan,—the latter absent by reason of wounds received at Nashville.

It having been determined to send the remnant of the Army of Tennessee to confront Sherman in Georgia and the Carolinas, to Lieutenant-General Taylor's troops, with the addition of Forrest's cavalry, was confided the defense of Mississippi and Alabama.

When Gen. Jos. E. Johnston was relieved at Atlanta President Davis had asserted that he would never again appoint him to important command; but after Sherman had made his march to the sea, captured Savannah and Columbia, and forced the evacuation of Charleston, and with his army spread out for sixty miles in width was pillaging, burning property, and harrying the defenseless citizens of South Carolina, members of Congress, State officials, and the newspapers united in the demand that General Johnston, in whom they had never lost confidence, should be reinstated to defend them. Gen. R. E. Lee, writing to the Secretary of War February 19, said:

3. *Ibid,* 216.
4. J. B. Hood, *Advance and Retreat,* 287.

> General Beauregard * * * has a difficult task to perform * * * and one of his best officers (General Hardee) is incapacitated by sickness. I have heard his own health is indifferent. * * * Should his strength give way, there is no one on duty in the departments that could replace him, nor have I any one to send there. Gen. J. E. Johnston is the only officer whom I know who has the confidence of the army and people, and if he was ordered to report to me, I would place him on duty there.[5]

General Lee had then recently been appointed General-in-Chief of all the Confederate armies, and to him General Johnston was ordered, by the War Department, to report, and on February 22 was by General Lee assigned to command of the departments of South Carolina, Georgia, Florida and Tennessee, and he immediately began active steps to concentrate his forces to oppose Sherman. The transfer of the Army of Tennessee was made as expeditiously as the weather and the limited and wretched condition of the railroads would permit. Cheatham's corps operated in South Carolina, and gradually approached Greensboro and Charlotte, North Carolina. A rendezvous camp was established in Augusta, Georgia, for the stragglers of the Army of Tennessee and the returning wounded and furloughed troops of both armies, until several thousand were thus assembled, when they were temporarily brigaded without reference to State or regimental organization. Lieutenant-General Lee was placed in chief command and General Govan in command of one of the brigades. Both of these generals were just recovering from wounds received in the Tennessee campaign. Thus this force left Augusta on March 18, and after marching through South Carolina, arrived at Rock Hill on the 29th, from which point the troops were sent by rail to Smithfield, North Carolina.

Upon the approach of the Federal left wing—the Fourteenth and Twentieth Corps—to Bentonville, North Carolina, where it was somewhat separated from the right wing, General Johnston determined to attack it with the troops of Bragg, Hardee, and such of the Army of Tennessee as had arrived. General Hardee led the advance

---

5. *O.R.,* XLVII, part 1, 1044.

at 3 P. M. of the 19th, and the enemy was routed in a few minutes; but about 6 o'clock P. M. the arrival of the Federal Seventeenth Corps, as reinforcements, stopped the pursuit of the Confederates, but they held the ground they had gained, which they retained until the night of the 21st. During the afternoon of that day, about 4 o'clock, the Seventeenth Corps penetrated the thin line of cavalry forming Johnston's extreme left, and moved upon Bentonville. This was met in front by General Hardee, with Cumming's Georgia brigade, while cavalry directed by Generals Hampton and Wheeler was thrown upon its flanks. In this affair Cumming's brigade and the Eighth Texas Cavalry distinguished themselves. In the latter General Hardee's only son, a promising youth of sixteen, fell mortally wounded while gallantly riding in the foremost ranks in the last charge made by the Army of Tennessee. The only two brigades of Cleburne's division engaged in the Bentonville battle were those of Smith and Govan, the latter commanded by Col. P. V. Green, Fifth Arkansas. The brigades of Lowrey and Granbury had not reached that point. Major-General Bate commanded the portion of Cheatham's corps present and Gen. J. A. Smith, the division. Both in their official reports speak in praise of the part taken by the brigades of Smith and Govan.

After the affair of March 21, finding that Sherman was heavily reinforcing in his front, on the 22d General Johnston withdrew to the vicinity of Smithfield. Here a reorganization of the army was effected. Gen. John C. Brown was assigned to command of Cleburne's division, which was once more placed in the corps of its old commander, General Hardee. In this reorganization the old division was virtually broken up and lost its identity. Some idea may be formed of the depletion of its ranks when the new formation of Brown's division was constituted by Smith's brigade.

First Florida formed by consolidation of First, Third, Fourth, Sixth and Seventh Infantry, and First Cavalry, Florida.

First Georgia formed by consolidation of First, Fifty-seventh, and Sixty-third Georgia Infantry.

Fifty-fourth Georgia formed by consolidation of Thirty-seventh and Fifty-fourth regiments and Fourth Battalion Georgia Sharpshooters.

Govan's brigade was consolidated into one regiment, viz.: First, Second, Fifth, Sixth, Seventh, Eighth, Thirteenth, Fifteenth, Nineteenth and Twenty-fourth Arkansas and Third Confederate, Col. E. A. Howell commanding.

Granbury's brigade, assigned to Govan, was consolidated in one regiment, viz.: Sixth, Seventh, Tenth and Fifteenth Texas Infantry, and Seventeenth, Eighteenth and Twenty-fourth, and Twenty-fifth Texas (dismounted cavalry), Lieut.-Col. William A. Ryan commanding.

Of Lowrey's brigade, the Sixteenth, Thirty-third, and Forty-fifth Alabama regiments were assigned to Shelley's brigade, Loring's division, Stewart's corps, and the Third, Eighth, Fifteenth, and Thirty-second Mississippi assigned to Sharp's brigade, Hill's division, Lee's corps.

On April 10 the army was put in motion in the direction of Raleigh, where it arrived on the morning of the 12th. From thence, on the 13th it marched to Chapel Hill, where it camped, and by the 16th reached and bivouacked near Salem, where the division remained until the 23d, when it moved and camped 10 miles in direction of Greensboro, the vicinity of which it reached on the evening of the 26th. While at Salem the first news of President Lincoln's assassination was received. On the 27th General Johnston's announcement of surrender was made, and on May 2, paroles were issued to the troops. The number to the division was 2,358.

* * * * *

Thus ended the military life of as gallant, brave, and patriotic an army as ever existed—an army equal to Cæsar's Tenth Legion, or the Old Guard of Napoleon, and not exceeded by them. The Confederate soldier, "a devoted lover of the cause, which, though lost, was garland with glories," was too intelligent not to understand at that period that with the immense disproportion of numbers it was but a question of time—and a very short time—when the Confederates would be overcome. Still, the rank and file were unwilling to admit this, even to themselves, and had the negotiations between Sherman and Johnston failed, and the old division been ordered to cut their way through, they would without doubt have responded unhesitatingly and not stopped to consider odds. But when their trusted leaders, Lee and Johnston, decided that only capitulation remained, their verdict was submitted to with grief, but without murmur. Their feelings may be likened to one who, having suffered the agonies of impending bankruptcy, experiences actual relief when final foreclosure ensues.

Truly the old "Stonewall Division of the West" "sat at the cradle of the Confederacy and followed its hearse." Since their last camp near Greensboro 43 years have elapsed, and the majority of those then present have since followed, as they did for four years in the field, their leaders "over the river," and against the names of the surviving remnant, in the course of nature, must soon be written

Finis.

BATTLE REPORTS

and

Appendices

MURFREESBORO

*Report of Maj.-Gen. Patrick R. Cleburne, C. S. A., Commanding Division.**

HEADQUARTERS CLEBURNE'S DIVISION,
HARDEE'S CORPS, ARMY OF TENNESSEE,
Tullahoma, Tenn., January 31, 1863.

On December 26, 1862, three brigades of my division were stationed at College Grove, near Eaglesville, about 20 miles west of Murfreesboro. The Fourth Brigade, under command of Brig.-Gen. S. A. M. Wood, was stationed at Triune, 4 miles north of College Grove, on the Nashville and Shelbyville turnpike.

On the evening of the same day I had information that the enemy had driven back the cavalry and occupied Nolensville, in my front.

During the night I received orders from General Hardee, who had gone in person to the front, to have everything in readiness for a movement and to be prepared for any emergency. I also received instructions as to the roads to be taken by my train and fighting force, respectively, in case of a retreat on Murfreesboro.

Early on the morning of the 27th, I received orders from the same source to take up a position on the turnpike about one mile north of my encampment. While making this disposition, I received orders from General Hardee to move the three brigades with me to Murfreesboro by the routes previously decided upon; also that Wood's brigade would remain at Triune and assist General Wharton's cavalry to retard the farther advance of the enemy.

For the proceedings of Wood's brigade under this order, I respectfully refer you to the report of Brig.-Gen. S. A. M. Wood, herewith transmitted.

I immediately moved as directed; marched all day, part of it over a miserable road and through a cold, drenching rain, and encamped after nightfall on the Salem turnpike, within one mile of Stone's River.

On the morning of the 28th, General Hardee ordered me to form line of battle north of Murfreesboro and east of Stone's River, my line to face north, its left resting on the river, its right near the Lebanon turnpike, 800 or 1,000 yards in rear of a line already occupied by Breckinridge's division.

Wood's brigade, falling back slowly before General McCook's army corps, impeding his advance wherever opportunity offered, finally reached Stone's River and rejoined the division on the morning of the 29th.

I law, inactive, in line of battle until the evening of the 30th, when I received orders to move from the right to the left of the army. Arriving at the fording place on Stone's River, I received orders to remain there until

---

**O.R.*, XX, part 1, 843-852.

General Hardee had examined the ground and determined my position. It was dark when staff officers were sent to order me forward and show me my position. The passage of the river in the night was attended with many difficulties, and my whole division was not in position before midnight. As well as I could judge from the camp-fires, my line was a prolongation to the left of Cheatham's line, and was 400 or 500 yards in rear of McCown's division.

Soon after midnight I received an order from General Hardee, on which I based and issued the following circular, viz:

"Generals of brigades will have their respective commands in readiness to move upon the enemy at 4:30 o'clock this morning. The several commands will fall into line without signal of bugle or drum."

Before daylight I formed line, placing Polk's brigade, with Calvert's battery, on the right; Johnson's brigade, with Darden's battery, in the center, and Liddell's brigade, with the Warren Light Artillery, commanded by Lieutenant [H.] Shannon, on the left. Wood's brigade I placed a short distance in rear of Polk's. This brigade had no battery in the fight, its battery (Semple's, of six Napoleon guns) having been detached the day before to support Hanson's brigade, of Breckinridge's division, and having remained with that brigade on the right of the army.

On account of the absence on duty of my chief of artillery, I ordered my chief of ordnance (Captain [T. R.] Hotchkiss) to act as chief of artillery, and Robert [D.] Smith, ordnance officer of Polk's brigade, to act as division ordnance officer.

It was not yet clear day when I received orders from General Hardee to advance. Swinging to the right as I moved forward, I rapidly communicated these instructions to brigade commanders, caused my division to load, and moved forward, stepping short upon the right and full upon the left, so as to swing round my left as directed. General Cheatham's left did not move forward at the same moment as my right, and my division, inclining to the left as it advanced, a gap was soon left between us, which General Hardee directed General Wood's brigade to fill. My whole division (Semple's battery excepted) was now advancing in line of battle, gradually wheeling to the right as it advanced. My left had not moved half a mile when heavy firing commenced near its front, supposed to be McCown's division engaging the enemy. A few moments more, and the enemy's skirmishers opened fire along the right and left center of my division, indicating that instead of being a second line supporting McCown's division, I was, in reality, the foremost line on this part of the field, and that McCown's line had unaccountably disappeared from my front. Skirmishers were immediately thrown forward, and I pressed on, continuing the difficult wheel under fire, through a country cut up with numerous fences and thickets. There was a great deal of crowding and improper opening out in the center of my line. Polk's and Johnson's brigades had to be moved by the flank more than once to regain their true positions. Driving back the enemy's skirmishers in the face of a heavy fire of shot and shell, I encountered his first solid line of battle at an average distance of three-fourths of a mile from the scene of my bivouac of last night. The left of his line (opposite Wood's and Polk's brigades) stretched through a large cedar brake; the right (opposite Liddell's and Johnson's) through open ground. In many parts of the brake the enemy found natural breastworks of limestone rock. In the open ground he covered most of his line behind a string of fence. Opposite my left, where the ground was open, a second line of the enemy, supported by artillery, could be seen a short distance in rear of his first. Here was my first important fight of the day. It extended along my whole line, and was participated in by McNair's brigade, of McCown's division, which had been placed on my left, and which a few moments before had surprised and driven the enemy from the ground over which my left had passed. The fight was short and bloody, lasting about twenty-five minutes, when the enemy gave way, both in the cedars and open ground, and fled back on his second line, which was immediately encountered in the woods, pastures, and open ground in rear of his former position. His second line soon gave way, and both went off together. My first fight may be said to have ended here. Its results were important.

The Eighth Arkansas, of Liddell's brigade, captured two stands of colors. They were handed to Colonel [John H.] Kelly on the field by Private James Riddle, of Company C, and Corpl. N. A. Horn, of Company E. In the rapid pursuit which followed, Colonel Kelly could not carry them; they were left on the field, and, I fear, appropriated by some person who had no title to them.

The Second Arkansas [Infantry], of Liddell's brigade, again encountered and defeated the Twenty-second Indiana (the same regiment it had so severely handled at the battle of Perryville), wounding and capturing its lieutenant-colonel. This brigade also captured two rifled cannon, with suitable ammunition; these Lieutenant Shannon added to his battery, and used on the enemy at subsequent periods of the battle. In Johnson's brigade, the Seventeenth Tennessee charged and captured a battery of four guns. In Wood's brigade, the Sixteenth Alabama wounded and captured the colonel and killed the lieutenant-colonel and major of the One hundred and first Ohio. My losses were very severe, especially on my left wing, where Johnson's and Liddell's brigades suffered more than in all the subsequent fighting of the day. In Johnson's brigade, Colonel [A. S.] Marks, of the Seventeenth

Tennessee (one of the best officers in the division), was severely wounded. Major [H. C.] Ewin, Forty-fourth Tennessee, was mortally wounded. Colonel [Moses] White and Lieutenant-Colonel [R. D.] Frayser, Thirty-seventh Tennessee, were wounded. Colonel [J. M.] Hughs, Twenty-fifth Tennessee, was wounded. In Polk's brigade, Majors [C. H.] Carlton and [R. A.] Duncan, Fifteenth and Thirteenth Arkansas, were wounded. In Wood's brigade, Lieutenant-Colonel [A. H.] Helvenston and Major [J. H.] McGaughy, Sixteenth Alabama, were wounded. In all, nine field officers, and a proportionate number of company officers, and non-commissioned officers, and privates were killed or wounded in this fight.

My division was now engaged in a rapid, but not very orderly, pursuit of the enemy, which was continued until a fresh line of his infantry and artillery came in view. This line was drawn up on the south side of, and parallel to, the Wilkinson turnpike, its right resting in open woods, its left in open fields. It checked or pushed back portions of my command, which, in the ardor of pursuit, had advanced beyond the general line. My whole division (the right of Johnson's brigade, which had delayed to replenish its ammunition, excepted) again engaged the enemy. Advancing steadily in the face of a heavy fire of infantry and artillery, Liddell's brigade, and the Seventeenth Tennessee, of Johnson's brigade, drove back the enemy's right. Wood's and Polk's brigades encountered a more obstinate and protracted resistance in the open fields where they fought; but here, too, success again rewarded the bravery of my men. The enemy were driven across the Wilkinson pike, and took refuge in the woods and heavy cedar brake on the north side. In this fight I captured 2 hospitals, nearly 1,000 prisoners, a train of ammunition wagons, 1 piece of artillery, 3 or 4 caissons, and 2 wagons loaded with medical stores. The Federal General [J. W.] Sill was killed near one of the hospitals. The Seventeenth Tennessee, of Johnson's brigade, and the Second Arkansas, of Liddell's brigade, contend for the honor of having first captured the hospital and killed General Sill.

My line was now far advanced beyond that of Withers and Cheatham. I began to discover from the firing that I was getting in rear of the right flank of the enemy's center. My right wing and left center were exposed to a heavy enfilading fire, as they crossed the open ground near the turnpike, from a powerful battery planted near the north side of the pike. Captain Hotchkiss, acting chief of artillery, placed Darden's and [J. H.] Calvert's batteries in position, and boldly attacked the Parrott and rifled artillery of the enemy. Wood's brigade having moved back to get a fresh supply of ammunition, Brigadier-General Polk moved forward, but was forced by the enfilading fire to change front forward on his first battalion, so as to place his line at right angles to the pike and facing eastwardly. This done, he advanced and attacked the supports of the battery, while Hotchkiss, though greatly overmatched in number and caliber of guns, continued to fire on them. The enemy abandoned the position, leaving several pieces of artillery. The Fifth Confederate and First Arkansas passed through and beyond these guns, and fairly deserve the honor of having captured them. Colonel [P. B.] Hawkins, of the Eleventh Kentucky, commanding a Federal brigade, was killed by the First Arkansas [Infantry] during this fight. Relieved of the enfilading fire, Brigadier-General Polk again changed front and resumed his original line of advance.

In the mean time, Wood's brigade had come up and been ordered by me to the left of Polk's brigade. Johnson's brigade had also come up, and, like Polk's, had been forced by the enfilading fire to change front. I had ordered Brigadier-General Johnson to throw forward a strong company of sharpshooters and advance on the battery to Polk's assistance; but just at this time the firing ceased, and I discovered the enemy had been driven back, as before stated. I then changed the direction of Johnson's advance to correspond with Polk's, and moved his brigade on the right of Polk's, whose guns were again heard in conflict with the enemy. On examination, I found the enemy had made another stand in a heavy cedar brake north of the Wilkinson pike, and in front of where my right crossed it. He had again found natural breastworks of limestone rock, and covered most of his line behind them. He made an obstinate and destructive resistance, during which Polk's brigade suffered a severe repulse; but he was finally dislodged and driven from the cedars. Towards the close of this fight, Smith's brigade, of Cheatham's division, under command of Colonel [A. J.] Vaughan, [Jr.,] came up on my left and rendered us material assistance.

In this fight Sergeant Lovin, of the Third Confederate Regiment, of Wood's brigade, captured a stand of colors, which I herewith transmit. Lieut.-Col. Don McGregor, of the First Arkansas, fell mortally wounded, and Major [J. T.] McReynolds, the last field officer of the Thirty-seventh Tennessee, was mortally wounded.

The commanding officers of Brigadier-General Wood's regiments again reported their ammunition expended; he moved the brigade in rear of the Wilkinson pike to procure a supply. While there information reached General Hardee that the enemy was threatening our left flank, and he ordered Wood's brigade to remain in the rear and protect the trains. This was the smallest brigade I had, numbering on the morning of the fight not over 1,100 officers and men. It was without a battery, as before explained; was on the extreme right of my line (the most exposed position) up to the time of crossing the pike, and at this time did not number 500.

The enemy was now driven out of the cedars in our front, but to the right of my division he still remained undisturbed, and as I again attempted to advance I found myself flanked on the right and again exposed to an enfilading fire. I therefore determined to advance on a line farther to the left, and where my right flank would not be so fearfully exposed. With this view, I ordered General Johnson to move his brigade to the left, where Liddell's brigade would again connect with him.

But here it would be proper to give a statement of the doings of Liddell's brigade since last mentioned as having driven back a line of the enemy on the south side of the Wilkinson pike. While my other brigades inclined to the right, as stated, Brigadier-General Liddell moved diagonally to the left for a considerable distance through open woods. He met the enemy on the far edge of these woods and drove him over the crest of the high ground beyond. Throwing forward skirmishers, it was found he had made another stand in the valley of Overall's Creek, 400 or 500 yards beyond the crest. Liddell moved his battery to the crest and drove him back until he disappeared from view behind the embankment of the Nashville railroad. From the high point where his battery now was, Liddell was in full view of the Nashville turnpike and the enemy's trains. He opened with his artillery on one portion of the train, while General Wharton, with the cavalry, charged another. The trains disappeared in haste and confusion. At this time Liddell's brigade was the extreme left of the infantry of the army, and there was a gap of three-quarters of a mile between his right and the left of the other portion of the division. I determined to unite the division opposite this gap and advance. I ordered Johnson to move on the left of Polk's brigade, and at the same time sent orders to Brigadier-General Liddell to move his brigade by the right flank until he had reconnected with Johnson's brigade.

While these commands were being executed, I met a brigade of McCown's division retreating in great disorder. I think this brigade must have attempted to advance through the gap in my division and been repulsed.

By moving inward and uniting in the gap mentioned, my division again advanced on a line midway between the diverging lines which the two portions had before pursued. I advanced with four brigades, disposed as follows: Polk's brigade on the right, Liddell's on the left, Smith's brigade, of Cheatham's division, the right center, Johnson's the left center. I had not moved 100 yards when Liddell's brigade became hotly engaged with a line of the enemy drawn up across a neck of woods and prolonged into the fields on each side. This, I think, was a continuation to the left of the same line which my other brigades had defeated farther to the right, or it may have been the line which caused the repulse of McCown's division (just mentioned) and which was pursuing. However this be, Liddell met the enemy here in force and engaged in the most obstinately contested and (to the enemy) most destructive fight which had yet occurred. Not until Liddell had closed within 25 paces of him would the portion of his line in the woods give way.

Colonel Kelly, of the Eighth Arkansas, and Colonel [S. G.] Smith, of the Sixth and Seventh Arkansas, were wounded here.

Lieutenant-Colonel [John E.] Murray, of the Fifth Arkansas, bore the colors of his regiment through the hottest of the fight, and by his own bright example encouraged his men to despise danger.

J. K. Leslie, a brave and intelligent private of Company C, of this regiment, captured a beautiful stand of colors belonging to one of the enemy's regiments of regulars. This flag I also herewith transmit.

The enemy gave way, and fled, leaving a large number of dead behind him. Johnson's, Smith's, and Polk's brigades moved rapidly in pursuit, obliquing to the left as they advanced. Liddell rapidly reformed his line and followed, *en échelon,* about 100 yards in rear of Johnson. My orders, frequently received from General Hardee during the day, being to push the enemy, and, if possible, give him no time to rally or select positions, I did not halt the division or lose any time in rectifying distances or alignments. The line had not advanced a quarter of a mile when a fresh line of the enemy was discovered in open fields. He was supported by numerous and well-served batteries. At this time I had but one battery (Liddell's). Polk's could not follow through the heavy woods and Johnson's had been ordered by General Hardee to remain in reserve near the Wilkinson pike. My line advanced steadily, pouring in a deadly fire, and drove the enemy across a small dirt road. That portion of his line opposite Johnson rallied behind a fence on the far side of the dirt road, but was driven from there also, when his whole line disappeared in the cedar woods, which here border the Nashville pike, and were close behind him. Still another line of the enemy showed itself on the edge of these cedars. A heavy fire of small-arms was immediately directed upon him. He fled back in the woods, leaving the ground in front of Johnson's brigade thickly covered with dead and wounded. Following up their success, our men gained the edge of the cedar's—Johnson's brigade capturing a battery of Parrott guns—and were almost on the Nashville turnpike, in rear of the original center of Rosecrans's army, sweeping with their fire his only line of communication with Nashville; but it was now after 3 o'clock; my men had had little or no rest the night before; they had been fighting since dawn, without relief, food, or water; they were comparatively without the support of artillery, for the advance had been too rapid to enable my single battery to get in position and answer the enemy; their ammunition was again nearly exhausted, and our ordnance trains could not follow.

At this critical moment the enemy met my thinned ranks with another fresh line of battle, supported by a heavier and closer artillery fire than I had yet encountered. A report also spread, which I believe was true, that we were flanked on the right. This was more than our men could stand. Smith's brigade was driven back in great confusion. Polk's and Johnson's followed. As our broken ranks went back over the fields before the fire of this fresh line, the enemy opened fire on our right flank from several batteries which they had concentrated on an eminence near the railroad, inflicting a heavier loss on Polk's brigade than it had suffered in all the previous fighting of the day. The division was rallied on the edge of the opposite woods, about 400 yards in the rear of the scene of disaster, though some of the men could not be stopped until they reached the Wilkinson pike. Liddell's brigade, *en échelon* on my extreme left, was not engaged in this last fight and was moved back in good order to the line where the other brigades rallied. Here I reformed my division as rapidly as possible, Polk's brigade on the right, Johnson's in the center, and Liddell's on the left. A fresh supply of ammunition was served out, and I waited in momentary expectation for an advance of the enemy in overwhelming force. He never advanced a foot, and the question presented itself, Ought I to again advance? I was now in possession of 3 miles of ground conquered from the enemy, large numbers of prisoners, cannon, and small-arms. Another repulse, and I might lose all these and cause the demoralization and destruction of my division. I immediately reported the situation to General Hardee, and was ordered by him to hold the ground I had won, rest, and reorganize my division and await further orders. Pushing my pickets well forward, I bivouacked in line of battle on the same line which the division rallied on after the repulse.

On the morning of January 1 there were rumors that the enemy was retreating. I was ordered by General Hardee to push forward, feel the enemy, and ascertain the true state of affairs in our front. Liddell's brigade was moved forward and to the left, and drove the enemy's skirmishers back at least a quarter of a mile, and beyond a white house used as a Federal hospital, and situated on the small dirt road near which our last fight of the day before occurred.

During this fight Lieutenant-Colonel [F. J.] Cameron, Sixth and Seventh Arkansas Regiment, was wounded.

Liddell again swept the Nashville turnpike with his artillery, and greatly disturbed the enemy's trains, which could be seen on and near it. Receiving another message from General Hardee to the effect that he had ordered me to feel the enemy, and could not hear my guns, and at the same time receiving information from General Liddell that he was in line of battle near the hospital just mentioned, and needed immediate support on his right, I ordered General Wood to move his brigade forward cautiously, and support Liddell on the right, but I also informed him that the object was merely to ascertain whether the enemy was still in force in our front, not to bring on a general battle. Wood's brigade moved forward, and I moved Johnson's skirmishers forward *en échelon* on Wood's right flank, so as to protect him as much as possible. Wood's brigade formed line close to the dirt road last mentioned, and immediately became hotly engaged with a very large force of the enemy, which advanced on him out of the cedars where our repulse of the day before occurred. He found that Liddell was not on his left, as expected, having previously fallen back; he also discovered that the enemy were flanking him on the left with another heavy force. At this time he received an order direct from General Hardee not to bring on a general battle. He ceased firing and fell back, leaving several killed and wounded on the ground. Some of the men of the Forty-fifth Mississippi Regiment had gone so far ahead that retreat was impossible; they remained where they were, and fell into the hands of the enemy. Wood must have lost nearly 100 killed, wounded, and prisoners in this fight. It was now clear the enemy was still in force in my front, and I so reported it.

On Friday morning, January 2, I was satisfied that the enemy was fortifying his position. On consultation with my brigade commanders, I addressed a note to General Hardee, which I requested him to forward to General Bragg, stating this important fact, and that I feared, if my single, and now reduced, line was pushed on the enemy in his fortified position, the result would prove very disastrous, but that I believed I could hold a defensible position against any assault of the enemy.

Semple's battery rejoined me on the 1st. On the 2d, Friday evening, I was ordered to send four of his guns to support an attack about to be made by Major-General Breckinridge's division. My acting chief of artillery, Captain Hotchkiss, having been twice wounded while gallantly discharging his duty, I ordered him to quit the field (which he reluctantly did) and directed Captain Semple to act as chief of artillery. Captain Semple sent four of his 12-pounders, under Lieutenant [E. J.] Fitzpatrick, to General Breckinridge's division. In the desperate conflict which took place on the right that evening, this battery bore a conspicuous part. Out of 45 men and officers, 20 were killed and wounded; among them Lieut. Joseph Pollard, who is represented as having fought most bravely, and only yielded when his leg and arm were both broken; 14 horses were killed and wounded, and one piece of artillery was lost. For details of the noble conduct of this battery in the fight, I refer you to the report of Captain Semple, herewith sent.

About 11 o'clock that night the enemy made a reconnaissance in force in front of my division; he was driven back by my skirmishers. Immediately afterwards I received orders to withdraw my pickets and resume the position held by me on the morning of December 30, on the right of the army, in rear of Breckinridge's division. Here I remained, enduring the incessant cold rain of that night and next day, until 11 P. M. of the 3d, when I commenced retreating on Manchester.

After the battles of Wednesday, I collected a large number of guns and sent them to General Bragg's chief of ordnance. I also got several artillery horses, with which I replaced most of the disabled horses in my batteries; also a large quantity of artillery ammunition, harness and other articles necessary in batteries.

To the courage and patriotism of the officers and men, the good discipline which existed among them, and the unexpected suddenness of the attack, are alone due the success which attended my advance upon the enemy's right. With the exception of the wheel of my division, directed by General Hardee, on the morning of the great battle, there was no strategic movement attempted. It was one determined charge, sometimes checked, and even repulsed, by the enemy; sometimes delayed to procure a fresh supply of ammunition, but ever renewed and successful, until McCook's Federal corps of 18,000 men, composing the right wing of Rosecrans's army, had been swept away, and two or three lines of his successors had shared the same fate.

To Brigadier-Generals Johnson, Wood, and Polk, and Colonel Vaughan, commanding Smith's brigade, of Cheatham's division, the country is indebted for their great exertions on this occasion. Brigadier-General Liddell led his brigade with a skill, courage, and devotion which, I believe, saved my left flank from being turned by the enemy.

I found the following officers of my staff very efficient in this battle; they were at their posts all the time, and discharged their difficult duties with a courage, promptness, and intelligence not often equaled, viz: Col. W. W. Kirkland, chief of staff; Maj. Calhoun Benham, assistant inspector-general; Capt. Irving A. Buck, assistant adjutant-general; Lieuts. J. W. Jetton and J. K. Dixon (the latter wounded); Capt. T. R. Hotchkiss (wounded); John M. Johnson, chief surgeon; Surg. J. H. Erskine, chief inspector. Dr. Johnson showed the same zeal, courage, and energy in this battle which has distinguished him on every other occasion, and made me feel that my division was very fortunate in having secured his services.

In addition to the officers and men already mentioned in my report, the following officers and men have been brought to my notice for distinguished services on the field. I hope it will be considered no disparagement of the services of other brave men of my division, some of whom laid down their lives or lost limbs on this field, if their gallant deeds have been overlooked in this report.

In Wood's brigade I must specially mention the following officers and men of the Sixteenth Alabama, viz: Col. W. B. Wood and Adjt. B. A. Wilson (wounded) ; Captain [William] Hodges, Company F; Lieutenant [C.] Davis, Company B; Lieutenant [G. W. W.] Jones, Company G; Lieutenant [G.] Pride, Company A; Lieutenant [C. F.] Carson, Company C, who remained fighting after he was wounded; Lieutenant [D. O.] Warren, Company F; Lieutenant [Thomas J.] Salter, Company D, who was wounded, but returned to the field the moment his wound was dressed; Sergt.-Maj. Robert H. Cherry and Private Harvey G. Sargent, of Company H; Privates William Boyce and James Peeden of Company C; Sergt. Bowen, Company H; Sergt. H. W. Rutland, Company A; Privates Peter White, Company F; Robert Williams, Company B, and H. D. Smith, Company A; the latter wounded in both legs, deserves promotion. In the Forty-fifth Mississippi: Lieutenant-Colonel [R.] Charlton, Major [E. F.] Nunn. Adjt. Frank Foster, Jr., Sergeants Asberry, Doolittle, Morrison, Vaughan, Stewart, Lieut. G. W. Williams, Sergeant-Major Kern, Corporals Mallett, Hackler, and Read, and Private McChadin. Corporal Read volunteered to carry the colors after the color-bearer had been shot down. He is well qualified as an officer, and ought to be promoted. In the Thirty-third Alabama: Colonel [Samuel] Adams, Captains [W. E.] Dodson and Thomas Seay (severely wounded, in advance), Sergeant Major Mizell(mortally wounded), Corp. Isaac R. Smith, Company C; Sergeant Stewart, Company H; Privates Byrd, Company I; Foster, Company E, and Riley, Company D. In the Third Confederate: Major [J. F.] Cameron. Wood's Sharpshooters: Captain [A. T.] Hawkins.

Polk's Brigade.—In Fifth Confederate: Col. J. A. Smith and Adjt. F. T. Smith. In First Arkansas: Colonel [John W.] Colquitt, Lieut.-Col. Don McGregor, Adjt. S. N. Greenwood, Captain [William A.] Alexander, Company B (wounded) ; Captain [W. H.] Scales, Company C (wounded) ; Captain [O. F.] Parrish, Company D (wounded) ; Lieut. John E. Letson (wounded) ; Corp. Green M. McKenzie, Company A (killed) ; John S. T. Hemphill, Company B (wounded) ; Privates G. W. Sallee, Company C:

J. C. Bogy, Company D; W. W. Chaney, Company E; Hardee J. Bullion, Company F, and A. P. Green, Company G (killed); James Beeson, Company H; John H. Curd, Company I (killed); Ocean C. Choat, Company K (killed). In Thirteenth and Fifteenth Arkansas: Capt. Thomas H. Osborne, Companies B and H, Fifteenth Arkansas; Lieut. John Dolan, Company A, Thirteenth Arkansas, ought to be promoted; Color-bearer Felix E. Lipe, Thirteenth Arkansas (wounded); First Sergt. J. M. Harkleroad, Company F, Fifteenth Arkansas; Private William Sanford, Company E, Thirteenth Arkansas (wounded), ought to be promoted; Lieut. William [H.] Pearce and Captain [W. H.] Kinsey, Fifteenth Arkansas. In Fifth Tennessee: Col. B. J. Hill, well worthy of promotion. Calvert's Battery: Joseph Lemon, color-bearer, deserves promotion.

Liddell's Brigade.—In Second Arkansas: Lieutenants [H. C.] Collier and [B. L.] Clegg, I fear killed; Lieutenant-Colonel [Reuben F.] Harvey, Captain [J. K.] Phillips, Company F. ought to be promoted; Lieutenants [C. S.] Emerson, Company A; [M. D.] Brown, Company K, and [R. E.] Smith, Company G. In Eighth Arkansas: Adjutant [H. J.] McCurdy, a brave young soldier (killed); Lieutenant [S. B.] Cole, Company I; Lieut. Calvin East, Company H; Lieut. T. H. Beard, Company F (killed); Lieut. [W. M.] Bass, Company E; Captain [W. H.] Lankford, Company A; Lieut. [B. A.] Terrett, Company E. In Fifth Arkansas: Captain [A. B.] Washington, Company K; Privates John Atkinson, Company C; B. W. Maret, Company I, and C. Mattix, Company F. This soldier was too badly wounded to carry his gun. He asked to be allowed to carry the colors, and did so through the rest of the day. Three color-bearers had been shot down previously. In Sixth and Seventh Arkansas: Captain [J. W.] Martin, Lieutenant [J. A.] Reeves, and Captain [S. C.] Brown, ever foremost in leading their men; Captains [J. G.] Fletcher, [W. E.] Wilkerson, and [M. M.] Duffie (wounded); Sergeant-Major Eddins, Sergeant Bratton, Company H; Private Hulse, Company K; the color-bearer, whose name has not been furnished to me.

Johnson's Brigade.—In Twenty-fifth Tennessee: Capt. A. Green, Company G; Capt. G. H. Swope, Company H; First Lieut. D. S. Walker, Company D. In Forty-fourth Tennessee: Maj. H. C. Ewin and Capt. Samuel Stiles, Company A; Adjt. R. G. Cross, Lieutenants [F. M.] Kelso, Company B; [J. W.] Dickins, Company C; [W. H.] Gibbs, Company F; A. P. Forester, Company K (wounded); Color-Sergt. M. J. Turner and Corp. I. S. Berry, Company I (wounded); Corp. John W. Gill, Company F (killed); Privates J. D. Stone, Company B; S. G. Heflin, Company C (killed); B. P. Hargroves, Company E (wounded); James D. Crenshaw, Company H (wounded), and J. M. Sellers, Company K. In Twenty-third Tennessee: Capt. N. R. Allen,

Company E; Capt. W. H. Harder, Company G; Privates Henry C. Haynes, Company E, and Stephen M. Foster, Company C. In Seventeenth Tennessee: Adjt. James [B.] Fitzpatrick.

I wish to call particular attention to the gallant conduct of Sergt. William N. Cameron, color-bearer of Twenty-fifth Tennessee Regiment. In the last fight he advanced in front of his regiment so far that when it fell back he was unable to follow, and was captured. He tore the colors from the staff, concealed them upon his person, and made his escape from Bowling Green, bringing with him the flag of the Twenty-fifth Tennessee Regiment.

In conclusion, I would state that I carried into the fight 6,045 men, out of which I lost 2,081 killed, wounded, and missing.

Very respectfully, your obedient servant,

P. R. CLEBURNE,
Major-General.

Maj. T. B. Roy,
Chief of Staff, Hardee's Corps.

LIBERTY GAP.

Report of Major-General P. R. Cleburne, C. S. Army, Commanding Division, Hardee's Corps.*

Hdrs. Cleburne's Division, Army of Tenn.,
Tyner's Station, Tenn., August 3, 1863.

Colonel: On June 24th last I was stationed at Wartrace, Tenn., with two brigades of my division. Polk's brigade was at Tullahoma, fifteen miles south of Wartrace, and Liddell's brigade was at Bellbuckle, a village 5 miles north of Wartrace. A range of hills dividing the headwaters of Duck River from the headwaters of Stone River separated our positions from those of the enemy. There were several gaps or good roads through these hills, two of which led directly on Liddell's position at Bellbuckle, viz: Railroad Gap, *via* New Fosterville, and Liberty Gap. Both of these gaps Liddell was ordered to picket. The former was 4, the latter 3 miles from Bellbuckle. Two other gaps—Dismal Hollow and Hoover's—gave ingress to the country immediately on the right of Liddell's position; these were held by some cavalry of Wheeler's division.

On the evening of June 24th I had information from the corps commander that the enemy had suddenly advanced in force simultaneously on Liberty and Hoover's Gaps and had carried both positions.

**O.R.*, XXIII, part 1, 186-187.

On the morning of the 25th, in pursuance of orders, I advanced Wood's brigade to Bellbuckle. I found Liddell still guarding the approaches *via* Liberty Gap and New Fosterville. He was holding two wooded hills a mile south of Liberty Gap. On the evening of the 25th Liddell, supposing the enemy retiring, advanced on the gap; but after some heavy fighting, in which he inflicted a considerable loss on the enemy and suffered little himself, he fell back to his former position. I was now satisfied the enemy was still in force at Liberty Gap; that he had at least a division of infantry, besides cavalry and artillery, so I ordered up three regiments of [S. A. M.] Wood's brigade and a section of [Henry C.] Semple's battery to Liddell's support. One regiment of Wood's and one of Liddell's brigade, with the other section of Semple's battery, were guarding the approaches *via* New Fosterville.

On the morning of the 26th this section of artillery and the two regiments rejoined their brigades in front of Liberty Gap, and were replaced by a regiment of Churchill's brigade, of my division, which arrived at Bellbuckle on the morning of the 26th. The remaining two regiments of Churchill's brigade I moved up as a reserve to the force in front of Liberty Gap. The enemy kept up a constant firing all day the 26th, and advanced twice with double lines of skirmishers. They were driven back and at night both parties held their former positions. I had no ammunition to spare, and did not reply to the continual fire of the enemy except with five Whitworth rifles, which appeared to do good service. Mounted men were struck at distances ranging from 700 to 1,300 yards. During the day the enemy, advancing in overwhelming force through Hoover's Gap, forced back Stewart's division almost to Fairfield, thus threatening to cut me off from Wartrace.

At night I received orders to retreat on Tullahoma *via* Schoefner's Bridge at daylight on the 27th, which I did without any loss, although my men were much wearied by the watching and fighting in front of the gaps, for it rained incessantly during most of the time. The men had no changes of clothing, no tents, and could not even light fires to dry themselves. Many had no shoes, and others left their shoes buried in the deep mire of the roads.

My entire loss in the several fights amounted to 121.

I respectfully submit this general report of these engagements, for the details of which I refer you to the report of General Liddell and his regimental commanders, forwarded herewith.

Very respectfully, your obedient servant,

P. R. CLEBURNE,
Major-General.

LIEUTENANT-COLONEL ARCHER ANDERSON,
Asst. Adjt.-Gen. Hill's Corps, Army of Tenn.

Organization of Cleburne's Division, December, 1862, Major-General Patrick R. Cleburne, Commanding

WOOD'S BRIGADE.

Brig.-Gen. S. A. M. Wood, Commanding.

32nd Mississippi Regiment,	Col. M. P. Lowrey.
45th Mississippi Regiment,	Col. A. B. Hardcastle.
16th Alabama Regiment,	Col. W. B. Wood.
33rd Alabama Regiment,	Col. Samuel Adams.
3rd Confederate Regiment,	Lieut.-Col. J. F. Cameron.
Hawkins's Sharpshooters,	Maj. A. T. Hawkins.
Semple's Battery,	Capt. H. C. Semple.

JOHNSON'S BRIGADE.

Brig.-Gen. Bushrod R. Johnson, Commanding.

17th Tennessee Regiment,	Col. A. S. Marks.
23rd Tennessee Regiment,	Col. R. H. Keeble.
25th Tennessee Regiment,	Col. J. M. Hughs.
37th Tennessee Regiment,	Col. Moses White.
44th Tennessee Regiment,	Col. John S. Fulton.
Darden's Battery,	Capt. Put. Darden.

LIDDELL'S BRIGADE.

Brig.-Gen. St. John R. Liddell, Commanding.

2nd Arkansas Regiment,	Col. D. C. Govan.
5th Arkansas Regiment,	Col. L. Featherston.
6th Arkansas Regiment,	Col. Samuel G. Smith.
7th Arkansas Regiment,	Col. D. A. Gillespie.
8th Arkansas Regiment,	Col. John H. Kelley.
Swett's Battery,	Capt. Chas. Swett.

POLK'S BRIGADE.

Brig.-Gen. Lucius E. Polk, Commanding.

1st Arkansas Regiment,	Col. J. W. Colquitt.
13th and 15th Arkansas Regiments,	Col. J. E. Josey.
2nd Tennessee Regiment,	Col. W. D. Robinson.
5th Tennessee Regiment,	Col. Benj. J. Hill.
48th Tennessee Regiment,	Col. G. H. Nixon.
5th Confederate Regiment,	Col. J. A. Smith.
Calvert's Battery,	Lieut. Thos. J. Key.

CHICKAMAUGA

*Report of Maj.-Gen. Patrick R. Cleburne, C. S. Army, Commanding Division.**

HEADQUARTERS CLEBURNE'S DIVISION,
HILL'S CORPS, ARMY OF TENNESSEE,
Missionary Ridge, near Chattanooga, Tenn., Oct. 18, 1863.

COLONEL: I have the honor to report the operations of my division in the battle of Chickamauga, fought on Saturday and Sunday, September 19 and 20.

During the afternoon of Saturday, the 19th ultimo, I moved my division in a westerly direction across the Chickamauga River at Thedford's Ford, and having received orders to report to Lieutenant-General Polk, commanding the right wing of the army, I did so, and was directed by him to form a second line in rear of the right of the line already in position. Accordingly, soon after sunset my division was formed partially *en échelon* about 300 yards in rear of the right of the first line. My right rested in front of a steam saw-mill known as Jay's Mill, situated on a small stream running between the Chickamauga and the road leading from Chattanooga to La Fayette. My line extended from the saw-mill almost due south for nearly a mile, fronting to the west. Polk's brigade, with Calvert's battery (commanded by Lieut. Thomas J. Key), composed my right wing; Wood's brigade, with Semple's battery, my center, and Deshler's brigade, with Douglas's battery, my left wing.

I now received orders from Lieutenant-General Hill to advance (passing over the line which had been repulsed) and drive back the enemy's left wing. In my front were open woods, with the exception of a clearing (fenced in) in front of my center, the ground sloping upward as we advanced. Ordering the brigades to direct themselves by Wood's (the center) brigade and preserve brigade distance, I moved forward, passing over the first line, and was in a few moments heavily engaged along my right and center. The enemy, posted behind hastily constructed breastworks, opened a heavy fire of both small-arms and artillery. For half an hour the firing was the heaviest I had ever heard. It was dark, however, and accurate shooting was impossible. Each party was aiming at the flashes of the other guns, and few of these shot from either side took effect. Major Hotchkiss, my chief of artillery, placed Polk's and Wood's artillery in position in the cleared field in front of my center. Availing themselves of the noise and the darkness, Captain Semple and Lieutenant Key ran their batteries forward within 60 yards of the enemy's

*O.R., XXX, part 2, 155-158.

line and opened a rapid fire. Polk pressed forward at the same moment on the right, when the enemy ceased firing and quickly disappeared from my front. There was some confusion at the time, necessarily inseparable, however, from a night attack. This, and the difficulty of moving my artillery through the woods in the dark, rendered a farther advance inexpedient for the night. I consequently halted, and, after readjusting my lines, threw out skirmishers a quarter of a mile in advance and bivouacked.

In this conflict the enemy was driven back about a mile and a half. He left in my hands 2 or 3 pieces of artillery, several caissons, 200 or 300 prisoners, and the colors of the Seventy-seventh Indiana and those of the Seventy-ninth Pennsylvania.

About 10 o'clock next morning, I received orders from Lieutenant-General Hill to advance and dress on the line of General Breckinridge, who had been placed on my right. Accordingly, directing each brigade to dress upon the right and preserve its distance, I moved forward. Breckinridge was already in motion. The effort to overtake and dress upon him caused hurry and some confusion in my line, which was necessarily a long one. Before the effects of this could be rectified, Polk's brigade and the right of Wood's encountered the heaviest artillery fire I have ever experienced. I was now within short canister range of a line of log breastworks, and a hurricane of shot and shell swept the woods from the unseen enemy in my front. This deadly fire was direct, and came from that part of the enemy's breastworks opposite to my right and right-center. The rest of my line, stretching off to the left, received an oblique fire from the line of breastworks, which, at a point opposite my center, formed a retiring angle running off toward the Chattanooga and La Fayette road behind.

The accompanying map, showing the shape of the enemy's line of works opposite my line, will explain our relative positions. Upon reference to it, it will be seen that opposite to my right and right center the enemy's works ran about half a mile north and south, and nearly parallel to the Chattanooga and La Fayette roads, which was about 300 yards behind; that at a point opposite my center, his works formed, as before stated, a retiring angle running in a westerly and somewhat oblique direction to the Chattanooga and La Fayette road, and that at a point nearly opposite my right his works formed another retiring angle running back also to the road. My right and right-center, consisting of Polk's brigade and Lowrey's regiment, of Wood's brigade, were checked within 175 yards of the advanced part of this portion of the enemy's works, and the rest of the line were halted in compliance with the order previously given to dress upon the right.

Passing toward the left at this time, I found that the line of advance of my division, which was the left of the right wing of the army, converged with the line of advance of the left wing of the army. The flanks of the two wings had already come into collision. Part of Wood's brigade had passed over Bate's brigade, of Stewart's division, which was the right of the left wing, and Deshler's brigade, which formed my left, had been thrown out entirely and was in rear of the left wing of the army. I ordered Wood to move forward the remainder of his brigade, opening at the same time in the direction of the enemy's fire with Semple's battery. That part of Wood's brigade to the left of Lowrey's regiment and to the left of the southern angle of the breastworks in its advance at this time entered an old field bordering the road (Chattanooga and La Fayette) and attempted to cross it in the face of a heavy fire from the works in its front. It had almost reached the road, its left wing being at Poe's house (known as the burning house), when it was driven back by a heavy oblique fire of small arms and artillery which was opened upon both its flanks, the fire from the right coming from the south face of the breastworks, which was hid from view by the thick growth of scrub-oaks bordering the field.

Five hundred men were killed and wounded by this fire in a few minutes. Upon this repulse (Lowrey's regiment having also in the meantime been forced to retire), I ordered the brigade still farther back to reform. Semple's battery, which had no position, I also ordered back.

I now moved Deshler's brigade by the right flank, with the intention of connecting it with Polk's left, so filling the gap left in my center by the withdrawal of Wood. This connection, however, I could not establish, as Polk's left had in its turn been also driven back. Finding it a useless sacrifice of life for Polk to retain his position, I ordered him to fall back with the rest of his line, and with his and Wood's brigade I took up a strong defensive position some 300 or 400 yards in rear of the point from which they had been repulsed. Deshler's brigade had moved forward toward the right of the enemy's advanced works, but could not go beyond the crest of a low ridge from which Lowrey had been repulsed. I therefore ordered him to cover himself behind the ridge and hold his position as long as possible. His brigade was now *en échelon* about 400 yards in front of the left of the rest of the division, which here rested for some hours.

In effecting this last disposition of his command, General Deshler fell, a shell passing fairly through his chest. It was the first battle in which this gentleman had the honor of commanding as a general officer. He was a brave and efficient one. He brought always to the discharge of his duty a warm zeal and a high conscientiousness. The army and country will long remember him.

At about 3:30 P. M. I received orders from Lieutenant-General Polk to move forward on a line with my left (Deshler), connecting my right with Jackson's brigade, and when I had formed my line, to remain and hold the position. I accordingly advanced with my center and right wing, drove in the enemy's skirmishers, and found his line behind the works from which he had repulsed us in the morning. The left wing of the army had been driving the enemy. The right wing now attacked, Lieutenant-General Polk ordering me to advance my heavy batteries and open on the enemy. Captain Semple, my acting chief of artillery (Major Hotchkiss, my chief of artillery, being disabled by a wound received the day before), selected positions in front of the line and placed his own and Douglas's batteries within 200 yards of the enemy's breastworks and opened a rapid and most effective fire, silencing immediately a battery which had been playing upon my lines. About the same time Brigadier-General Polk charged and soon carried the northwestern angle of the enemy's works, taking in succession three lines of breastworks. In this brilliant operation he was materially aided by Key's battery, and toward its close by Douglas's battery, which had been moved by my orders to my extreme right, where it was run into position by hand. A large number of prisoners (regulars) were here captured. The enemy abandoned his works and retired precipitately. Brigadier-General Polk pursued to the Chattanooga and La Fayette road, where he captured another piece of artillery. I here received directions from Lieutenant-General Hill to halt my command until further orders.

I cannot close this report without an acknowledgment of distinguished services rendered by various officers and men which would otherwise pass unnoticed.

I have already incidentally called attention to the gallant conduct of Brigadier-General Polk, but it is due to him and to the country, which wishes to appreciate its faithful servants, to say that to the intrepidity and stern determination of purpose of himself and men, I was principally indebted for the success of the charge on Sunday evening which drove the enemy from his breastworks and gave us the battle.

Colonel Mills, also, is entitled to be remembered. Leading his men through the battle until the fall of his brigadier (the lamented Deshler), he was then called, by seniority, to command the brigade, which he did with gallantry and intelligence.

To my staff—Maj. Calhoun Benham, assistant adjutant-general (who received a contusion on the right shoulder from a grape-shot or fragment of shell); Capt. Irving A. Buck, assistant adjutant-general (whose horse was shot under him); Maj. Joseph K. Dixon, assistant inspector-general; Capt. B. F. Philips, assistant inspector-general; Lieut. J. W. Jetton, aide-de-camp and acting assistant inspector-general; Maj. T. R. Hotchkiss, chief of artillery (who received a wound from a Minie ball in the foot on Saturday, which deprived me of his valuable services afterwards); Capt. Henry C. Semple, who replaced Major Hotchkiss as chief of artillery when disabled; Capt. C. F. Vanderford, chief of ordnance; Lieut. L. H. Mangum, aide-de-camp, and Lieut. S. P. Hanly, aide-de-camp (who received a contusion from a grape-shot)—I am indebted for the faithful and indefatigable manner in which they performed their vital, though perhaps not showy, duties throughout these operations.

Maj. T. R. Hotchkiss, chief of artillery; Captain Semple, with his battery, and Lieut. Thomas J. Key, commanding Calvert's battery, rendered invaluable service and exhibited the highest gallantry on Saturday night in running their pieces up as they did within 60 yards of the enemy. In this they were ably sustained by Lieut. Richard W. Goldthwaite, of Semple's battery. Here Major Hotchkiss received his wound.

Captain Semple also displayed skill and judgment as acting chief of artillery, particularly in the selection of a position for his own and Douglas's batteries on Sunday evening, which gave an oblique fire upon the enemy in his works, contributing to the success of the final charge by Polk's brigade.

Capt. O. S. Palmer, assistant adjutant-general of Wood's brigade, was conspicuous for his coolness and attention to duty on the field, and has my thanks.

I am much indebted also to Dr. D. A. Linthicum, chief surgeon of my division. The completeness of his arrangements, his careful supervision of subordinates, both on the field under fire and elsewhere, and in the hospitals, secured our gallant wounded prompt attention, and all the comfort and alleviation of pain attainable in the exigencies of battle.

Surg. A. R. Erskine, then acting (now actual) medical inspector of my division, rendered most efficient service.

Asst. Surg. Alfred B. De Loach particularly distinguished himself by his unselfish devotion, going repeatedly far forward under fire and among the skirmishers to attend the wounded.

James P. Brady and Melvin L. Overstreet, privates in the Buckner Guards (my escort), specially detailed to attend me through the battle, went with me wherever my duty called me. Brady was wounded in the hand; Overstreet had his horse shot.

To Capt. C. F. Vanderford, my chief of ordnance, my thanks are specially due. His trains were always in the best order and in the most accessible position, and to his care in this respect I am indebted for a prompt supply of ammunition in every critical emergency which arose.

I carried into action on Saturday (the 19th) 5,115 officers and men, 4,875 bayonets.

On Sunday (the 20th) I carried in 4,671 officers and men, 4,437 bayonets.

In the two days my casualties were 204 killed, 1,539 wounded, 6 missing; making in all, 1,749.

Respectfully,

P. R. CLEBURNE,
Major-General.

Lieut. Col. ARCHER ANDERSON,
Assisatnt Adjutant-General, Hill's Corps.

---

*Report of Col. Daniel C. Govan, Second Arkansas Infantry, commanding Liddell's brigade.**

HEADQUARTERS LIDDELL'S BRIGADE,
Missionary Ridge, October 6, 1863.

CAPTAIN: I have the honor to submit the following report of the part taken by this brigade in the recent battle of Chickamauga, on September 19 and 20:

On September 18, about 2 P. M., I, with General Walthall's brigade forming a reserve division, commanded by Brigadier-General Liddell, in Walker's corps, arrived in front of Alexander's Bridge, on West Chickamauga Creek. I was ordered to move forward, supporting General Walthall's brigade in an attack to gain possession of the bridge, then held by the enemy. Walthall's brigade, moving forward, soon engaged the enemy, who occupied a dense thicket on the south side of the creek, near the bridge. After firing several volleys he hastily retreated, leaving us in possession of the bridge, which was, however, rendered useless, the planks having been removed. The brigade was not actively engaged excepting the skirmishers, who were thrown forward on General Walthall's left to the creek, sustaining a loss of 1 killed and 5 wounded.

Moving down the creek 1½ miles, I crossed at Byram's Ford and bivouacked about 1 mile from the ford.

Early on the morning of the 19th, I moved in a southwesterly direction and halted in a position nearly opposite Alexander's Bridge. While here awaiting orders it was ascertained that a heavy column of the enemy was moving around to turn our right flank. Wilson's and Ector's brigades were

---

**O.R.*, XXX, part 2, 259-61.

already engaged and were being heavily pressed. About 12 M. I was ordered to move forward to their support, Walthall's brigade being on my right, forming a line of battle facing northward. Moving forward about one-quarter of a mile I engaged the enemy, and succeeded by a charge in driving him from his position, capturing his artillery and 300 or 400 prisoners. Pursuing this advantage, I encountered his second line, which was also routed after a hotly contested fight, again leaving his artillery in our possession. I had previously been cautioned by General Liddell to look well to my left flank, as a force of the enemy were reported advancing in that direction. I accordingly instructed Colonel Gillespie, commanding the left regiment of the brigade, to protect his left by throwing skirmishers well on his flank, and in case of being attacked from that direction to change his front so as to meet the attack.

About the time, or just previous to engaging the third line, a heavy column of the enemy moved on my left flank. The left regiment, according to my instructions, changed front so as to meet it, while the other regiments of the brigade engaged him in front. The overwhelming force which attacked my left flank and had gained my rear forced me to retire, which movement I executed by the flank in order to prevent the capture of a portion of the brigade, and reformed my line in rear of General Cheatham's division, then moving into position. It was afterwards ascertained that we had engaged the whole of General Thomas's (Federal) corps. The two lines which I had driven back in confusion were composed in part of the Fifth, Fourteenth, Fifteenth, Sixteenth, and Twenty-first Regiments Regulars, U. S. Army. Four hundred men and some officers belonging to these regiments were captured and safely sent to the rear, together with three Parrott guns, composing a part of Loomis's battery, designated as Company H, Fifth Artillery, U. S. Army, which were sent to the rear under charge of 3 men, belonging to the First Louisiana Regiment, and delivered to Major Palmer, chief of artillery, Walker's corps. One piece, a James rifled gun, captured by the Second and Fifteenth Arkansas Regiments, was carried to the rear by hand by men belonging to that regiment and delivered to Lieutenant Shannon, commanding Swett's battery. The other pieces from which the enemy had been driven (the horses attached to them being either killed or disabled) we were compelled to leave behind when we retired. This engagement lasted nearly two hours.

In the fight many gallant officers and privates were killed and wounded. Among the first was Col. L. Featherston, commanding Fifth and Thirteenth Arkansas Regiments, who fell mortally wounded while gallantly leading his regiment, and Lieutenant-Colonel Baucum, commanding Eighth Arkansas and First Louisiana Regiments, severely wounded while carrying the colors at the head of his regiment.

Late in the evening I was ordered to the extreme right on the prolongation of the line occupied by General Cheatham, facing westward, with Walthall's brigade on my left. Moving forward, I ascertained that there was no considerable force of the enemy in my front, the firing indicating him to be in the immediate front of General Walthall in force. My left regiment (the Sixth and Seventh Arkansas) gave way and moved about 200 yards to the rear, being, as they informed me, enfiladed and fired into. While in this position one of our own batteries in the rear fired over my lines and slightly wounded several of my men. The fire from the battery continuing, I moved a short distance to the rear and by the left flank and formed on Walthall's right, in which position we remained during the night. I was informed by several officers that there was a battery immediately in front of the last position occupied, which the enemy had abandoned, and which I might have had conveyed to the rear if I had ascertained the fact sooner.

On the morning of the 20th, about 9 o'clock, I was ordered to take a position on the extreme right, supporting Major-General Breckinridge's division. About noon I was ordered to advance, making a slight change of direction to the left. While executing this movement I was ordered by one of Lieutenant-General Polk's staff officers to the assistance of Gist's brigade, who was heavily pressed by the enemy. The officer could only give me general directions as to where General Gist's brigade was engaged. Encountering no enemy in my front, I commenced changing direction to the left, so as to meet the enemy, who had opened fire upon me from the edge of the woods immediately on my left flank. This movement, difficult at all times, was executed across an open field in an exposed position, and under a heavy fire of musketry. The brigade pressed gallantly forward and succeeded in driving the enemy from his position in the woods. Continuing this circular movement to the left, the left regiment pressed up to an angle of the enemy's fortifications, while the right continued to press the enemy across an open field until I had reached a position forming an acute angle with our original direction, and almost immediately in rear of a line of the enemy's strongest breastworks. Gist's brigade, which I had not succeeded in finding, had fallen back about the time I had engaged the enemy. I was thus completely isolated from our line. I would here state that Walthall's brigade had previously been sent to another part of the field. The enemy being massed in heavy force behind his breastworks and perceiving the interval between my left and our line, made a vigorous attack upon my left and succeeded, by enfilading and overlapping it, in breaking it, and thus while the right was driving the enemy, it was in danger of being captured. This was only obviated by the greatest efforts on the part of the regimental commanders, who, after they had succeeded in halting their commands, moved by the right flank and by a circuitous route succeeded in rejoining the command. I immediately reformed the line, and was placed in position in the front line on the left of General Walthall's brigade.

About 5 P. M. orders were received to advance. There was a considerable interval between me and Jackson's brigade, next on my left, which fact was represented to General Liddell and by him communicated to General Walker. The movement commenced, I, in obedience to orders, conforming my movements to those of General Walthall, next on my right. I passed on, moving square to the front, two of the regiments passing through an open field, through which I had executed the change of direction to the left in the engagements last mentioned. The skirmishing in my front developed no enemy. Just before reaching the Chattanooga and La Fayette road, Captain Stringfellow, First Louisiana Regiment, in command of the skirmishers, reported to me that he saw two of the enemy's batteries in position about 250 yards from my left flank on either side of the above-mentioned road, supported by a long line of infantry. Jackson's brigade, which was some distance to my left and rear, having engaged the enemy in his front, had halted, thus leaving my left entirely unprotected.

Upon examination I found the report of Captain Stringfellow to be correct, discovering the enemy to be in position as he represented. It was impossible from the disposition of the enemy's forces for me to extricate myself by changing my front. Reaching a position just across the road and on a line with General Walthall's left, I ordered the men to lie down. The enemy immediately opened fire from the two batteries on my left, also with small-arms, while two batteries, afterwards ascertained to be on General Walthall's right, opened almost at the same time. Under this heavy and galling fire no other alternative was left but to withdraw the brigade as speedily as possible to save it from annihilation or capture.

The brigade retreated in considerable confusion, but was promptly rallied and reformed 300 or 400 yards in rear. Shortly thereafter I again advanced to a position near the house of Mr. McDonald, on the Chattanooga and La Fayette road, and some distance to the right of the position from which I had just been driven. Just about this time the enemy's lines gave way in every quarter and the battle was ended.

The loss in officers and privates was very heavy, being over 50 per cent. of the number carried into the fight, a report* of which is herewith forwarded.

*Not found.

For instances of individual bravery and skill among company officers and privates, I refer you to reports of regimental commanders. Among the field officers Lieut.-Cols. John E. Murray and R. F. Harvey, the former commanding the Fifth and Thirteenth Arkansas Regiments, the latter the Second and Fifth Arkansas Regiments, were particularly distinguished for their gallantry during the engagement, and by their coolness and skill on two occasions saved their regiments from capture. I strongly recommend the first (Lieutenant-Colonel Murray) to the favorable consideration of the President as one particularly distinguished for his skill and gallantry in the battle of Chickamauga.

To Lieutenant-Colonel Harvey, then commanding the Second and Fifteenth Regiments, an equal meed of praise is due, but, unfortunately for the service, this gallant officer died on the 30th instant, of disease contracted by overexertions on the field, lamented by all who knew him.

To Captain Fletcher, Company A Thirteenth Arkansas Regiment, I am indebted for saving one piece of Swett's battery, which had several horses disabled, and, but for his timely efforts would have fallen into the enemy's hands. He seized the colors of the Second and Fifteenth Arkansas Regiments and rallied enough men to drive back the enemy, whose skirmishers were within a short distance of the gun. Lieutenant Shannon, commanding Swett's battery, handled it with distinguished skill and gallantry, and most effectively whenever an opportunity offered.

The members of my staff—Lieut. J. G. Warfield, acting assistant inspector-general; Lieut. W. S. Sawrie, acting assistant adjutant-general, and Lieut. G. T. Snowden, aide-de-camp—rendered me efficient aid and were always at my command.

In conclusion, as an act of justice to the brigade which I had the honor to command, and with which I have been associated in all the hard-contested battles in the west, from Shiloh to this last memorable one, I beg leave to state that they never failed to drive the enemy in their front, and advanced each time with a single line unsupported, and with one or the other of my flanks unprotected, and that on no former occasion was their courage and endurance more severely tested, nor in any previous battle did they ever exhibit more determined bravery and gallantry.

I am, captain, very respectfully, your obedient servant,

D. C. GOVAN,
Colonel, Commanding Brigade.

Capt. G. A. WILLIAMS,
Assistant Adjutant-General.

MISSIONARY RIDGE

Reports of Maj.-Gen. Patrick R. Cleburne, C. S. Army, commanding division, etc., with thanks of the Confederate Congress.*

HEADQUARTERS CLEBURNE'S DIVISION.

COLONEL: On the morning of the 23d November, 1863, I was with my division at Chickamauga Station, on the Western and Atlantic Railroad, attending to the transportation of Buckner's and my own division by rail to Loudon, E. Tenn., where, with both divisions, I was ordered to report to Lieutenant-General Longstreet, then besieging Knoxville.

I had sent off all of Buckner's division except Reynolds's brigade, when I received the following order from army headquarters, viz:

"The general commanding desires that you will halt such portions of your command as have not yet left at Chickamauga; such as may have left halt at Charleston. Do not, however, separate brigades; if parts of brigades have gone, let the remaining portion of the brigade go, but halt at Charleston."

In compliance with the above, I sent forward the remainder of Johnson's brigade, but took a portion of Reynolds's brigade off the cars as it was about to start. I also telegraphed to Brig. Gen. Bushrod Johnson, commanding Buckner's division, directing him to halt the division at Charleston.

I immediately after received the following dispatch from army headquarters, viz:

"Order Johnson's troops at Charleston back here. Move up rapidly with your whole force."

I despatched General Johnson accordingly.

In a few minutes after I received the following, viz:

"We are heavily engaged. Move up rapidly to these headquarters.

BRAXTON BRAGG."

Instructing Brigadier-General Polk to bring up the division, I galloped forward to headquarters for further instructions. I was ordered to rest for the night immediately behind Missionary Ridge, and placed my division accordingly. Returning to General Bragg's headquarters, he informed me that my division would act as reserve for the army and would report directly to him. I ordered Reynolds's brigade, which I brought back with me from Chickamauga, to be reported directly to General Bragg, and had no further control of it.

During the night our line along the western front of Missionary Ridge was abandoned, and at early dawn I commenced to construct a new line of defense along the top of the ridge from the Shallow Ford road to General Bragg's headquarters. Before this was completed General Bragg informed me

**O.R.*, XXXI, part 2, 745-53.

that the enemy had crossed the Tennessee River, both above and below the mouth of the Chickamauga, and directed me to send a brigade and battery to the East Tennessee and Georgia Railroad bridge over the Chickamauga to guard that point. I sent Brigadier-General Polk's command and Semple's battery.

About 2 P. M. on the 24th November, I received orders to proceed with the remaining three brigades and the batteries of my division to the right of Missionary Ridge, near the point where the tunnel of the East Tennessee and Georgia Railroad passes through Missionary Ridge, where I would find an officer of General Hardee's staff, who would show me my position. At the same time General Bragg informed me that the enemy had already a division in line opposite the position I intended to occupy; that he was rapidly crossing another, and had nearly completed a pontoon bridge over the Tennessee opposite my position. He also told me I must preserve the railroad bridge in my rear, where Brigadier-General Polk was stationed, at all hazards. Galloping forward ahead of my command, I found Major Poole, of General Hardee's staff, at the tunnel, who informed me he had been left by General Hardee to show me my position.

I will attempt here a description of the ground. The right of Missionary Ridge, to which I was ordered, runs nearly north and south, parallel to the Tennessee River, which is about 1½ miles west of it. From the tunnel north along the ridge it is about a mile to the Chickamauga River, which bounds the ridge on that side, flowing thence westwardly into the Tennessee River. To simplify the description, the two rivers and the ridge may be said to form three sides of a square. The Tennessee Valley, between the rivers and the ridge, is mostly level, with a continuation of cleared fields bordering the ridge, but immediately in front of the center of my position, about 1,200 yards north and 600 yards west of the railroad tunnel, was a high detached ridge, which in a military point of view dominated over every point within cannon range.

After passing through the tunnel the railroad runs in a northeasterly direction to the Chickamauga, which it crossed on the bridge Brigadier-General Polk was guarding. From the east side of the main ridge there projected two spurs, one, on the north boundary, with its precipitous north side washed by the Chickamauga; the other, jutting out just north of the tunnel, did not run directly back, but northeasterly for 1,000 yards, forming an acute angle with the parent ridge. Opposite the right of this spur, the main ridge was intersected by a little valley, through which came a road from the Tennessee Valley, where the enemy now was. The highest point on my line, and the point of chief interest in the battle on the right, and which I shall designate in this report as Tunnel Hill, was situated on the main ridge 250 yards north of the tunnel. The position pointed out for my command by Major Poole was to occupy, with one brigade, the detached ridge in the Tennessee Valley, and with the remainder of my command to stretch from the top of Tunnel Hill to the right of Walker's division, three-quarters of a mile south of the tunnel.

I sent Major Poole to inform General Hardee that I had but three brigades, and could not cover so long a line. The head of my division, Smith's (Texas) brigade, was now at hand, and at the same moment reported to me from the detached ridge. Private Henry Smith, of the signal corps of my division, informed me he was just from that point; that the enemy was advancing on it in line of battle. I ordered Smith to move his brigade rapidly and try to get possession of it before the enemy had gained a foothold, but if he found the enemy in possession to fall back on the main ridge. General Smith moved into the valley, but was fired on from the top of the detached ridge as he approached its foot. Smith was too late. The enemy had crowned the ridge. He therefore marched by his right flank on to the main or Missionary Ridge, and formed on its top, his two left regiments facing the detached ridge, his right regiment thrown back in an easterly direction to protect his flanks. Smith had scarcely thrown out skirmishers before he was briskly attacked by the skirmishers of the enemy.

In the mean time, I had placed Lowrey's brigade in position south of the tunnel and was about placing Govan's brigade on his left so as to complete my connection with Walker's division, when my attention was attracted to the fighting on my right. It was evident the enemy was endeavoring to turn my right flank and get possession of the main ridge between my right and the Chickamauga. If he succeeded, my connection with Brigadier-General Polk and my line of retreat by the bridge he was guarding was cut, and the safety of the whole army was endangered. Instead of placing Govan's brigade on the main ridge, I placed him on that spur in rear of it which jutted out just north of the tunnel and covered the valley and road before described, which led over the main ridge from the direction of the enemy. Govan rapidly threw skirmishers across this road and between it and the Chickamauga.

Lieutenant-General Hardee was soon on the ground in person. He approved my dispositions, directed the destruction of a bridge which crossed the Chickamauga close in rear of my right flank, and ordered two regiments of Lowrey's brigade and some artillery into position in rear of my right flank. Between the left of Smith's brigade and Walker's division, a distance of near a mile, there were now but two regiments of Lowrey's brigade, and it so remained all night and until 7 A. M. next day.

It was now dark; the fighting had ceased in front of Smith's; he had maintained his position. Hearing of the disaster at Lookout, I supposed our army would fall back beyond the Chickamauga, and accordingly had sent my ordnance and artillery across that river, with the exception of the two pieces of cannon planted beyond my right flank. I sent Captain Buck, my assistant adjutant-general, to headquarters of the army so as to receive any orders that might be given as quickly as possible. About midnight he returned with the information that it was determined to await the enemy's attack on Missionary Ridge. I now ordered my artillery and ordnance to join me at daylight, sent to my train for the axes belonging to the division in order to throw up some defenses, and rode out myself to make a moonlight survey of the ground and line of retreat. I found a hill on the north bank of the Chickamauga, between my right and the railroad bridge, guarded by General Polk, which completely commanded my line of retreat.

I ordered Brigadier-General Polk to occupy this hill at once with two regiments of infantry and a section of artillery. Discovering the facility which it afforded for turning me on the extreme right, I determined to immediately throw a line across the other east spur of Missionary Ridge, which jutted out from the north point of the ridge, and was washed by the Chickamauga. I placed the two regiments of Lowrey's brigade, left near the tunnel, on this line. In the mean time, Smith had thrown up some defenses in his front, but at my suggestion he now abandoned them and took up position as follows, viz: his left resting on the crest of the main ridge about 150 yards north of the tunnel, and running north along the crest for the length of one regiment, the Sixth, Tenth, and Fifteenth Texas (consolidated), Col. R. Q. Mills commanding. The right of this regiment rested close under the crest of Tunnel Hill. On the top of Tunnel Hill a space was left clear of infantry, and Swett's battery of four Napoleon guns, commanded by Lieut. H. Shannon, was placed on it so as to sweep north in the direction of Smith's old position. Northwest of the detached ridge, or west into the Tennessee Valley as occasion might require, at a point about 60 yards northeast of the right of Mills's regiment, Smith's line recommenced, but instead of continuing north, it now ran but slightly north of east down the side of the hill for the length of two regiments, the Seventh Texas, Col. H. B. Granbury commanding, and the Seventeenth, Eighteenth, Twenty-fourth, and Twenty-fifth Dismounted Cavalry (consolidated), Maj. W. A. Taylor commanding. This formation made the angle on the apex of Tunnel Hill, where Swett's battery was planted, the weak point in Smith's line, but it secured Smith's flank, by throwing his extreme right back within 200 yards of Govan's left, bringing the latter officer's line nearly at right angles to his north front, thus enabling each line to assist the other if attacked. At a favorable point of Govan's line, selected by General Hardee, I placed Douglas's battery, commanded by Lieut. John H. Bingham, so as to enfilade any line attempting to charge Smith's north front. Lowrey's position, across the spur before mentioned, was *en échelon* about 200 paces in front of Govan. I ordered the whole of his brigade to occupy this position, and completed my line from Tunnel Hill to Chickamauga. Lowrey had no artillery, the spur being too steep to admit of its being brought up. Calvert's battery, commanded by Lieut. Thomas J. Key, I placed directly over the tunnel, and between the tunnel and left of Smith's brigade were placed three regiments of Brown's brigade, of Stevenson's division. I was determined to construct a slight work in front of my line. I was prevented for some time by an eclipse of the moon, which rendered the morning very dark, but at length, distributing our few axes, we went to work.

The day broke hazy, so that it was some time before the enemy could discover our operations. As soon as he did, he commenced a heavy fire on General Smith's working party, and prevented us from erecting any work whatever in front of the battery on the top of Tunnel Hill. Up to 10:30 A. M. the enemy contented himself with severe skirmishing, and a heavy artillery fire from batteries erected by him during the night on the detached hill. About this hour he drove in Smith's skirmishers, and possessed himself of the breastworks which Smith had abandoned that morning. A heavy attack on the tunnel and on Smith's line was now imminent. General Hardee sent me directions to take my position at the tunnel, and to take charge of everything in that quarter and to the right of it. The enemy was now in sight, advancing in two long lines of battle, his right stretching far beyond my left, his left stretching beyond Smith's right, where further view of it was prevented by the woods that covered and bordered the detached hill. For the full understanding of the fierce conflict that followed, it would be proper for me in this place to give a statement of the force of the enemy opposite my position as ascertained at a later hour from prisoners and other sources. It consisted of the divisions of Maj.-Gen. Jeff C. Davis, three divisions of the army brought by Sherman from Vicksburg, and Howard's (Eleventh) corps, of the Army of the Potomac, all under the command of Major-General Sherman.

At 11 A. M. the first serious fight of the day commenced. It was heavy along Smith's whole line, and extended some distance south of the tunnel. The right of the enemy's line, exposed to the fire of several pieces of artillery planted over the tunnel, and met by a brigade sent by General Hardee to the foot of the ridge, swayed backward and forward for some time, but did not dare to advance nearer than 400 yards, and finally lay down, contenting itself with sending forward a large body of skirmishers and sending to the rear a much larger number of stragglers. The enemy's left, however, under shelter of Smith's abandoned works of the night before, and protected by the woods on that flank, and by the precipitous, heavily wooded sides of Tunnel Hill, advanced rapidly on Smith's line, and finally made a heavy charge on Swett's battery on the apex of the hill. The artillerymen stood bravely to their guns under a terrible cross-fire, and replied with canister at short range, but still the enemy advanced. When he had reached within 50 steps of the battery, Brigadier-General Smith charged him with the right of Mills's regiment and the left of the Seventh Texas, Smith's north front pouring into him from the breastworks a close volley at the same time. The enemy was routed and driven back to his cover behind the hill-side and abandoned work.

In this charge Brigadier-General Smith and Colonel Mills were both severely wounded at the head of their men. Col. H. B. Granbury, Seventh Texas, now assumed command of Smith's brigade. In less than half an hour the enemy made another desperate charge. He was met by the Texas men and artillery in front. Douglas's battery enfiladed him from Govan's hill, and Lowrey's extreme left regiment got a long-range volley on his flank. He was driven back in confusion as before.

In these attacks Lieut. H. Shannon, commanding Swett's battery, was wounded. The command devolved on Lieut. Joseph Ashton; in a few minutes he was mortally wounded.* The command then fell on Corp. F. M. Williams. So many non-commissioned officers and men had been killed and disabled in the battery, Colonel Granbury was forced to make a detail from the infantry to work the guns. There was now a short lull in the battle, during which, at the request of Colonel Granbury, I detailed the Second, Fifteenth, and Twenty-fourth Arkansas (consolidated), under Lieutenant-Colonel Warfield, from Govan's left, and posted them immediately in rear of the battery on top of the Tunnel Hill. I sent two of Swett's 12-pounders to report to Colonel Govan, as Douglas's guns were too light to be effective in their present position. I ordered Key's battery of four light field pieces to move up and replace the guns sent off, and put Lieutenant Key in command of all the artillery on Tunnel Hill.

About 1 P. M. it was evident that another grand attack was soon to be made on my division. In a few minutes after it commenced. The enemy again

*Corporal Joseph Ashton had just been promoted lieutenant, and I handed him his commission as he rode into this battle. An hour later he was a corpse. He was mentioned in official reports for conspicuous gallantry at Chickamauga by Lieutenant Shannon, his battery commander.—I. A. B.

lined Smith's abandoned works, and from them kept up a close, incessant fire on Smith's north front, and particularly on the artillery on top of the hill. Simultaneously a charge was made on the west face of Tunnel Hill. Warfield's regiment was thrown forward outside of the work to the crest of the hill, looking into the Tennessee Valley, to meet this charge. Key fired rapidly into the charging line as it crossed the open ground at the west foot of the ridge, but it was soon under shelter. At the steep the enemy's line now seemed to form into a heavy column on the march and rushed up the hill in the direction of the batteries. Warfield's fire stopped the head of the charging column just under the crest. Here the enemy lay down behind trees, logs, and projecting rocks, their first line not 25 yards from the guns, and opened fire. Tier after tier of the enemy, to the foot of the hill and in the valley beyond, supplied this fire and concentrated the whole on a space of not more than 40 yards, till it seemed like one continuous sheet of hissing, flying lead. This terrific fire prevented Warfield's men from moving sufficiently forward to fire with effect down the hill, but otherwise it only swept over our heads. The crossfire from Smith's abandoned work was, however, more fatal. It took Warfield in flank and was constantly disabling men near the top of the hill.

This desperate attack had now lasted more than half an hour. Key was depressing his guns to the utmost and firing shell and canister down the hill in the face of the enemy's fire. Discovering the impossibility of reaching the enemy by a direct fire, the officers of Warfield's regiment were pitching down heavy stones, apparently with effect.

General Hardee, from a hill south of the tunnel, seeing the stubbornness of the fight, had placed some pieces of artillery in position and was endeavoring to dislodge the enemy with a flank fire, but his right flank was protected by an intervening projection of the hill he was on and this fire was not effective. General Hardee also sent a brigade to move north along the west face of the ridge to strike the enemy in flank, but this brigade returned without accomplishing anything. At this point of the fight Colonel McConnell, commanding a Georgia regiment of Cumming's brigade, came up to the threatened point, and moved his regiment forward to where Warfield's men were fighting. McConnell was shot through the head, and his regiment fell back or was withdrawn. Brigadier-General Cumming, of Stevenson's division, now reported to me with the remainder of his brigade, and was posted in rear of the threatened point. Brigadier-General Maney, of Walker's division, also reported to me with his brigade, and was posted in rear of Smith's line and parallel to it, with instructions to support the Texas brigade behind the works and the artillery at the angle.

The fight had lasted unceasingly for an hour and a half, and the enemy seemed to be constantly reinforcing. The First and Twenty-seventh Tennessee, of Maney's brigade, Colonel Field commanding, was moved in front of the work, and placed on Warfield's right, the latter officer and his gallant regiment still nobly holding their exposed position, although the regiment was diminished in numbers and almost out of ammunition. It was at this critical period of the day that Lieutenant-Colonel Warfield suggested to me that our men were wasting ammunition and becoming disheartened at the persistency of the enemy, and proposed a charge down upon them with the bayonet. Brigadier-General Cumming gallantly proposed to lead the charge with two of his regiments. I immediately consented, and directed General Cumming to prepare for the charge, and went to the left to see that a simultaneous charge was made on the enemy's right flank. I now ordered the left of Mills's (Texas) regiment, being the extreme left of my division, to make the charge on the enemy's flank the moment that Cumming charged them in front, and I remained at the breastwork myself to see the execution of the order.

In the mean time, General Cumming, having placed the Fifty-sixth Georgia in line for the charge, and supported it by placing the Thirty-sixth Georgia 10 paces in rear, moved forward to the charge; twice he was checked and had to reform. Warfield's (Arkansas) regiment with empty guns, and the gallant First and Twenty-seventh Tennessee prepared to share his next effort. At the command the whole rushed forward with a cheer, Lieutenant-Colonel Sanders simultaneously leading the left of Mills's (Texas) regiment on the enemy's flank. The enemy, completely surprised, fled down the foot, the Texas troops on the left pursuing him beyond the foot and nearly across the open ground in front. Our charging columns returned with many prisoners and stands of colors; a fresh force of the enemy, attempting to follow us as we returned from this charge, was quickly met and routed by the Fiftieth Tennessee and with troops of my division. Immediately on his last repulse the enemy opened a rapid and revengeful artillery fire on Tunnel Hill from his batteries on the detached hill, and under cover of this fire he went to work felling trees and fortifying his position.

It is but justice for me to state that the brunt of this long day's fight was borne by Smith's (Texas) brigade and the Second, Fifteenth, and Twenty-fourth Arkansas (consolidated), of Govan's brigade, together with Swett's and Key's batteries. The remainder of my division was only engaged in heavy skirmishing. The final charge was participated in and successful through the timely appearance and gallant assistance of the regiments of Cumming's and Maney's brigades before mentioned.

Out of the eight stands of colors shown by me to have been captured, four were presented to me by Mills's (Texas) regiment, two were presented by the Fifty-sixth and Thirty-sixth Georgia Regiments, of Cumming's brigade; one flag was presented by the First Tennessee, of Maney's brigade, and one by the Second, Fifteenth, and Twenty-fourth Arkansas (consolidated) of Govan's brigade; in all, eight colors, six of which I herewith transmit. Among them are the flags of the Twenty-seventh Pennsylvania and Ninety-third Illinois. About 500 prisoners were captured. At a critical moment of the battle I lost two of the bravest officers of my division—Brig.-Gen. J. A. Smith, commanding the Texas brigade, and Col. R. Q. Mills, the same officer who commanded it in the battle of Chickamauga, after General Deshler fell. Including these gallant officers, other noble officers and men, some of whose names are handed down to history in the reports of brigade and regimental commanders.

I suffered the following losses in three brigades of my division engaged, viz, 42 killed, 178 wounded, and 2 missing.

Colonel Sugg, of the Fiftieth Tennessee Regiment, Maney's brigade, was dangerously wounded in the last charge. Colonel McConnell, of Cumming's brigade, and other gallant soldiers who fell in front of my works, I can but lament. I did not personally know them, but I saw and can bear witness to their gallant bearing and noble deaths.

The enemy must have suffered severely, the hill-side and the valley were thickly strewn with his dead, and if we may credit his published reports of casualties in this fight, he lost 1 major-general, John E. Smith, wounded; 3 brigadier-generals, Corse, Matthies, and Giles Smith, wounded, the latter mortally, and 1 colonel commanding brigade, Colonel Raum, mortally wounded.*

Soon after the final defeat of the enemy in front of Smith's position, I received a dispatch from General Hardee to send to the center all the troops I could spare, as the enemy were pressing us in that quarter. I immediately ordered Generals Cumming and Maney, with their respective brigades, to report accordingly, and went myself to push them forward. Before I had gone far, however, a dispatch from General Hardee reached me, with the appalling news that the enemy had pierced our center, and were on Missionary Ridge, directing me to take command of my own, Walker's and Stevenson's divisions and form a line across the ridge, so as to meet an attack upon my flank, and take all other necessary measures for the safety of the right wing. I ordered Brigadier-General Gist, commanding Walker's division, to form it across the ridge; ordered all vehicles which could be spared, to cross the Chickamauga. Sent Brigadier-General Polk orders to despatch a

---

*Neither Smith nor Raum was mortally wounded.

force to the Shallow Ford Bridge, and hold it at all hazards, and sent Govan's brigade to dispute the enemy's advance on the Shallow Ford road.

Soon after night was upon us, and General Hardee ordered an immediate retreat across the Chickamauga, and that Smith's (Texas) brigade should remain in position and bring up the rear. General Lowrey attacked and drove back the enemy's skirmishers in his front and then retreated. By 9 P. M. everything was across except the dead and a few stragglers lingering here and there under the shadow of the trees for the purpose of being captured, faint-hearted patriots succumbing to the hardships of the war and imagined hopelessness of the hour. I now ordered Smith's brigade to move in retreat. Sadly, but not fearfully, this band of heroes left the hill they had held so well and followed the army across the Chickamauga.

To Brigadier-Generals Smith, Cumming, and Maney, and Colonel Granbury, I return my thanks for the able manner in which they managed their commands. My thanks are also due to Brigadier-Generals Polk and Lowrey, and Colonel Govan, commanding brigades; although not actively engaged, they were rendering good service in holding important positions.

Swett's battery, under command of Lieut. H. Shannon, and Calvert's battery, commanded by Lieut. Thomas J. Key, were bravely fought and did great execution. Swett's battery was hotly engaged the whole day and lost some noble officers and men.

A section of Barrett's battery, under command of Lieut. Isaiah Lightner, in position where the road crosses the hill, did much towards driving back the right of the enemy's line in its attempted advance across the open fields.

Brig. Gen. John C. Brown's brigade, on my left flank, was engaged in heavy skirmishing most of the day.

The following officers of my staff—Maj. Calhoun Benham, assistant adjutant-general; Maj. J. K. Dixon, assistant inspector-general; Capt. Irving A. Buck, assistant adjutant-general; Capt. Charles S. Hill, ordnance officer (whose horse was shot under him); Surg. D. A. Linthicum, Lieuts. L. H. Mangum and S. P. Hanly, aides-de-camp, and Capt. C. H. Byrne, volunteer aide-de-camp (whose horse was shot under him)—acted with their usual gallantry and discharged their duties with zeal and intelligence.

Messrs. Henry Smith and William Rucker, of the signal corps, volunteered on my staff for the battle, and were very efficient.

Very respectfully, your obedient servant,

P. R. CLEBURNE,

Major-General, Provisional Army, C. S.

COL. KINLOCH FALCONER,

Assistant Adjutant-General.

It will be noticed that during this engagement, in addition to his own division, Cleburne had command of Cumming's and Maney's brigades—and Barrett's battery—at least a corps. And after the piercing of the Confederate left-center he was placed in command, with his own, of the divisions of Walker and Stevenson.

RINGGOLD GAP*

HEADQUARTERS CLEBURNE'S DIVISION,
Tunnel Hill, Ga., December 9, 1863.

COLONEL: On the retreat of the Army of Tennessee from Missionary Ridge, Tennessee, to Ringgold, Georgia, my division covered the retreat of Hardee's corps, arriving safely on the west bank of the East Chickamauga River at 10 P. M. on November 26. At this point the river had to be forded. It was nearly waist-deep and the night was freezing cold. I therefore determined to postpone crossing until the morning and bivouacked on the hills near by.

At 3 A. M. on the 27th I received the following order, viz:
"Major-General CLEBURNE.

"GENERAL: The General desires that you will take strong position in the gorge of the mountain and attempt to check pursuit of enemy. He must be punished until our trains and the rear of our troops get well advanced. The reports from the rear are meager and the General is not thoroughly advised of the state of things there. Will you be good enough to report fully?

"Respectfully,

GEORGE WM. BRENT,
"Assistant Adjutant-General."

Leaving staff officers to conduct the troops across the river to the position designated, I went forward myself to examine the ground and form a plan for its defense.

The town of Ringgold, a place of 2,000 or 3,000 inhabitants, stands on a plain between the East Chickamauga River and the range of hills known as Taylor's Ridge. It is on the Western and Atlantic Railroad, about 20 miles southeast of Chattanooga. Taylor's Ridge, which rises up immediately back of the town, runs in a northerly and southerly direction. Opposite the town the ridge is intersected by a narrow gap, which admits the railroad, a wagon road, and a good sized creek, a tributary of the Chickamauga. The creek hugs the southernmost or left-hand hill as you face Ringgold. The wagon and railroad run close to the creek. At its western mouth, next to Ringgold the

*O.R., XXXI, part 2, 753-58.

gap widens out to a breadth of over 100 yards, leaving room for a patch of level wooded land on each side of the roads. The gap is about half a mile through, but the plain immediately in front of its east or rear mouth is so cut up by the windings of the creek that three bridges, or three fords, have to be crossed in the first half mile of road leading from the gap to Dalton. It will be perceived at once that this was a most dangerous position to be caught in if the enemy should succeed in turning either flank.

The gap and the hills on either hand are thinly wooded, except the base of the right-hand hill, along which, next to the town, a heavy fringe of young timber extends from the gap northward for 300 or 400 yards. Behind this fringe of trees I placed two regiments of Smith's (Texas) brigade, Col. H. B. Granbury, Seventh Texas, commanding; the Sixth, Tenth, and Fifteenth Texas (consolidated), Capt. John R. Kennard commanding, on the left; the Seventeenth, Eighteenth, Twenty-fourth, and Twenty-fifth Texas Dismounted Cavalry (consolidated), Maj. W. A. Taylor commanding, on the right; the remaining regiment of the brigade, the Seventh Texas, Capt. C. E. Talley commanding, I sent to the top of the right-hand hill, with instructions to keep out of view, but watch well the right flank of its brigade at the foot. On the precipitous hill to the left of the gap and creek I placed the Sixteenth Alabama, Maj. F. A. Ashford commanding, of Lowrey's (Alabama and Mississippi) brigade, with instructions to conceal itself and guard well the left flank. I also sent on the face of this hill fronting Ringgold three companies of the Sixth and Seventh Arkansas (consolidated), of Liddell's (Arkansas) brigade, under charge of Lieutenant Dulin, of General Liddell's staff. For the defense of the gap itself, I disposed the rest of the Arkansas brigade, under command of Col. D. C. Govan; the Fifth and Thirteenth Arkansas (consolidated), Col. John E. Murray commanding, I placed in a small ravine running across the mouth of the gap from the right-hand hill to the railroad embankment; the Eighth and Nineteenth Arkansas (consolidated), under command of Lieut. Col. A. S. Hutchison, 50 paces in rear and parallel to the former regiment; the Sixth and Seventh Arkansas (consolidated), under command of Lieut. Col. Peter Snyder, and the Second, Fifteenth, and Twenty-fourth Arkansas Regiments (consolidated), under Lieut. Col. E. Warfield, at suitable distances in rear and covered as well as the nature of the ground would permit, thus giving me four short lines across the gap. From these regiments I sent a body of skirmishers to occupy the patch of woods at the mouth of the gap and left of the railroad and that portion of the bank of the creek close to the mouth of the gap. In front of the mouth of the gap, supported by Govan's foremost regiment in the ravine, I placed a section of Semple's battery, two Napoleon guns, commanded by

Lieutenant Goldthwaite. I had screens of withered branches built up in front of these, so as to effectually conceal them from view, and made the artillerymen shelter themselves in the ravine close by. The remaining three regiments of Lowrey's brigade—consisting of the Thirty-second and Forty-fifth Mississippi Regiments (consolidated), under command of Col. A. B. Hardcastle: the Thirty-third Alabama, under command of Col. Samuel Adams, and the Forty-fifth Alabama, Lieut.-Col. H. D. Lampley commanding—I placed in reserve in the center of the gap. The portion of Polk's (Tennessee and Arkansas) brigade with me—consisting of the First Arkansas, Col. J. W. Colquitt commanding; the Second Tennessee, Col. W. D. Robinson commanding, and the Third and Fifth Confederate Regiments (consolidated), under Lieut.-Col. J. C. Cole—I ordered to take position temporarily near the rear mouth of the gap with directions to observe my right flank and prevent the enemy from turning me in that quarter.

I had scarcely half an hour to make these dispositions, when I was informed that the enemy's skirmishers were crossing the Chickamauga, driving our cavalry before them. Immediately after the cavalry retreated through the gap at a trot, and the valley in front was clear of our troops, but close in rear of the ridge our immense train was still in full view, struggling through the fords of the creek and the deeply cut-up roads leading to Dalton, and my division, silent, but cool and ready, was the only barrier between it and the flushed and eager advance of the pursuing Federal army.

Shortly after 8 A. M. the enemy's skirmishers were in view, advancing. He opened fire, and under cover of it his lines of battle were placed and moved with the utmost decision and celerity against the ridge on the right of the gap. So quick and confident was this attack, the enemy must have been acting on a concerted plan, and must have had guides who knew well the nature of the country. As the first line moved towards the ridge its right flank became exposed at canister range to my artillery in the mouth of the gap. Five or six rapid discharges broke the right of this line to pieces and caused them to run for shelter under the railroad embankment. Farther to his left, however, he continued to advance, and made a heavy attack on the right-hand ridge. He continued to advance in the face of a deadly fire from Major Taylor's regiment, with the determination to turn the right flank of the Texas Brigade. Major Taylor deployed skirmishers up the hill at right angles to his line of battle, and held him in check, while he informed Colonel Granbury of the state of affairs. Colonel Granbury sent two companies of his left regiment to reinforce his right. With three companies of his own regiment Major Taylor charged down the hill upon the force attempting to turn him, and routed it, capturing between 60 and 100 prisoners and the colors of the Twenty-ninth Missouri Regiment.

In the mean time, I had ascertained that the enemy was moving another line of battle some distance beyond my present right with the view of ascending the ridge in that quarter. I instantly notified Brigadier-General Polk, stationed in the rear of the gap, to ascend the ridge and meet this attempt of the enemy. Luckily General Polk had already heard of this movement from a breathless straggler of our army who was fleeing before the enemy, and, anticipating my order, sent the First Arkansas up the hill and met the enemy's skirmishers within a few yards of the top. With the assistance of the Seventh Texas, after an obstinate fight, the enemy was driven down the hill. By this time large bodies of the enemy had crossed the Chickamauga, and it was evident that the main attack was about to be made upon the right. I ordered General Lowrey to move his command up the hill and assist General Polk in defending that position. Moving rapidly ahead of his command, General Lowrey found the First Arkansas again heavily engaged, but heroically holding its ground against great odds. Assuring the regiment that support was at hand, he brought up the Thirty-second and Forty-fifth Mississippi in double time, and threw them into the fight at the critical moment. The enemy gave way and went down the ridge in great confusion. Lowrey now brought up the two remaining regiments of his brigade and Polk the two other regiments of his command. The enemy, constantly reinforcing, made another powerful effort to crown the ridge still farther to the right.

A peculiarity of Taylor's Ridge is the wavy conformation of its north side. The enemy, moving up in a long line of battle, suddenly concentrated opposite one of the depressions in this wavy surface and rushed up it in heavy column. General Polk, with the assistance of General Lowrey, as quickly concentrated a double line opposite this point, at the same time placing the Second Tennessee in such a position as to command the flank of any force emerging from it. The attack was again defeated and the enemy hurled down the hill, with the loss of many killed on the spot, several prisoners, and the colors of the Seventy-sixth Ohio Regiment. The colors and most of the prisoners were captured by the First Arkansas.

In a fight where all fought nobly I feel it my duty to particularly compliment this regiment for its courage and constancy. In the battle the officers fought with pistols and with rocks, and so close was the fight that some of the enemy were knocked down with the latter missiles and captured. Apprehending another attack, General Polk rapidly threw up some slight defenses in his front.

But I must now return to the extreme left which the enemy attempted to turn. He sent what appeared to be a brigade of three regiments to the creek upon my left, and crossed over some companies of skirmishers. These were promptly met and stopped by a detachment from the Sixteenth Alabama, posted on the left-hand hill, and the main body was for some time held in check by Dulin's skirmishers, on the face of the left-hand hill, and the other skirmishers of Govan's brigade, on the creek bank and in the patch of woods to the left of the railroad. He got possession, however, of some houses and barns opposite this point, from which he annoyed me with a constant and well-directed fire of sharpshooters. At length, collecting in large numbers behind these houses, he made a charge on Govan's skirmishers on the left of the railroad. Lieutenant Goldthwaite quickly trained round his guns and swept them at quarter range with a load of canister and a solid shot. They ran back, leaving several dead and a stand of colors on the ground. Lieutenant Goldthwaite then shelled the houses, and greatly relieved us of the firing from that quarter. The stand of colors lay temptingly within 60 yards of my line, and some of the officers wanted to charge and get it, but as it promised no solid advantage to compensate for the loss of brave soldiers, I would not permit it.

About 12 M. I received a dispatch from Lieutenant-General Hardee, to the effect that the train was now well advanced, and I might safely withdraw. On consultation with Generals Breckinridge and Wheeler, both of whom were present lending me their personal assistance, I determined to withdraw from Taylor's Ridge and take up a new position on some wooded hills 1 mile in rear.

About 1 P. M. I rebuilt the screen in front of the artillery, which had been partially blown away, and then withdrew both pieces by hand without loss. By this time the enemy had concentrated a large portion of his army at Ringgold, and was doubtless preparing to throw an overwhelming force on my flanks. He opened a rapid artillery fire down the gap and on the crest of the ridge, but showed no disposition to advance in front. I now simultaneously withdrew the brigades, leaving a few skirmishers to hold the front, which they did without difficulty.

Soon after 2 P. M. I withdrew my skirmishers, fired the bridges in my rear, and proceeded to form line of battle in my new position. The enemy was visible on the ridge in about half an hour after I had withdrawn my skirmishers. He saw my new dispositions for defense, but showed no further inclination to attack, and ceased from all further pursuit of our army.

I took into the fight: In Polk's brigade, 545; Lowrey's brigade, 1,330; Smith's (Texas) brigade, 1,266; Liddell's brigade, 1,016 effective men, making a total of 4,157 bayonets.

My loss was 20 killed, 190 wounded, and 11 missing. I am confident the enemy's loss was out of all proportion greater than mine.

The conduct of the officers and men in this fight needs no comment; every man, as far as I know, did his whole duty.

To Brigadier-Generals Polk and Lowrey and Colonels Govan and Granbury, I must return my thanks. Four better officers are not in the service of the Confederacy.

Lieutenant Goldthwaite, of the artillery, proved himself a brave and skillful officer.

The following officers of my staff have my thanks for the efficient manner in which they discharged their responsible and dangerous duties: Maj. Calhoun Benham, assistant adjutant-general; Maj. J. K. Dixon, assistant inspector-general; Capt. Irving A. Buck, assistant adjutant-general; Capt. C. S. Hill, ordnance officer; Surg. D. A. Linthicum; Lieuts. L. H. Mangum, S. P. Hanly, aides-de-camp; Capt. C. H. Byrne, volunteer aide-de-camp; also Messrs. Henry Smith and William Rucker, of the signal corps, who volunteered their services, and who I found very efficient and useful.

I forward herewith the reports of the brigade, regimental, and battery commanders. General Liddell was absent on leave, but hearing of the fight returned and rendered me all the assistance in his power. He selected and reformed the new line after we withdrew from our first position.

Respectfully, your obedient servant,

P. R. CLEBURNE,
Major-General.

COL. GEORGE WILLIAM BRENT,
Assistant Adjutant-General, Army of Tennessee.

No. 16.—JOINT RESOLUTION of thanks to Maj-Gen. Patrick R. Cleburne, and the officers and men under his command, for distinguished service at Ringgold Gap, in the State of Georgia, November 27, 1863.

Resolved, That the thanks of Congress are due, and are hereby tendered to Maj.-Gen. Patrick R. Cleburne, and the officers and men under his command, for the victory obtained by them over superior forces of the enemy at Ringgold Gap, in the State of Georgia, on the 27th day of November, 1863, by which the advance of the enemy was impeded, our wagon train and most of our artillery saved, and a large number of the enemy killed and wounded.

Resolved, That the President be requested to communicate the foregoing resolution to Major-General Cleburne and his command.

Approved February 9, 1864.

PICKETT'S MILL*

Report of Maj.-Gen. P. R. Cleburne, C. S. Army, Commanding Division, of the Battle of New Hope Church (Pickett's Mill).

HEADQUARTERS CLEBURNE'S DIVISION,
PAULDING COUNTY, GA., *May 30, 1864.*

COLONEL: In compliance with orders I submit the following account of the operations of my division on the afternoon and night of the 27th instant:

About 2 or 3 o'clock of the afternoon of the 26th I arrived with my division on the extreme right of the then line of the army, when I was sent to support Major-General Hindman. At that point our lines, the general bearing of which was north and south, retired for a few yards to the east. In continuation of this retiring line I placed [L. E.] Polk's brigade, of my division, in and diagonally across it upon a ridge *en échelon* by battalion to avoid an artillery enfilade from a neighboring position held by the enemy. Resting on Polk's right was placed Hotchkiss's artillery, consisting of four Napoleons, four Parrott guns, and four howitzers. Supporting Hotchkiss on the right was one regiment of [D. C.] Govan's, of my division. The remainder of my division was disposed in rear as a second line in support of Hindman's right brigades and my first line. Intrenchments were thrown up in the afternoon and night of the 26th and in the morning of the 27th. The position was, in the main, covered with trees and undergrowth, which served as a screen along our lines [and] concealed us, and were left standing as far as practicable for that purpose.

On the morning of the 27th at about 7 o'clock Govan was sent to the north front on a reconnaissance, with directions to swing to the left in his advance. From time to time while engaged in this reconnaissance Govan sent

---

O.R., XXXVIII, part 3, 720-26; This report, in Captain Buck's handwriting and signed by Cleburne, is now (1958) in a collection of papers of General Joseph E. Johnston in the Henry E. Huntington Library, San Marino, Cal. It may have been forwarded to General Johnston, while he was still in command of the Army of Tennessee, by General J. B. Hood, to whom it was addressed. Apparently, this is *not* the report to which Major Benham refers as being in the possession of Miss Sue Tarleton of Mobile, General Cleburne's fiance (see *ante,* pages 54-57). Miss Norma Cuthbert of the Huntington Library writes: "In my opinion this document [Cleburne's report of May 30, 1864, given above] never was in the possession of [Miss] Sue Tarleton." The question remains as to the present whereabouts of the report Major Benham refers to as "a report which I also prepared and he [Cleburne] examined and approved and which gives the history of his division in the Dalton-Atlanta campaign." (see *ante,* page 55).

me word that the enemy was moving to the right (his own left). At 11 A. M. upon my order to that effect, Govan came in, leaving his skirmishers about three-quarters of a mile in front. I at once placed him on the right of Polk, where he covered himself in rifle-pits.

About 4 P. M., hearing that the enemy's infantry in line of battle were pressing the cavalry on my right—they had already driven in my skirmishers —I placed [H. B.] Granbury on Govan's right. He had but just gotten into position and a dismounted cavalry force, in line behind a few disconnected heaps of stones loosely piled together, had passed behind him when the enemy advanced. He showed himself first, having driven back my skirmishers, in the edge of an open field in front of Govan about 400 yards across, where he halted and opened fire. From the point on the ridge where Govan's right and Granbury's left met there made off a spur, which at about a hundred yards from it turned sharply to the northeast, running then in a direction almost parallel with it and maintaining about an equal elevation. Between this spur and the parent ridge, beginning in front of Granbury's left, was a deep ravine, the side of which next to Granbury was very steep, with occasional benches of rock, up to line within 30 or 40 yards of Granbury's men, where it flattened into a natural glacis. This glacis was well covered with well grown trees, and in most places with thick undergrowth. Here was the brunt of the battle, the enemy advancing along this front in numerous and constantly reinforced lines. His men displayed a courage worthy of an honorable cause, pressing in steady throngs within a few paces of our men, frequently exclaiming, "Ah! damn you, we have caught you without your logs now." Granbury's men, needing no logs, were awaiting them, and throughout awaited them with calm determination, and as they appeared upon the slope slaughtered them with deliberate aim. The piles of his dead on this front, pronounced by the officers of this army who have seen most service to be greater than they had ever seen before, were a silent but sufficient eulogy upon Granbury and his noble Texans. In the great execution here done upon the enemy, Govan, with his two right regiments, disdaining the enemy in his own front, who were somewhat removed, and Key, with his two pieces of artillery, run up by hand upon my order to a convenient trench made in our breastworks, materially aided Granbury by a right-oblique fire, which enfiladed the masses in his front.

In front of a prolongation of Granbury's line and abutting upon his right was a field about three hundred yards square. The enemy, driving back some cavalry at this point, advanced completely across the field and passed some forty or fifty yards in its rear. Here, however, they were confronted by the Eighth and Nineteenth Arkansas, consolidated, commanded by [Colonel

G. F.] Baucum, hastily sent by Govan upon Granbury's request and representation of the exigency. In a sweeping charge Baucum drove the enemy from the ridge in his front, and with irresistible impetuosity forced him across the field and back into the woods from which he had at first advanced. Here he fixed himself and kept up a heavy fire, aided by a deadly enfilade from the bottom of the ravine in front of Granbury.

When Baucum was about to charge, Lowrey, of my division, who had been hastened up from his distant position (upwards of a mile and a half from my right as finally established), came into line, throwing his regiments in successively as they unmasked themselves by their flank march. His arrival was most opportune, as the enemy was beginning to pour around Baucum's right. Colonel [S.] Adams, with the Thirty-third Alabama, which was the first of Lowrey's regiments to form into line, took position on Baucum's right and advanced with him, his seven left companies being in the field with Baucum and his other four in the woods to the right. Baucum and Adams finding themselves suffering from the enemy's direct and oblique fire, withdrew, passing over the open space of the field behind them. The right companies of Adams, which were in the woods, retired to a spur which rises from the easterly edge of the field about 200 yards from its southerly edge, where Baucum's and Adams's left companies rested. Here they halted, Captain [Wm. E.] Dodson with fine judgment perceiving the importance of the position—it would have given the enemy an enfilading fire upon Granbury, which would have dislodged him—and making his company the basis of alignment for the remainder of Lowrey, now coming into position.

This retrograde movement across the field was not attended with loss, as might have been expected, the enemy not advancing as it was made. It was mistaken, however, for a repulse, and some of my staff-officers, hearing that my line had broken, hastened forward Quarles's brigade, of Stewart's division (just then providentially sent up by General Hood) to reestablish it. Lowrey being under the same impression, detached his two right regiments (which had not been engaged) under Colonels [W. H. H.] Tison and [A. B.] Hardcastle, and had them quickly formed in support of Baucum and Adams. The error, however, was soon discovered, and my line being ascertained to remain in its integrity, Quarles's brigade was conducted to the rear of Lowrey and formed as a second line.

The Fourth Louisiana (Colonel [S. E.] Hunter) finding itself opposite an interval between the two regiments of Lowrey's line, caused by Baucum's resting closer upon Granbury on his return from the advance than he had done at first, under the immediate superintendence of General Quarles advanced into the field, halted, and delivered a very effective fire upon the enemy in his front. After some minutes Quarles withdrew this regiment and formed it behind the field, where they continued their fire across it. General Quarles and his brigade have my thanks.

During these movements the battle continued to rage on Granbury's front and was met with unflagging spirit.

About the time of Quarles getting into position night came on, when the combat lulled. For some hours afterwards a desultory dropping fire, with short, vehement bursts of musketry, continued, the enemy lying in great numbers immediately in front of portions of my line, and so near it that their footsteps could be distinctly heard.

About 10 P. M. I ordered Granbury and Lowrey to push forward skirmishers and scouts to learn the state of things in their respective fronts. Granbury, finding it impossible to advance his skirmishers until he had cleared his front of the enemy lying up against it, with my consent charged with his whole line, Walthall, with his brigade from Hindman's division, whom I sent to his support, taking his place in the line as he stepped out of it. The Texans, their bayonets fixed, plunged into the darkness with a terrific yell, and with one bound were upon the enemy; but they met with no resistance. Surprised and panic-stricken, many fled, escaping in the darkness; others surrendered and were brought into our lines. It needed but the brilliancy of this night attack to add lustre to the achievements of Granbury and his brigade in the afternoon. I am deeply indebted to them both.

My thanks are also due to General Lowrey for the coolness and skill which he exhibited in forming his line. His successive formation was the precise answer to the enemy's movement in extending his left to turn our right. Time was of the essence of things and his movement was the quickest. His line was formed under heavy fire on ground unknown to him and of the most difficult character, and the stern firmness with which he and his men and Baucum's regiment drove off the enemy and resisted his renewed attacks, without doubt, saved the right of the army, as Granbury had already done before.

During the progress of the battle much service was rendered by the rifle battery and two remaining howitzers of Key's battery, in position on Polk's right. They were trained in enfilade upon the enemy's reserves massed behind the hill in front of the spur we occupied. I regretted I did not have more guns for this service. I had sent the Napoleon guns to the right, where they were unable to find positions, and so were useless. During these operations Polk was not engaged, but it was a source of strength and confidence to the rest of the division to know that he had charge of the weakest and most delicate part of our line.

It is due to the following officers of my staff that I should acknowledge the industry, zeal and activity they manifested in the battle—Maj. Calhoun Benham, assistant adjutant-general; Maj. J. K. Dixon, assistant inspector-general; Capt. Irving A. Buck, assistant adjutant-general; Capt. Robert McFarland, Lieutenants L. H. Mangum, S. P. Hanly, and J. W. Jetton, aides-de-camp, and Capt. C. H. Byrne, volunteer aide-de-camp. They did their full duty with ability, gallantry, and enthusiasm. I am indebted to them for their co-operation.

My ordnance, under Capt. C. S. Hill, and my medical department, under Surgeon D. A. Linthicum, and my artillery, under Maj. T. R. Hotchkiss, were well administered.

My casualties in this battle were few. I had 85 killed, 363 wounded, carrying into the engagement 4,683 muskets. The enemy's losses were very heavy. The lowest estimate of his dead is 500. We captured 160 prisoners, who were sent to Army Headquarters, exclusive of 72 of his wounded carried to my field hospital. He could not have lost in all less than 3,000 killed and wounded. I took upwards of 1,200 small-arms.

This battle was fought at a place known as the Pickett Settlement, and about two miles east of New Hope Church.

Very respectfully,

P. R. CLEBURNE,
Major-General.

Lieutenant-Colonel [W. H.] SELLERS,
Assistant Adjutant-General, Hood's Corps.

APPENDIX A

[Letters of Cleburne dated July 15 and 16, 1864, have not been located in the *Official Records*. Perhaps these were copies of letters retained by Captain Buck.—Editor]

"COLUMBIA, TENNESSEE,
"May 30, 1908.

"MY DEAR CAPTAIN BUCK:

*   *   *   *   *   *   *   *   *

"I enclose you General Cleburne's farewell address to my Regiment, (48th Tennessee), and his endorsement of my ability and worthiness of promotion. * * * While General Sherman was commander of the Army [and] stationed in New York, [at] Governor's Island, in 1884, I met him [and] was introduced by a mutual friend. General Sherman asked, 'Are you in the Regular Army, Colonel?' I laughingly replied not, and he said, 'Were you ever in the Army: (you) look too young to have been '61-'65. I said, 'Yes, I have fronted you before this, General, on many occasions'; and he asked me when, where, and whose command? I told him with General Cleburne, and he then said, 'I want to shake hands with you again, and hats off in memory of Pat Cleburne, the ablest division commander in your army. When we met with Cleburne's division, we always had to fight' * * *

"Sincerely your friend and comrade,

H. G. EVANS,
"Col. 48th (Nixon's) Tenn. Infantry."

The following are copies of the two papers referred to:

"HEADQUARTERS CLEBURNE'S DIVISION,
"IN THE FIELD, *July 15, 1864.*

"Special Orders
No.

"By direction of General Johnston, the Forty-eighth Tennessee Regiment is relieved from duty with this Division, and will report to Brigadier-General Quarles, for incorporation with Colonel Voorhees, Forty-eighth Tennessee.

"In severing his connection with the small, but noble remnant of this regiment, justice, as well as feeling, prompts General Cleburne to express his admiration of the gallant and soldierly conduct its members have ever manifested. While under his command, Richmond, Ky., Perryville, Murfreesboro, Chickamauga, Ringgold Gap have been inscribed upon its colors, and the names of the victories of the present trying campaign may justly be placed there.

"As a battalion of sharpshooters, its courage, skill and endurance have been tested and proven in innumerable bloody skirmishes. The handful to which it is reduced attests how conspicuous a part it must have borne in building up the glorious reputation of the brigade and division which it is about to be separated from.

"General Cleburne bids you a soldier's farewell, and trusts that he may deserve and retain through life the good will and kind feeling which he bears to each surviving member of the Forty-eighth Tennessee.

"By command of Major-General Cleburne.

"I. A. BUCK,
"A. A. Gen.

"For Capt. H. G. EVANS,
"Commanding Forty-eighth Tennessee."

"HEADQUARTERS CLEBURNE'S DIVISION,
"July 16, 1864.

"Captain H. G. Evans, Forty-eighth Tennessee Regiment, having been ordered to appear before the board for promotion, I take pleasure in stating that he has been under my immediate command since soon after the battle of Shiloh, a portion of which time he has been in command of his regiment, and has proven himself fully competent for the position for which he is to be examined. He is brave and intelligent in action, and a good disciplinarian in camp, and I have no hesitation in recommending his case for the favorable consideration of the board.

"P. R. CLEBURNE,
"Major-General."

APPENDIX B

Gen. John H. Morgan was killed by a deserter from Cleburne's Division.

Upon surrender of General Johnston at Greensboro, North Carolina, the paroled soldiers were formed into organizations of those from neighboring sections, on certain lines of March, and put under command of officers of rank, and as each company or command reached the vicinity of home, it dropped out of line. One of these organizations was placed under General Govan, and its route was via Asheville and Knoxville to Chattanooga. When near Knoxville the column was met by a company of Federal cavalry, which after greetings were exchanged passed on. Turning to the adjutant of the Second Arkansas, General Govan said, "Sawrie, the face of the captain of that company seemed very familiar." The reply was, "Why, General, I recognized him; it is Campbell, the sergeant of your old regiment, who deserted at Wartrace." Subsequently Govan met Campbell in Arkansas, who told him that he deserted because of some injustice done him by his captain; that he entered the enemy's lines, and being unable to return to Arkansas, and with no means of subsistence, enlisted in the Federal army, won a commission, finally reaching the grade of captain. He also said that he fired the shot which killed Gen. John H. Morgan, under the following circumstances as related by Campbell: On September 4, 1864, his command was in the vicinity of Greenville, Tennessee; and he was informed by a woman that General Morgan and staff had quartered for the night at a house in town, unguarded, and his command was some distance away. Campbell's company surrounded the house, and at about dawn demanded surrender. He observed a man attempting to escape through the shrubbery in the garden, who refused to stop when ordered, upon which Campbell fired and the man fell. In the dim light of breaking dawn the body was not first recognized as that of General Morgan. Campbell asserted that when he fired he had no idea as to whom it was he was shooting at. It is singular that the gallant Morgan should have fallen by the hand of a Confederate deserter.

This statement may be relied upon as authentic, as the author had this account from General Govan's lips, in the presence of Capt. Geo. A. Williams, of New Orleans, in May, 1906.

APPENDIX C

Correspondence regarding Cleburne's advocating freeing and enlistment of negroes in the Army.

"NEAR DALTON, *January 12, 1864.*

"HIS EXCELLENCY, JEFFERSON DAVIS,

"President of the Confederate States:

"I feel it my duty as an officer of the army to lay before the Chief Magistrate of the Southern Confederacy the within document [Cleburne's Memorial] which was read on the night of the 2d of January, 1864, at a meeting which I attended in obedience to the following order:

" 'HEADQUARTERS HARDEE'S CORPS,
" '*Dalton, Georgia, January 2, 1864.*

" 'Major-General WALKER,

" 'Commanding Division.

" 'GENERAL: Lieutenant-General Hardee desires that you will meet him at General Johnston's headquarters this evening at 7 o'clock.

" 'Very respectfully, your obedient servant,

" 'D. H. POOLE,
" '*Assistant Adjutant General.*'

"Having, after the meeting adjourned, expressed my determination to apply to General Cleburne for a copy of the document to forward to the War Department, some of the gentlemen who were present at that meeting insisted upon their sentiments on so grave a subject being made known to the Executive. I informed them that I would address a letter to each of the gentlemen present at the meeting, which I did. I addressed a note to General Cleburne, asking him for a copy of the document, informing him that I felt it my duty to forward it to the War Department; that should he do so, I would, of course, give him a copy of the endorsement I made on it. He furnished me with a copy, and avowed himself its author. I applied to the commanding general for permission to send it to the War Department, through the proper official channel, which, for reasons satisfactory to himself, he declined to do; hence the reason for it not reaching you through the official channel. The gravity of the subject, the magnitude of the issues involved, my strong convictions that the further agitation of such sentiments and propositions would ruin the efficiency of our army, and involve our cause in ruin and disgrace constitute my reasons for bringing the documents before the Executive.

"W. H. T. WALKER, *Major-General.*"[1]

"(Circular)

"DALTON, *January 31, 1864.*

"Lieutenant General HARDEE, Major-Generals CHEATHAM, HINDMAN, CLEBURNE, STEWART, WALKER. Brigadier-Generals BATE and P. ANDERSON.

"GENERAL: I have just received a letter from the Secretary of War in reference to Major-General Cleburne's memoir read in my quarters about the 2d instant. In this letter the honorable Secretary expresses the earnest conviction of the President 'That the dissemination or even promulgation of such opinion under the present circumstances of the Confederacy, whether in the army or among the people, can be productive only of discouragement, distraction and desertion. The agitation and controversy which must spring from the presentation of such views of officers high in the public confidence are to be deeply deprecated, and while no doubt or mistrust is for a moment entertained of the patriotic intents of the gallant author of the memorial, and such of his brother officers as may have favored his opinions, it is requested that you communicate to them, as well as all others present on the occasion, the opinions, as herein expressed, of the President, and urge on them the suppression, not only of the memorial itself, but likewise of all discussion and controversy respecting or growing out of it. I would add that the measures advocated in the memorial are considered to be little appropriate for consideration in military circles, and indeed in their scope pass beyond the bounds of Confederate action, and could under our Constitutional systems neither be recommended by the Executive to Congress nor be entertained by that body. Such views can only jeopard among the States and people unity and harmony, when for successful co-operation and the achievement of independence both are essential.'

"Most respectfully, your obedient servant,

"J. E. JOHNSTON,

"*General.*

"P. S. Major-General Cleburne: Be so good as to communicate the views of the President, expressed above, to the officers of your division who signed the memorial.

"J. E. JOHNSTON."[2]

---

1. *O.R.*, LII, part 2, 595.
2. *O.R.*, LII, part 2, 608.

Later on the opinion of the President, expressed in the above, underwent a radical change, for an Act of Congress, authorizing enrollment of negroes, received Executive approval on March 13, 1865, but *too late* to do any good. Had Cleburne's wise counsel of January, 1864, been promptly put into effect, and with from fifty to one hundred thousand men, which could thus have been added to the Confederate forces, it is probable the result of the war would have been reversed.

The following is a copy of War Department order as to enrollment of negroes:

"ADJUTANT AND INSPECTOR-GENERAL'S OFFICE,
"RICHMOND, VIRGINIA, *April 1, 1865.*

"Special Orders
No. 78

* * * * * * * *

"XIV. Colonel K. Otey, Eleventh Regiment, Virginia Volunteers, is assigned to duty at Lynchburg, Virginia, with authority to recruit, muster, and organize negro troops for the Army, under provisions of the Act of Congress approved March 13, 1865, promulgated in General Orders No. 14, Current Series.

"By Command of the Secretary of War.

"JOHN W. RIELY,
"Assistant Adjutant-General."[3]

"Among the blind, the one-eyed are kings."

APPENDIX D

Return of captured flag of Third Iowa Infantry.

"ST. LOUIS, *July 28, 1883.*

"TO THE ADJUTANT-GENERAL, STATE OF IOWA, DES MOINES:

"DEAR SIR:—In overhauling some old articles a few days ago we discovered an old battle-scarred flag of the Third Iowa, captured by General Pat Cleburne before Atlanta, Georgia, and by him given to my sister, who was then living in Georgia. It was folded, put away as a relic of the war, and forgotten until resurrected a few days ago. If the Third Iowa still exists and would like to have this flag that so plainly shows how gallantly its bearer carried it, my sister will be glad to send it to the regiment.

"Yours very respectfully,
"H. F. MASSENGALE."

---

3. *O.R.*, Series 4, III, 1193.

General Alexander wrote at once asking to have the flag sent to him, and saying he would see that it was given a place among the other old flags in the State Arsenal, and that it would gladden the eyes of the regiment, which would have their reunion at Cedar Falls, the following September. The flag was sent to General Alexander by express.

The lady referred to, at the time the flag was given her by General Cleburne was Miss Laura J. Massengale, afterwards Mrs. Laura J. Pickett, of St. Louis.

APPENDIX E

The following were the assistant adjutants-general of Hardee's corps and Cleburne's division:

HARDEE'S HEADQUARTERS

1. Col. T. B. Roy. Died November 20, 1910.
2. Maj. D. H. Poole. Died after close of war.

CLEBURNE'S HEADQUARTERS

3. Maj. Calhoun Benham. Died June 12, 1884.
4. Capt. Irving A. Buck. Died Front Royal, Va., September 18, 1912

POLK'S BRIGADE

5. Capt. Wm. A. King. Died after close of war.

LOWREY'S BRIGADE

6. Capt. O. S. Palmer. Killed in battle of Franklin.

GRANBURY'S BRIGADE

7. Capt. J. T. Hearne. Killed in battle of Pickett's farm.

GOVAN'S BRIGADE

8. Capt. George A. Williams. Born 1842; died December 29, 1929—

Of the eight adjutants-general of Hardee's corps and Cleburne's division at this date (April, 1908), but three survive—Colonel Roy, Captains Buck and Williams. All of these were from Front Royal, Virginia, and originally enlisted as privates in Company B, Seventeenth Virginia Infantry. They were school-mates and related to each other. The major of the Seventeenth Virginia Regiment, Geo. Wm. Brent, was made adjutant-general of the Army of Tennessee, and thus members of that regiment furnished the adjutants general of the army and one each to the corps, division and brigade of the Western Army.

PUBLISHER'S ACKNOWLEDGMENT

The generous assistance given us in the compilation of this volume has been heart-warming. The editor, Thomas Robson Hay, has expressed his thanks in his introduction.

The publisher also owes a debt of gratitude to many who have given aid and comfort while Buck's book was in process.

Special thanks go to the ladies of Carter House Association at Franklin for their treasured photographs and for the use of the Kurz and Allison print used on the dust jacket; to Robert Quarles, archivist and president of the Tennessee Historical Society and to Fred Estes, director of the State Museum for furnishing the pictures of Cleburne's war relics including that of the cap he was wearing on the day of his death; to Dan Robison, State Librarian and his assistant, Gertrude Parsley, for their help and encouragement in many phases of the work; to Robert H. White, State Historian for advice in the early stages of production; to L. H. Parks of Newbern, Tennessee, for first suggesting that we reprint this title; to Walton Folk of Marietta, Georgia, for relinquishing a prior and recognized claim to its publishing rights; to Walter Diffee and Aubrey Hamilton of our staff for their help in designing the physical book; and above all, thanks to Jennelyn Perkins, alter ego, for her continued help and patience in making this book a reality.

MAPS

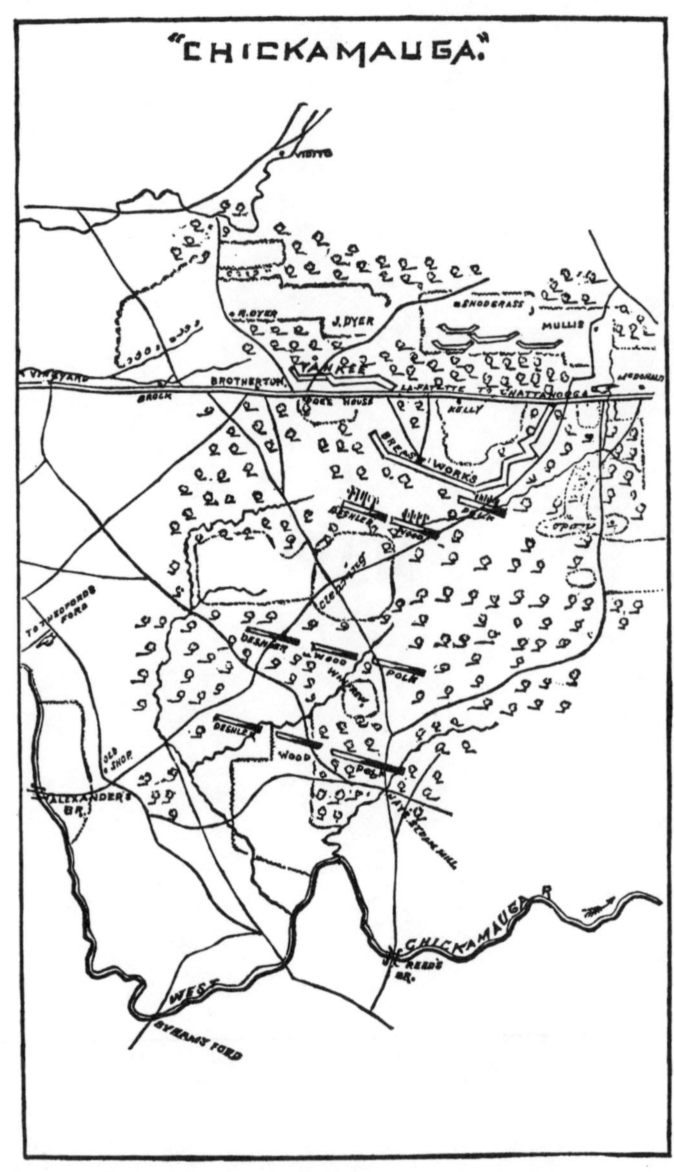

Map 1

Cleburne's battle map of the battle of Chickamauga, September 19-20, 1863

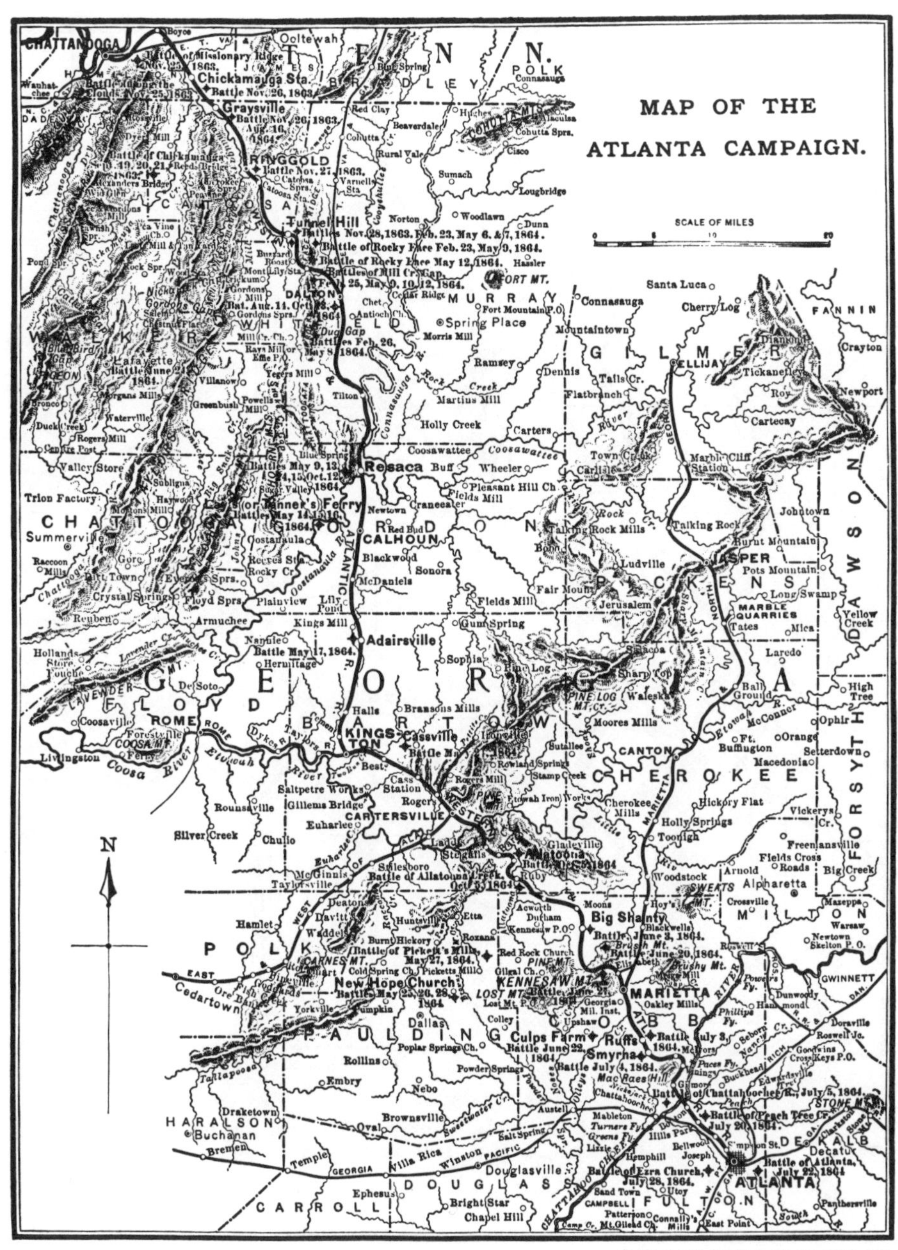

—Battles and Leaders of the Civil War

Map 2
The Atlanta Campaign, May to July 1864

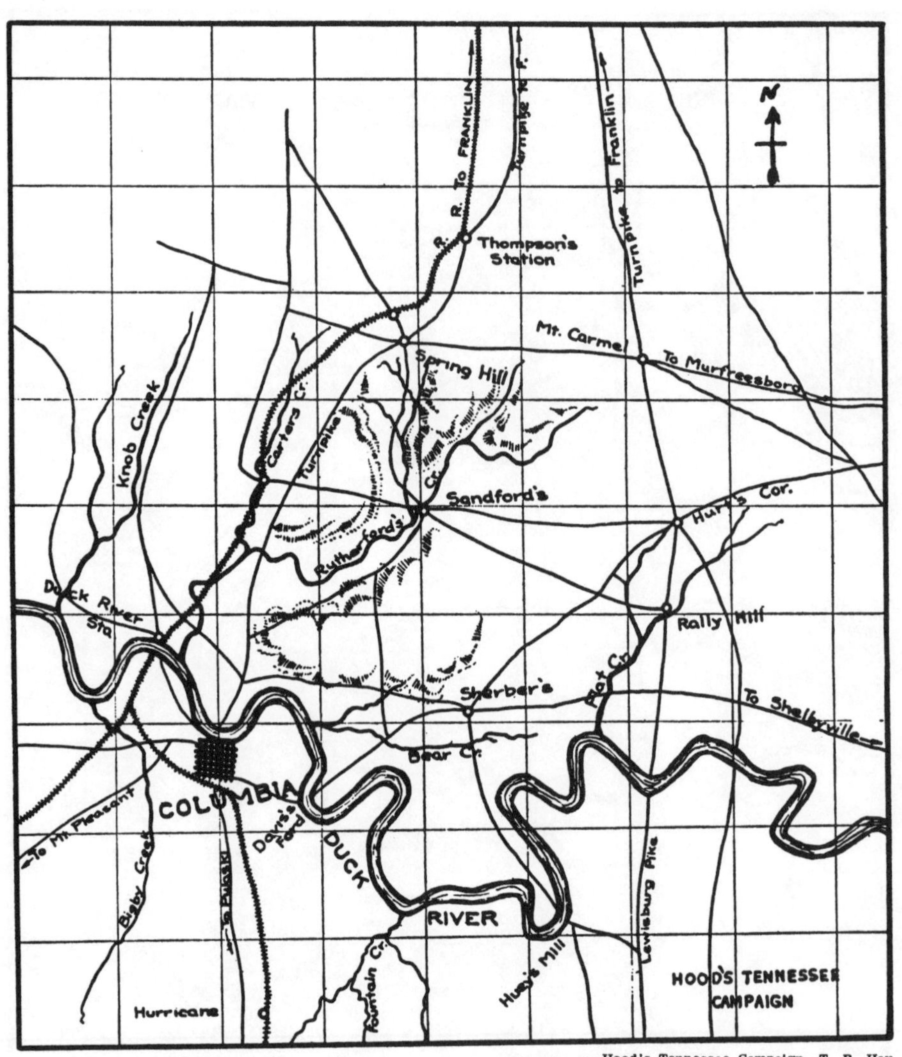

—Hood's Tennessee Campaign, T. R. Hay

MAP 3

The vicinity of Columbia, Tennessee, showing the relation of Columbia, Spring Hill, and Franklin to each other.

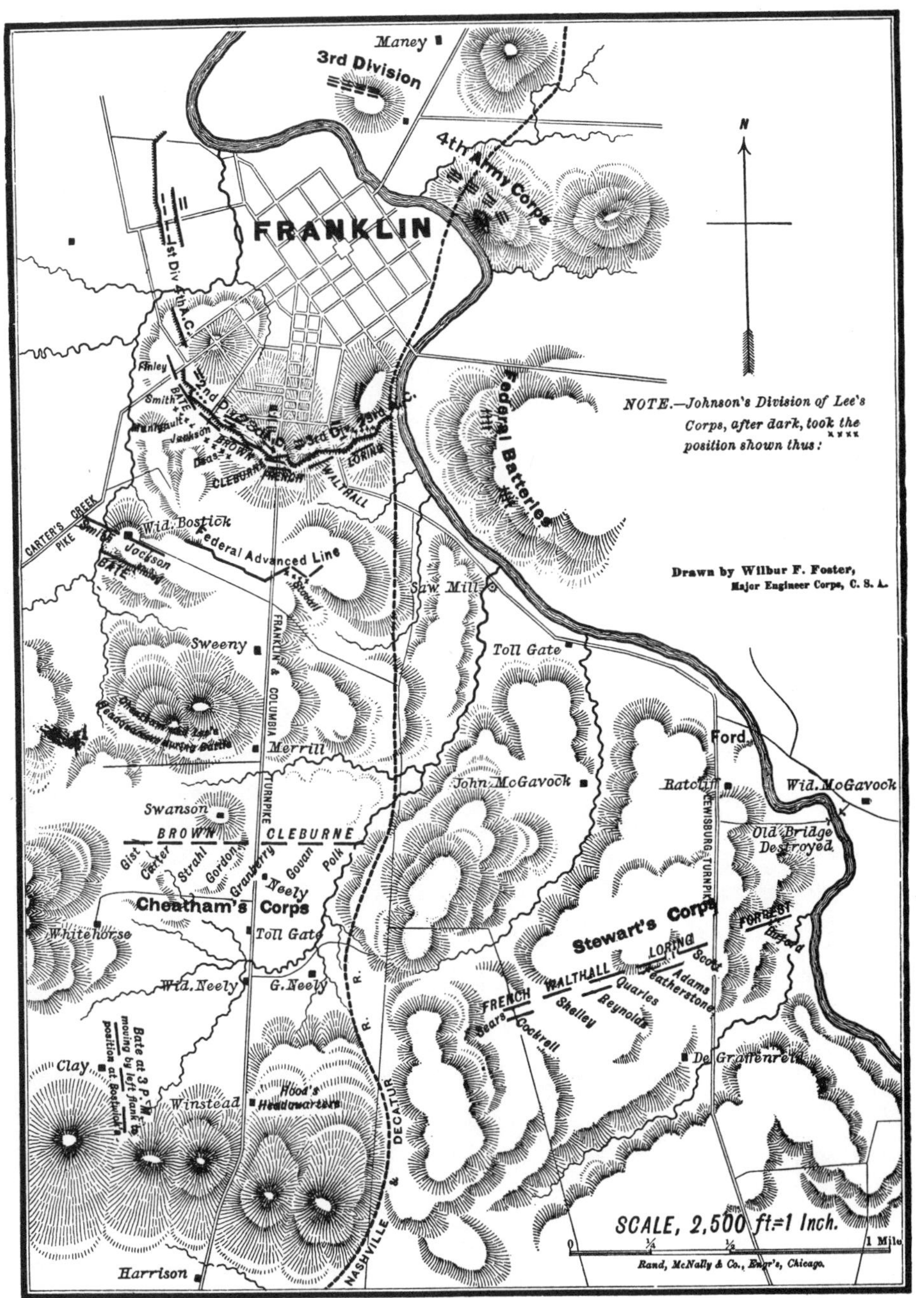

Map 4

The Battlefield of Franklin, Tenn., November 30, 1864. By Major W. F. Foster, Engineer Corps, C. S. Army, in *Southern Bivouac,* June 1885. The original of this map is in the Atlas accompanying the *Official Records,* plate LXXIII, No. 3.

INDEX

D

E

F

G

R

S

T